D0044896

CASSELL
Dictionary of Proverbs

CASSELL

Dictionary
of Proverbs

David Pickering

CASSELL

This edition first published in the UK 1997 by
Cassell
Wellington House
125 Strand
London WC2R 0BB

Distributed in the United States by
Sterling Publishing Co. Inc.
387 Park Avenue South
New York NY 10016-8810

British Library Cataloguing-in-Publication Data
A catalogue record for this book is available from the British Library

ISBN 0-304-34911-9

Designed by Geoff Green
Typeset by Geoff Green
Printed and bound in Great Britain by
Mackays of Chatham

Preface

Dictionary definitions of the word 'proverb' vary considerably, and it is inevitable that reference sources should differ when it comes to deciding what should qualify for inclusion and what should not. In compiling this latest addition to the proverbs library, possible inclusions were judged on the following grounds. To be included, a proverb had – in most cases, at least – to be concise, memorable (usually traditional) and expressive of a commonplace truth or perceived fact of experience.

The best proverbs, most readers will agree, are short, pithy sayings that are redolent of vanished eras, but that still have something to communicate to the contemporary age. A good proverb neatly summarizes what might otherwise be difficult to express and is immediately understood by the person to whom it is addressed (regardless of whether he or she agrees with it or not). Proverbs represent a shorthand route in conversation – an invaluable tool in this modern era of sound-bites and linguistic functionality. This does not mean, however, that defunct proverbs of purely historical interest have been neglected – they have not, unless they are so obscure that their meaning has long since been lost.

Dictionaries of proverbs may be divided into those that adopt a wholly alphabetical approach and those that rely solely on thematic organization. Some consist of little more than lists of citations, while others go into such detail on a small number of proverbs that relatively few are covered. This book attempts to combine elements of both approaches, gathering often large numbers of related proverbs around key headwords and incorporating within the entries copious cross-references (indicated by small capitals) to associated sayings, all within a strict alphabetical framework. Thus, the reader benefits from the convenience of an easily accessible source of reference while still enjoying the opportunity to read in some detail about a particular proverb's origins or history.

With over 3000 entries, every attempt has been made to ensure a high degree of comprehensivity, with proverbs being gleaned from a wide range of cultures and all periods of history, including our own. Where possible, some indication has been given of the actual country of origin (though this may sometimes reflect only a proverb's earliest known history rather than its actual beginnings). Meanings are fully explained and are supported by information about early usage (specifically in the English language), usually when the proverb in question first appeared in something approximating to its modern form. Where appropriate, a full commentary is then offered, together with variant forms, cross-references to related entries and, in many cases, examples of usage (with full citations).

It would be both churlish and unrealistic to contemplate the compilation of a new dictionary of proverbs without acknowledging that it will, by necessity, build upon the knowledge amassed in other celebrated collections over the years. Notable authorities to which all modern collections must inevitably owe a debt include: R. Taverner's *Proverbs or Adages of Erasmus* (1539), J. Heywood's *A Dialogue containing ... the Proverbs in the English Tongue* (1546), Randle Cotgrave's *A Dictionary of the French and English Tongues* (1611), T. Draxe's *Bibliotheca Scholastica* (1616), J. Clarke's *Paroemiographia Anglo-Latina* (1639), George Herbert's *Jacula Prudentum* (1640), John Ray's *A Collection of English Proverbs* (1670), James Kelly's *A Complete Collection of Scottish Proverbs* (1721), Thomas Fuller's *Gnomologia* (1732), Benjamin Franklin's *Poor Richard's Almanack* (1733), W.C. Hazlitt's *English Proverbs* (1869), and *The Oxford Dictionary of English Proverbs* (1935 and later editions). Among more recent publications of note are the dictionaries of proverbs compiled by G.L. Apperson and by Linda and Roger Flavell.

This volume in its turn humbly adds to the common store a modest number of 'new' proverbs, renders some old ones in forms now current, and in some instances casts a new light on the history, meaning and origins of already collected sayings.

Finally, thanks are also due to the editors and production staff for their assistance and, as ever, to Jan, Edward and Charles.

DAVID PICKERING

a

abhors. *See* NATURE abhors a vacuum

a-borrowing. he that goes a-borrowing, goes a-sorrowing (English) Those who borrow are fated to regret doing so. Wright and Halliwell, *Reliquiae Antiquae, c.*1470. *See also* neither a BORROWER nor a lender be.

Ah, him that goes a borrowin' goes a sorrowin'!... An' there isn't hardly a neighbour in the whole street that hasn't lent him money on the strength of what he was going to get.
Sean O'Casey, *Juno and the Paycock*, 1924

Abraham. *See* there's no LEAPING from Delilah's lap into Abraham's bosom

abroad. go abroad and you'll hear news of home (English) When far afield the traveller is sure to hear news from home. John Ray, *A Collection of English Proverbs*, 1678.

You must go into the country to hear what news at London.
John Ray, *A Collection of English Proverbs*, 1678

absence makes the heart grow fonder (English) Separation from a loved one serves only to intensify the feelings of one partner for another. In this form, the sentiment was first expressed c.1830 in the song 'Isle of Beauty', written by Thomas Haynes Bayly (1797–1839). It has been sug-

gested, however, that the identical line appeared as the opening of an anonymous poem published in 1602, and certainly the same feeling was expressed in a range of variant forms in various seventeenth-century literary works. Other variants in which it appeared included 'absence sharpens love, presence strengthens it' and 'absence works wonders'. Another variant runs 'absence is a shrew'. The French, meanwhile, know the proverb in the form 'a little absence does much good'. *See also* OUT of sight, out of mind.

I dote upon his very absence.
William Shakespeare, *Othello, c.*1602

absent. the absent are always wrong (French) It is easy to lay the blame on others not present to defend themselves. John Lydgate, *The Fall of Princes, c.*1440. Originally known in the French version 'les absents ont toujours tort'.

The absent are never without fault, nor the present without excuse.
Benjamin Franklin, 1736

accidents will happen in the best regulated families (English) Misfortunes may befall anyone, regardless of conduct, station or family background. George Colman, *The Deuce is in Him*, 1763. In common currency by the mid-eighteenth century, when it was frequently applied in the discussion of such domestic disasters as unwanted pregnancies or scandalous romantic liaisons among the most upstanding in society, the proverb is now often heard in the truncated form 'accidents will happen' (in which form George Colman rendered it in *The Deuce is in Him* as early as 1763). Variants have included the waggish 'actresses will happen in the best regulated families'.

'Copperfield,' said Mr Micawber, 'accidents will occur in the best-regulated families; and in families not regulated by ... the influence of Woman, in the lofty character of Wife, they must be expected with confidence, and must be borne with philosophy.'
Charles Dickens, *David Copperfield*, 1850

accounting. there is no accounting for tastes (*English*) There is no explaining divergence of taste. J. Minsheu, *A Spanish Grammar*, 1599. Originally given in the Latin form '*De gustibus non est disputandum*' (there is no disputing about tastes). Variants include 'all meat is not the same in every man's mouth'. *See also* one man's MEAT is another man's poison.

De gustibus non est disputandum; men may be convinced, but they cannot be pleased, against their will.
Samuel Johnson, *Lives of the Poets*, 1781

accuser. *See* a GUILTY conscience needs no accuser

accuses. *See* he who EXCUSES himself, accuses himself

accusing the times is but excusing ourselves (*English*) It is no excuse to blame the times in which one lives

rather than one's own failings when things go wrong. Thomas Fuller, *Gnomologia*, 1732.

acolyte. the acolyte at the gate reads scriptures he has never learnt (*Japanese*) Those anxious to please will profess all manner of things they do not really believe.

acorns. *See* GREAT oaks from little acorns grow

act quickly, think slowly (*Greek*) Be decisive in action, but think carefully before acting.

actions speak louder than words (*US*) A person may be judged more tellingly by his deeds than by his words. *Melancholy State of Province*, 1736, in A. M. Davis, *Colonial Currency*, 1911. Though popularized in this form initially in the USA, much the same sentiments have been expressed in different words through the centuries, as far back as the Roman poet Ovid, who wrote 'no need of words, trust deeds'. In 1659 James Howell, in *English Proverbs*, gave the version 'a man of words and not of deeds, is like a garden full of weeds'. *See also* FINE words butter no parsnips; HANDSOME is as handsome does; PRACTISE what you preach.

'Actions speak louder than words' is the maxim; and, if true, the South now distinctly says to the North, 'Give us the measures, and you take the men.'
Abraham Lincoln, 1856, quoted in *Works*, 1953

Adam. Adam's ale is the best brew (*English*) The best drink of all is water, the only drink available to the biblical Adam. The Scottish sometimes refer to water as 'Adam's wine'.

when Adam delved and Eve span, who was then the gentleman?

(English) When only Adam and Eve populated the world, what meaning then had class and rank? Richard Rolle of Hampole, c.1340 (quoted in G. G. Perry, *Religious Pieces*). According to the fifteenth-century writer Thomas Walsingham, in his *Historia Anglicana*, this argument was employed by John Ball when he delivered a famous speech at Blackheath during the Peasants' Revolt of 1381.

When Adam dalfe and Eve spanne
To spire of thou may spede,
Where was then the pride of man,
That now marres his meed?
Richard Rolle of Hampole, c.1340, quoted in
G. G. Perry, *Religious Pieces*

adder. if the adder could hear and the blindworm could see, neither man nor beast would ever go free (English) If circumstances were different, the overall situation would be much altered. *Notes and Queries*, 1856. Variants include 'if the adder could hear and the blindworm could see, no poor man's children could go their way free'.

adventures are to the adventurous (English) Only those who show some daring are likely to have exciting, adventurous lives. Benjamin Disraeli, *Coningsby*, 1844.

'I fear that the age of adventures is past.' ...
'Adventures are to the adventurous,' said the stranger.
Benjamin Disraeli, *Coningsby*, 1844

adversity makes strange bedfellows (English) Circumstances sometimes oblige a person to forge unlikely alliances. William Shakespeare, *The Tempest*, c.1610. The proverb is variously applied to politics and poverty among other contexts. Other proverbs concerning adversity include 'adversity flattereth no man' and 'adversity makes a man wise, though not rich'.

Misery acquaints a man with strange bedfellows.
William Shakespeare, *The Tempest*, c.1610

advertise. it pays to advertise (US) Advertising one's wares in some way will assuredly improve sales. The premise upon which the whole advertising industry is based, this sloganistic advice probably entered common currency around the 1870s, when the power of advertising was first acknowledged on a big scale. One form in which it was recorded around 1870 was 'the man who on his trade relies must either bust or advertise'. Cole Porter wrote a song titled 'It pays to advertise' while still at Yale University, around 1912.

The codfish lays ten thousand eggs,
The homely hen lays one.
The codfish never cackles
To tell you what she's done.
And so we scorn the codfish,
While the humble hen we prize,
Which only goes to show you
That it pays to advertise.
Anonymous, quoted in *Bartlett's Familiar
Quotations*, 1980

advice should be viewed from behind (Swedish) Quality of advice will become apparent in after days.

advice. *See also* GIVE neither counsel nor salt till you are asked for it

Africa. *See* always something NEW out of Africa

after. *See* after DINNER rest a while, after supper walk a mile; after DROUGHT cometh rain; after a STORM comes a calm; it is easy to be WISE after the event

Agamemnon. *See* BRAVE men lived before Agamemnon

age. age and wedlock bring a man to his nightcap (English) Men are tamed by age and marriage. William Shakespeare, *The Taming of the Shrew*, c.1592. Sometimes encountered (as in *The Taming of the Shrew*) with reference to winter rather than age and wedlock. Related proverbs include 'age and wedlock tame man and beast', 'marriage and want of sleep tame both men and beast' and 'age and wedlock we all desire and repent of'.

But, thou knowest, winter tames man, woman and beast.
William Shakespeare, *The Taming of the Shrew*, c.1592

age can be a bad travelling companion (English) Many ills are attendant on old age. Similar sentiments are implicit in the saying 'age breeds aches'.

age does not give sense – it only makes one go slowly (Finnish) Wisdom does not necessarily come with experience.

age. *See also* the age of MIRACLES is past

agree. agree, for the law is costly (English) It is better to settle a dispute before going to court, to save on legal bills. William Camden, *Remains Concerning Britain*, 1605. Frequently repeated in the seventeenth and eighteenth centuries.

Come to a composition with him, Turfe, the law is costly.
Ben Jonson, *A Tale of a Tub*, 1633

agree. *See also* BIRDS in their little nests agree; TWO of a trade never agree

agues come on horseback, but go away on foot (English) Fevers and other minor ailments develop suddenly, but fade away slowly. Randle Cotgrave, *A Dictionary of the French and English Tongues*, 1611.

ale in, wit out *See* when the DRINK is in, the wit is out; when the WINE is in, the wit is out

all. *See* all's for the BEST in the best of all possible worlds; all CATS are grey in the dark; all things COME to those who wait; DEATH pays all debts; why should the DEVIL have all the best tunes?; don't put all your EGGS in one basket; all's FAIR in love and war; all FELLOWS at football; all FISH are not caught with flies; all is FISH that comes to the net; all FLESH is not venison; you may FOOL all of the people some of the time, some of the people all of the time, but not all of the people all of the time; all that GLITTERS is not gold; all GOOD things must come to an end; all is GRIST that comes to the mill; HEAR all, see all, say nowt; all lay LOADS on a willing horse; there is MEASURE in all things; all MEN are mortal; MODERATION in all things; it will all be ONE in a hundred years' time; all PUBLICITY is good publicity; to the PURE all things are pure; all ROADS lead to Rome; all are not SAINTS that go to church; it takes all SORTS to make a world; all STUARTS are not sib; all THINGS are possible with God; the THIRD time pays for all; all things grow with TIME, except grief; all's WELL that ends well; you can't WIN them all; all WORK and no play makes Jack a dull boy

almost was never hanged (English) No person can be condemned for something they might have considered doing but never actually committed. J. Clarke, *Paroemiographia Anglo-Latina*, 1639.

alms quencheth sin (Hebrew) Those who give to the poor atone for any sins they have committed. Bible, Ecclesiastes 3:30.

alone. See he TRAVELS fastest who travels alone; a WISE man is never less alone than when he is alone

alter. See CIRCUMSTANCES alter cases

although. See although the SUN shine, leave not thy cloak at home

always. See the CUSTOMER is always right; always LOOK on the bright side; there is always ROOM at the top; the UNEXPECTED always happens

ancient. with the ancient is wisdom; and in the length of days understanding (Hebrew) Wisdom comes with experience. One of many proverbs taken from the Bible, Job 12:12

ands. See IF ifs and ands were pots and pans, there'd be no work for tinkers' hands

angels. See FOOLS rush in where angels fear to tread

anger. anger can be an expensive luxury (Italian) Outbursts of anger can cost dear. Variations include 'anger and haste hinder good counsel' and 'anger is a short madness'.

anger without power is folly (German) Unless one can act on them, displays of anger are always a mistake.

angered. I was angered, for I had no shoes – then I met a man who had no feet (Chinese) Keep your own problems in perspective and count your blessings. Attributed to Confucius.

angry. an angry man is not fit to pray (Yiddish) A man in the heat of anger is incapable of rational thought and in a wrong frame of mind to come before his God.

he who has been angry becomes cool again (Greek) Anger is a tem-

porary state and will eventually subside. Another proverb on similar lines is 'anger dieth quickly with a good man'.

no man is angry that feels not himself hurt (English) For a man to be truly angry he must have suffered some personal affront. Coined or repeated by Francis Bacon.

angry. See also a HUNGRY man is an angry man

annuity. See GIVE a man an annuity and he'll live for ever

answer. See a SOFT answer turneth away wrath

ant. an ant hole may collapse an embankment (Japanese) An apparently insignificant event may have important repercussions.

ants. in the ants' house the dew is a flood (Persian) What might seem an insignificant event to one person might be crucial to someone in a more vulnerable position. Another proverb observes that when ants are unusually busy with building walls then rain is imminent: 'if ants their walls do frequent build, rain will from the clouds be spilled'.

anvil. See the CHURCH is an anvil which has worn out many hammers

any. See any PORT in a storm; any PUBLICITY is good publicity

anyone can kill a trussed foe (Turkish) There is no glory in accomplishing an easy task.

anything. anything may be spoken if it be under the rose (English) You may speak without fear of your confidences being betrayed. This old English proverb, often abbreviated to 'sub rosa' ('under the rose') may have originated in the Classical myth in

5

which Cupid bribed Harpocrates, the god of silence, with the gift of a rose so that he would not speak of Venus's love affairs. The rose subsequently came to symbolize silence, and in Tudor times the rose, also a symbol of kingship, was carved on the ceilings of banquet halls, confessionals and other meeting-places to remind those present of their duty not to reveal what they heard in confidence.

anything will fit a naked man (Irish) In extreme necessity, any aid should be gratefully accepted. *See also* BEGGARS can't be choosers.

if anything can go wrong, it will (US) 'Murphy's Law', concerning the inevitability of disaster, which was promulgated by George Nichols, a project manager working for the Northrop aircraft company, in 1949. 'Murphy' was Captain E. Murphy, an employee of the Wright Field-Aircraft Laboratory, with whom Nichols worked. The celebrated observation was first expressed in *Aviation Mechanics Bulletin*, May-June 11, 1955, thus: 'Murphy's Law: If an aircraft part can be installed incorrectly, someone will install it that way.' Subsequent decades have dubbed the same principle 'Sod's law'.

ape. an ape's an ape, a varlet's a varlet, though they be clad in silk or scarlet (Greek) Dressing up in fine clothes will not disguise baseness of character. The proverb was quoted by the ancient Greek satirist Lucian in the first century AD in the form 'an ape is an ape ... even if it has gold insignia'. According to other proverbs, 'an ape is never so like an ape as when he wears a doctor's cap' and 'apes are never more beasts than when they

wear men's clothes'. *See also* the HIGHER the monkey climbs the more he shows his tail.

apes. *See* OLD maids lead apes in hell

apparel makes the man (English) A man may be judged by the clothes he wears. John Florio, *Second Fruites*, 1591. *See also* NINE tailors make a man.

For the apparel oft proclaims the man.
William Shakespeare, *Hamlet*, c.1600

appear. *See* TALK of the Devil and he is bound to appear

appearances are deceptive (Greek) Trust should not be placed on superficial appearances, as the underlying reality might be quite different. G. Torriano, *Italian Proverbs*, 1666. Known to the ancient Greeks, but not commonly encountered in England before the eighteenth century. Often heard in the USA in the form 'appearances are deceiving'. *See also* BEAUTY is only skin deep; the COWL does not make the monk; all that GLITTERS is not gold; never JUDGE by appearances; STILL waters run deep

Egad, appearances are very deceitful.
Tobias Smollett, *Gil Blas*, 1750

appetite comes with eating (French) The more one indulges in something, the more one wants to continue to indulge. Rabelais, *Gargantua*, 1534. The proverb was originally almost exclusively applied to the consumption of food, but has since been applied to greed for conquest and for sex, among other cravings. *See also* HUNGER is the best sauce.

Why, she would hang on him,
As if increase of appetite had grown
By what it fed on.
William Shakespeare, *Hamlet*, c.1600

apple. an apple a day keeps the doctor away (English) Consuming an apple every day will improve the health and ward off illness. *Notes & Queries*, 1866. Though the apple has long been considered magically potent, being employed in a variety of ways in love magic and divination, this proverb is of relatively recent coinage. Modern science approves the sentiment, as apples contain vitamins, fibre and boron and by aiding absorption of calcium promote strong teeth and healthy bones.

the apple never falls far from the tree (German) Children will inevitably echo their parents in traits, appearance, interests and so forth and will in all likelihood never stray far from the parents. Ralph Waldo Emerson, letter, 22 December 1839. Possibly of Eastern origin, though first recorded in Germany in the sixteenth century. *See also* like FATHER, like son.

As men say the apple never falls far from the stem, I shall hope that another year will draw my eyes and steps to this old deaar odious haunt of the race.
Ralph Waldo Emerson, letter, 22 December 1839

apple. *See also* the ROTTEN apple injures its neighbours

apples. apples, pears and nuts spoil the voice (Italian) Those who wish to preserve their voice should avoid apples, pears and nuts. J. Howell, *Paroemiographia*, 1659.

apples taste sweetest when they are going (Roman) Apples (and many other foodstuffs and pleasures) are best enjoyed at the moment of greatest ripeness, just before they go rotten.

how we apples swim (Greek) How well you think you've done – intended to deflate someone who boasts unwontedly of his or her achieve-

ments. J. Withals, *A Short Dictionary in Latin and English*, 1586. The origins of the proverb, now little heard, are indicated by the fuller form in which it was formerly known: 'see how we apples swim!, quoth the horse-turd'. According to Aesop's *Fables*, some lumps of horse dung were washed into a stream by heavy rain and found themselves floating among apples, prompting them to congratulate themselves with the line 'how we apples swim!'

And even this, little as it is, gives him so much self-importance in his own eyes that he assumes a consequential air, sets his arms akimbo, and, strutting among the historical artists, cries, 'How we apples swim!'
William Hogarth, *Works*, 1768

your neighbour's apples are the sweetest (Yiddish) What belongs to another always seems more desirable than what one has oneself. *See also* FORBIDDEN fruit tastes sweetest.

apples. *See also* there is SMALL choice in rotten apples

April showers bring forth May flowers (English) A wet April promises a good show of flowers the following month. T. Wright, *Songs and Ballads*, c.1560. This piece of horticultural wisdom dates from the sixteenth century or earlier, but is not, according to the experts, always borne out by experience. This is but one of a series of similar rural traditions. If it rains on Saint Paul's Day (25 January) there will be a poor harvest of corn; if it rains at Easter the grass will grow lush but there will be little hay; if it rains on Saint Peter's Day (29 June) there will be a good crop of apples. The proverb is also encountered in the longer form

'March winds and April showers bring forth May flowers'. *See also* SAINT Swithin's day, if thou dost rain, for forty days it will remain; Saint Swithin's Day, if thou be fair, for forty days 'twill rain no more.

I believe, if showers fall in April, that we shall have flowers in May.
Walter Scott, *Kenilworth*, 1821

April. *See also* a COLD April the barn will fill

arm. *See* STRETCH your arm no further than your sleeve will reach; YORKSHIRE born and Yorkshire bred, strong in the arm and weak in the head

arms. *See* KINGS have long arms

army. an army marches on its stomach (French) The progress of an army depends directly upon the quality and quantity of its provisions. *Windsor Magazine*, January 1904. This military maxim has been variously attributed to both Napoleon and to Frederick the Great. Also found as 'an army, like a serpent, goes on its belly'.

arrive. *See* it is better to TRAVEL hopefully than to arrive

art. art consists in concealing art (Roman) The true artist conceals the technique by which he gets his effects. B. Melbancke, *Philotimus*, 1583. This old adage, sometimes rendered in Latin as *'ars est celare artem'*, has been heard less frequently in the twentieth century with the new emphasis on deliberate deconstruction of technique in full public view, to the point where exploration of technique and materials and so on becomes the whole point of the work in question. Variants include 'art must be deluded by art'.

In oratory the greatest art is to hide art.
Jonathan Swift, *The Faculty of the Mind*, 1707

art has no enemy but ignorance (Roman) Only the ill-educated fail to appreciate art. Ben Jonson, *Every Man Out of His Humour*, 1599.

Arte hath an enemy cal'd Ignorance.
Ben Jonson, *Every Man Out of His Humour*, induction, 1599

art helps nature, and experience art (English) Art can improve on nature and is improved itself by experience. R. Rainoldes, *Foundation of Rhetoric*, 1563. Also given as 'art improves nature'.

art is long, life is short (Greek) A lifetime is too short to achieve a mastery of art. Geoffrey Chaucer, *The Parlement of Foules*, c.1374. Often given in its Latin form 'ars longa, vita brevis', a reworking of Seneca's 'vita brevis est, ars longa', this proverb provided the basis of the Hippocratic Oath that is sworn by members of the modern medical profession. It was the ancient Greek physician Hippocrates himself who first applied the saying to the medical profession, lamenting that as regards learning medicine 'life is short, the art long, opportunity fleeting, experience treacherous, judgement difficult'. It made its first appearance in English as early as the fourteenth century, and it has since been applied to many other forms of art other than medicine (though often somewhat inaccurately conveying the idea that it is about the survival of artistic works beyond the lifetime of their creators).

The lyf so short, the craft so long to lerne,
Th'assay so hard, so sharp the conqueriynge.
Geoffrey Chaucer, *The Parlement of Foules*, c.1374

artful speech and an ingratiating demeanour rarely accompany

virtue (Chinese) The silver-tongued and the charming are not necessarily to be trusted. Attributed to Confucius.

ash. See beware of the OAK, it draws the stroke; avoid the ash, it courts the flash; when the OAK is before the ash, then you will get only a splash

ask. ask a silly question and you'll get a silly answer (English) Stupid questions deserve meaningless answers.

ask much to have a little (English) Ask for more than you need and you stand a chance of getting sufficient. R. Taverner, *Proverbs or Adages of Erasmus*, 1545.

ask no favour during the solano (Spanish) Do not ask for favours in troubled times. *Brewer's Phrase and Fable*, 1959. The *solano* is a hot, dusty wind that blows through Spain from the south-east, causing much discomfort to those caught in it.

ask no questions and hear no lies (English) To make enquiries is an invitation to deceive. Oliver Goldsmith, *She Stoops to Conquer*, 1773. Related proverbs include 'he that asketh nothing, nothing learneth'.

Ask me no questions and I'll tell you no fibs.
Oliver Goldsmith, *She Stoops to Conquer*, 1773

a-sorrowing. See he that goes A-BORROWING, goes a-sorrowing

ass. every ass loves to hear himself bray (English) A fool loves the sound of his own voice. Related proverbs add 'the ass brays when he pleases' and 'the ass that brays most eats least'.

he that makes himself an ass must not take it ill if men ride him (English) A man who freely allows others to take advantage of him must

not complain when such advantage is taken. Thomas Fuller, *Gnomologia*, 1732.

the ass loaded with gold still eats thistles (Roman) A fool is a fool, however rich he may be. George Chapman, *Widow's Tears*, 1612. Possibly German in origin, though a similar sentiment was recorded in the writings of Plutarch. Variants include 'an ass is but an ass, though laden with gold'. Another proverb observes that 'an ass laden with gold will go lightly uphill', the way ahead being cleared by virtue of the wealth it carries.

Or wilt thou, being keeper of the cash, like an ass that carries dainties, feed on thistles?
Philip Massinger, *The City Madam*, 1632

when an ass climbs a ladder we may find wisdom in women (English) Only when an ass climbs a ladder will women be presumed clever, and not before. John Ray, *A Collection of English Proverbs*, 1678. This inflammatory saying is unsurprisingly little heard today; the root of it ('when the ass climbs to the tiles') was known to the Romans.

atheist. an atheist is one point beyond the Devil (English) An atheist is worse than the Devil himself, because the Devil at least believes in God. T. Adams, *Sermons*, 1629.

atheists. there are no atheists in foxholes (US) When under extreme threat to life and limb, many professed non-believers will suddenly rediscover their religious faith. This rather cynical observation was first voiced in a sermon delivered by Father W. T. Cummings, a US Army chaplain stationed in Bataan during the Second World War.

attack is the best form of defence

(US) If threatened, it is best to attack rather than to wait passively to be attacked. W. H. Drayton, 1775 (quoted in R. W. Gibbes, *Documentary History of the American Revolution*, 1855). This militaristic slogan was heard with increasing frequency after the American War of Independence, when its adherents included the US commander George Washington.

Make them believe, that offensive operations, often times, is the surest, if not the only ... means of defence.
George Washington, *Writings*, 1799 (published 1940)

aunt. if my aunt had been a man, she'd have been my uncle (English) If circumstances were otherwise it would be pointless having the discussion in progress, as the causes that gave rise to it would not have existed

– said in response to anyone who, in the course of an argument, postulates what might happen in a different situation. John Ray, *A Collection of English Proverbs*, 1813.

aunt. See also visit your aunt, but not every day of the year

avoidance is the only remedy (English) Some problems have no solution, and the only way to overcome them is to avoid them in the first place. Geoffrey Chaucer, *Minor Poems*, c.1380.

away. away goes the Devil when he finds the door shut against him (English) Those who intend evil will achieve nothing when others refuse all temptations they offer. James Howell, *Paroemiographia*, 1659.

away. *See also* when the CAT's away, the mice will play

b

---

babes. *See* out of the MOUTHS of babes and sucklings

baby. don't throw the baby out with the bathwater (German) Take care not to reject what is valuable or essential when instituting change or reform. Thomas Carlyle, *The Nigger Question*, 1853 (also quoted in German by J. Kepler in *Tertius Interveniens*, 1610). The proverb was first introduced into English by the historian Thomas Carlyle, who was an authority on German language. In Germany it is given as '*Das Kind mit dem Bade ausschütten*'.

When changing we must be careful not to empty the baby with the bath in mere reaction against the past.
George Bernard Shaw, *Everybody's Political What's What*, 1944

the baby comes out of the parsley-bed (English) Babies are born in beds of parsley. R. Brome, *Antipodes*, 1640. Curious children were formerly told by their parents that baby girls issued from parsley beds, while baby boys were found under gooseberry bushes or in beds of nettles.

bachelors' wives and maids' children be well taught (English) Those who do not have wives and children of their own envisage the ones they might have as perfect in every regard. John Heywood, *A Dialogue containing ... the Proverbs in the English Tongue*, 1546.

What a pity it is that nobody knows how to manage a wife, but a batchelor.
George Colman, *The Jealous Wife*, 1761

back. the back door robs the house (English) It is through the unobserved back door that one's possessions tend to disappear, in the hands of servants and family members etc. Thomas Fuller, *Gnomologia*, 1732.

back. *See also* GOD makes the back to the burden; what is GOT over the Devil's back is spent under his belly; it is the LAST straw that breaks the camel's back; you SCRATCH my back, and I'll scratch yours

bacon. *See* CHILD's pig but father's bacon

bad. a bad bush is better than an open field (French) Meagre possessions are better than nothing at all (just as the shelter of a sparse bush is better than none at all). 1300 or earlier.

These evil showers make the low bush better than no bield.
Walter Scott, *The Monastery*, 1820

a bad custom is like a good cake, better broken than kept (English) Rules and habits that are unhelpful should be discarded. Randle Cotgrave, *A Dictionary of the French and English Tongues*, 1611.

a bad excuse is better than none (English) In the absence of a better reason, a poor excuse may serve better than none at all. Ralph Udall, *Roister Doister*, c.1550.

Yea Custance, better (they say) a badde scuse than none.
Nicholas Udall, *Ralph Roister Doister*, 1553

a bad penny always turns up (English) Unwelcome people have a tendency to turn up time and time again. Early nineteenth century. Originally, the proverb referred to miscreants who attempted to pass counterfeit money, warning them that their debased coinage was sure to find its way back to them, to their own detriment.

She had not seen him for thirty-six years. He must be over seventy years of age, and he had turned up again like a bad penny, doubtless a disgrace!
Arnold Bennett, *The Old Wives' Tale*, 1908

a bad woman is worse than a bad man (English) A woman given to wickedness will prove far more evil than any male counterpart. Henry Liddon, *Sermons*, 1893. Another proverb along the same lines runs 'a wicked woman and an evil is three halfpence worse than the Devil'.

a bad workman blames his tools (English/French) A slipshod worker will seek to avoid culpability for bungled work by blaming it on the tools or some other interfering factor. Randle Cotgrave, *A Dictionary of the French and English Tongues*, 1611. Also encountered in the form 'an ill workman quarrels with his tools' and, in agricultural circles, as 'a bad shearer never had a good sickle'.

Never had ill workman good tools.
George Herbert, *Jacula Prudentum*, 1640

bad is the best (English) In some circumstances, something that is bad is the best that can be hoped for. Bullein, *Dialogue*, 1564.

Bad is the best (this English is flat).
Edmund Spenser, *The Shepheardes Calendar*, 1579

bad luck is fertile (Russian) Misfortunes breed more quickly than blessings.

bad money drives out good (English) When good and bad currencies mix, the bad currency will prevail. V. S. Lean, *Collecteana*, 1902–4. Known as Gresham's Law, this principle was first voiced by Sir Thomas Gresham (c.1519–79), founder of the Royal Exchange, when he wrote to Elizabeth I in 1558 to stress the need to defend the purity of the coinage at a time when much debased currency was in circulation. The proverb has since been applied in many fields other than finance.

bad news travels fast (Greek) News of disasters or other setbacks spreads much faster than any other kind of news. Thomas Kyd, *The Spanish Tragedy*, 1592 (also found in essence in the writings of Plutarch). Also encountered in the form 'ill news comes apace'.

Evil news flies faster still than good.
Thomas Kyd, *The Spanish Tragedy*, 1592

it is a bad cause that none dare speak in (English) If no one will speak in defence of something then it can only be assumed that it has nothing at all to recommend it. J. Clarke, *Paroemiologia Anglo-Latina*, 1639.

bad. *See also* GIVE a dog a bad name and hang him; a GOOD horse cannot be of a bad colour; HARD cases make bad law; HOPE is a good breakfast but a bad supper; KEEP bad company and you'll soon be of their number; NOTHING so bad but it might have been worse; THREE removals are as bad as a fire

bag. *See* there's many a GOOD cock come out of a tattered bag

bagpipe. he is like a bagpipe; he never talks till his belly be full (English) He does not speak until he has been fed (just as a bagpipe will not sound until the bag is filled with air). T. Draxe, *Bibliotheca Scholastica*, 1616.

A baggepipe will not lightly speake, untill his belly be full.
T. Draxe, *Bibliotheca Scholastica*, 1616

bairns. *See* FOOLS and bairns should never see half-done work

bait. the bait hides the hook (English) Fair appearances conceal a hidden threat. John Lyly, *Euphues: The Anatomy of Wit*, 1578.

Beauty ... was a deceitful bayte with a deadly hooke.
John Lyly, *Euphues: The Anatomy of Wit*, 1578

bake. as you bake, so shall you brew (Roman) The better something is prepared, the better it will turn out. Edward Hall, *Hall's Chronicle*, 1542 (also quoted by Terence in Phormio). *See also* as you BREW, so shall you bake; as you MAKE your bed, so you must lie in it; as you SOW, so shall you reap.

As they bake they shall brew.
Old Nick and his crew.
David Garrick, *May-Day*, 1775

baker. *See* PULL devil, pull baker

bald. a bald head is soon shaven (English) It takes little time to complete the task when there is little to be done. *Reliquae Antiquae*, c. 1450.

bald. *See also* EXPERIENCE is a comb which nature gives us when we are bald

bale. when bale is highest, boot is nighest (Icelandic) When evil (bale) does its worst, help (boot) is most likely to be at hand. *The Owl and the Nightingale*, 1250.

Did you never hear, that when the need is highest the help is nighest?
Sir Walter Scott, *Nigel*, 1822

balm. is there no balm in Gilead? (Hebrew) Is there no remedy? A reference, first given in this form in the Geneva Bible of 1560, to the gold-coloured resin 'balm of Gilead', the glutinous substance exuded by the mastic tree *Pistacia lentiscus*, which was supposed to have medicinal properties.

There are two guineas to buy a new frock. Come, Cary, never fear: we'll find balm in Gilead.
Charlotte Brontë, *Shirley*, 1849

bare. *See* there goes more to MARRIAGE than four bare legs in a bed

barefoot. *See* the SHOEMAKER's son always goes barefoot

bargain. the bargain is ill made where neither party gains (English) A bargain by virtue of which nobody gains anything is of no use to anyone. c. 1597, A. Douglas, quoted in *Notes and Queries*.

bargain. *See also* it takes TWO to make a bargain

bark. *See* the DOGS bark but the caravan

goes on; put not thy HAND between the bark and the tree; why KEEP a dog and bark yourself?

barking. a barking dog never bites (English) A dog that barks at a stranger is unlikely to attack him. *Proverbs of Alfred*, c.1275 (also recorded in thirteenth-century France). The proverb is frequently applied not to dogs, but to people, implying that the most vociferous individuals are in fact often quite harmless. Also known in the forms 'great barkers are no biters' and 'his bark is worse than his bite', it may be found in Latin, French, Italian, German and sundry other languages.

A barking dog doth seldom strangers bite. *Locrine*, 1595

Barnaby bright, Barnaby bright, the longest day and the shortest night (English) Traditionally, according to the Old Style calendar, the longest day of the year was held to be Saint Barnabas' Day (11 June). Edmund Spenser, *Epithalamion*, 1595. The rhyme fell into disuse after the adoption of the New Style calendar in 1752.

Barnaby bright All day and no night. Edith Holden, *The Country Diary of an Edwardian Lady* (published 1977)

basket. *See* don't put all your EGGS in one basket

bate me an ace, quoth Bolton (English) Allow me some advantage. Richard Edwards, *The Excellent Comedie of Damon and Pithias*, 1571. The Bolton in the proverb was John Bolton, a courtier who once played cards and dice with Henry VIII. By asking the king to deal him an ace, Bolton played the monarch a deft compliment, in effect asking for an advantage to counter the king's implied greater

playing skills. The proverb acquired a new interpretation, however, in the reign of Elizabeth I, after the queen was presented with a new collection of proverbs with the boast that it included all the proverbs in the language. The queen replied only with 'bate me an ace, quoth Bolton', which had been omitted by the author. From then on the proverb was also used to imply that it is wise to exercise caution before making brash boasts.

bathes. he who bathes in May will soon be laid in clay; he who bathes in June, will sing a merry tune; he who bathes in July, will dance like a fly (English) Those who bathe in May (with its uncertain weather) will soon perish, while those who bathe in the warmer months of June and July will flourish. William Hone, *Table-Book*, 1827. *See also* ne'er CAST a clout till May be out; MARRY in May and rue the day; a SWARM of bees in May is worth a load of hay

bathwater. *See* don't throw the BABY out with the bathwater

baton. *See* every SOLDIER has the baton of a field-marshal in his knapsack

battalions. *See* GOD is always on the side of the big battalions

Battersea. go to Battersea to get your simples cut (English) You are so foolish you should go to Battersea for a cure. F. Grose, *A Provincial Glossary*, 1787. Battersea was where market gardeners grew medicinal herbs ('simples') for the London apothecaries, who were quick to sell them to their more gullible customers. Also found as 'go to Battersea to be cut for the simples'.

battle. *See* the RACE is not to the swift, nor the battle to the strong

be what you would seem to be (English) Be true to your nature. W. Baldwin, *Treatise of Moral Philosophy*, 1547. The proverb echoes the biblical injunction 'I am what I am'. Variant forms include 'Be what thou wouldst be called'.

It's a vegetable. It doesn't look like one, but it is ... the moral of that is – 'Be what you would seem to be'.

Lewis Carroll, *Alice's Adventures in Wonderland*, 1865

beans. *See* CANDLEMAS DAY, put beans in the clay, put candles and candlesticks away; he KNOWS how many beans make five

bear (noun). **as a bear has no tail, for a lion he'll fail** (English) One cannot aspire to greatness if one lacks the essential qualities necessary (applied against those who aspire to stations beyond their natural reach). Thomas Fuller, *The History of the Worthies of England*, 1662. The story goes that the ambitious Robert Dudley, Earl of Leicester, who sought dominion over the Netherlands in 1585, claimed descent from the noble Warwick family and accordingly exchanged his own crest, featuring a two-tailed lion, for the bear and ragged staff of the Warwicks. When his crest was set up in public, a wag scrawled beneath it 'Your bear for lion needs must fail, because your true bears have no tail'.

bear. *See also* CALL the bear 'uncle' till you are safe across the bridge

bear (verb). **bear and forbear** (Greek) Endure with patience. J. Sandford, *Hours of Recreation*, 1576. The so-called 'golden rule' of Epictetus.

You must take two bears to live with you – Bear and Forbear.

H. W. Thompson, *Body, Boots and Britches*, 1940

bear wealth, poverty will bear itself (French) It is more difficult to cope with wealth, because of the temptations it brings with it, than it is to adjust to poverty. David Fergusson, *Scottish Proverbs*, 1641.

bear with evil and expect good (French) Endure the bad and hope for better things to come. George Herbert, *Jacula Prudentum*, 1640.

beard. if the beard were all, the goat might preach (Greek) If physical appearances were all-determining, the most dimwitted might aspire to greatness. Thomas Fuller, *The History of the Worthies of England*, 1662.

it is not the beard that makes the philosopher (English) A learned appearance does not necessarily reflect a learned mind. E. Gayton, *Festivious Notes on Don Quixote*, 1654. *See also* APPEARANCES are deceptive; never JUDGE by appearances.

beards. *See* 'tis MERRY in hall when beards wag all

beast. *See* when the WIND is in the east, 'tis neither good for man nor beast

beat. if you can't beat 'em, join 'em (US) If one's opponents are invincible, it is advisable to change sides or to adopt a similar position to theirs. Quentin Reynolds, *The Wounded Don't Cry*, 1941. Often heard in the USA in the form 'if you can't lick 'em, join 'em'.

beat. *See also* one ENGLISHMAN can beat three Frenchmen; it is easy to find a STICK to beat a dog; a WOMAN, a dog and a walnut tree, the more you beat them the better they be

beats. one beats the bush, another takes the bird (English) One man does the work, while his master takes the profit. *Ipomadon, c.* 1300.

And while I at length debate and beate the bushe, there shall steppe in other men, and catche the burdes.

John Heywood, *A Dialogue containing the Proverbs in the English Tongue,* 1546

beautiful. *See* BIG is beautiful; SMALL is beautiful

beauty. beauty and honesty seldom agree (English) A woman who is both beautiful and honest is very rare, because beauty invites temptation. John Lyly, *Euphues and His England,* 1580.

Beawtie and honesty seldome agree, for of beautie comes temptation, of temptation dishonour.

John Florio, *Second Fruites,* 1591

beauty is in the eye of the beholder (English) The judgement of beauty is subjective and not likely to be the same between one individual and another. F. Brooke, *History of Emily Montague,* 1769. Recorded in this form for the first time towards the close of the nineteenth century, but known in variant forms for some 200 years previously. *See also* one man's MEAT is another man's poison.

Most true is it that 'beauty is in the eye of the gazer'.

Charlotte Brontë, *Jane Eyre,* 1847

beauty is no inheritance (English) Beauty is not necessarily passed from one generation to the next. T. Draxe, *Bibliotheca Scholastica,* 1633.

beauty is only skin deep (English) Physical beauty is in the final analysis superficial and cannot be relied upon as an indication of underlying character. First recorded in English in the poem 'A Wife' by Sir Thomas Overbury in 1613 but also found in Classical literature, including the works of Virgil. Authorities observe that it is an expression most often heard on the lips of those who are not themselves outwardly beautiful. Variants include 'beauty is only skin deep, but ugly goes to the bone'. *See also* APPEARANCES are deceptive; HANDSOME is as handsome does; never JUDGE by appearances.

I'm tired of all this nonsense about beauty being only skin-deep. That's deep enough. What do you want — an adorable pancreas?

Jean Kerr, *The Snake Has All the Lines,* 1960

beauty is potent, but money is omnipotent (English) Money exerts more power than beauty. John Ray, *A Collection of English Proverbs,* 1670.

beauty provoketh thieves sooner than gold (English) Beauty has a greater lure than things of purely monetary value. William Shakespeare, *As You Like It, c.* 1599.

beauty without virtue is a flower without perfume (French) Good looks are worthless if unsupported by good character.

because is a woman's reason (English) Referring to an opinion that is illogically held without any supporting argument and purely from personal prejudice. William Shakespeare, *The Two Gentlemen of Verona, c.* 1594.

I have no other but a woman's reason: I think him so because I think him so.

William Shakespeare, *The Two Gentlemen of Verona, c.* 1594

bed. bed is the poor man's opera (Italian) The poor man cannot afford to go to the opera, so finds a parallel passion in his sex life.

'Bed', as the Italian proverb succinctly puts

it, 'is the poor man's opera.'
Aldous Huxley, *Heaven and Hell*, 1956

go to bed with the lamb and rise with the lark (English) Go to sleep early and get up early. Wright, *Songs*, c.1555. *See also* the EARLY bird catches the worm.

We were compelled to rise, having been perhaps not above four hours in bed – (for we were no go-to-beds with the lamb, though we anticipated the lark oft times in her rising).
Charles Lamb, *The Last Essays of Elia*, 1833

bed. *See also* EARLY to bed and early to rise, makes a man healthy, wealthy and wise; as you MAKE your bed, so you must lie in it; there goes more to MARRIAGE than four bare legs in a bed

bedfellows. *See* ADVERSITY makes strange bedfellows

bee. a dead bee will make no honey (English) You cannot expect someone who is dead or otherwise defunct to produce what you want. John Florio, *First Fruites*, 1578. Related proverbs include 'when bees are old they yield no honey'.

where the bee sucks honey the spider sucks poison (English) Some will find good things while others find only bad from the same source. G. Harvey, *Letter-book*, 1573.

Sweet poetry's a flower, where men, like bees and spiders, may bear poison, or else sweets and wax away.
Francis Beaumont and John Fletcher, *Four Plays* (published 1905), 1614

beer. *See* LIFE isn't all beer and skittles; TURKEY, heresy, hops and beer came into England all in one year

bees. bees that have honey in their mouths have stings in their tails (English) Something may be desirable, but carries with it the risk of an unpleasant surprise. *Passe forth, pilgrime*, c.1440.

There are some things which are pleasant but not good, as youthful lusts and worldly delights. These bees carry honey in their mouths, but they a sting in their tails.
W. Secker, *Nonsuch Professor* 1660

bees. *See also* a SWARM of bees in May is worth a load of hay

begets. *See* LENGTH begets loathing; LOVE begets love

beggar. a beggar is never out of his way (English) A beggar has no reason to be in one place rather than another, as he may pursue his way of life anywhere. T. Adams, *Works*, 1630.

a beggar may sing before a pickpocket (Roman) A beggar need not worry about pickpockets, because he has nothing in his pocket to be stolen. Juvenal, *Satires*, first century AD. Also found in the form 'a beggar may sing before a thief'.

The last prerogative of beggary, which entitled him to laugh at the risk of robbery.
Walter Scott, quoted in Lockhart's *Life*, 1829

a beggar's purse is bottomless (English) No amount of wealth will satisfy some people. R. Taverner, *Proverbs or Adages of Erasmus*, 1539.

one beggar does not hate another as much as one doctor hates another (Polish) In terms of professional rivalry, there is nothing to match that between doctors.

set a beggar on horseback, and he'll ride to the Devil (Roman) Give power or opportunity to one not used to it and the person concerned will be overcome with pride and arrogance. G. Pettie, *Petite Pallace*, 1576. The proverb is known in various forms: according to these, a beggar on horseback will never alight, ride a gallop, ride to the gallows, run his horse out of breath or run his horse to death.

It needs not ... proud queen; unless the adage must be verified, that beggars mounted run their horse to death.
William Shakespeare, *Henry VI, Part 3*, c.1591

sit a beggar at your table and he will soon put his feet on it (Russian) Show kindness to the undeserving and they will only abuse it.

sue a beggar and get a louse (English) There is no point in suing someone with no assets with which to compensate you. R. Wilson, *The Cobblers Prophecy*, 1594.

I guess it is some law phrase – but sue a beggar, and – your honour knows what follows.
Walter Scott, *The Bride of Lammermoor*, 1819

beggars. beggars breed and rich men feed (English) The offspring of beggars find work as servants of the rich. John Ray, *A Collection of English Proverbs*, 1670.

Poor people's children find a support in the service of the rich and great.
James Kelly, *A Complete Collection of Scotish Proverbs*, 1721

beggars can't be choosers (English) Those in need cannot afford to question what is offered to them, even if it is not quite what they hoped for. John Heywood, *A Dialogue containing ... the Proverbs in the English Tongue*, 1546. The date of the proverb suggests it might have arisen in connection with the huge increase in vagrancy that occurred in sixteenth-century England when social and economic changes, coupled with the decline of the medieval feudal system, forced many people into a condition of indigence. *See also* never LOOK a gift horse in the

mouth; NEEDS must when the Devil drives.

For all this we were to pay at a high rate; but beggars cannot be choosers.
Robert Louis Stevenson, *The Master of Ballantrae*, 1889

beggars. *See also* who DAINTIES love shall beggars prove; if WISHES were horses, beggars would ride

begin. *See* when THINGS are at the worst they soon begin to mend

begins. he begins to die that quits his desires (English) Any person who abandons all ambitions and hopes for the future might as well be dead. Randle Cotgrave, *A Dictionary of the French and English Tongues*, 1611.

he who begins too much accomplishes little (German) Those who set their sights too high may end up achieving nothing.

begins. *See also* CHARITY begins at home; LIFE begins at forty

begun. *See* WELL begun is half done

beholder. *See* BEAUTY is in the eye of the beholder

believe. believe nothing of what you hear, and only half of what you see (English) Question the truth of everything you learn. Layamon, *Brut*, c.1205. In the simplified form 'don't believe all you hear' it was recorded well before 1300, and has even been attributed to King Alfred the Great himself.

we soon believe what we desire (Roman) We are easily deceived by our desires. Geoffrey Chaucer, *Melibeus*, c.1386 (also quoted by Seneca and other Classical writers).

We soon believe that we would have.
T. Draxe, *Bibliotheca Scholastica*, 1616

believing. *See* SEEING is believing

bellowing. a bellowing cow soon forgets her calf (English) Exaggerated displays of grief soon subside. T. Wilson, *The Art of Rhetoric*, 1553.

When a woman, newly widowed, had tried to throw herself into her husband's grave at his funeral ... some one ... said drily ... 'Ah, you wait. The bellowing cow's always the first to forget its calf.'
Flora Thompson, *Lark Rise to Candleford*, 1945

belly. a belly full of gluttony will never study willingly (English) The student works best on an empty stomach. George Pettie, *Guazzo*, 1586.

the belly carries the legs and not the legs the belly (English) A person must be well fed before they can hope to walk far or meet demanding physical challenges. T. Shelton, *Cervantes' Don Quixote*, 1620.

the belly hath no ears (English) No amount of words will make a hungry man forget he is hungry. R. Taverner, *Proverbs or Adages of Erasmus*, 1539. Another related proverb runs 'the belly is not filled with fair words'.

when the belly is full the mind is among the maids (English) When a man's appetite for food is satisfied, his mind turns inevitably to sex. H. Estienne, *World of Wonders*, 1607.

When the belly is full, the breech would be frigging.
Randle Cotgrave, *A Dictionary of the French and English Tongues*, 1611

belly. *See also* he is like a BAGPIPE; he never talks till his belly be full; the EYE is bigger than the belly; what is GOT over the Devil's back is spent under his belly

belongs. what belongs to everybody belongs to nobody (Spanish) No one can claim ownership of something that is common property.

bend. better bend than break (English) It is better to compromise than to be defeated utterly because one will not yield ground. Geoffrey Chaucer, *Troilus and Criseyde*, c.1385.

I have had ... sorrows ... but I have borne them ill. I have broken where I should have bent.
Charles Dickens, *Barnaby Rudge*, 1840

bent. *See* as the TWIG is bent, so is the tree inclined

Bernard. the good Bernard does not see everything (English) Even the wise and good cannot know everything. Geoffrey Chaucer, *The Legend of Good Women*, c.1385. Saint Bernard of Clairvaux (1091–1153) was a French theologian and reformer, who was dubbed the 'Mellifluous Doctor' and the last of the fathers of the Catholic Church. He founded over 70 monasteries and was canonized in 1174. *See also* even HOMER sometimes nods.

Bernard the monk ne say nat al pardee!
Geoffrey Chaucer, *The Legend of Good Women*, c.1385

best. all's for the best in the best of all possible worlds (French) Everything that happens is for a purpose, namely the ultimate good of the world. Voltaire, *Candide*, translated by W. Rider, 1759.

Pangloss would sometimes say to Candidus: 'All Events are linked together in this best of all possible Worlds.'
Voltaire, *Candide*, translated by W. Rider, 1759

the best go first, the bad remain to mend (English) It is always those of better character who perish first, leaving behind lesser men. John Donne, 'Sonnet on Death', 1631. *See also* only the GOOD die young; whom the GODS love die young.

And soonest our best men with thee doe goe.
John Donne, 'Sonnet on Death', 1631

the best is the enemy of the good
(English) The exceptional eclipses what is merely very good. William Shakespeare, *King Lear*, 1605. *See also* the GOOD is the enemy of the best.

the best laid schemes of mice and men gang oft agley (*Scottish*) The most carefully prepared plans all too often turn out not as intended. Robert Burns, *Poems*, 1786.

I am sorry the book-binding has gone pop. But there 'The best laid schemes' etc. etc.
D. H. Lawrence, letter, 1911

the best manure is under the farmer's foot (*English*) It is human nature to reserve the best of something for yourself.

the best of friends must part (English) All friendships come to an end. Geoffrey Chaucer, *Troilus and Criseyde*, c.1385.

Friends must part, we came not all together, and we must not goe all together.
George Chapman, *May-Day*, 1611

the best of men are but men at best (English) Even the greatest of men have human failings. John Aubrey, letter, 15 June 1680. *See also* even HOMER sometimes nods.

I remember one sayeing of Generall Lambert's, that 'the best of men are but men at best'.
John Aubrey, letter, 15 June 1680

the best things come in small packages (English) The modest size of the package does not necessarily reflect the value of what is inside. J. Howell, *Paroemiographia*, 1659.

the best things in life are free (English) The greatest pleasures in life are not to be bought for money, but are freely available to all. Popularized by the song 'The best things in life are free', written by B. G. De Silva in 1927.

best. *See also* ACCIDENTS will happen in the best regulated families; ATTACK is the best form of defence; why should the DEVIL have all the best tunes?; the best DOCTORS are Dr Diet, Dr Quiet and Dr Merryman; EAST, west, home's best; EXPERIENCE is the best teacher; the best FISH swim near the bottom; he is the best GENERAL who makes the fewest mistakes; the GOOD is the enemy of the best; HONESTY is the best policy; HOPE for the best and prepare for the worst; HUNGER is the best sauce; the best MIRROR is an old friend; be OFF with the old love before you are on with the new; an old POACHER makes the best gamekeeper; it is best to be on the SAFE side; SECOND thoughts are best; SILENCE is a woman's best garment; it is the best SWIMMERS who drown

betrothed. the betrothed of good is evil, the betrothed of life is death, the betrothed of love is divorce (*Malay*) Every good thing in life has its undesirable but inseparable counterpart.

better. the better the day, the better the deed (English) Work done on a Sunday or other holy day will be doubly blessed. Thomas Middleton, *Michaelmas Term*, 1607. Also recorded in similar form in French in the early fourteenth century.

Ask Mr Landless to dinner on Christmas Eve (the better the day the better the deed).
Charles Dickens, *The Mystery of Edwin Drood*, 1870

better. *See also* better BEND than break; it is better to be BORN a beggar than a fool; better a CLOUT than a hole out;

better the DEVIL you know than the devil you don't know; better a DINNER of herbs than a stalled ox where hate is; DISCRETION is the better part of valour; better no DOCTOR at all than three; better an EGG today than a chicken tomorrow; better be ENVIED than pitied; better a little FIRE to warm us than a great one to burn us; better be FIRST in a village than second at Rome; better GIVE a penny than lend twenty; it is better to GIVE than to receive; better a GOOD cow than a cow of a good kind; the GREY mare is the better horse; better one HOUSE spoiled than two; better LATE than never; a LIVE dog is better than a dead lion; better LOST than found; better a LOUSE in the pot than no flesh at all; 'tis better to have LOVED and lost, than never to have loved at all; it is better to be born LUCKY than rich; better a MISCHIEF than an inconvenience; better be an OLD man's darling than a young man's slave; better be OUT of the world than out of fashion; better SAFE than sorry; better SAY nothing, than nothing to the purpose; it is better to TRAVEL hopefully than to arrive; better to WEAR out than to rust out; better WED over the mixen than over the moor

between two stools you fall to the ground (Latin) He who hesitates between two choices may miss the chance of either. Seneca, Controversia, first century AD.

While the two stools her sitting-part confound, between 'em both fall squat upon the ground.
Henry Fielding, Tom Thumb, 1730

beware. beware of Greeks bearing gifts (Roman) Be suspicious of those who curry favour with presents and favours. Virgil, Aeneid, 19 BC. The proverb is an allusion to the legend of the wooden horse, by means of which Greek soldiers were smuggled into the midst of their enemies, the Trojans. Rendered in Latin as 'timeo Danaos et dona ferentes' ('I fear the Greeks even when they bring gifts').

Tell Mrs Boswell that I shall taste her marmalade cautiously at first. Timeo Danaos et dona ferentes.
Samuel Johnson, letter, 3 May 1777

beware. See also let the BUYER beware; beware of the OAK, it draws the stroke; avoid the ash, it courts the flash

big. big fish eat little fish (English) It is part of the natural order of things that the strong prey on those weaker than themselves. Old English Homilies, 1200.

Third Fisherman Master, I marvel how the fishes live in the sea.
First Fisherman Why, as men do a-land; the great ones eat up the little ones.
William Shakespeare, Pericles, c.1608

big fleas have little fleas upon their backs to bite them, and little fleas have lesser fleas, and so ad infinitum (English) Those who prey upon others are themselves preyed upon. Jonathan Swift, Poems, 1733.

big is beautiful (US) The bigger something is, the greater the advantages. Commonly applied in discussion of large business enterprises. See also SMALL is beautiful.

however big the whale may be, the tiny harpoon can rob him of life (Malay) The largest opponent or hardest task may still be overcome by an apparently insignificant effort. See also the BIGGER they are, the harder they fall.

big. See also GOD is always on the side of the big battalions

bigger. the bigger they are, the harder they fall (English) The more powerful an opponent, the greater the impact when overthrown. H. Parker, *Dives and Pauper*, 1493. Popularized around 1900 after it was used by the boxer Robert Fitzsimmons in discussing a forthcoming bout. Variants include 'the highest tree hath the greatest fall'.

billet. See every BULLET has its billet

bind. See SAFE bind, safe find

bird. a bird in the hand is worth two in the bush (Greek) Something of modest value but securely held is more valuable than something of potentially greater worth that has yet to be firmly seized. *Harleian MS*, c.1470 (also quoted by Theocritus). The sentiment of the proverb was commonly expressed in various forms as far back as ancient Greece, when Aesop used it as the basis of several of his fables. It has since been recorded in a host of European languages, including French ('a bird in the hand is worth two in the hedge') and Italian ('better a sparrow in the pan than a hundred chickens in the priest's yard'). Other European variants include 'a sparrow in the hand is worth a pheasant that flyeth by', which was recorded in England in 1732, 'a pullet in the pen is worth an hundred in the fen' and 'a pound in the purse is worth two in the book'.

That proverb, *A bird in the hand is worth two in the bush*, is of more authority with them than are all ... testimonies of the good of the world to come.
John Bunyan, *Pilgrim's Progress*, 1678

a bird never flew on one wing (Scottish) One should always take a balanced view of things (often used as a justification for taking a second drink). James Kelly, *A Complete Collection of Scottish Proverbs*, 1721. Sometimes formerly given as 'the bird must flighter [flutter] that flies with one wing'.

bird. See also one BEATS the bush, another takes the bird; the EARLY bird catches the worm; it's an ILL bird that fouls its own nest; in vain the NET is spread in the sight of the bird

birds. birds in their little nests agree (English) The young should not argue among themselves. I. Watts, *Divine Songs*, 1715.

'Birds in their little nests agree,' she said, smiling ... She knew nothing at all about birds.
Laura Ingalls Wilder, *Little Town on the Prairie*, 1941

birds of a feather flock together (Greek) People of similar character tend to come together. W. Turner, *Rescuing of the Romish Fox*, 1545 (also quoted by Homer and Cicero). Commonly heard since the sixteenth century; usually said disparagingly of more dubious sorts, typically the criminal classes. See also a MAN is known by the company he keeps.

Clifford and the haught Northumberland, and of their feather many more proud birds.
William Shakespeare, *Henry VI, Part 3*, c.1591

there are no birds in last year's nest (English) Things change as time passes, just as each season the birds build new nests rather than re-use those of the previous year. T. Shelton, *Cervantes' Don Quixote*, 1620. Sometimes quoted in reference to those who are of advanced years and cannot be expected to come out with new ideas or physical feats (as an old man Winston

Churchill quoted it on one occasion when someone pointed out that he had absentmindedly forgotten to do up his flies). Also encountered in the form 'there are no birds of this year in last year's nest'.

birds. *See also* you cannot CATCH old birds with chaff; FINE feathers make fine birds; LITTLE birds that can sing and won't sing must be made to sing

birth is much but breeding more (English) A person's character is partly inherited, but the influences to which they are exposed in childhood will ultimately have the greater impact. John Clarke, *Paroemiologia Anglo-Latina*, 1639.

bite. don't bite the hand that feeds you (English) It is foolhardy, as well as ungrateful, to attack a person or organization on whom you are dependent.

if you cannot bite, never show your teeth (English) Never threaten to act unless you are prepared to follow the threat through. Thomas Fuller, *The History of the Holy War*, 1639.

bite. *See also* a BLEATING sheep loses a bite; DEAD men don't bite; every DOG is allowed one bite; big FLEAS have little fleas upon their backs to bite them

biter. the biter is sometimes bit (Greek) Those who criticize or attack others must expect to be attacked in return on occasion. Thomas D'Urfey, *The Richmond Heiress*, 1693 (also quoted by Lucian).

bites. *See* a BARKING dog never bites

bitten. he who has been bitten by a snake fears a piece of string (Persian) Bitter experience can cause a person to

hesitate in the future, even when there is no real risk. John Ray, *Adages of the Hebrews*, 1678.

once bitten, twice shy (English) Bad experiences teach a person to be more cautious another time. R. S. Surtees, *Sponge's Sporting Tour*, 1853. *See also* a BURNT child dreads the fire.

Once bit twice shy. He had no mind to be kidnapped.
Joseph Conrad, *Rescue*, 1920

bitter pills may have blessed effects (English) Hard lessons, like sour medicines, may yield the best results. Geoffrey Chaucer, *Troilus and Criseyde*, c.1385. A proverb related to the principle 'the more desperate the disease, the more desperate the remedy'. Variants include 'bitter pills may have wholesome effects'.

The medicine, the more bitter it is, the more better it is in working.
John Lyly, *Euphues: The Anatomy of Wit*, 1578

black. there's a black sheep in every family (English) Every family has its rebel, whose conduct is a cause of disgrace and regret. Walter Scott, *Old Mortality*, 1816. Originally often given in the form 'there are black sheep in every flock/fold'. Superstition had it that if the first lamb born into a flock in the spring was black, this brought bad luck to the owner (though in other circumstances the presence of a black sheep promoted the luck of the flock). The birth of twin black sheep was considered particularly ominous as regards the luck of the shepherd. In practical terms, the birth of a black sheep was unwelcome because its fleece could not be dyed, thus rendering the creature relatively worthless.

I suppose every family has a black sheep.

Tom had been a sore trial to his for twenty years.
W. Somerset Maugham, *Cosmopolitans*, 'The Ant and the Grasshopper', 1926

black. *See also* the DEVIL is not as black as he is painted; the POT calls the kettle black

blacks. *See* TWO blacks don't make a white

blames. *See* a BAD workman blames his tools

bleating. a bleating sheep loses a bite (English) Time wasted in talking could be better used. J. Minsheu, *Dialogues in Spanish*, 1599.

He said something about a bleating sheep losing a bite; but I should think this young man is not much of a talker.
T. Hughes, *Tom Brown at Oxford*, 1861

blessed. blessed are the dead that the rain rains on (English) If it rains at a funeral this is a portent that the angels are mourning the passing of the deceased and further constitutes a sign that he or she has been allowed entry into Heaven. *The Puritan*, 1607. *See also* HAPPY is the bride the sun shines on.

I could only remember, without resentment, that Daisy hadn't sent a message or a flower. Dimly I heard someone murmur, 'Blessed are the dead that the rain falls on'.
F. Scott Fitzgerald, *The Great Gatsby*, 1925

blessed is he who expects nothing, for he shall never be disappointed (English) Those who adopt a pessimistic outlook to life thus safeguard themselves from disappointment of their hopes. Alexander Pope, letter, 6 October 1727.

blessing. *See* a CHILD may have too much of his mother's blessing

blessings. blessings brighten as they take their flight (English) It is only when some benefit is gone that its full worth is appreciated. T. Fuller, *Gnomologia*, 1732. Also heard as 'blessings are not valued till they are gone'.

How blessings brighten as they take their flight.
Edward Young, *Night Thoughts*, 1742

blessings do not come in pairs; misfortunes never come singly (Chinese) Strokes of bad luck seem to fall more frequently than strokes of good fortune.

blind. a blind man cannot judge colours (English) Someone who is ignorant of a subject should not be expected to understand it. Geoffrey Chaucer, *Troilus and Criseyde*, c.1385.

A blind man can nat juggen wel in hewis.
Geoffrey Chaucer, *Troilus and Criseyde*, c.1385

a blind man's wife needs no paint (Spanish) It is pointless and even suspicious if a person goes to some trouble that in normal circumstances will not be appreciated (in this case, a blind man's wife putting on make-up, presumably in order to impress someone other than her husband). c.1627, quoted in Correas, *Vocabulary*, 1906.

For whom does the blind man's wife paint herself?
T. Fuller, *Gnomologia*, 1732

if the blind lead the blind, both shall fall into the ditch (Hebrew) Disaster will befall those who put their faith in the leadership of others who know no better than themselves. *Anglo-Saxon Gospel*, AD 995 (also quoted in the Bible, Luke 6:39). Also found in numerous variants in Classical literature. Hieronymus Bosch, Breughel the Elder and Breughel the Younger are among the artists to have produced celebrated works of art on the theme of the blind leading the blind. Now often heard in the shortened form 'the blind leading the blind'. British theatre critic Kenneth Tynan produced his own variation of the proverb when about to join the *New Yorker* magazine in 1958: 'They say the *New Yorker* is the bland leading the bland.'

When the blind leads the blind, no wonder they both fall into – matrimony.
George Farquhar, *Love and a Bottle*, 1699

men are blind in their own cause (English) If a person has a vested interest in something he or she is likely to dismiss arguments that appear to run contrary to that interest, however well founded they might be. John Heywood, *A Dialogue containing ... the Proverbs in the English Tongue*, 1546.

there are none so blind as those who will not see (English) Some people fail to see the truth of the matter simply because they refuse to contemplate the possibility that they may be wrong. John Heywood, *A Dialogue containing ... the Proverbs in the English Tongue*, 1546. *See also* there are none so DEAF as those who will not hear.

'None so blind as those that won't see.' Baxter was credulous and incredulous for precisely the same reason ... A single effort of the will was sufficient to exclude from his view whatever he judged hostile to his immediate purpose.
Edward Fitzgerald, *Polonius*, 1852

blind. *See also* in the COUNTRY of the blind, the one-eyed man is king; a DEAF husband and a blind wife are always a happy couple; LOVE is blind; a NOD is as good as a wink to a blind horse; NOTHING so bold as a blind mare

blindworm. *See* if the ADDER could hear and the blindworm could see, neither man nor beast would ever go free

bliss. *See* where IGNORANCE is bliss, 'tis folly to be wise

blister. a blister will rise upon one's tongue that tells a lie (English) A lie is betrayed by blisters upon the tongue, or by some other telling sign. John Lyly, *Sapho and Phao*, 1584.

I have a blister on my tongue; yet I don't remember I told a lie.
Jonathan Swift, *A Complete Collection of Polite and Ingenious Conversation*, 1738

blood. blood is thicker than water (German) Loyalty felt to one's blood relations will always outweigh loyalty to friends. John Ray, *A Collection of English Proverbs*, 1813.

Weel – blude's thicker than water – she's welcome to the cheeses.
Walter Scott, *Guy Mannering*, 1815

blood will have blood (English) Violence begets violence. *Mirror for Magistrates*, 1559. *See also* an EYE for an eye, and a tooth for a tooth.

It will have blood; they say blood will have blood.
William Shakespeare, *Macbeth*, c.1604

blood will tell (English) Individuals inherit certain traits of character from their ancestors, and these will inevitably show themselves. G. H. Boker, *World a Mask*, 1850.

the blood of the martyrs is the seed of the Church (Roman) The persecution of Christian martyrs through the ages inspired the growth of the Church. T. Adams, *Works*, 1630 (also quoted by Tertullian in *Apologeticus* in the second century AD).

And hanged he had been, had not Harry Marteyn told them that *sanguis martyrum est*

semen ecclesiae, and that way would do them more mischief.
John Aubrey, *Brief Lives*, 1697

you cannot get blood from a stone (Roman) There is no point trying to extract some benefit where there is no benefit to be had. John Lyly, *Euphues and His England*, 1580 (also quoted by Plautus). Originally, the word 'water' often appeared in the place of 'blood', and the 'stone' might be given as 'pummice' or 'flint'.

Blood cannot be obtained from a stone, neither can anything on account be obtained ... from Mr Micawber.
Charles Dickens, *David Copperfield*, 1850

bloom. *See* when the FURZE is in bloom, my love's in tune; when the GORSE is out of bloom, kissing's out of fashion

blow. *See* the FIRST blow is half the battle; SEPTEMBER blow soft, till the fruit's in the loft

blows. *See* it's an ILL wind that blows nobody any good; STRAWS tell which way the wind blows

blue. blue are the hills that are far away (Scottish) Some things look better at a distance than they do at close quarters. T. H. Hall Caine, *Deemster*, 1887. *See also* DISTANCE lends enchantment to the view.

blue. *See also* TRUE blue will never stain

blushing is a sign of grace (English) Only those with finer feelings will have the sensitivity to blush when they are embarrassed and thus a blush may be taken as a sign of nobility of character. *A Quest of Enquirie*, 1595.

Well, however, blushing is some sign of grace.
Jonathan Swift, *Polite Conversation*, 1738

blustering. a blustering night, a fair day follows (Spanish) A stormy night

presages a fine day. George Herbert, *Jacula Prudentum*, 1640.

boaster. a boaster and a liar are all one (English) There is no difference in morality between a boast and a lie. Geoffrey Chaucer, *Troilus and Criseyde*, c.1385. Also encountered as 'a boaster and a liar are cousins'.

boatmen. too many boatmen will run the boat up to the top of the mountain (Japanese) An overmanned ship (or organization) will surely come to grief. *See also* too many COOKS spoil the broth.

bodies. *See* CORPORATIONS have neither bodies to be punished nor souls to be damned

boils. *See* a WATCHED pot never boils

bold. he was a bold man that first ate an oyster (English) It takes courage to be the first to do something that, lacking the knowledge of hindsight, appears to be very risky. T. Fuller, *The History of the Worthies of England*, 1662.

King James was wont to say, 'he was a very valiant man who first adventured on eating of oysters'.
T. Fuller, *The History of the Worthies of England*, 1662

it is a bold mouse that breeds in the cat's ear (English) To survive in a position of potential danger requires much cunning and wariness. John Lydgate, *Minor Poems*, c.1430.

Let Philautus behave himself never so craftely, he shal know that it must be a wyly Mouse that shall breede in the Cats eare.
John Lyly, *Euphues: The Anatomy of Wit*, 1578

bold. *See also* NOTHING so bold as a blind mare

boldness in business is the first, second and third thing (English) A determined, resolute approach is the one essential in all business matters. Thomas Fuller, *Gnomologia*, 1732.

bolted. *See* it is too LATE to shut the stable-door after the horse has bolted

Bolton. *See* BATE me an ace, quoth Bolton

bond. *See* an ENGLISHMAN's word is his bond

bone. *See* what's BRED in the bone will come out in the flesh; a DOG that will fetch a bone will carry a bone; the NEARER the bone, the sweeter the flesh

bones. *See* you BUY land you buy stones, you buy meat you buy bones; FAIR words break no bones; HARD words break no bones; STICKS and stones may break my bones, but names will never hurt me

book. you can't judge a book by its cover (US) One cannot judge inner character by outward appearances. *American Speech*, 1929. *See also* APPEARANCES are deceptive.

book. *See also* a GREAT book is a great evil

books. books and friends should be few and good (English) One should be selective in both one's reading and in one's friends.

books. *See also* YEARS know more than books

boot. *See* when BALE is highest, boot is nighest

boots. *See* a LIE travels around the world while truth is putting on her boots

born. if you're born to be hanged then you'll never be drowned (French) A lucky escape may simply be a sign that one is destined for a worse fate later on. A. Barclay, translation of

*Gringore's Castle of Labour, c.*1503.

Go, go; begone to save your ship from wreck,
Which cannot perish, having thee aboard,
Being destined to a drier death on shore.
William Shakespeare, *The Two Gentlemen of Verona*, c.1594

it is better to be born a beggar than a fool (Spanish) It is better to be born poor than stupid. R. Percyvall, *A Spanish Grammar*, 1599.

It is better to be a beggar than an Ignoramus.
G. Torriano, *Select Italian Proverbs*, 1642

we are born crying, live complaining and die disappointed (English) It is man's lot to suffer at all stages of life. Thomas Fuller, *Gnomologia*, 1732.

born. *See also* it is better to be born LUCKY than rich; the MAN who is born in a stable is a horse; YORKSHIRE born and Yorkshire bred, strong in the arm and weak in the head

borrowed garments never fit well (English) The clothes, position, responsibilities of one person will never fit another person perfectly. Thomas Fuller, *Gnomologia*, 1732.

borrower. neither a borrower nor a lender be (English) Borrowing or lending money, especially from or to one's friends, is but an invitation to trouble. William Shakespeare, *Hamlet, c.*1600. The proverb doubtless descends from such biblical injunctions as 'the borrower is servant to the lender' (Proverbs, 22:7). *See also* LEND your money and lose your friend.

Neither a borrower nor a lender be;
For loan oft loses both itself and friend,
And borrowing dulls the edge of husbandry.
William Shakespeare, *Hamlet, c.*1600

borrowing. *See* he that goes A-BORROW-ING, goes a-sorrowing

borrows. *See* the EARLY man never borrows from the late man

both. you can't have it both ways (*English*) In some circumstances choosing to enjoy one particular benefit necessarily precludes a person from enjoying an alternative one. *See also* you can't HAVE your cake and eat it.

bottles. *See* you can't put NEW wine in old bottles

bottom. *See* TRUTH lies at the bottom of a well; every TUB must stand on its own bottom

boughs. the boughs that bear most hang lowest (*English*) The truly great are often the most humble in discussing their achievements. Thomas Fuller, *Church History of Britain*, 1655.

The vines that bear much fruit are proud to stoop with it.
Elizabeth Barrett Browning, *Aurora*, 1856

bought. bought wit is the best (*English*) Knowledge is only of any worth if someone else is prepared to pay for it. H. Medwall, *Nature*, c.1490. Also encountered in the forms 'bought wit is dear', 'wit once bought is the best' and 'wit is never good till it be bought'.

We say, Wisdom is not good till it is bought; and he that buys it ... usually smarts for it.
John Bunyan, *Accept Sacrifice*, 1688

bought. *See also* GOLD may be bought too dear

bound. the bound must obey (*English*) Those who have no other choice are obliged to do what is demanded of them. Layamon, *Brut*, 1205.

Wo is hym that is bun, ffor he must abyde.
Towneley Plays, c.1410

bow. *See* DRAW not your bow till your arrow is fixed

Bowden. not every man can be vicar of Bowden (*English*) It is impossible for all men to occupy the best positions. John Ray, *A Collection of English Proverbs*, 1678. Bowden was celebrated as one of the best livings in Cheshire. *See also* the VICAR of Bray will be vicar of Bray still.

bowl. *See* LIFE is just a bowl of cherries

bowls. *See* those who PLAY at bowls must look out for rubbers

boys. boys will be boys (*Roman*) It is in the nature of young boys to be at times boisterous and mischievous, and such behaviour should therefore be excused. W. Robertson, *Phraseology Generalis*, 1681. The proverb was known to the Romans in the form 'pueri sunt pueri, pueri puerilia tractant' ('children are children and employ themselves with childish things'), and it has been suggested that the modern form of the proverb limited to boys alone may have arisen from a mistranslation of the Latin 'pueri', which actually signified children of both sexes. Variants include 'boys will be men' (meaning, all boys will grow to manhood, with all its responsibilities, in time).

Would old Anstruther consider an outrage perpetrated on the person of Bertram Wooster a crime sufficiently black to cause him to rule Thos out of the race? Or would he just give a senile chuckle and mumble something about boys being boys?
P. G. Wodehouse, *Very Good Jeeves!*, 1930

two boys are half a boy, and three boys are no boy at all (*English*) The greater the number of boys that help in doing something, the less effective their assistance becomes. Flora Thompson, *Country Calendar*, c. 1930. *See also* too many COOKS spoil the broth.

Their parents do not encourage the joining of forces ... we have a proverb here: 'Two boys are half a boy, and three boys are no boy at all'.

Flora Thompson, *Country Calendar*, c. 1930

brae. *See* put a STOUT heart to a stey brae

brag. Brag is a good dog, but Holdfast is better (English) Quietly determined action counts for more than boastful and conceited talk. A. Munday, *Zelanto*, 1580. Not unrelated is the proverb of seventeenth-century origins, 'Brag's a good dog but dares not bite', which underlines the idea that some people make threats or boasts that they are not brave or resolute enough to carry through. Other variants include 'Brag's a good dog but that he hath lost his tail', 'Brag is a good dog but dares not bite' and 'Brag's a good dog if he be well set on'. *See also* they BRAG most that can do least.

When I envied the finery of any of my neighbours, [my mother] told me, that 'brag was a good dog, but holdfast was a better'.

Samuel Johnson, *The Rambler*, 4 February 1752

they brag most that can do least (English) Those who boast loudest of their powers are the least likely to possess them. R. Taverner, *Proverbs or Adages of Erasmus*, 1545. *See also* BRAG is a good dog, but Holdfast is better.

brain. *See* an IDLE brain is the Devil's workshop

Bran. if not Bran, it is Bran's brother (English) Compliment that suggests that someone or something is so good as to be indistinguishable from an original of fabled excellence. Walter Scott, *Waverley*, 1814. Bran was the celebrated dog belonging to Fingal, the hero of Gaelic legend.

'Mar e Bran, is e a brathair, if it be not Bran, it is Bran's brother,' was the proverbial reply of Maccombich.

Walter Scott, *Waverley*, 1814

brass. where there's muck, there's brass *See* where there's MUCK, there's money

brave. brave men lived before Agamemnon (Greek) Our own age should not be accepted as the only time when great men and women lived and great things were done (as the ancient Greeks might have been tempted to do). Horace, *Odes*, first century BC. In Horace, the proverb appears in the form '*vixere fortes ante Agamemnon*'; it was later famously reworked by Byron. In 1902 Dean Hole contributed '*vixere fortes ante Agamemnon* – there was splendid cricket before Grace'.

Brave men were living before Agamemnon
And since, exceeding valorous and sage,
A good deal like him too, though quite the
    same none:
But then they shone not on the poet's page,
And so have been forgotten.

George Gordon, Lord Byron, *Don Juan*, 1819

none but the brave deserve the fair (English) Only those of heroic character should aspire to win the most beautiful women. John Dryden, *Poems*, 1697.

All the proverbs were on his side. 'None but the brave deserve the fair,' said his cousin.

Anthony Trollope, *Phineas Redux*, 1873

brave. *See also* FORTUNE favours the brave; ROBIN Hood could brave all weathers but a thaw wind

brawling curs never want sore ears (English) Those who are quick to pick quarrels with others will find they are frequently at the receiving end of others' wrath. Randle Cotgrave, *A Dictionary of the French and English Tongues*, 1611.

Come, come, sir, babling curs never want sore ears.
Thomas D'Urfey, *Quixote*, 1694

Bray. *See* the VICAR of Bray will be vicar of Bray still

bread. bread is the staff of life (English) Bread has a unique value, being a staple food of life. Jonathan Swift, *Tale of a Tub*, 1704. Another proverb goes a little further: 'bread is the staff of life, but beer's life itself'.

'Bread,' says he, 'dear brothers, is the staff of life.'
Jonathan Swift, *Tale of a Tub*, 1704

he who has no bread has no authority (Turkish) Only those who have something to offer can hope to enjoy influence over others.

the bread never falls but on the buttered side (English) When things go awry, ill luck will ensure that the worst happens. John Ray, *A Collection of English Proverbs*, 1678. Originated in the north of England. *See also* if ANYTHING can go wrong, it will.

We express the completeness of ill-luck by saying 'the bread never falls but on its buttered side'.
John Lockwood Kipling, *Man and Beast in India*, 1891

bread. *See also* EATEN bread is soon forgotten; HALF a loaf is better than no bread; it is HARD to pay for bread that has been eaten; MAN cannot live by bread alone

break. *See* better BEND than break; never GIVE a sucker an even break; HARD

words break no bones; if it were not for HOPE, the heart would break; STICKS and stones may break my bones, but names will never hurt me

breakfast. *See* HOPE is a good breakfast but a bad supper

breaking. *See* you cannot make an OMELETTE without breaking eggs

breaks. a man that breaks his word bids others be false to him (English) A person who does not behave honestly towards others cannot expect them to behave honestly in return. Edward Hall, *Hall's Chronicle*, 1548.

breaks. *See also* it is the LAST straw that breaks the camel's back

breath. *See* SAVE your breath to cool your porridge

bred. what's bred in the bone will come out in the flesh (English) A person's true character, inherited traits or long ingrained habits will inevitably reveal themselves. William Caxton, *Reynard*, 1481. The proverb has undergone a gradual change from its original form, which suggested something slightly different: 'what's bred in the bone will not out of the flesh'. In this earlier form, the proverb implies rather that there is no faking the kind of qualities that one has to be born with.

Sir Launcelot smyled and said hard hit is to take oute of the flesshe that is bred in the bone.
Thomas Malory, *Morte d'Arthur*, 1485

bred. *See also* YORKSHIRE born and Yorkshire bred, strong in the arm and weak in the head

breeding rather than birth (Japanese) Upbringing is more important than ancestry.

breeds. *See* FAMILIARITY breeds contempt; LIKE breeds like

brevity is the soul of wit (English) Wit is best when pithy and concise. William Shakespeare, *Hamlet*, *c.*1600 (much the same sentiment was expressed by many writers of the Classical world, among them Plautus and Horace). In Shakespeare's time the word 'wit' did not necessarily imply humour, but understanding of all kinds. To US wit Dorothy Parker is attributed the *bon mot* 'brevity is the soul of lingerie'.

Since brevity is the soul of wit – I will be brief. Your noble son is mad.
William Shakespeare, *Hamlet*, *c.*1600

brew. as you brew, so shall you bake (English) As you sow, so must you reap. 1264, quoted in C. Brown, *English Lyrics of the XIIIth Century*, 1932. *See also* as you BAKE, so shall you brew; as you MAKE your bed, so you must lie in it.

Bot we must drynk as we brew
And that is bot reson.
Towneley Play of the Second Shepherd, *c.*1450

bribe. a bribe will enter without knocking (English) Through bribery a person may gain immediate access where a more honest approach would be of no avail. B. Rich, *Irish Hubbub*, 1619.

bricks. you can't make bricks without straw (English) The right materials (or knowledge etc.) must be acquired before certain tasks can be successfully accomplished. Robert Burton, *The Anatomy of Melancholy*, 1624. The proverb is loosely derived from a passage in Exodus 5:7, which runs 'yee shall no more give the people straw to make bricke, as heretofore: let them goe and gather straw for themselves'. The background to this passage was that

the Israelites, then under the Egyptians, asked for time off to make a pilgrimage into the desert; the Egyptians, impressed by the fact that their slaves now dared to ask for time off, decided they were not being kept busy enough and so ordered that as well as making bricks as before the Israelites would also have to collect the straw for them themselves.

You can only acquire really useful general ideas by first acquiring particular ideas ... you cannot make bricks without straw.
Arnold Bennett, *Literary Taste*, 1909

bride. *See* HAPPY is the bride the sun shines on

bridge. it is good to make a bridge of gold to a flying enemy (Greek) When an enemy is defeated, it is wise to let him make good his escape, lest he turn to fight again because his route has been cut off. Plutarch, *Themistocles*, first century AD. The proverb is attributed originally to Aristides, who advised the victorious Themistocles to allow the vanquished Xerxes to escape via a bridge of boats across the Hellespont. In some instances it is a bridge of silver, rather than one of gold.

You may have heard a military proverb: that it is a good thing to make a bridge of gold to a flying enemy.
Robert Louis Stevenson, *The Master of Ballantrae*, 1889

bridge. *See also* don't CROSS the bridge until you get to it

bright. *See* always LOOK on the bright side

brighten. *See* BLESSINGS brighten as they take their flight

bring. he who would bring home the wealth of the Indies, must carry the wealth of the Indies with

him (*Spanish*) To attract wealth, one must be wealthy in the first place. James Boswell, *Life of Johnson*, 1791. The proverb had its roots in the days when Spanish adventurers sought to make their fortune in the West Indies, though success depended largely upon substantial financial backing for their voyages.

bring. *See also* the WORTH of a thing is what it will bring

broke. if it ain't broke, don't fix it (*US*) If something is working perfectly well it should not be interfered with just for the sake of change. Tim Rice, quoted in the *Independent*, 12 November 1988. There seems to be no record of this proverb before 1977, when President Carter's Director of Management and Budget, Bert Lance, apparently said it when discussing the possibility of governmental reform.

broken. *See* the PITCHER goes so often to the well that it is broken at last; PROMISES, like pie-crust, are made to be broken

broom. a new broom sweeps clean (*English*) A person newly promoted to a post will show greater zeal than his or her predecessor. John Heywood, *A Dialogue containing ... the Proverbs in the English Tongue*, 1546. Although the proverb was recorded in the sixteenth century, popular tradition derives it from an incident that occurred during the first Dutch War of 1652. The story goes that the Dutch admiral Van Tromp lashed a broom to the mast of his flagship as a warning that he would 'sweep' the English navy from the seas; in reply, the English admiral Robert Blake had a horsewhip bound to the mast of his own flagship – and

subsequently drove the Dutch ships off (sailors also tied brooms to the mast to indicate that their ship was for sale). In reality, the proverb almost certainly arose from the fact that old-fashioned brooms, comprising a bundle of green stems tied to a long handle, rapidly lost their effectiveness as the sticks dried out and became far less efficient than when new. New appointees are often succinctly described as 'new brooms'. An Irish proverb, however, adds the rider: 'a new broom sweeps clean, but the old brush knows all the corners'.

broth. *See* every COOK praises his own broth; too many COOKS spoil the broth

build. *See* FOOLS build houses and wise men live in them; it is easier to PULL down than to build up; where GOD builds a church, the Devil will build a chapel

built. *See* ROME was not built in a day

bullet. every bullet has its billet (*English*) Fate dictates all things, including whether a bullet will strike its target or not (in other words, whether a person is killed or survives). George Gascoigne, *Fruits of War*, 1575. Tradition ascribes the proverb to William of Orange (though there is some doubt as to which particular William of Orange is meant, with William III of England being a favourite contender for the honour). The same notion inspired the fanciful belief that a person would die by shooting only if a particular bullet 'had his name' on it. Napoleon often repeated this idea, boasting that the bullet that would kill him had yet to be cast.

He never received one wound. So true is

the odd saying of King William, that 'every bullet has its billet'.

John Wesley, *Journal*, 6 June 1765

bully. a bully is always a coward (English) Those who use others cruelly usually lack courage themselves. Maria Edgeworth, *Harrington and Ormond*, 1817.

Mrs M'Crule, who like all other bullies was a coward, lowered her voice.

Maria Edgeworth, *Harrington and Ormond*, 1817

bung-hole. *See* SPARE at the spigot, and let out at the bung-hole

burden. *See* GOD makes the back to the burden

burdensome. *See* NOTHING is burdensome as a secret

burn. you cannot burn the candle at both ends (English) If a person works too hard or too long at something he or she will have no energy (or health) left to apply to anything else. Francis Bacon, *Promus*, 1592.

By sitting up till two in the morning, and rising again at six ... Frank Headley burnt the candle of life at both ends.

Charles Kingsley, *Two Years Ago*, 1857

burnt. a burnt child dreads the fire (Roman) We learn from experience to avoid that which harms us. *Proverbs of Hending*, c.1250 (also quoted by Cicero). Parallel proverbs in other languages include the French 'a scalded dog fears cold water', the Italian 'a dog which has been beaten with a stick fears its own shadow' and the Jewish 'one bitten by a serpent is afraid of a rope's end'. *See also* once BITTEN, twice shy; he who has once BURNT his mouth always blows his soup; a SCALDED cat fears cold water.

The burnt child fears the fire, and bitter experience had taught Pongo Twistleton to view with concern the presence in his midst of Ickenham's fifth earl.

P. G. Wodehouse, *Uncle Dynamite*, 1948

he who has once burnt his mouth always blows his soup (German) We learn from bad experiences to be cautious the next time. *See also* once BITTEN, twice shy.

burnt. *See also* if you PLAY with fire you get burnt

bury. *See* let the DEAD bury the dead

bush. *See* a BAD bush is better than an open field; a BIRD in the hand is worth two in the bush; good WINE needs no bush; one BEATS the bush, another takes the bird

bushel. *See* don't HIDE your light under a bushel; don't MEASURE other people's corn by one's own bushel

busiest. the busiest men have the most leisure (English) Those whose lives are the fullest are often also those who find the most time for pleasure (presumably because they are obliged by necessity to keep their affairs in good order). S. Smiles, *Self-Help*, 1866. Not unrelated was the now neglected proverb 'who is more busy than he that hath least to do?' *See also* IDLE people have the least leisure.

business. business before pleasure (English) Business matters should be dealt with before one turns to pleasure. *Grobiana's Nuptials*, c.1640. The wisdom of the proverb was underlined in ancient times when news of a plot to murder him was brought to the Spartan garrison commander Archias at Thebes: Archias, who was in the midst of a banquet, put the message under a cushion with the words 'business tomorrow', without reading it. Before the next day dawned he was dead.

business is business (English) Business should be tackled in a businesslike way, without sentiment or emotion. William Thackeray, *The Virginians*, 1857. Another proverb advises that 'business is the salt of life'.

Business is business, my dear young sir.
William Thackeray, *The Virginians*, 1857

one business begets another (English) If one business prospers it promotes the establishment of further related enterprises. Thomas More, *Works*, 1528.

who likes not his business, his business likes not him (English) No man will prosper in a business for which he has no liking. T. Wright, *Essays on the Middle Ages*, 1846. Related proverbs include 'he that thinks his business below him will always be above his business'.

business. *See also* EVERYBODY's business is nobody's business; PUNCTUALITY is the soul of business

butter. butter is mad twice a year (English) Some things, though usually reliable, may be counted upon to go awry at certain times or under certain circumstance (just as butter made in July was supposed to be too thin and butter made in December too hard). Ben Jonson, *Staple of News*, 1625.

Butter is said to be mad twice a year; once in summer ... when it is too thin and fuild; and once in winter ... when it is too hard and difficult to spread.
John Ray, *A Collection of English Proverbs*, 1678

butter. *See also* FINE words butter no parsnips; there are more WAYS of killing a dog than choking it with butter

buttered. *See* the BREAD never falls but on the buttered side

button up to the chin till May comes in (English) Do not discard winter clothing before the month of May. *See also* ne'er CAST a clout till May be out.

buy. buy in the cheapest market and sell in the dearest (English) In business there are profits to be made by buying merchandise at a low price and selling it for more. T. Lodge, *A Fig for Momus*, 1595.

Buy in the cheapest market? – yes; but what made your market cheap? ... Sell in the dearest? ... but what made your market dear?
John Ruskin, *Unto this Last*, 1862

why buy a cow when milk is so cheap? (English) It is illogical to go to great lengths to enjoy something that is readily available without such trouble. J. Howell, *Proverbs*, 1659. Often quoted by those opposed to marriage, on the grounds that sex is easily obtainable elsewhere.

Who would keep a Cow of their own, that can have a quart of milk for a penny? Meaning, Who would be at the charge to have a Wife, that can have a Whore when he listeth?
John Bunyan, *Mr Badman*, 1680

you buy land you buy stones, you buy meat you buy bones (English) Many purchases necessitate acquiring things one does not want as they are inseparable from what is desired. John Ray, *A Collection of English Proverbs*, 1670. In its fullest form, the proverb compares the purchase of land or meat and so on with the purchase of good ale, which brings with it no such refuse.

He that buys Land, buys Stones; He that buys Nuts, buys shells: He that buys good Ale, buys nought else.

James Kelly, *A Complete Collection of Scottish Proverbs*, 1721

buyer. let the buyer beware (*Roman*) It is the buyer's responsibility to ensure that he does not allow himself to be duped in a business transaction. J. Fitzherbert, *Husbandry*, 1523. Often quoted in the Latin form, '*caveat emptor*'. The fullest form of the maxim runs '*caveat emptor, quia ignorare non debuit quod ius alineum emit*' ('let the buyer beware, for he ought not to be ignorant of the nature of the property which he is buying from another'). Modern consumer law provides some protection for the purchaser by insisting that any item offered for sale should be of a quality 'proper for the purposes for which it is required'.

the buyer has need of a hundred eyes, the seller of but one (*Italian*) In business, it is the purchaser rather than the vendor who runs all the risks and has the most need of vigilance. George Herbert, *Jacula Prudentum*, 1640.

He taught him ... to get ... from customers by taking advantage of their ignorance ... He often repeated ... 'The buyer has need of a hundred eyes; the seller has need of but one.'
Maria Edgeworth, *The Parent's Assistant*, 1800

by the street of by and by one arrives at the house of never (*Spanish*) If one is always procrastinating, things will never get done. R. C. Trench, *On the Lessons in Proverbs*, 1853. *See also* PROCRASTINATION is the thief of time.

bygones. let bygones be bygones (*Greek*) Past arguments with others should be consigned to history. John Heywood, *A Dialogue containing ... the Proverbs in the English Tongue*, 1546 (similar sentiments may be found in various forms in the writings of Epictetus, Homer and other Classical authors). *See also* FORGIVE and forget.

Let us adopt a Scotch proverb ... 'Let bygones be bygones, and fair play for the future'.
Walter Scott, *Guy Mannering*, 1815

C

cabbage twice cooked is death (*Greek*) Some things, like cabbage, should be discarded if not consumed or otherwise dealt with at once. R. Taverner, *Proverbs or Adages of Erasmus*, 1545 (also quoted by Juvenal).

Which I must omitte, least I set before you, colewortes twice sodden.
John Lyly, Euphues: The Anatomy of Wit, 1578

Caesar. Caesar's wife must be above suspicion (*Roman*) The spouses of those in the public eye need to preserve untarnished reputations. Plutarch, *Lives*, first century AD. The proverb refers to Pompeia, the wife of Roman dictator Julius Caesar, who became embroiled in a scandal involving Publius Clodius, a notorious libertine who was supposed to have seduced her after gaining entrance to the all-female Feast of the Great Goddess disguised as a woman. Though Caesar declared himself to be convinced of his wife's innocence, he went ahead and divorced her, explaining that even the taint of suspicion rendered her position as his wife untenable: 'I will not, sayd he, that my wife be so much as suspected'.

Your moral character must be not only pure, but, like Caesar's wife, unsuspected.
Lord Chesterfield, Letters, 1774

Caesar. *See also* RENDER unto Caesar that which is Caesar's

cake. *See* you can't HAVE your cake and eat it

calf. *See* a BELLOWING cow soon forgets her calf; there are many WAYS of dressing a calf's head

call. call a man a thief and he will steal (*English*) Give a person a bad reputation and they will be inclined to live up to it. Thomas Carlyle, *Sartor Resartus*, 1838.

In a very plain sense the proverb says, Call one a thief, and he will steal.
Thomas Carlyle, Sartor Resartus, 1838

call a spade a spade (*English*) Call things by their proper names, so that their real nature is revealed. William Rastell, *The Four Elements*, 1519 (also quoted by Erasmus).

call no man happy till he dies (*Greek*) A life that ends badly cannot be called happy, however good it may have been up to that point. *The Proverbs or Adages of Erasmus*, 1545 (also quoted by Sophocles in *Oedipus Rex*, fifth century BC, by Herodotus, by Sophocles, by Aristotle and by Ovid in *Metamorphoses*).

'Call no man happy until he is dead' ... He was seventy-two, and yet there was still time for this dream ... to change to a nightmare.
C. S. Forester, *Hornblower and Crisis*, 1967

call the bear 'uncle' till you are safe across the bridge (Turkish) Do not provoke those who can harm you until you are safe from any retaliation on their part. *Times Weekly*, 12 April 1912.

I wouldn't call the king my cousin (English) I am content with things as they are (and would be no better off even if related to the monarch himself). James Kelly, *A Complete Collection of Scotish Proverbs*, 1721.

Added when we say, Had I such a thing, could I get such a place, or effect such a project: I would think myself so happy, that I would flatter no body.
James Kelly, *A Complete Collection of Scotish Proverbs*, 1721

calls. *See* he who PAYS the piper calls the tune

calm. in a calm sea every man is a pilot (Roman) When there is no threat or challenge to test one's skills, any man may claim mastery of a subject safe in the knowledge that it will not be challenged. John Ray, *A Collection of English Proverbs*, 1670 (also quoted by Seneca in his *Epistles*). Variants include 'in a calm sea every passenger is a pilot'. Also recorded in Spanish and several other European languages.

In a calm sea everyone can steer.
Thomas Fuller, *Gnomologia*, 1732

calm. *See also* after a STORM comes a calm

camel. *See* it is EASIER for a camel to go through the eye of a needle than it is for a rich man to enter into the king-

dom of heaven; it is the LAST straw that breaks the camel's back

camomile. the more camomile is trodden on, the faster it grows (English) Some things, such as love and virtue, grow stronger the harsher they are treated (just as camomile lawns are supposed to grow better when walked upon). William Shakespeare, *Henry IV, Part 1*, c.1597.

For ne'er was simple camomile so trod on, yet still I grow in love.
James Shirley, *Hyde Park*, 1637

can. he who can does, he who cannot teaches (English) Only those who have failed to realize their ambitions of practising an art or craft themselves end up teaching it to others. George Bernard Shaw, *Maxims for Revolutionaries*, 1903.

candle. a candle lights others and consumes itself (English) Some people sacrifice themselves in inspiring others. J. Minsheu, *A Spanish Grammar, now augmented ... by J. Minsheu*, 1599.

The painful preacher, like a candle bright, consumes himself in giving others light.
Benjamin Franklin, *Poor Richard's Almanack*, 1742

candle. *See also* you cannot BURN the candle at both ends.

candles *See* CANDLEMAS Day, put beans in the clay, put candles and candlesticks away

candlelight. *See* never CHOOSE your women or your linen by candlelight

Candlemas. Candlemas Day, put beans in the clay, put candles and candlesticks away (English) Candlemas Day (the festival of the Virgin Mary, 2 February), traditionally the halfway point through the winter, marks the date on which candles and candlesticks used in religious services should be put away and the first planting of broad beans should take place. John Ray, *A Collection of English Proverbs*, 1678. The proverb dictates that on this day, the anniversary of Christ's first visit to the Temple with his mother, candles and candlesticks used in services of vespers and litanies should be put away until the following All Hallow's Mass in October. Candles blessed on Candlemas Day were formerly particularly valued as protectives against witchcraft.

Broad beans were planted ... on Candlemas Day. *Candlemas Day, stick beans in the clay, Throw candle and candlestick right away*, they would quote.
Flora Thompson, *Still Glides the Stream*, 1948

if Candlemas Day be sunny and bright, winter will have another flight; if Candlemas Day be cloudy with rain, winter is gone, and won't come again (English) The weather on Candlemas Day (2 February) may be interpreted to foretell what weather is in store. John Skelton, *Works*, 1523. The wording of the proverb varies from one source to another. Variants include 'if Candlemas Day be fair and fine, half the winter is left behind; if Candlemas Day be dull and gloom, half the winter is yet to come' and 'if Candlemas Day be cloudy and black, 'twill carry cold winter away on its back; but if Candlemas Day be fine and clear, then half the winter's to come this year'. A starker version insists 'on Candlemas Day, if the sun shines clear, the shepherd had rather see his wife on the bier'. In practical terms, farmers tended to regard Candlemas Day as marking the halfway point through the winter, and would husband their livestock rations so that there was still at least half left at this date. This piece of folk wisdom was rendered in proverb form as 'on Candlemas Day, you must have half your straw and half your hay'. Other proverbs offer more detail about the weather to come: 'as much ground as is covered with snow on Candlemas Day will be covered with snow before Lady-Day', alternatively: 'when the wind's in the east on Candlemas Day, there it will stick to the second of May'. *See also* SAINT Swithin's Day, if thou dost rain, for forty days it will remain; Saint Swithin's Day, if thou be fair, for forty days 'twill rain no more.

If Candlemas Day be fair and bright Winter will have another flight but if Candlemas Day be clouds and rain Winter is gone and will not come again.
Edith Holden, *The Country Diary of an Edwardian Lady*, 1906

canoe. *See* PADDLE your own canoe

cap. if the cap fits, wear it (English) If you are guilty of some act of blame or folly, then you should acknowledge it. N. Breton, *Pasquil's Fools-Cap*, 1600. The proverb has its origins in the fool's cap (often adorned with bells) that was worn in medieval times by fools and jesters as a symbol of their craft. The last fools disappeared in the early eighteenth century, but the fool's cap is still remembered as a symbol of stupidity or folly. In former times anyone who became the butt of a company's jokes might be said to be 'wearing the cap and bells'. The proverb is usually quoted in an aggressive context, suggesting to the recipient of the remark that they should recognize their own foolishness.

If indeed thou findest ... that the cap fits thy own head, why then ... e'en take and clap it on.
Samuel Richardson, *Clarissa*, 1748

capacity. *See* GENIUS is an infinite capacity for taking pains

caravan. *See* the DOGS bark but the caravan goes on

carcase. where the carcase is, there shall the eagles be gathered together (*Hebrew*) The wicked and the avaricious will gather where circumstances allow them to prosper. Bible, Matthew 24:28. The meaning of the proverb becomes clearer when it is appreciated that in the original Hebrew 'eagles' could signify vultures. Also found in the form 'where the carcase is, the ravens will gather'. *See also* BIRDS of a feather flock together.

Where carcasses are, eagles will gather, And where good laws are, much people flock thither.
Benjamin Franklin, *Poor Richard's Almanack*, 1734

cards are the Devil's books (*English*) Those who indulge in gambling lay themselves open to all manner of evil. *Poor Robin's Almanack*, 1676. The phrase was much used by Presbyterian opponents of card-playing and similar trivial 'ungodly' pastimes, partly in response to the older name for a pack of cards – 'the King's books' (derived from the French *livre des quatre rois*, the book of the four kings). Alternatively, a deck of cards might be referred to on occasion as the 'Devil's Bible'. Particularly ominous among gamblers is the four of clubs, which is dubbed the Devil's bedpost (any hand including this card is called the Devil's four-poster).

He thought that cards had not without

reason been called the Devil's Books.
Robert Southey, *The Doctor*, 1834

care. care and diligence bring luck (*English*) Good fortune is the product of hard work and careful attention. R. Taverner, *Flores aliquot sententiarum*, 1540.

Diligence is the mother of good fortune.
W. Stepney, *The Spanish Schoolmaster*, 1591

care is no cure (*English*) Kindness and good intentions cannot cure all ills. William Shakespeare, *Henry VI, Part 1*, c.1590.

Care is no cure, but rather corrosive, for things that are not to be remedied.
William Shakespeare, *Henry VI, Part 1*, c.1590

care killed the cat (*English*) Excessive worrying or anxiety is self-defeating, particularly if one is set on enjoying oneself. William Shakespeare, *Much Ado About Nothing*, c.1598. *See also* CURIOSITY killed the cat.

What, courage, man! What though care killed a cat.
William Shakespeare, *Much Ado About Nothing*, c.1598

care. *See also* take care of the PENNIES and the pounds will look after themselves; a POUND of care will not pay an ounce of debt

careful. *See* if you can't be GOOD, be careful

cares. *See* CHILDREN are certain cares, but uncertain comforts

carpenter. a carpenter is known by his chips (*English*) The best craftsmen may be distinguished by the small amount of waste they leave as they work. Thomas Coryat, *Coryats Crudities*, 1611.

They say a carpenter's known by his chips.
Jonathan Swift, *Polite Conversation*, 1738

carries. he carries fire in one hand

and water in the other (Roman) Spoken of a person who says one thing but means another (usually deceiving others for his own nefarious ends). John Lydgate, *Troy Book*, 1412–20 (also recorded in Plautus).

Whatsoever I speake to men, the same also I speake to women, I meane not ... to carye fire in the one hand and water in the other.
John Lyly, *Euphues: The Anatomy of Wit*, 1578

carrion crows bewail the dead sheep, and then eat them (English) The hypocritical bemoan the fate of others, then set about profiting from their misfortune. George Herbert, *Outlandish Proverbs*, 1640.

carry. See a DOG that will fetch a bone will carry a bone

cart. don't put the cart before the horse (Greek) Don't do things in the wrong order. Sir Thomas More, *Works*, 1528 (also quoted by Lucian). A variant warns of the dangers of putting the plough before the oxen.

Excuse me, that the Muses force the cart to stand before the horse.
Edward Ward, *Hudibras Redivivus*, 1705

the best cart may overthrow (English) Accidents may befall the best people or things just as easily as they befall the less perfect. John Heywood, *A Dialogue containing ...the Proverbs in the English Tongue*, 1546.

cases. See CIRCUMSTANCES alter cases; HARD cases make bad law

cask. the cask savours of the first fill (Roman) A person or project begun badly will never be rid of the taint of that first evil (just as a wine cask will preserve an echo of the wine it first contained). Horace, *Epistles*, c. AD 19. Variants include 'every cask smells of

the wine it contains'. See *also* WINE savours of the cask.

With what the maiden vessel is season'd first – you understand the proverb.
Beaumont and Fletcher, *The Custom of the Country*, c. 1615

cast. don't cast your pearls before swine (Hebrew) Don't bestow valuable things upon those who will not appreciate them. Bible, Matthew 7:6. It has been suggested that 'pearls' in the original biblical context was a mistranslation for 'crumbs'. A Chinese equivalent is 'don't play the lute before a donkey'.

Give not that which is holy unto the dogs, neither cast your pearls before swine, lest they trample them under their feet and turn again and rend you.
Bible, Matthew 7:6

it is in vain to cast your net where there is no fish (English) There is no point speculating where there is nothing to be gained. Thomas Fuller, *Gnomologia*, 1732.

ne'er cast a clout till May be out (English) Do not discard winter clothing until after the month of May, as the weather may still turn wintry. J. Stevens, *Spanish and English Dictionary*, 1706 (also recorded in Spanish, c. 1627). 'Clout' here signifies a rag or patch of material, hence clothing. Less well-known proverbs expressing similar sentiments include 'who doffs his coat on a winter's day will gladly put it on in May'. May is traditionally considered the unluckiest of all the months and the worst possible time to come down with a cold due to chilly weather. The notion that the proverb refers to hawthorn blossom (often called may), suggesting that not till the blossoms are over is it safe to wear less, is probably erroneous. In much the same vein in many areas it was considered unwise even to bathe the body in the month of May, as the loss of a protective coat of grime acquired over the winter would render the person concerned vulnerable to sudden cold snaps. *See also* he who BATHES in May will soon be laid in clay; MARRY in May and rue the day; a SWARM of bees in May is worth a load of hay.

The wind at North and East
Was never good for man nor beast,
So never think to cast a clout
Until the month of May be out.
F. K. Robinson, *Whitby Glossary*, 1855

though you cast out nature with a fork, it will still return (Roman) Any attempt to deny the true nature of something or someone is futile, as underlying character will always reveal itself. Horace, *Epistles*, fifth century BC. *See also* TRUTH will out.

Mr Crotchet ... seemed ... to settle down ... into an English country gentleman ... but, though, you expel nature with a pitchfork, she will always come back.
Thomas Love Peacock, *Crotchet Castle*, 1831

cast. *See also* COMING events cast their shadows before; OLD sins cast long shadows

castle. a castle that speaketh is near a surrender (English) If one party is prepared to negotiate, then this may be taken as a sign that it may soon come to terms. John Lyly, *Euphues and His England*, 1580. The proverb was formerly commonly quoted in reference to the courting of women, suggesting that any woman who allowed herself to engage in wordplay with a suitor would soon surrender to his advances.

castle. *See also* an ENGLISHMAN's home is his castle

cat. a cat has nine lives (Indian) Some people seem to lead charmed lives, just as cats are supposed to die only after they have survived the threat of imminent death nine times (a notion probably inspired by the cat's ability to survive falls from considerable heights). 'The Greedy and Ambitious Cat', *Fables of Pilpay* (first recorded in English by John Heywood in *A Dialogue containing ... the Proverbs in the English Tongue*, 1546). As a child the philosopher and statesman Francis Bacon tried to test the superstition that cats have nine lives by tossing cats from an upper-storey window (history does not record what became of them). In former times the sentiment was often expressed of cats and women together. *See also* he is like a CAT; fling him which way you will, he'll light on his legs.

A cat has nine lives, and a woman has nine cats' lives.
Thomas Fuller, *Gnomologia*, 1732

a cat in gloves catches no mice (French/Italian) A person who holds back will not gain his objective (said particularly of those who do their work in gloves in order to keep their hands clean). J. Sandford, *The Garden of Pleasure*, 1572 (recorded in France in the fourteenth century). Variant forms include the words 'gloved', 'muffled' and 'muzzled'. Known in Italian as 'gatta guantata non piglia sorce'.

A muffled cat was never good mouser.
William Camden, *Remains concerning Britain*, 1623

a cat may look at a king (English/French/German) Matters of rank and status are irrelevant in some circumstances (a humble cat has no regard for human rank and may cast its gaze as readily upon a king as on any less distinguished person). John Heywood, *A Dialogue containing ... the Proverbs in the English Tongue*, 1546. Usually said in retaliation to someone who assumes a superior air to his or her supposed inferiors or in circumstances where a person is accused of showing a lack of deference or respect. A famous political pamphlet was published with this title in 1652. An equivalent proverb in French runs 'un chien regarde bien un évêque' ('even a dog may look at a bishop'). This is said to hark back to a decree of the sixth century AD, under which bishops were prohibited from keeping dogs, so that petitioners might not be bitten. In Germany, this proverb also exists in the form 'Darf doch die Katze den Kaiser ansehen' ('even a cat may look at an Emperor'). The tradition is that when Maximilian I paid a visit to a woodcarver's workshop the man's cat stared openly at the monarch, regardless of his high standing.

A cat may look at a king, and so may I at her.
Thomas Heywood, *The Wise Woman of Hogsdon*, 1638

he is like a cat; fling him which way you will, he'll light on his legs (English) Some people will always emerge unscathed from the most perilous adventures, just as cats always land on their feet after a fall. Horman, *Vulgaria*, 1519.

Not hurt him,
He pitcht upon his legs like a cat.
Beaumont and Fletcher, *Monsieur Thomas*, 1616

the cat and dog may kiss, yet are none the better friends (English) A public show of friendship does not necessarily reflect genuine feelings. *Trinity MS*, c.1225.

the cat knows whose lips she licks (English) Some people reserve their affections or praise for those from whom they might expect some benefit. Wright, *Essays on the Middle Ages*, c.1210.

when the cat's away, the mice will play (English) When authority is absent, others will engage in mischief. *Harley MS*, c.1470. Similar sentiments are found in many other languages. The French version may be translated as 'when the cat runs on the roofs, the mice dance on the floors'. The Spanish and Italians know the proverb in the form 'when the cat is not in the house, the mice dance', while the Germans have 'cat outside the house, repose for the mouse'.

So it is, and such is life. The cat's away, and the mice they play.
Charles Dickens, *Bleak House*, 1852

cat. *See also* it is a BOLD mouse that breeds in the cat's ear; CARE killed the cat; CURIOSITY killed the cat; there are more WAYS of killing a cat than choking it with cream

catch. catch not at the shadow and lose the substance (English) In concentrating on something trivial you might neglect what is most important. John Lyly, *Euphues: The Anatomy of Wit*, 1578.

Like the dog in the fable, to throw away the substance in catching at the shadow.
Thomas Love Peacock, *Nightmare Abbey*, 1818

never catch at a falling knife or friend (Scottish) Take care in offering assistance to friends in trouble, as their troubles might pull you down also. J. H. Friswell, *Gentle Life*, 1864.

you cannot catch old birds with chaff (English) The experienced and the wily are not easily deceived (just as birds will not be deceived if they are thrown chaff rather than birdseed). William Caxton, *Reynard the Fox*, 1481.

Tis well — an olde birde is not caught with chaffe.
William Shakespeare, *Timon of Athens*, c.1607

catch. *See also* EAGLES don't catch flies; FIRST catch your hare; if you RUN after two hares you will catch neither; set a THIEF to catch a thief

catches. *See* HONEY catches more flies than vinegar; the EARLY bird catches the worm

catching fish is not the whole of fishing (English) There is more to fishing (and many other pursuits and enterprises) than simply the climactic moment of final success. *Times Literary Supplement*, 1913.

cats. all cats are grey in the dark (English) When matters are obscured (as at night) or confused, it is impossible to tell one thing from another. John Heywood, *A Dialogue containing ... the Proverbs in the English Tongue*, c.1549.

He knew not which was which; and, as the saying is, all cats in the dark are grey.
Tobias Smollett, *Humphry Clinker*, 1771

all cats love fish but fear to wet their paws (English) There are those who desire something but are not prepared to endure the discomfort or risk required to obtain it. Trinity MS, c.1225.

Letting 'I dare not' wait upon 'I would', like the poor cat i' the adage.
William Shakespeare, *Macbeth*, c.1604

he that plays with cats must expect to be scratched (English) Any person who engages in potentially risky enterprises must not be surprised if they suffer some harm as a result. S. Palmer, *Moral Essays on Proverbs*, 1710.

cats. *See also* KEEP no more cats than will catch mice; WANTON kittens make sober cats

cause. *See* it is a BAD cause that none dare speak in; no one should be JUDGE in his own cause

causes. that which a man causes to be done, he does himself (English) Responsibility for an action rests with the person who ordered it done, as well as with his agent. Roger L'Estrange, *Aesop's Fables*, 1692. Sometimes encountered in the Latin version 'Qui facit per alium facit per se'. *See also* if you WANT a thing done well, do it yourself.

That which a man causes to be done, he does himself, and 'tis all a case whether he does it by practice, precept, or example.
Roger L'Estrange, *Aesop's Fables*, 1692

cease. *See* WONDERS will never cease

certain. *See* CHILDREN are certain cares, but uncertain comforts; NOTHING is certain but death and taxes; NOTHING is certain but the unforeseen

chaff. *See* you cannot CATCH old birds with chaff

chain. a chain is no stronger than its weakest link (English) A single flaw may compromise the strength of the whole. Charles Kingsley, letter, 1856. *See also* the THREAD breaks where it is weakest.

chamber. the chamber of sickness is the chapel of devotion (English) Those who are ill are prone to turn to religion for comfort, regardless of any previous lack of conviction. T. Draxe, *Bibliotheca Scholastica*, 1616. *See also* the DEVIL sick would be a monk.

change. a change is as good as a rest (English) Doing something different can be as therapeutic as doing nothing at all. J. Thomas, *Randigal Rhymes*, 1895. Variants include 'a change of work is as good as touch-pipe', a 'touch-pipe' signifying a short period of rest.

don't change horses in mid-stream (US) Don't switch allegiances half way through whatever you are doing. Abraham Lincoln, 1864 (quoted in *Collected Works*, 1953). Lincoln himself, who is largely responsible for popularizing the proverb, claimed to be quoting an old Dutch farmer. He quoted the proverb on 9 June 1864 while explaining his reasons for accepting renomination as US President despite doubts voiced by others about his handling of the US Civil War.

Don't change horses in mid-stream ... if we think it necessary to make changes, we must choose the right moment to make them.
Ridout and Witting, *English Proverbs Explained*, 1967

plus ça change, plus c'est la même chose (French) The more things change, the more they stay the same. Alphonse Karr, *Les Guêpes*, 1849. Often encountered in the abbreviated form 'plus ça change'.

to change the name and not the letter, is a change for the worse, and not for the better (English) Any woman who marries a man whose surname begins with the same letter as her maiden name will experience bad luck in her married life. Chambers, *Book of Days*, 1862. Conversely, a woman who marries a man who happens to share the same surname as her own will be blessed with powers of healing (according to Cheshire superstition).

change. *See also* a LEOPARD can't change its spots; TIMES change and we with time

chapel. *See* the CHAMBER of sickness is the chapel of devotion; where GOD builds a church, the Devil will build a chapel

charity. charity begins at home (Greek) Those keen to do good works should begin by doing what they can to improve the circumstances of those immediately around them. John Wycliffe, *Of Prelates*, c.1380 (also quoted by Theocritus and Terence). A possible origin of the proverb may be the biblical passage in Timothy 5:4: 'Let them learn first to show piety at home, and to requite their parents'. In modern times this somewhat over-used proverb has assumed a cynical overtone and is often used in reference to those who, eschewing acts of charity towards strangers, have directed their largesse towards their friends and business acquaintances, perhaps in the hope of promoting some self-interest.

But charity begins at home, and justice begins next door.
Charles Dickens, *Martin Chuzzlewit*, 1850

charity covers a multitude of sins (Hebrew) Those who perform generous acts may be compensating for evil acts that they have committed. Bible, Peter 4:8. In the original context 'charity' signified Christian love rather than acts of generosity to others.

Ah, you always were one for a pretty face, weren't you? Covers a multitude is what I always say.
Kingsley Amis, *Lucky Jim*, 1954

chase. *See* a STERN chase is a long chase

cheap. it is as cheap sitting as standing (English) An invitation to sit. G. Torriano, *Italian Proverbs*, 1666.

cheap. *See also* why BUY a cow when milk is so cheap?

cheapest. *See* BUY in the cheapest market and sell in the dearest

cheat. he that will cheat at play, will cheat you anyway (English) A person who disobeys the rules in trivial matters should not be trusted to behave honourably in more serious contexts. James Kelly, *A Complete Collection of Scotish Proverbs*, 1721.

cheats never prosper (English) Those who cheat will not profit by their dishonesty in the long run. John Harington, *Epigrams*, 1612.

cheeping. *See* MAY chickens come cheeping

cheerful. a cheerful look makes a dish a feast (English) A meal, however modest, that is eaten in jovial company will be much more enjoyable than one eaten in an atmosphere of gloom. George Herbert, *Jacula Prudentum*, 1640.

cheese. cheese digests all things but itself (English) The consumption of cheese at the end of the meal aids the digestion of the previous courses, but may prove indigestible itself. John Lyly, *Sapho and Phao*, 1584.

They say, cheese digests everything but itself.
Jonathan Swift, *Polite Conversation*, 1738

cheese. *See also* 'tis an OLD rat that won't eat cheese

cherry. a cherry year, a merry year; a plum year, a dumb year (English) A good show of cherry blossom (or a good crop of cherries) bodes well for the coming months, while plentiful plum blossom (or fruits) bodes ill. John Ray, *A Collection of English Proverbs*, 1678.

chestnuts. take the chestnuts out of the fire with the cat's paw (French) Use an unwitting partner to gain some benefit for yourself, thus avoiding any risk involved. G. Whitney, *Emblems*, 1586. The proverb is illustrated by a fable told by La Fontaine in which a monkey, taking a fancy to a chestnut roasting in a fire, uses a cat's paw to retrieve the morsel, thus escaping injury to itself (regardless of damage to the cat). The proverb is sometimes given with a dog rather than a cat being thus abused.

He makes her ... become herself the cat's paw to help him to the ready roasted chestnuts.
Samuel Richardson, *Sir Charles Grandison*, 1753

chicken. *See* CHILDREN and chicken must always be pickin'

chickens. *See* CURSES, like chickens, come home to roost; don't COUNT your chickens before they are hatched; MAY chickens come cheeping

child. a child may have too much of his mother's blessing (English) A child may easily be spoiled by an over-indulgent mother. John Clarke, *Paroemiologia Anglo-Latina*, 1639.

Mothers are oftentimes too tender and fond of their children. Who are ruined and spoiled by their cockering and indulgence.
John Ray, *A Collection of English Proverbs*, 1670

child's pig but father's bacon (English) What one person may like to consider their pet or plaything may be regarded as a business opportunity by another and a possible source of profit. *Douce MS, c.*1350.

Child's pig, but father's bacon. Parents usually tell their children, this pig or this lamb

is thine, but when they come to be grown up and sold, parents themselves take the money for them.
John Ray, *A Collection of English Proverbs*, 1678

the child is the father of the man (English) The eventual character of an adult can be determined largely by the influences to which he or she is exposed while still very young. Also this character is discernible in youth. William Wordsworth, 'My heart leaps up', *Poems*, 1807.

child. *See also* a BURNT child dreads the fire; GIVE me a child for the first seven years, and you may do what you like with him afterwards; MONDAY's child is fair of face; PRAISE the child, and you make love to the mother; SPARE the rod and spoil the child; it is a WISE child that knows its own father

children. children and chicken must always be pickin' (English) Children and chicken alike are always hungry. T. Tusser, *Five Hundred Points of Good Husbandry*, 1573.

children and fools must not play with edged tools (English) The young and the mad should not be allowed to tamper with anything that is potentially dangerous. Roger Ascham, *The Scholemaster*, 1570.

'Oh dear, what an edged tool you are!' 'Don't play with me then,' said Ralph impatiently, 'You know the proverb.'
Charles Dickens, *Nicholas Nickleby*, 1839

children and fools tell the truth (English) The young (or in some versions drunkards) and the mad are incapable of telling untruths. R. Taverner, *Proverbs or Adages of Erasmus*, 1545. Another proverb observes 'children and fools have merry lives'.

Fools and children always speak truth, they say.
George Colman, *Man and Wife*, 1769

children are certain cares, but uncertain comforts (English) Children are bound to cause their parents heartache, but will not necessarily provide compensating pleasure. *How the Good Wife*, c.1460.

children are poor men's riches (English) The poor man might consider himself rich because he has children. Randle Cotgrave, *A Dictionary of the French and English Tongues*, 1611. Also encountered in the form 'children are the parents' riches'.

They say barnes are blessings.
William Shakespeare, *All's Well That Ends Well*, c.1602

children are to be deceived with comfits and men with oaths (Greek) Sweets will distract children and promises will satisfy men, however hollow they are. Plutarch, *Lysander*, first century AD.

That other principle of Lysander, That children are to be deceived with comfits, and men with oaths: and the like evil and corrupt positions.
Francis Bacon, *The Advancement of Learning*, 1605

children have wide ears and long tongues (English) The young have a habit of hearing all manner of things they perhaps should not hear and then repeating them. Thomas Fuller, *Gnomologia*, 1732. Equivalent proverbs include 'children pick up words as pigeons pease, and utter them again as God shall please'.

children should be seen and not heard (Greek) Well-behaved children should refrain from making noise in the presence of adults. George Bernard

Shaw, *Misalliance*, 1914 (also quoted by Aristophanes in *The Clouds* in 423 BC). In its original English form, first recorded in the fourteenth century, the proverb was often directed at 'maidens' rather than 'children' (the more common form from the mid-nineteenth century). *See also* SPEAK when you are spoken to.

Father heard the children scream,
So he threw them in the stream,
Saying as he drowned the third,
'Children should be seen, not heard!'
Harry Graham, *Ruthless Rhymes for Heartless Homes*, 1899

children suck the mother when they are young, and the father when they are old (English) In their infancy children rely on mother's milk for sustenance, but when older are inclined to dip into their father's wallet for maintenance. John Ray, *A Collection of English Proverbs*, 1678.

he that has no children knows not what is love (Italian) Only parents know the meaning of true love. G. Torriano, *Select Italian Proverbs*, 1642.

what children hear at home soon flies abroad (English) Children who overhear private conversations at home are likely to repeat them elsewhere. Randle Cotgrave, *A Dictionary of the French and English Tongues*, 1611. Variants include 'the child says nothing but what it heard by the fire'.

Children pick up words as pigeons peas,
And utter them again as God shall please.
John Ray, *A Collection of English Proverbs*, 1670

when children stand still they have done some ill (English) Uncharacteristic quiet in a child is ominous, as it may signify that the child in question is up to no good. George Herbert, *Jacula Prudentum*, 1640.

I remember a wise old gentleman who used to say, 'when children are doing nothing, they are doing mischief.'
Henry Fielding, *Tom Jones*, 1749

children. *See also* the DEVIL's children have the Devil's luck; HEAVEN protects children, sailors, and drunken men; LATE children, early orphans

chink. so we get the chink, we'll bear with the stink (Roman) Providing we get paid, we will put up with any accompanying taint. Sir John Harington, *The Metamorphosis of Ajax*, 1596 (also quoted by Suetonius in *Vespasian* in the second century AD). According to Suetonius, the Emperor Vespasian made the remark 'Non olet' ('it does not smell') when taking receipt of his taxes on urine.

But the gain smells not of the excrement.
John Dryden, *To Mr Southern*, 1692

choice. *See* you PAYS your money and you takes your choice; there is SMALL choice in rotten apples

choke. *See* it is idle to SWALLOW the cow and choke on the tail

choking. *See* there are more WAYS of killing a cat than choking it with cream; there are more WAYS of killing a dog than choking it with butter

choose. never choose your women or your linen by candlelight (English) Do not select something without being able to see it clearly (for example, not by flattering candlelight). J. Sandforde, *Garden of Pleasure*, 1573. Equivalent proverbs are found in other European languages, including Swedish ('one should choose one's bedfellow whilst it is daylight').

Fine linnen, girls and gold so bright. Chuse not to take by candlelight.
Benjamin Franklin, *Poor Richard's Almanack*, 1737

choose. *See also* of TWO evils choose the lesser

choosers. *See* BEGGARS can't be choosers

chose. *See* plus ça CHANGE, plus c'est la même chose

Christmas comes but once a year (English) Christmas coming only once in the year should be enjoyed to the fullest (often spoken to justify some act of supposed extravagance or self-indulgence). T. Tusser, *Five Hundred Points of Good Husbandry*, 1573.

church. church work goes on slowly (English) Projects connected with the Church, especially building, always proceed at a notoriously slow pace. Thomas Fuller, *Holy War*, 1639.
The fifty new churches will ... mend the prospect; but church-work is slow!
Joseph Addison, *Spectator*, 1712

the church is an anvil which has worn out many hammers (English) The Church, though attacked from many quarters, has outlasted its many enemies. Alexander MacLaren, *Acts of the Apostles*, 1908.

church. *See also* the BLOOD of the martyrs is the seed of the Church; where GOD builds a church, the Devil will build a chapel; he is a GOOD dog who goes to church; the NEARER the church, the further from God; all are not SAINTS that go to church

churchyard. a piece of a churchyard fits everybody (English) All mortals must die. George Herbert, *Jacula Prudentum*, 1640.

churchyard. *See also* a GREEN winter makes a fat churchyard

cider is treacherous because it smiles in the face and then cuts the throat (English) Cider tastes pleasant and innocuous in the mouth, but

when swallowed quickly overcomes the drinker with its alcoholic power. T. Adams, *Works*, 1653.

circumstances alter cases (English) Different decisions may be necessitated by changed circumstances. Thomas Rymer, *The Tragedies of the Last Age*, 1678.
It is undoubtedly true that circumstances alter cases. I do feel ... that in the present circumstances decisions may have to be reconsidered.
Agatha Christie, *Appointment with Death*, 1938

circus. *See* if you can't RIDE two horses at once, you shouldn't be in the circus

city. *See* if every man would SWEEP his own doorstep the city would soon be clean

civility. civility costs nothing (English) Good manners and politeness cost nothing. J. Stevens, *Spanish and English Dictionary*, 1706.

civility. *See also* there is NOTHING lost by civility

clartier. the clartier the cosier (Scottish) The dirtier the quarters, the more comfortable they are likely to prove. Walter Scott, *Antiquities*, 1816.
There was dirt good store. Yet ... an appearance of ... comfort, that seemed to warrant their old sluttish proverb, 'The clartier the cosier'.
Walter Scott, *Antiquities*, 1816

clay. *See* CANDLEMAS Day, put beans in the clay, put candles and candlesticks away

clean. clean heels, light meals (English) Cows reared on clay, which promotes the growth of lush grass, will yield more milk than cows reared on lighter sandy soils. R. Holland, *Cheshire Glossary*, 1886.

clean. *See also* a new BROOM sweeps clean; if every man would SWEEP his own doorstep the city would soon be clean

cleanliness is next to godliness (English) Keeping the body pure and living life in a blameless fashion is sure to win the approval of Heaven. Francis Bacon, *The Advancement of Learning*, 1605. The origins of the proverb have been traced back to the writings of the ancient rabbi Phinehas ben Yair. Acceptance of this notion has been so widespread that at times in the past some religious figures, such as Christian Scientist Mary Baker Eddy, have sought to play down the link between cleanliness and godliness because of their worry that members of their flocks would consider a quick wash alone sufficient to restore their spiritual health.

Slovenliness is no part of religion; neither this, nor any text of Scripture, condemns neatness of apparel. Certainly this is a duty, not a sin; 'cleanliness is indeed next to godliness'.
John Wesley, *Sermons: On Dress*, c.1780

clergymen's sons always turn out badly (English) Those brought up by strict religious rules are certain to rebel against them. E. J. Hardy, *How to be Happy though Married*, 1885.

clerk. the clerk makes the justice (English) It is often the humble clerk or assistant who does the real work, rather than his master. A. Brome, 'The Leveller', 1660.

So makeing good the old proverb that the clark makes the justice, while the master does just nothing.
Daniel Defoe, *The Complete Gentleman*, 1729

clerk. *See also* the CLOCK goes as it pleases the clerk

clerks. the greatest clerks be not the wisest men (English/French) Education

does not necessarily imply wisdom. Geoffrey Chaucer, 'The Reeve's Tale', *The Canterbury Tales*, c.1387 (also found, as 'the greatest scholars are not the wisest men', in Rabelais).

It is true that I long syth haue redde and herde that the best clerkes ben not the wysest men.
William Caxton, *Reynard the Fox*, 1481

client. *See* a man who is his own LAWYER has a fool for his client

climb. *See* he that would EAT the fruit must climb the tree

climbed. he that never climbed never fell (English) Those who never risk themselves will never come to grief as a result. John Heywood, *A Dialogue containing ... the Proverbs in the English Tongue*, 1546. A related proverb adds 'who climbs high his fall is great'. *See also* NOTHING ventured, nothing gained.

Crabshaw replied ' ... who never climbed, never fell.'
Tobias Smollett, *Sir Launcelot Greaves*, 1762

climbs. *See* the HIGHER the monkey climbs the more he shows his tail

clock. the clock goes as it pleases the clerk (English) Bureaucrats often determine how time is to be governed and spent, following their own inclination. John Ray, *A Collection of English Proverbs*, 1678.

clogs. from clogs to clogs is only three generations (English) A newly rich family can all too easily be reduced to poverty within the space of three generations. *Notes & Queries*, 1871. This salutary proverb, perhaps meant to console those not newly rich, is thought to have arisen in Lancashire, where clogs were worn by factory and manual workers. Also found as 'twice clogs, once boots'. An alternative

Lancashire saying runs 'rags to riches to rags'. *See also* from SHIRTSLEEVES to shirtsleeves in three generations.

close. a close mouth catches no flies (Italian) Those who keep their own counsel will not experience unpleasant consequences. J. Minsheu, *A Spanish Grammar, now augmented ... by J. Minsheu,* 1599. Variants include 'a close mouth makes a wise head'.

Not flattering lies shall soothe me more to sing with winking eyes,
And open mouth, for fear of catching flies.
John Dryden, *Fables,* 1700

cloth. *See* CUT your coat according to your cloth

cloud. every cloud has a silver lining (English) There is no situation so lamentable that does not offer some consoling hope for the future (just as the sun or the moon behind a raincloud will give it a striking silver edge). John Milton, *Comus,* 1634. Equivalents from other parts of the world include the Indian saying 'there is no evil without its advantages'. *See also* HOPE springs eternal in the human breast; where there's LIFE there's hope; always LOOK on the bright side.

Don't let's be downhearted. There's a silver lining to every cloud.
W. S. Gilbert, *The Mikado,* 1885

clouds. when the clouds go up the hills, they'll come down by the mills (English) Rain will quickly follow after clouds gather round hilltops. John Ray, *A Collection of English Proverbs,* 1678. Also found as 'when the clouds are upon the hills, they'll come down by the mills' and 'A misty morning may prove a good day'.

cloudy mornings turn to clear afternoons (English) A dull morning promises a brighter afternoon (or,

alternatively, evening). *Ancrene Riwle,* c.1200.

Thus cloudy mornynges turne to cleere after noones.
John Heywood, *A Dialogue containing ... the Proverbs in the English Tongue,* 1546

clout. better a clout than a hole out (English) It is better to accept a possibly unsightly repair than to risk more serious damage to something. William Camden, *Remains concerning Britain,* 1605.

clout. *See also* ne'er CAST a clout till May be out

clubs are trumps (English) Force of arms will overwhelm all opposition. Robert Greene, *Pandosto,* 1588.

Taking up a cudgel ... sware solemnly that she would make clubs trump if hee brought any bastard brat within her dores.
Robert Greene, *Pandosto,* 1588

clutch. *See* a DROWNING man will clutch at a straw

coat. it is not the gay coat that makes the gentleman (English) There is more to gentility than a fine appearance. W. Goddard, *Nest of Wasps,* 1615.

coat. *See also* CUT your coat according to your cloth; NEAR is my coat but nearer my skin

cobbler. let the cobbler stick to his last (Greek) One should confine one's opinions to what one actually knows about (just as a cobbler should restrict his views to business connected with his last, the foot-shaped wooden or metal device round which he builds his shoes). Pliny, *Natural History,* first century AD (first recorded in English literature in the sixteenth century). The proverb is traditionally ascribed to the Greek painter Apelles, a friend of Alexander the Great, who lived in the fourth century BC. The story goes that a cobbler, unaware of the painter's presence, found fault with one of his portraits, criticizing the execution of a shoe – the artist acted upon the man's comments and altered the shoe accordingly, but when the cobbler ventured to criticize the painting of a leg he refused to countenance the artesan's opinion, on the grounds it was beyond the province of his expertise (none of his paintings survive). Variants of the proverb run 'the shoemaker must not go above his latchet, nor the hedger meddle with anything but his bill' and 'the cobbler to his last and the gunner to his linstock' (a linstock being the staff that musketeers formerly used to steady their guns in battle).

Let not the shoemaker go beyond hys shoe.
R. Taverner, *Proverbs or Adages of Erasmus*, 1539

cobwebs. where cobwebs are plenty, kisses are scarce (English) No one loves a slovenly housewife. *Notes & Queries*, 1864.

cock. every cock crows on his own dunghill (Roman) Any man may be tempted to arrogance on what he feels is his home ground, where he is unlikely to be challenged. *Ancrene Riwle*, c.1225 (also quoted by Seneca in *Ludus de Morte Claudii* in AD 55). Also encountered as 'every cock is bold on his own dunghill' and recorded in parallel forms in other European languages.

Cock of the dunghill. He's got to be cock – even if it's only of the tiniest Fabian dunghill. Poor old Mark! What an agony when he can't get to the top of his dunghill!
Aldous Huxley, *Eyeless in Gaza*, 1936

if the cock crows on going to bed, he's sure to rise with a watery head (English) If a cock crows in the evening, it will rain the following morning. M. A. Denham, *A Collection of Proverbs ... relating to the Weather*, 1846.

cock. *See also* there's many a GOOD cock come out of a tattered bag; the ROBIN and the wren are God's cock and hen

coffin. the coffin is the brother of the cradle (German) Death is as much a part of life as birth is.

coin. *See* MUCH coin, much care

cold. a cold April the barn will fill (English) Cold weather in April is a sign of a good harvest to come. J. Howell, *Paroemiographia*, 1659. Another proverb, though, warns 'a sharp April kills the pig'. Also found as 'April cold and wet fills barn and barrel'.

cold hands, warm heart (English) Those who keep their feelings to themselves may turn out to be the most passionate of all (just as a lover with cold hands may well harbour the sincerest love). V. S. Lean, *Collecteana*, 1903.

I knew you would be on my side ... cold hand – warm heart. That is the saying, isn't it?
J. M. Barrie, *Shall We Join the Ladies?*, 1927

cold. *See also* as the DAY lengthens, so the cold strengthens; FEED a cold and starve a fever; REVENGE is a dish that is best eaten cold

colour. *See* a GOOD horse cannot be of a bad colour

comb. *See* EXPERIENCE is a comb which nature gives us when we are bald

come. all things come to those who wait (English) Patience will be rewarded. A. Barclay, *Eclogues*, 1530.

I have got it at last, everything comes if a man will only wait.
Benjamin Disraeli, *Tancred*, 1847

come day, go day, God send Sunday (English) May the working week pass quickly until Sunday (the traditional pay-day for servants) arrives. T. Draxe, *Bibliotheca Scholastica*, 1616.

Spoken to lazy, unconscionable servants, who only mind to serve out their time, and get their wages.
James Kelly, *A Complete Collection of Scotish Proverbs*, 1721

come with the wind, go with the water (Scottish) Riches or possessions that have been acquired dishonestly will be dissipated with no real benefit to those who possess them. James Kelly, *A Complete Collection of Scotish Proverbs*, 1721.

Onyway, Deacon, ye'd put your ill-gotten gains to a right use: they might come by the wind but they wouldna gang wi' the water.
William Henley and Robert Louis Stevenson, *Deacon Brodie*, 1880

come. *See also* EASY come, easy go; FIRST come, first served; come LIVE with me and you'll know me; many go out for WOOL and come home shorn

comes. he that comes first to the hill, may sit where he will (Scottish) Those who arrive first may take first choice. David Fergusson, *Scottish Proverbs*, 1641. *See also* FIRST come, first served.

He that is first on the midding [dunghill], may sit where he will.
James Kelly, *A Complete Collection of Scotish Proverbs*, 1721

comes. *See also* TOMORROW never comes

comforter. the comforter's head never aches (English) Though others may offer sympathy for the afflicted, they can never actually share the grief or pain that the real sufferer is experiencing. George Herbert, *Jacula Prudentum*, 1640.

comforts. *See* CHILDREN are certain cares, but uncertain comforts

coming. coming events cast their shadows before (English) The imminence of change often inspires change itself. T. Campbell, *Lochiel's Warning*, 1802.

'Tis the sunset of life gives me mystical love, And coming events cast their shadows before.
T. Campbell, *Lochiel's Warning*, 1802

coming. *See also* NO coming to heaven with dry eyes

command. he is not fit to command others that cannot command himself (English) No one should assume control over others when incapable of controlling their own behaviour. Stanbridge, *Vulgaria*, c.1510. Related proverbs include 'he that commands well shall be obeyed well'.

Cato ... would say, 'No man is fit to command another, that cannot command himself'.
William Penn, *No Cross, No Crown*, 1669

commend not your wife, wine, nor house (Italian) It is immodest to boast of one's own possessions. G. Torriano, *Select Italian Proverbs*, 1642. *See also* SELF-praise is no recommendation.

common fame is a common liar (English) Rumours are often based on falsehoods. B. Rich, *Faultes*, 1606. Another proverb, however, insists 'common fame is seldom to blame'.

But common fame, Magnus considered, was a common liar.
Walter Scott, *The Pirate*, 1821

communications. *See* EVIL communications corrupt good manners

companion. he is an ill companion that has a good memory (English) No one likes a companion who remembers everything that is said or done when others are intoxicated or otherwise inclined to let slip things they would rather were forgotten. White Kennett, *Erasmus' Praise of Folly*, 1683.

company. it is good to have company in misery (English) Those who face hardship of some kind will find solace in the companionship of others. Geoffrey Chaucer, *Troilus and Criseyde*, c.1385. Variants include 'company's good if you are going to be hanged'.

'Tis some comfort to have a companion in our sufferings.
Susannah Centlivre, *The Busy Body*, 1709

the company makes the feast (English) An enjoyable meal with others depends primarily upon who one's fellow-guests are, rather than upon the fare on offer. Izaak Walton, *The Compleat Angler*, 1653.

'Tis the company and not the charge that makes the feast.
Izaak Walton, *The Compleat Angler*, 1653

company. *See also* a MAN is known by the company he keeps; MISERY loves company; TWO's company, three's a crowd

comparisons are odious (French/English) Comparing one thing or person with another is not necessarily helpful and may cause offence. John Lydgate, *Debate Between the Hors, Shepe and Ghoos*, c.1430 (also recorded in French in the thirteenth century and found in other European languages). In 1598 Shakespeare turned the proverb into a joke in *Much Ado About Nothing*, with Dogberry delivering it as the malapropism 'comparisons are odorous'.

But comparisons are odious; another man may write as well as he.

Henry Fielding, *An Apology for the Life of Mrs Shamela Andrews*, 1742

complains. he complains wrongfully on the sea who twice suffers shipwreck (English) Anyone who suffers a setback has only themselves to blame if they risk a repetition of that same setback. Edmund Spenser, *The Shepheardes Calender*, 1579 (also recorded in the writings of Publius Syrus). Variants include 'he who is shipwrecked the second time cannot lay the blame on Neptune'. *See also* let another's SHIPWRECK be your seamark.

The Soveraigne of the Seas he blames in vain That, once sea-beate, will to sea again.
Edmund Spenser, *The Shepheardes Calender*, 1579

complies. he that complies against his will is of his own opinion still (English) A person obliged to co-operate against his will should not be assumed thereby to have given up their former views. Samuel Butler, *Hudibras*, 1678.

No one should submit their mind to another mind: He that complies against his will is of his own opinion still – that's my motto. I won't be brainwashed.
Muriel Spark, *Mandelbaum Gate*, 1965

conceal. it is better to conceal one's knowledge than to reveal one's ignorance (Spanish) In attempting to demonstrate one's knowledge one may only reveal how little one really knows.

confess and be hanged (English) A man may be hanged on the strength of his own confession. 'Misophonus', *De Caede Gallorum*, 1589.

Handkerchief – confessions – handkerchief! To confess, and be hanged for his labour.
William Shakespeare, *Othello*, c.1602

confessed. *See* a FAULT confessed is half redressed

confession. *See* OPEN confession is good for the soul

conscience. conscience makes cowards of us all (English) Those with something to hide are less likely to take risks. William Shakespeare, *Richard III*, c.1592.

Where's thy conscience now? – I'll not meddle with it – it makes a man a coward.
William Shakespeare, *Richard III*, c.1592

conscience. *See also* a GUILTY conscience needs no accuser

consent. *See* SILENCE means consent

constant. constant dropping wears away the stone (Roman) Perseverance and patient effort will achieve its object in the end, however puny the effort might seem when considered singly (just as a stone will be gradually worn away by dripping water). Ovid, *Epistolae ex Ponto*, first century AD (also found in the writings of Choerilus of Samos). *See also* SLOW but sure wins the race.

Time's office is to ... waste huge stones with little water-drops.
William Shakespeare, *Lucrece*, c.1594

constant. *See also* a constant GUEST is never welcome

contempt. *See* FAMILIARITY breeds contempt

content. content is more than a kingdom (English) A person with a contented mind has more riches than any monarch possesses. John Clarke, *Paroemiologia Anglo-Latina*, 1639. Variants include 'content is happiness' and 'content is worth a crown'.

he who is content in his poverty is wonderfully rich (English) Those who can reconcile themselves to what

they lack are guaranteed to be happy. R. Dallington, *Aphorisms*, 1613. Related proverbs include 'contentment is the greatest wealth'.

contented. a contented mind is a continual feast (English) Those who find content in themselves will find interest in many things. Miles Coverdale, Bible, Proverbs, 1535.

A quiet heart is a continual feast.
Miles Coverdale, Bible, Proverbs, 1535

contraries. *See* DREAMS go by contraries

conversation. although there exist many thousand subjects for elegant conversation, there are persons who cannot meet a cripple without talking about feet (Chinese) Some people lack any sense of tact in sensitive situations.

cook. every cook praises his own broth (English) Any worker may be expected to praise his own achievements. Gerbier, *Counsel*, 1663.

he is a poor cook that cannot lick his own fingers (English) Those who are unable (or otherwise unwilling) to enjoy the fruits of their labours in even the most modest fashion should be pitied. Stanbridge, *Vulgaria*, c.1510. The implication is that it is in human nature for someone acting to promote or safeguard the interests of another party to be tempted to glean some benefit for themselves.

He's a sarry cook that may not lick his own fingers. Apply'd satirically to receivers, trustees, guardians, and other managers. Signifying that they will take a share of what is among their hands.
James Kelly, *A Complete Collection of Scotish Proverbs*, 1721

cooks. too many cooks spoil the broth (English) If too many people interfere in a job only chaos and confusion will result (as will happen in any kitchen when more than one person attempts to supervise the cooking). *The Life of Carew*, 1575. The proverb is known in other European languages, including Dutch ('too many cooks make the porridge too salt'). A Turkish equivalent runs 'two captains will sink the ship'.

She professes to keep her own counsel ... 'Too many Cooks spoil the Broth'.
Jane Austen, *The Watsons*, c.1805

cooks. See also GOD sends meat, but the Devil sends cooks

cool. See SAVE your breath to cool your porridge

cord. the cord breaketh at the last by the weakest pull (*Spanish*) When something is already greatly weakened, it takes only a slight effort to complete its destruction. Francis Bacon, *Essays*, 1625. See also it is the LAST straw breaks the camel's back.

Corinth. it is not given to every man to go to Corinth (*Roman*) Some rare pleasures or privileges are only to be enjoyed by the rich or the very lucky. Horace, *Epistles*, c.19 BC. Horace was referring to Lais, the famous courtesan of Corinth, who charged the highest prices for her favours.

Lais an harlot of *Corinthe* ... was for none but lordes and gentlemen that might well paie for it. Whereof came up a proverbe, that it was not every man to go unto *Corinthe*.
Nicholas Udall, 1542

corn. there is corn in Egypt (*Hebrew*) There is a plentiful supply of something. Charles Lamb, *Letters*, 1834. The proverb is derived from the biblical story of Joseph in Egypt (Genesis, 43:2).

There is corn in Egypt while there is cash at Leadenhall.
Charles Lamb, *Letters*, 1834

up corn, down horn (*English*) If corn prices go up, then the price of beef will come down (because people will have less money to spend on it and demand will be reduced). A contrasting proverb (first recorded by John Ray in *A Collection of English Proverbs* in 1678) runs 'corn and horn go together', suggesting that the prices of the two commodities rise and fall together.

corn. See also don't MEASURE other people's corn by one's own bushel

corporations have neither bodies to be punished nor souls to be damned (*English*) Large organizations are impervious to the threat of physical punishment or the dictates of morality, in contrast to individuals. E. Bulstrode, *Reports*, 1658.

corrupt. See EVIL communications corrupt good manners

corrupts. See POWER corrupts

cosier. See the CLARTIER, the cosier

cost. the more cost the more honour (*Scottish*) The more expensive a thing is, the more desirable it is to some. David Fergusson, *Scottish Proverbs*, 1641. Expressing much the same sentiment is the English proverb 'what costs little, is less esteemed'.

Spoken to them that propose an expensive thing, when a cheaper would do.
James Kelly, *A Complete Collection of Scotish Proverbs*, 1721

costs. See CIVILITY costs nothing

cough. See LOVE and a cough cannot be hid

councils of war never fight (*English*) Committees (especially councils of war) typically fail to commit themselves to battle – or any other course of action – as promptly as individuals might. H. W. Halleck, telegram, 1863 (popularly attributed originally to Solomon).

Act upon your own judgment and make your Generals execute your orders. Call no counsel of war. It is proverbial that counsels of war never fight.
H. W. Halleck, telegram, 13 July 1863

counsel. if the counsel be good, no matter who gave it (English) Good advice should be welcome, regardless of what quarter it comes from. Thomas Fuller, *Gnomologia*, 1732. Another proverb rather sourly observes 'good counsel is lacking when most needed'. *See also* a FOOL may give a wise man counsel.

counsel. *See also* GIVE neither counsel nor salt till you are asked for it

counselled. he that will not be counselled cannot be helped (English) There is no helping those who will not listen to advice. J. Clarke, *Paroemiologia Anglo-Latina*, 1639.

count. don't count your chickens before they are hatched (Greek) Never presume that something will turn out well before it has actually happened. T. Howell, *New Sonnets*, c.1570 (also quoted by Philemon). The sentiment behind the proverb was the subject of 'The Milkmaid and the Pail', one of Aesop's *Fables* of the sixth century BC. In this tale, a milkmaid, walking along with her pail of milk balanced on her head, daydreams about the eggs she will buy with the money she gets for the butter she is going to make with the milk – how she will sell the chickens these hatch into to buy a pretty dress and how, with this, she will attract the attention

of well-heeled young men. These, she fancies, she will be in a position to reject, on the basis of her new-found wealth as a raiser of chickens. Unfortunately, in practising the flounce with which she will turn down all but the most desirable suitors, she loses her balance and the pail of milk falls to the ground. According to Walter Scott, in his journal for 20 May 1829, it is foolhardy to presume one's 'chickens' will hatch out as intended 'even though they are chipping the shell now'. A related Dutch proverb runs 'you can't hatch chickens from fried eggs'. Other equivalents in English advise 'make not your sauce before you have caught the fish' and 'don't sell the bear's skin before the bear has been caught'. *See also* FIRST catch your hare; don't HALLOO till you are out of the wood; there's MANY a slip 'twixt cup and lip.

To swallow Gudgeons ere th'are catch'd,
And count their Chickens ere th'are hatch'd.
Samuel Butler, *Hudibras*, 1664

countries. so many countries, so many customs (Greek) Every country boasts its own distinctive cultural identity. *Anglo-Saxon Gnomic Verses*, c.1100 (also recorded in a hymn by the Greek poet Pindar in the fifth century BC). Equivalent proverbs are found in several other European languages. *See also* OTHER times, other manners; so many MEN, so many opinions.

In sondry londes, sondry ben usages.
Geoffrey Chaucer, *Troilus and Criseyde*, c.1385

country. in the country of the blind, the one-eyed man is king (English) When all others are totally ignorant (or foolish), a man who possesses even slight knowledge (or slight cunning) may claim precedence. Erasmus, *Adagia*, 1536. Also found in several other languages besides English. H. G. Wells wrote a short story on the theme suggested by the proverb, under the title 'The Country of the Blind' (1911).

A man were better be half blind than have both his eyes out.
John Ray, *A Collection of English Proverbs*, 1678

our country, right or wrong (English) Expressing unswerving support for one's native country, regardless of whether that country is in the right or not. S. Decatur, *Toast*, 1816. Also encountered in the form 'my wife, right or wrong'.

country. *See also* GOD made the country, and man made the town; HAPPY is the country which has no history; a PROPHET is not without honour save in his own country

couple. *See* a DEAF husband and a blind wife are always a happy couple

course. another course would have done it (English) A little more would have completed the job. This proverb has its origins in a celebrated story concerning some Yorkshire peasants who attempted to trap a cuckoo by building a wall round it (thinking that by so doing they would enjoy eternal spring). The cuckoo escaped by simply flying over the top of the wall, prompting one of the disappointed workers to comment 'another course would have done it'. Ever since, the phrase has been applied to any ridiculous project that no sensible person would undertake.

the course of true love never did run smooth (English) Love affairs are typically tempestuous and likely to encounter difficulty. William

Shakespeare, *A Midsummer Night's Dream*, c.1596.

Ay me! for aught that I could ever read,
Could ever hear by tale or history,
The course of true love never did run
  smooth.
William Shakespeare, *A Midsummer Night's Dream*, c.1596

courses. *See* HORSES for courses

court. *See* HOME is home, as the Devil said when he found himself in the Court of Session

cousin. *See* I wouldn't CALL the king my cousin

cover. *See* you can't judge a BOOK by its cover

coverlet. *See* everyone STRETCHES his legs according to the length of his coverlet

cow. the cow knows not the worth of her tail till she loses it (English) The value of some things is apparent only when they are gone. George Herbert, *Jacula Prudentum*, 1640. Another proverb runs 'if you buy the cow, take the tail into the bargain'.

cow. *See also* a BELLOWING cow soon forgets her calf; why BUY a cow when milk is so cheap?; a CURST cow has short horns; better a GOOD cow than a cow of a good kind; many a GOOD cow hath an evil calf; it is idle to SWALLOW the cow and choke on the tail

coward. *See* a BULLY is always a coward

cowards. cowards die many times before their death (English) Those who lack courage imagine the terror of death often before they actually experience it. William Shakespeare, *Julius Caesar*, 1599 (also found, as 'every houre he dyes, which ever feares', in Michael Drayton's *Mortimeriados* in 1596). Also found as 'cowards die often'.

Cowards die many times before their deaths: The valiant never taste of death but once.
William Shakespeare, *Julius Caesar*, 1599

cowards. *See also* CONSCIENCE makes cowards of us all

cowl. the cowl does not make the monk (French) Do not rely upon appearances as an indication of character. *Ayenbite of Inwit*, 1340. Also found as 'the habit does not make the monk' and 'the hood does not make the monk'. *See also* APPEARANCES are deceptive.

Such impostures are sure of support from the sort of people ... who think that it is the cowl that makes the monk.
George Bernard Shaw, *Music in London*, 1891

cradle. *See* the COFFIN is the brother of the cradle; the HAND that rocks the cradle rules the world

creaking doors hang the longest (English) Those who long suffer ill health often outlive those who are in apparently rude health. T. Coggan, *John Buncle, Junior*, 1776. Alternative versions run 'cracked pots last longest' and 'a creaking cart goes long on the wheels'.

cream. *See* there are more WAYS of killing a cat than choking it with cream

credit. *See* GIVE credit where credit is due

creditors have better memories than debtors (English) It is easier to forget what one owes than what one is owed. J. Howell, *Paroemiographia*, 1659.

When you have got your bargain; you may, perhaps, think little of payment, but ... Creditors ... have better memories than Debtors.
Benjamin Franklin, *English Garner*, 1758

cries. *See* NO man cries stinking fish

crime. *See* POVERTY is not a crime

cripple. *See* although there exist many thousand subjects for elegant CONVERSATION, there are persons who cannot meet a cripple without talking about feet

crop. *See* good SEED makes a good crop

cross. don't cross the bridge until you get to it (English) Don't worry about possible future problems until they actually arise. Henry Wadsworth Longfellow, *Journal*, 29 April 1850. Earlier variants of the proverb include 'you must not leape over the stile before you come to it', recorded in Henry Porter's *The Two Angrie Women* in 1599. *See also* SUFFICIENT unto the day is the evil thereof.

crosses are ladders that lead to heaven (English) It is through coping with troubles and suffering that a person may prove his worth and finally earn his heavenly reward. T. Draxe, *Adages*, 1616.

crow. a crow on the thatch, soon death lifts the latch (English) If a crow (or raven) perches on the roof of a house then a member of the household will soon die. M'Crie, *Scotch Church History*, 1841. This time-honoured superstition, dating back to Classical times, has its origins in the notion that all black birds are portents of evil. It is also supposed to be ominous if a crow taps at the windowpane or settles in the churchyard. A counter-charm recorded in northern England runs 'crow, crow, get out of my sight, or else I'll eat thy liver and thy lights'.

By the will of the Fates ... your respective lots have been assigned ... to the raven prophecy, unfavourable omens to the crow.
Phaedrus, *Fables*, AD 35

the crow thinks her own birds

fairest (English) Every mother thinks her own offspring the most beautiful of all, regardless of how others may see them. Gavin Douglas, *Aeneis*, 1513.

You think you never heard of this wonderful son of mine, Miss Hale. You think I'm an old woman whose ... own crow is the whitest ever seen.

Elizabeth Gaskell, *North and South*, 1855

crow. *See also* ONE for the mouse, one for the crow, one to rot, one to grow

crowd. *See* TWO's company, three's a crowd

crowing. *See* a WHISTLING woman and a crowing hen are neither fit for God nor men

crowns. *See* the END crowns the work

crows. *See* every COCK crows on his own dunghill; on the FIRST of March, the crows begin to search

cruel. you've got to be cruel to be kind (French) In some circumstances it is necessary to act in what appears a harsh manner in order to save another from greater harm in the long run. Early variants of the proverb include the Italian saying 'sometimes clemency is cruelty and cruelty is clemency'. Similar sentiments were expressed by writers as far back as the Classical world, with Sophocles quoting something along similar lines in 409 BC. Legend has it that Catherine de Medici quoted the proverb on the eve of Saint Bartholomew's Day (24 August 1572) to justify her son Charles IX's massacre of the French Huguenots, which led to some 50,000 deaths. *See also* SPARE the rod and spoil the child.

I must be cruel, only to be kind.
William Shakespeare, *Hamlet*, c.1600

cry. *See* MUCH cry and little wool

crying. it's no use crying over spilt

milk (English) There is no point lamenting over some setback when there is nothing that can be done about it. J. Howell, *Paroemiographia*, 1659. Originally given as 'no weeping for shed milk'.

cuckold. it is better to be a cuckold and not know it, than be none, and everybody say so (English) Bearing the reputation of having a faithless wife, even when the rumour is false, is worse than actually having a faithless wife and no one knowing about it. J. Howell, *Paroemiographia*, 1659. Another proverb comments 'to be a cuckold and know it not is no more than to drink with a fly in the cup and see it not'.

cuckoo. the cuckoo comes in April, and stays the month of May; sings a song at midsummer, and then goes away (English) Traditional rhyme delineating the months in which the cuckoo may be found in England. W. C. Hazlitt, *English Proverbs*, 1869. One variant runs 'the cuckoo comes in mid-March, sings in mid-April, struts in mid-May and in mid-June flies away', while yet another insists that 'in April, come he will; in May, he sings all day; in June he alters his tune; in July, he prepares to fly; in August, go he must; if he stay till September, 'tis as much as the oldest man can ever remember'.

cup. *See* FULL cup, steady hand; the LAST drop makes the cup run over; there's MANY a slip 'twixt cup and lip

Cupar. he that will to Cupar maun to Cupar (Scottish) Obstinate persons cannot be dissuaded from pursuing their course, however misguided it may be. Walter Scott, *Rob Roy*, 1818. The proverb has its origins in the historical fact that the Fife Courts of Justice were formerly sited at Cupar, a town in Fife, which thus became a risky place to be.

The Heccate ... ejaculated, 'A wilfu' man will hae his way: them that will to Cupar maun to Cupar!'
Walter Scott, Rob Roy, 1818

cure. See CARE is no cure; PREVENTION is better than cure

cured. what can't be cured must be endured (English) What cannot be changed must be put up with. William Langland, Piers Plowman, 1377.

What was over couldn't be begun, and what couldn't be cured must be endured.
Charles Dickens, Pickwick Papers, 1837

curiosity killed the cat (English) There are risks in being too inquisitive. Eugene O'Neill, Diff'rent, 1921. The origins of this proverb are obscure, though there is clearly a reference to the natural curiosity for which cats are notorious (though one variant replaces the cat with a monkey). Complementary proverbs include 'curiosity is ill manners in another's house' (first recorded in 1622). See also CARE killed the cat.

curried. See a SHORT horse is soon curried

curses, like chickens, come home to roost (English) Those who wish ill on others will only find their malice eventually rebounds on them (just as chickens return to their roosts at the end of the day). Robert Southey, Curse of Kehama, 1809 (also found in an early form in Geoffrey Chaucer's 'The Parson's Tale', c.1387). Some variants have the curses, like arrows or stones, rising into the air and then falling back down onto the head of the person who uttered them: 'I have heard a good man say, that a curse was like a stone flung up to the heavens, and maist like to return on the head that sent it' (Walter Scott, Old Mortality, 1816).

Curses, like rookses, flies home to nest in bosomses and barnses.
Stella Gibbons, Cold Comfort Farm, 1932

curst. a curst cow has short horns (English) Vengeful persons are rarely in a position to do as much mischief as they would like. Geoffrey Chaucer, Eight Goodly Questions, 1475. Sometimes encountered in Latin, as 'Dat Deus immiti cornua curta bovi'.

A curst cow hath oftentimes short hornes, and a willing minde but a weake arm.
Robert Greene, Pandosto, 1588

customer. the customer is always right (English/US) In business, the wishes of the customer must always be paramount. Carl Sandburg, Good Morning, America, 1928. There is much debate over who coined this business axiom, with authorities arguing both British and US claims for the honour. Those credited with coining it include the business tycoon H. Gordon Selfridge, who was born in the USA but later took British citizenship and who adopted the proverb as the motto for his Selfridges retail store. It has also been attributed to US retailer John Wanamaker, whose stores bear his name.

customs. See so many COUNTRIES, so many customs

cut. cut your coat according to your cloth (English) Compromise according to what is reasonable, bearing in mind your resources (financial or otherwise). John Heywood, A Dialogue Containing ... the Proverbs in the English Tongue, 1546. Historically, the proverb may well reflect the laws that governed the amount of cloth that English citizens were permitted to wear (laid down according to social rank by an Act of Parliament passed in 1533). These laws were introduced in the wake of the Black Death, as a result of which surviving labourers had been able to demand higher wages and thus pay for better clothes, thereby obscuring class distinctions (which the higher classes naturally wished to retain).

I love your wit well, sir, but I must cut my coat according to my cloth.
John Dryden, The Wild Gallant, 1669

don't cut off your nose to spite your face (French) Do not indulge in petty or more serious acts of malice that will ultimately result only in harm to yourself. *Deceit of Women*, c.1560 (also recorded in the writings of Peter of Blois, 1200, and, in variant forms in the works of Roman authors). Other versions include 'He that biteth his nose off, shameth his face', and Chinese equivalents include 'don't burn down your house even to annoy your chief wife's mother' and 'don't thrust your fingers through your own lantern'.

He cut off his nose to be revenged of his face, said of one who, to be revenged of his neighbour, has materially injured himself.
F. Grose, *Dictionary of the Vulgar Tongue*, 1788

cut. *See also* a SLICE off a cut loaf isn't missed

d

dainties. who dainties love, shall beggars prove (English) Those with expensive tastes will soon be reduced to penury. T. Tusser, *Five Hundred Points of Good Husbandry*, 1573. On similar lines are 'dainty makes dearth', 'dear bought and far fetched are dainties for ladies' and 'the dainties of the great are the tears of the poor'.

You know the proverb – those that are dainty …
Hannah Cowley, *More Ways Than One*, 1783

daisies. *See* it is not SPRING until you can plant your foot upon twelve daisies

dance. they that dance must pay the fiddler (US) Those who want to enjoy themselves must be prepared to pay for their enjoyment themselves. J. Taylor, *Taylor's Feast*, 1638. Related proverbs include 'he'll dance to nothing but his own pipe', 'he dances well to whom fortune pipes' and 'those who dance are thought mad by those who hear not the music'. *See also* he who PAYS the piper calls the tune.

I am decidedly opposed to the people's money being used to pay the fiddler. It is an old maxim and a very sound one, that he that dances should always pay the fiddler.
Abraham Lincoln, speech, 11 January 1837

dances. *See* he that LIVES in hope dances to an ill tune

danger. a danger foreseen is half avoided (English) Knowledge of a threat goes a long way to enabling a person to escape it. R. Franck, *Northern Memoirs*, 1658.

the danger past and God forgotten (English) Those in trouble may call on God to help them, but neglect to show any gratitude afterwards or to remember any promises made. Randle Cotgrave, *A Dictionary of the French and English Tongues*, 1611. *See also* the DEVIL sick would be a monk.

In time of danger and affliction men will address themselves earnestly to God for relief.
James Kelly, *A Complete Collection of Scotish Proverbs*, 1721

danger. *See also* OUT of debt, out of danger; the POST of honour is the post of danger

dangerous. *See* DELAYS are dangerous; a little LEARNING is a dangerous thing

dark. *See* all CATS are grey in the dark

darkest. the darkest hour is just before the dawn (English) Things may seem their worst just before they get better. Thomas Fuller, *A Pisgah-Sight of*

Palestine, 1650. The same sentiment may be found in various forms in numerous other languages, including, to take just one example, Persian: 'it is at the narrowest part of the defile that the valley begins to open'. *See also* when BALE is highest, boot is nighest; HOPE springs eternal in the human breast; NEVER say die

It is usually darkest before day break. You shall shortly find pardon.
John Wesley, *Journal*, 1760

darling. *See* better be an OLD man's darling than a young man's slave

daughter. he that would the daughter win, must with the mother first begin (English) To court a girl successfully, a young man does well to win the approval of her mother first. John Ray, *A Collection of English Proverbs*, 1670. *See also* PRAISE the child and you make love to the mother.

daughter. *See also* like MOTHER, like daughter; my SON is my son till he gets him a wife, but my daughter's my daughter all the days of her life

daughters and dead fish are no keeping wares (English) Daughters, like the flesh of caught fish, do not improve with long keeping, but need to be disposed of (through marriage) while still at their best. Thomas Fuller, *Gnomologia*, 1732.

dawn. *See* the DARKEST hour is just before the dawn

day. as the day lengthens, so the cold strengthens (English) The weather at the start of the year, when the days are growing longer, is often colder than the weather before the New Year. E. Pellham, *God's Power*, 1631. Another proverb advises 'as the days grow longer, the storms grow stronger', while another claims 'as the days

begin to shorten, the heat begins to scorch them'.

At the time of writing we have just enjoyed a virtually frost-free January, and it was followed by two mild winter months and then heat-waves and drought in April, May and June. *As the day lengthens, so the cold strengthens* is usually correct, however.
Ralph Whitlock, *March Winds and April Showers*, 1993

no day without a line (Roman) Each day has its work to be done. John Lyly, *Euphues: The Anatomy of Wit*, 1578. Lyly attributed it to the Classical painter Apelles, who never let a day pass without doing some work on his paintings. Sometimes encountered in its Latin form, as 'nulla dies sine linea'. A gloomier proverb insists 'no day passeth without some grief'.

Nulla dies sine linea. But never a being, from my infancy upwards, hated task-work as I hate it.
Walter Scott, *Journal*, 1 December 1825

day. *See also* an APPLE a day keeps the doctor away; BARNABY bright, Barnaby bright, the longest day and the shortest night; the BETTER the day, the better the deed; every DOG has his day; FAIR and soft goes far in a day; ROME was not built in a day; SUFFICIENT unto the day is the evil thereof; TOMORROW is another day; there are only TWENTY-FOUR hours in the day

days. *See* FISH and guests stink after three days

dead. dead men don't bite (English) There is nothing to be feared from a corpse. Edward Hall, *Hall's Chronicle*, 1542 (also found in the writings of Erasmus). Also encountered in the form 'dead dogs bark/bite not'.

Yet am I glad he's quiet, where I hope He will not bite again.

Beaumont and Fletcher, *The Knight of the Burning Pestle*, 1611

dead men tell no tales (English) Secrets are never divulged by the dead. John Wilson, *Andronicus Commenius*, 1663.

Where are the stories of those who have not risen − ... who have ended in desperation? ... Dead men tell no tales.
Charles Kingsley, *Alton Locke*, 1850

let the dead bury the dead (Hebrew) There comes a point when the living should forsake the dead, in order to get on with their own lives. Bible, Matthew 8:22.

Jesus said unto him, Follow me, and let the dead, bury their dead.
Bible, Matthew 8:22

dead. *See also* BLESSED are the dead that the rain rains on; the only GOOD Indian is a dead one; it's ILL waiting for dead men's shoes; QUEEN Anne is dead; never SPEAK ill of the dead; STONE-dead hath no fellow; THREE may keep a secret, if two of them are dead

deadly. *See* the FEMALE of the species is more deadly than the male

deaf. a deaf husband and a blind wife are always a happy couple (English) Those who are unconscious of the failings of their spouse or partner will enjoy a peaceful life together. John Florio, *First Fruits*, 1578.

there are none so deaf as those who will not hear (English) Those who are determined not to listen are the hardest to persuade. John Heywood, *A Dialogue containing ... the Proverbs in the English Tongue*, 1546. The proverb is rendered in French as 'il n'y a de pire sourd que celui qui ne veut pas entendre'. *See also* there are none so BLIND as those who will not see.

dear. *See* EXPERIENCE keeps a dear school; GOLD may be bought too dear

dearest. *See* BUY in the cheapest market and sell in the dearest

death. death devours lambs as well as sheep (English) Death claims with equal impartiality the young and the innocent as well as the older and more worldly wise. T. Shelton, *Don Quixote*, 1620.

death is the great leveller (Roman) Death erases all marks of distinction between classes, races, sexes, etc. T. Shelton, *Don Quixote*, 1620 (also quoted by Claudian in *De Raptu Proserpinae* in the fourth century AD). Also found as 'death is the grand leveller'.

Death is the grand leveller.
Thomas Fuller, *Gnomologia*, 1732

death keeps no calendar (English) Death strikes regardless of the date or of the age of the victim. George Herbert, *Jacula Prudentum*, 1640.

death pays all debts (English) All financial obligations to others cease at death. William Shakespeare, *The Tempest*, c.1610. Also encountered as 'death squares all accounts', in which form it was quoted by Shirley in *Cupid and Death* in 1653. Another proverb claims 'death cancels everything but truth'.

The Laird's dead − aweel, death pays a' scores.
Walter Scott, *Guy Mannering*, 1815

death. *See also* CABBAGE twice cooked is death; COWARDS die many times before their death; NOTHING is certain but death and taxes; there is a REMEDY for everything except death

debt. *See* OUT of debt, out of danger; a POUND of care will not pay an ounce of debt

debts. *See* DEATH pays all debts; SPEAK not

of my debts unless you mean to pay them

deceit. *See* TRUST is the mother of deceit

deceive. if a man deceive me once, shame on him; but if he deceive me twice, shame on me (English) If a person allows himself to be duped twice by the same party then they have only themselves to blame. Nathan Bailey, *An Universal Etymological English Dictionary*, 1736.

to deceive a deceiver is no deceit (English) It is no sin to pull the wool over the eyes of someone who is seeking to deceive others. Fulwell, *Ars Adulandi*, c. 1580.

deceptive. *See* APPEARANCES are deceptive

deed. *See* the BETTER the day, the better the deed

deeds are fruits, words are but leaves (English) It is not words but deeds that count. T. Draxe, *Bibliotheca Scholastica*, 1633. Equivalents sayings include 'deeds are males, words are females' and 'deeds not words'.

deep. *See* BEAUTY is only skin deep; STILL waters run deep

deeper. the deeper the sweeter (English) The further a person probes into something they enjoy, the more pleasure they will get from it. Ben Jonson, *Every Man in His Humour*, 1596.

Stir it up with the spoon, miss; for the deeper the sweeter.
Jonathan Swift, *Polite Conversation*, 1738

defence. *See* ATTACK is the best form of defence

deferred. *See* HOPE deferred makes the heart sick

delays are dangerous (English) Putting something off allows more time for something to go wrong. John Lyly, *Euphues:The Anatomy of Wit*, 1578. Similar

sentiments were expressed by Geoffrey Chaucer in *Troilus and Criseyde* back in 1385: 'That peril is with dreeching in y-drawe'. *See also* PROCRASTINATION is the thief of time.

Delay, they say, begetteth peril.
Robert Louis Stevenson, *The Black Arrow*, 1888

Delilah. *See* there's no LEAPING from Delilah's lap into Abraham's bosom

delved. *See* when ADAM delved and Eve span, who was then the gentleman?

demand. when the demand is a jest, the answer is a scoff (English) If one is faced with a ludicrous request the only possible response is to mock what has been suggested. John Clarke, *Paroemiologia Anglo-Latina*, 1639.

denying a fault doubles it (English) Refusing to recognize your own misdeeds only makes them worse. *Politeuphuia*, 1669.

depends. he who depends on another dines ill and sups worse (English) Those who depend on others for their maintenance will find their fare may be less satisfactory than they might hope for. John Ray, *A Collection of English Proverbs*, 1813. Another proverb remarks 'dependence is a poor trade'.

deserve. *See* none but the BRAVE deserve the fair

deserves. *See* one GOOD turn deserves another

desire hath no rest (English) Passion allows no peace for those afflicted by it. W. Baldwin, *Beware the Cat*, 1551.

A true saying it is, desire hath no rest.
Richard Burton, *The Anatomy of Melancholy*, 1621

desires. he that desires honour is not worthy (English) Those who value fame and glory for their own sake are thereby less deserving of such recognition. William Shakespeare, *Henry V*, c.1598.

But if it be a sin to covet honour, I am the most offending soul alive.
William Shakespeare, *Henry V*, c.1598

desperate diseases call for desperate remedies (English) The worse a problem is the more radical the solution must be. R. Taverner, *Proverbs or Adages of Erasmus*, 1539 (also recorded in the form of a maxim in the *Aphorisms* of the Greek physician Hippocrates around 400 BC). In historical terms, quack doctors, witches and other practitioners of folk medicine learnt to recommend cures for physical ailments that incorporated all manner of unusual and even revolting ingredients, knowing that the more outlandish the remedy was the more impressed the patient would be, and thus more likely to agree to pay a high price for it. Tradition has it that Guy Fawkes quoted the proverb to James I on 6 November 1605 to explain his motives on his arrest following the failed Gunpowder Plot. Variants include 'desperate cuts must have desperate cures'.

Diseases desperate grown by desperate appliance are reliev'd, or not at all.
William Shakespeare, *Hamlet*, c.1600

destroy. *See* whom the GODS would destroy, they first make mad

Devil. better the devil you know than the devil you don't know (English) When faced with a choice between a known evil and an unknown evil, most people will settle for the evil that is at least familiar. Anthony Trollope, *Barchester Towers*, 1857 (though also recorded in variant forms in writings of the Classical authors). In the sixth century Aesop

illustrated the proverb in a fable about some frogs. These frogs asked Jupiter for a king, but were given a lump of wood and when they scorned the log and asked for a new king from Jupiter, he sent them a frog-eating water snake. The moral of the story was rendered as 'likewise, you must bear the evil that you have, lest a greater one befall you'. *See also* of TWO evils choose the lesser.

The dread of something after death ... makes us rather bear those ills we have, Than fly to others that we know not of.
William Shakespeare, *Hamlet*, c.1600

every devil has not a cloven hoof (English) It is not always obvious by superficial appearances that a person is evil-minded. Daniel Defoe, *The History of the Devil*, 1726.

the Devil always leaves a stink behind him (English) Wickedness always leaves its taint behind. Henry Smith, *Sermons*, 1591. Superstition had it that when the Devil materialized at witches' covens he often took the form of a rank-smelling male goat.

the Devil can quote scripture for his own purpose (English) The ill-intentioned can easily turn well-meaning maxims and writings to their own evil or unworthy ends. William Shakespeare, *The Merchant of Venice*, c.1596. The proverb has its origins in the biblical story of the Devil's temptation of Christ, though Shakespeare may also have been influenced by a line in Christopher Marlowe's *The Jew of Malta* (c.1592), 'What, bring you scripture to confirm your wrongs.'

Does anyone doubt the old saw, that the Devil (being a layman) quotes

Scripture for his own ends?
Charles Dickens, *Martin Chuzzlewit*, 1850

the Devil dances in an empty pocket (English) Those who have no money are vulnerable to temptation. Thomas Hoccleve, *The Regiment of Princes*, 1412. Related proverbs include 'the Devil's mouth is a miser's purse'.

The devil sleeps in my pocket; I have no cross [with which coins were once marked] to drive him from it.
Philip Massinger, *The Bashful Lover*, 1636

the Devil finds work for idle hands (English) Those with nothing better to do will soon be tempted to mischief. Isaac Watts, *Divine Songs*, 1715 (a similar sentiment is expressed in the letters of Saint Jerome). *See also* an IDLE brain is the Devil's workshop; IDLENESS is the root of all evil.

If the Devil find a man idle, he'll set him to work.
Thomas Fuller, *Gnomologia*, 1732

the Devil gets up to the belfry by the vicar's skirts (English) The wicked may work hand in hand with the good in order to achieve their evil aims. J. Howell, *Paroemiographia*, 1659. Related proverbs include 'the Devil lurks behind the cross'.

the Devil is a busy bishop in his own diocese (English) Acts of evil multiply where men are disposed to wickedness. Hugh Latimer, *Sermon on Ploughers*, 1549.

the Devil is at home (English) The source of much wickedness is often to be found in the home. Thomas Middleton, *Works*, 1620.

A foolish proverb says, 'The devil's at home'.
George Crabbe, *The Borough*, 1810

the Devil is not as black as he is painted (English) Some things (or people) are not as bad as commonly believed. Thomas More, *Dialogue of Comfort*, 1535. Also encountered in the form 'the Devil is not so ill as he's called'. *See also* GIVE the Devil his due.

Fear kills more people than the yellow fever … The devil's not half so black as he's painted – nor the yellow fever half so yellow, I presume.
Captain Frederick Marryat, *Peter Simple*, 1834

the Devil looks after his own (English) The Devil protects those who have devoted themselves to mischief and evil. J. Day, *Isle of Gulls*, 1606. Also encountered in the form 'the Devil is kind to his own'.

The Dee'ls ay good to his own … Spoken when they whom we affect not, thrive and prosper in the World; as if they had their Prosperity from the Devil.
James Kelly, *A Complete Collection of Scotish Proverbs*, 1721

the Devil lurks behind the cross (English) Evil attends closely upon religion, awaiting opportunities. T. Shelton, *Don Quixote*, 1612.

the Devil makes his Christmas-pies of lawyers' tongues and clerks' fingers (Italian) Evil prospers through the immorality and cunning of lawyers and the corruption of clerks. John Florio, *Second Fruits*, 1578.

Sir Robert Pye, attorney of the court of wards, … happened to die on Christmas day: the news being brought to the serjeant, said he 'The devil has a Christmas pie'.
John Aubrey, *Brief Lives*, 1669–96

the Devil rides upon a fiddlestick (English) Sometimes a great deal of fuss and trouble may arise from the most trivial grounds. William Shakespeare, *Henry IV, Part 1*, c.1597.

Heigh, heigh! The Devil rides upon a

fiddlestick: what's the matter?
William Shakespeare, *Henry IV, Part 1, c.1597*

the Devil sick would be a monk
(English) Ill health or other adverse circumstances prompt many people to make rash promises that are forgotten as soon as their health or fortunes are restored. L. Evans, *Withals Dictionary Revised*, 1586. Also encountered in the form 'the Devil was sick, the Devil a saint would be; the Devil was well, the devil a saint was he!' or, more concisely, 'the Devil was sick'. Equivalent proverbs may be found in many other European languages and even in Chinese ('when times are easy we do not burn incense, but when trouble comes we embrace the feet of Buddah'). *See also* the CHAMBER of sickness is the chapel of devotion.

The old, the irrepressible adage ... was to live again between them: 'When the devil was sick the devil a saint would be; when the devil was well the devil a saint was he!'
Henry James, *A Small Boy and Others*, 1913

the Devil to pay and no pitch hot
(English) Trouble looms, and there seems no immediate way to counter it. *c.1400*, published in *Reliquae Antiquae*, 1841. The proverb alludes to the business of sealing ('paying') with pitch the seam (the 'devil') between the outboard plank and waterways of a ship – a particularly awkward operation.

If they hurt but one hair of Cleveland's head, there will be the devil to pay, and no pitch hot.
Walter Scott, *The Pirate*, 1821

the Devil's children have the Devil's luck (English) It is often those least deserving of good fortune who seem to enjoy the best luck, as if the Devil himself is helping them. John Ray, *A Collection of English Proverbs*, 1678.

The Dee'ls Bairns have Dee'ls luck. Spoken enviously when ill People prosper.
James Kelly, *A Complete Collection of Scotish Proverbs*, 1721

there is a devil in every berry of the grape (English) Alcohol brings with it opportunities for evil and temptation. J. Howell, *Letters*, 1647 (sometimes attributed to a Turkish original).

when it rains and the sun shines at the same time the Devil is beating his wife (French) Weather superstition, seeking to provide an explanation for contrary climatic conditions. G. Torriano, *Select Italian Proverbs*, 1642.

The Devil was beating his wife behind the door with a shoulder of mutton.
Jonathan Swift, *Polite Conversation*, 1738

when the Devil is dead, he never lacks a chief mourner (English) When some nefarious practice is brought to an end there is always someone who will regret it, because they profited by it. R. C. Trench, *On the Lessons in Proverbs*, 1853.

where no one else will, the Devil must bear the cross (English) If no one better is available, tasks that must be done have to be entrusted to those one would not normally select. John Lyly, *Euphues: The Anatomy of Wit*, 1578.

Where none will, the Divell himselfe must beare the crosse.
John Lyly, *Euphues: The Anatomy of Wit*, 1578

why should the Devil have all the best tunes? (English) Why should music and other amusements (together with other characteristics of the secular world) be reserved for the wicked alone? W. Chappell, *Popular Music*, 1859. The phrase is often quoted in discussion of church music set to popular secular tunes (as controversially espoused by the early Methodists) and may have first been used by evangelist and hymn writer Rowland Hill – according to his biographer E. W. Broome – in reference to Charles Wesley, who adapted popular tap-room tunes for his songs. Later, the proverb was quoted by General Booth, founder of the Salvation Army, when he borrowed the tunes of many well-known music-hall songs to accompany religious lyrics.

Devil. *See also* an ATHEIST is one point beyond the Devil; AWAY goes the Devil when he finds the door shut against him; CARDS are the Devil's books; GIVE the Devil his due; to GIVE a thing, and take a thing, is to wear the Devil's gold ring; GOD sends meat, but the Devil sends cooks; where GOD builds a church, the Devil will build a chapel; what is GOT over the Devil's back is spent under his belly; HASTE is from the Devil; HOME is home, as the Devil said when he found himself in the Court of Session; an IDLE brain is the Devil's workshop; every MAN for himself, and the Devil take the hindmost; NEEDS must when the Devil drives; PARSLEY seed goes nine times to the Devil; PULL Devil, pull baker; it is easier to RAISE the Devil than to lay him; he who SUPS with the Devil should have a long spoon; TALK of the Devil and he is bound to appear

devotion. *See* the CHAMBER of sickness is the chapel of devotion

diamond cuts diamond (English) Cunning can outwit cunning, denoting a clash between two equally acute minds. John Marston, *The Malcontent*, 1604. Because diamonds are so hard,

only by rubbing one against another will the stones be scratched.

Wit must be foiled by wit; cut a diamond with a diamond.
William Congreve, *The Double Dealer*, 1693

die. *See* COWARDS die many times before their death; you've got to EAT a peck of dirt before you die; only the GOOD die young; a MAN can die but once; OLD habits die hard; OLD soldiers never die, they simply fade away; YOUNG men may die, but old men must die

dies. *See* CALL no man happy till he dies; whom the GODS love die young; he who LIVES by the sword dies by the sword

diet. *See* the best DOCTORS are Dr Diet, Dr Quiet and Dr Merryman

differ. *See* TASTES differ

difficult. the difficult we do at once, the impossible takes a little longer (English/French) Nothing is impossible, but some things will take longer to achieve (often delivered sarcastically when requested to perform an impossible task). Anthony Trollope, *Phineas Redux*, 1873. Formerly often repeated in military and naval circles.

difficult. *See also* it is the FIRST step that is difficult

difficulty. *See* ENGLAND's difficulty is Ireland's opportunity

diligence. *See* CARE and diligence bring luck

dinner. after dinner rest a while, after supper walk a mile (English) For the sake of good health, the diner is recommended to take things easy after a large dinner but to take a walk to aid the digestion after taking supper. Cogan, *Haven of Health*, 1588.

As the proverb says, for health sake, after dinner, or rather after supper, willingly

then I'll walk a mile to hear thee.
Philip Massinger, *The Unnatural Combat*, 1639

better a dinner of herbs than a stalled ox where hate is (Hebrew) It is preferable to dine off modest fare in friendly company than to feast in a hostile atmosphere. Bible, Proverbs 15:17. The fuller form of the proverb, as given in the 1560 translation of the Bible, runs 'better is a dinner of grene herbes where love is, then a stalled oxe and hatred therewith'. A 'stalled ox', incidentally, is an ox fattened in a stall and ready for slaughter.

dirt. *See* FLING enough dirt and some will stick; you've got to EAT a peck of dirt before you die

dirty. dirty water will quench fire (English) Certain desires – especially sexual ones – are readily sated by less than what might be ideally hoped for (for instance, through the use of an ugly prostitute in the place of an idealized lover). John Heywood, *A Dialogue containing ... the Proverbs in the English Tongue*, 1546.

As this proverbe saieth, for quenchyng hot desire, Foul water as soone as fayre, wyl quenche hot fire.
John Heywood, *A Dialogue containing ... the Proverbs in the English Tongue*, 1546

don't throw out your dirty water until you get in fresh (English) Do not part with what you have before you have made certain of your possession of its better replacement. David Fergusson, *Scottish Proverbs*, 1641. Also encountered in the form 'cast not out your foul water until you get in clean'.

Mrs Giddy has discarded Dick Shuttle ... she was a fool to throw out her dirty water before she got clean.
Jonathan Swift, *A Complete Collection of Polite and Ingenious Conversation*, 1738

dirty. *See also* don't WASH your dirty linen in public

disappointed. *See* BLESSED is he who expects nothing, for he shall never be disappointed

discretion is the better part of valour (English) It is sometimes wiser to back down than to risk a course of action in which one may come off worst. William Caxton, *Jason*, c.1477 (also recorded in the writings of Euripides and other Classical authors). It has been suggested that originally 'discretion' signified tactics or strategy, throwing a rather different light upon the meaning. *See also* he who FIGHTS and runs away, lives to fight another day.

The better part of valour is discretion: in the which better part, I have saved my life.
William Shakespeare, *Henry IV, Part 1*, c.1597

disease. a disease known is half cured (English) By recognition of the nature of a disease, or some other problem, one is halfway to curing it. James Wright, *Country Contentments*, 1694.

disease will have its course (English) Some diseases must run their full course before there can be any hope of effecting a recovery. T. Muffett, *Healths Improvement*, 1655.

disease. *See also* the DOCTOR is often more to be feared than the disease; the REMEDY may be worse than the disease

diseases. diseases are the price for ill pleasures (English) Diseases are provoked by over-indulgence in vice. John Ray, *A Collection of English Proverbs*, 1670.

diseases. *See also* DESPERATE diseases call for desperate remedies

dish. See REVENGE is a dish that is best eaten cold

dismount. See he who RIDES a tiger is afraid to dismount

disposes. See MAN proposes, but God disposes

distance lends enchantment to the view (English) Some situations or things look better when considered from a detached position. T. Campbell, *Pleasure of Hope*, 1799.

ditch. See if the BLIND lead the blind, both shall fall into the ditch

divide and rule (Roman) By setting your opponents against each other you can establish your own supremacy over both. Phineas Fletcher, *Purple Island*, 1633. Rendered in Latin as 'divide et impera'.

As Machiavel taught 'em, divide and ye govern.
Jonathan Swift, *Poems*, 1732

divided. See a HOUSE divided against itself cannot stand; UNITED we stand, divided we fall

divine. See to ERR is human, to forgive divine

do. do as I say, not as I do (Hebrew) Do as I advise, but do not expect me to be restrained by the same rules myself. Bible, Matthew, 23:3. Often delivered sarcastically in reference to those who hypocritically fail to live up the standards they espouse. Variants include 'do as the friar saith, not as he doth'. A defence available to those who find themselves incapable of realizing these ideals is offered in the proverb 'he that may not do as he would, must do as he may'.

It is as folke dooe, and not as folke say.
John Heywood, *A Dialogue containing ... the Proverbs in the English Tongue*, 1546

do as you would be done by (Hebrew/Chinese/Hindu) Treat others as you would like to be treated yourself. A. Munday and others, *Sir Thomas More*, c.1596 (also attributed to Confucius and as the 'Golden Rule' a maxim of the Hindu, Judaic and Christian religions). The version given in Matthew 7:12 runs 'therefore all things whatsoever ye would that men should do to you, do ye even so to them: for this is the law and the prophets'. Luke 6:31 has 'as yee would that men should doe to you, doe yee also to them likewise'. Sometimes encountered in the form 'do unto others as you would they should do unto you'. Charles Kingsley introduced the characters Mrs Doasyouwouldbedoneby and Mrs Bedonebyasyoudid in *The Water Babies*, 1863. In 1898, in *David Harum*, Edward N. Westcott added his own variation on the theme: 'Do unto the other feller the way he'd like to do unto you an' do it fust'.

'Do as you would be done by', is the surest method that I know of pleasing.
Lord Chesterfield, letter, 16 October 1747

do on the hill as you would do in the hall (English) Always behave well, regardless of your surroundings. A. Barclay, *The Ship of Fools*, 1509.

Accustom yourself to act with discretion and good manners at all times.
James Kelly, *A Complete Collection of Scotish Proverbs*, 1721

do right and fear no man (English) Do what is good and do not allow yourself to be cowed by any other person. *Book of Precedence*, c.1450.

never do things by halves (English) If you are going to do something, do it properly. Hanway, *Travels*, 1753.

do. See also the KING can do no wrong;

whatever MAN has done, man may do; when in ROME, do as the Romans do; if you WANT a thing done well, do it yourself

doctor. better no doctor at all than three (Polish) Doctors can always be relied upon to give contrary advice about a person's condition and treatment, so the fewer consulted the better. Related proverbs include the Czech saying 'many doctors, death accomplished'.

the doctor is often more to be feared than the disease (English) The courses of treatment recommended by doctors may be more harmful than the diseases they are meant to cure. Richard Burton, *The Anatomy of Melancholy*, 1621.

Paupers got sick and got well as Nature pleased; but woe betided the rich in an age when, for one Mr Malady killed three fell by Dr Remedy.
Charles Reade, *The Cloister and the Hearth*, 1861

doctor. *See also* an APPLE a day keeps the doctor away

doctors. the best doctors are Dr Diet, Dr Quiet and Dr Merryman (English) Rest, a sensible diet and a cheerful outlook are the best treatment for many ailments. W. Bullein, *Government of Health*, 1558.

doers. *See* EVIL doers are evil dreaders

does. *See* he who CAN does, he who cannot teaches; it's DOGGED as does it; EASY does it

dog. a dog that will fetch a bone will carry a bone (English) A gossip who shares others' confidences with you is in turn equally likely to divulge your own confidences to others. R. Forby, *Vocabulary of East Anglia*, 1830.

So Nellie twisted what you said and told it

to Miss Wilder … 'A dog that will fetch a bone, will carry a bone'.
Laura Ingalls Wilder, *Little Town on the Prairie*, 1941

dog does not eat dog (Roman) Like does not attack like (just as animals of the same species rarely attack one another). W. Turner, *The Hunting of the Romish Fox*, 1543 (similar sentiments may be found in the writings of Juvenal and Shakespeare, among others). Also found in the form 'wolf does not eat wolf'. *See also* there is HONOUR among thieves.

Dogs are hard drove, when they eat dogs. It is an hard Winter, when Dogs eat Dogs.
Thomas Fuller, *Gnomologia*, 1732

every dog has his day (Roman) Though currently oppressed, even the lowliest and most humble will eventually get their chance to enjoy a moment of glory (typically by avenging wrongs done to them). R. Taverner, *Proverbs or Adages of Erasmus*, 1546. Erasmus traced the saying back to the death of the Greek playwright Euripides, who is reputed to have been mauled to death by dogs set on him by his rivals Arrhidaeus and Crateuas. It was often given in Latin as 'hodie mihi, cras tibi' ('today to me, tomorrow to thee'). A variation recorded in Essex in 1864 runs 'every dog has his day, and a cat has two Sundays'.

Let Hercules himself do what he may, the cat will mew, and dog will have his day.
William Shakespeare, *Hamlet*, c.1600

every dog is a lion at home (English) Many people who brag of their courage while safe at home find their courage deserts them when in public. N. R. Gent, *Proverbs English, French, Dutch etc*, 1659.

every dog is allowed one bite
(English) Every person should be allowed to make one mistake before any action is taken in retribution. V. S. Lean, *Collecteana*, 1902–04. The proverb harks back to the common law maxim that no action should be taken against those who keep domestic animals that are accused of biting someone, unless it is at least a second offence.

the dog returns to its vomit
(Hebrew) The wicked and the foolish often return to the scene of their past misdeeds. *Romance of the Rose*, c. 1400 (also quoted in the Bible, in Proverbs 26:11).

Le chien est retourné à son propre vomissement.
William Shakespeare, *Henry IV, Part 2*, c. 1598

dog. *See also* a BARKING dog never bites; BRAG is a good dog, but Holdfast is better; the CAT and dog may kiss, yet are none the better friends; GIVE a dog a bad name and hang him; a GOOD dog deserves a good bone; he is a GOOD dog who goes to church; why KEEP a dog and bark yourself?; a LIVE dog is better than a dead lion; LOVE me, love my dog; a MAN's best friend is his dog; it is easy to find a STICK to beat a dog; TAKE the hair of the dog that bit you; you can't TEACH an old dog new tricks; there are more WAYS of killing a dog than choking it with butter; there are more WAYS of killing a dog than hanging it; a WOMAN, a dog and a walnut tree, the more you beat them the better they be

dogged. it's dogged as does it (English) Perseverance pays off in the end. M. B. Chesnut, *Diary*, 6 August 1864.

There ain't nowt a man can't bear if he'll only be dogged ... It's dogged as does it. It's not thinking about it.

Anthony Trollope, *The Last Chronicle of Barset*, 1867

dogs. the dogs bark but the caravan goes on (Arabian) Protests about something may be made, but will not last long (just as the barking of dogs at the passing of a caravan of travellers in the desert soon dies away). Marcel Proust, *A l'Ombre des Jeunes Filles en Fleurs*, 1918. A favourite saying of South African politician Jan Smuts, it was also quoted – as 'the dogs bark, but the caravan passes by' – by British theatre director Sir Peter Hall in response to his critics in the 1970s.

In the words of a fine Arab proverb, 'The dogs may bark; the caravan goes on!'
Marcel Proust, *A l'Ombre des Jeunes Filles en Fleurs*, 1918; translated as *Within a Budding Grove*, 1924, by C. K. Scott Moncrieff

dogs. *See also* if you LIE down with dogs, you will get up with fleas; let SLEEPING dogs lie

doing. *See* if a THING is worth doing, it's worth doing well

done. what's done by night appears by day (English) Deeds committed in secrecy will inevitably come to light eventually. John Gower, *Confessio Amantis*, c. 1390.

Day ... night's scapes doth open lay.
William Shakespeare, *Lucrece*, c. 1594

what's done cannot be undone
(Greek) There is no changing past deeds. Geoffrey Chaucer, *The Book of the Duchess*, c. 1369 (also found, as 'things could not now be otherwise' in Sophocles).

Things without all remedy
Should be without regard: what's done is done.
William Shakespeare, *Macbeth*, c. 1604

done. *See also* DO as you would be done

by; whatever MAN has done, man may do; WELL begun is half done

door. a door must either be shut or open (*French*) It must be one way or the other (there is no third option). Brueys and Palaprat, *Le Grondeur*, 1691. Rendered in French as 'il faut qu'une porte soit ouverte ou fermée'. In the original play, a servant is scolded for leaving the door open, to which he complains bitterly that last time, when he closed the door, he had also been scolded.

There are but the two ways; the door must either be shut, or it must be open.
Oliver Goldsmith, *Citizen of the World*, 1762

when one door shuts, another opens (*English/Irish*) When one opportunity disappears another is sure to present itself. D. Rowland, *Lazarillo*, 1586. A rather cynical modern reworking of the proverb runs, 'one door closes and another door closes'. *See also* every CLOUD has a silver lining.

door. *See also* a GOLDEN key can open any door; it is too LATE to shut the stable-door after the horse has bolted; OPPORTUNITY seldom knocks twice at any man's door; a POSTERN door makes a thief; when POVERTY comes in at the door, love flies out of the window

doors. *See* CREAKING doors hang the longest

doorstep. *See* if every man would SWEEP his own doorstep the city would soon be clean

doubt. when in doubt, do nowt (*English*) When uncertain what course to take, the best policy is to do nothing. G. Weatherly, 'Little Folks' Proverb Painting Book, 1884. *See also* NOTHING ventured, nothing gained.

draw not your bow till your arrow is fixed (*English*) Do not start doing something until the necessary first steps have been made. *See also* don't put the CART before the horse.

draws. whosoever draws his sword against the prince must throw the scabbard away (*English*) Those who lead rebellions against established powers will never be able to relax their constant vigilance against attack themselves. R. Dallington, *View of France*, 1604.

dreaders. *See* EVIL doers are evil dreaders

dreads. *See* a BURNT child dreads the fire

dream of a funeral and you hear of a marriage (*English*) Dreams of death presage good events (typically news of a wedding) in one's waking life. John Clarke, *Paroemiologia Anglo-Latina*, 1639. Sometimes encountered in the reverse form. *See also* DREAMS go by contraries.

My wife had the most lucky dreams in the world ... It was one night a coffin and cross-bones, the sign of an approaching wedding.
Oliver Goldsmith, *The Vicar of Wakefield*, 1766

dreams. dreams go by contraries (*English*) In the interpretation of dreams, the opposite of what is dreamed may be expected to come true. *Tale of Beryn*, c.1400 (also found in the first century AD writings of Apuleius). *See also* DREAM of a funeral and you hear of a marriage.

I took your letter last night to bed with me. In the morning I found your name on the sealing wax obliterated. I was startled at the bad omen till I recollected that it must have happened in my dreams, and they you know fall out by contraries.
John Keats, letter to Fanny Brawne, 15 July 1819

dreams. *See also* MORNING dreams come true

dressing. *See* there are many WAYS of dressing a calf's head

dries. *See* nothing dries sooner than TEARS.

drink. when the drink is in, the wit is out (Roman) The more a person has to drink, the less quick-witted they are and the less subtle and clever their sense of humour becomes. John Gower, *Confessio Amantis*, c.1390 (also quoted by Pliny). Also encountered in the form 'drink in, wit out'. Warburton, Bishop of Gloucester in the eighteenth century, offered an alternative version with his own 'those who drink beer will think beer' (to which a resentful drinker replied 'and those that drink water will think water'). *See also* when the WINE is in, the wit is out.

But after dinner is after dinner – an old saying and a true, 'much drinking, little thinking'.
Jonathan Swift, *Journal to Stella*, 1712

drink. *See also* you can lead a HORSE to water, but you can't make him drink

drinketh. he that drinketh well sleepeth well, and he that sleepeth well thinketh no harm (English) Alcohol promotes sleep and through healthy sleep generosity of spirit. J. Palsgrave, *L'Éclaircissement de la langue française*, 1530.

dripping. a dripping June sets all in tune (English) Wet weather in June promises well for crops and flowers later in the season. *Agreeable Companion*, 1742. Also encountered as 'a dry May and a dripping June bringeth all things into tune' and (from the Isle of Man) 'a dry May and a leaking June

makes the farmer whistle a merry tune'. Another proverb insists 'a leaky May and a June, brings on the harvest very soon'.

drive. drive gently over the stones (English) Take things slowly and carefully when troubled times loom. Jonathan Swift, letter, 30 June 1711. Originally a piece of advice to riders, but later applied in other contexts.

you can drive out nature with a pitchfork, but she keeps on coming back (Roman) The inbred character of a man will come to the surface, despite all efforts to change (just as weeds and other plants will always reappear despite all attempts to eradicate them). Horace, *Epistles*, first century BC.

Mr Crotchet ... seemed ... to settle down ... into an English country gentleman ... But as, though you expel nature with a pitchfork, she will always come back.
Thomas Love Peacock, *Crotchet Castle*, 1831

drives. *See* BAD money drives out good; HUNGER drives the wolf out of the wood; NAIL drives out nail; NEEDS must when the Devil drives

drop. *See* the LAST drop makes the cup run over

dropping. *See* CONSTANT dropping wears away the stone

drops. many drops make a shower (English) Tiny things may combine to make something much more significant. George Pettie, *A Petite Pallace of Pettie His Pleasure*, 1576. Related proverbs include 'many drops of water will sink a ship'. *See also* look after the PENNIES and the pounds will look after themselves.

drought. after drought cometh rain (English) Even the most long-lasting periods of hardship or adversity will eventually come to an end. *Reliquae Antiquae*, fifteenth century.

drought never bred dearth in England (English) Lack of rain never brought famine in England. John Heywood, *Play of Weather*, 1533. The sentiment is supported by another proverb, which runs 'a dry year never starves itself'.

Drought never brought dearth.
George Herbert, *Jacula Prudentum*, 1640

drowned. *See* if you're BORN to be hanged then you'll never be drowned

drowning. a drowning man will clutch at a straw (English) When in desperate straits a person will grasp at any hope of relief, however slim. Thomas More, *Dialogue of Comfort*, 1534. The proverb, or variants of it, is known in many languages. The Italian version has the drowning man clutching at razors.

We drift down time, clutching at straws. But what good's a brick to a drowning man?
Tom Stoppard, *Rosencrantz and Guildenstern are Dead*, 1966

drums. where drums beat, laws are silent (Roman) When a country is torn by warfare, the normal safeguards of the civil law no longer apply in practical terms. Cicero, *Pro Milone*, first century BC.

For the laws are dumb in the midst of arms.
Cicero, *Pro Milone*, first century BC

drunk. he that is drunk is as great as a king (English) Drunkards believe they are more capable and more powerful than they really are. *Westminster Drollery*, 1672.

drunkards. *See* there are more OLD drunkards than old doctors

drunken. *See* HEAVEN protects children, sailors and drunken men

drunkenness reveals what soberness conceals (Roman) What sober men keep secret is revealed when they are drunk. Geoffrey Chaucer, *The Canterbury Tales*, c.1387 (also quoted by Horace).

It is an old proverbe, whatsoever is in the heart of the sober man, is in the mouth of the drunkarde.
John Lyly, *Euphues: The Anatomy of Wit*, 1578

dry. dry bread at home is better than roast meat abroad (English) Something modest but certainly held is preferable to something better but still to be secured. George Herbert, *Jacula Prudentum*, 1651. *See also* a BIRD in the hand is worth two in the bush.

dry. *See also* you never MISS the water till the well runs dry; put your TRUST in God and keep your powder dry

duck. if it looks like a duck, walks like a duck and quacks like a duck, it's a duck (US) If something acts in a certain, unmistakeable way there is no denying its true identity. Walter Reuther, 1950s. This relatively modern addition to the proverbial stock was introduced by Reuther, a union leader who was suggesting how a communist might be identified.

due. *See* GIVE credit where credit is due; GIVE the Devil his due

dumb. the dumb man gets no land (English) A person who is not prepared to stand up for his own interests cannot expect to gain reward. John Gower, *Confession Amantis*, c.1390.

dumb. *See also* a CHERRY year, a merry year; a plum year, a dumb year

dunghill. *See* every COCK crows on his own dunghill

dust. while the dust is on your feet,

sell what you have bought (English)
It is good business practice to sell on
stock you have acquired as quickly as
possible (before even brushing away
the dust of the journey taken to get
the goods). John Ray, *A Collection of
Scotish Proverbs*, 1678.

The meaning is that we should sell quickly
(though with light gaines) that we may
trade for more.
John Ray, *A Collection of Scotish Proverbs*, 1678

dust. *See also* a PECK of March dust is
worth a king's ransom

duty. *See* the FIRST duty of a soldier is
obedience

**dwarf. a dwarf on a giant's shoulders
sees further of the two** (Roman)
By taking advantage of the achievements or knowledge of great men, a
lesser person may surpass them.
Richard Burton, *The Anatomy of
Melancholy*, 1621.

I say with Didacus Stella 'A dwarf standing
on the shoulders of a giant may see farther
than a giant himself'; I may ... farther than
my predecessors.
Richard Burton, *The Anatomy of Melancholy*,
1621

dying. *See* you cannot SHIFT an old tree
without it dying

e

eagles. eagles don't catch flies
(English) The great are not interested in
trifles. *Mirror for Magistrates*, 1563 (also
found in the writings of Erasmus).
Also related, and indicative of the for-
bearance of the great towards the
humble and lowly, is 'the eagle suffers
little birds to sing'.

With regard to slight insults ... 'They sting
one (says he) but as a fly stings a horse; and
the eagle will not catch flies.'
Hester Piozzi, *Anecdotes of Johnson*, 1786

eagles fly alone (English) People with
inner strength and self-confidence
tend to remain independent of others,
pursuing their course alone. J. Clarke,
Paroemiographia Anglo-Latina, 1639.

Eagles commonly fly alone: they are crows,
daws, and starlings that flock together.
John Webster, *The Duchess of Malfi*, 1623

eagles. *See also* where the CARCASE is,
there shall the eagles be gathered
together

ear. *See* you can't make a SILK purse out
of a sow's ear

early. early sow, early mow (English)
The sooner you start on something,
the sooner you will see results from
your efforts. J. Clarke, *Paroemiographia
Anglo-Latina*, 1639. Confirming the
notion that the early sower does best

comes another proverb, 'the early
sower never borrows of the late'.

**early to bed and early to rise,
makes a man healthy, wealthy and
wise** (English) Those who avoid late
nights and get up at an early hour will
benefit in all ways. *Treatise of Fishing with
Angle*, 1496. The sentiment did not
find favour with US humorist James
Thurber who, in *Fables for Our Time*,
coined his own version of it: 'early to
rise and early to bed makes a male
healthy and wealthy and dead'.

Early to bed and early to rise being among
Mr Sponge's maxims, he was enjoying the
view ... shortly after daylight.
R. S. Surtees, *Sponge's Sport*, 1853

early wed, early dead (English) Those
who marry young are fated to die prematurely. *Notes & Queries*, 1895.

the early bird catches the worm
(English) Those who set about their
work promptly will prosper most.
William Camden, *Remains concerning
Britain*, 1605. Related proverbs include
'the early bird gets the late one's
breakfast'. An Indian variant noted by
Rudyard Kipling runs 'who sleeps late
gets the bull-calf, he who rises early
the cow-calf' – the cow-calf being
preferable.

And it's the early bird, as the saying goes, that gets the rations.
Robert Louis Stevenson, *Treasure Island*, 1883

the early man never borrows from the late man (English) Those who get their work done promptly will never have need to borrow from those who do not. J. Howell, *Proverbs*, 1659.

Oats, too, benefit from early sowing ... Another agricultural proverb ... declares that, 'the early man never borrows from the late man'.
Ralph Whitlock, *Calendar of Country Customs*, 1978

earned. *See* a PENNY saved is a penny earned

ears. *See* FIELDS have eyes, and woods have ears; LITTLE pitchers have big ears; WALLS have ears

earth must to earth (English) All living things (including men and animals as well as plants, literally born of the earth) are fated to return to earth when they die. c.1480, *Early Miscellany*, 1855. A less concise version of the proverb runs 'the earth produces all things and receives all again'.

earthen. the earthen pot must keep clear of the brass kettle (Hebrew) Weaker persons (or states etc.) should avoid clashing with those who are stronger. Thomas Fuller, *Gnomologia*, 1732 (also quoted in the Bible, Apocrypha, Ecclesiasticus 13).

Buckingham is Lord of the Ascendant ... you are the vase of earth; beware of knocking yourself against the vase of iron.
Walter Scott, *The Fortunes of Nigel*, 1822

easier. easier said than done (Roman) It is one thing to discuss doing something, but quite another actually to get it done. *Religious and Love Poems*, c.1450 (also recorded in the writings of Plautus and Livy).

That is (quoth she) sooner said then doone, I dreede.
John Heywood, *A Dialogue containing ... the Proverbs in the English Tongue*, 1546

it is easier for a camel to go through the eye of a needle than it is for a rich man to enter into the kingdom of heaven (Hebrew) The lowly and humble are favoured in the eyes of heaven, whereas the wealthy will find it more difficult to prove their worth. Bible, Matthew 19:24 and Mark 10:25. The proverb is also to be found in the Koran: 'the impious shall find the gates of heaven shut; nor shall he enter till a camel shall pass through the eye of a needle'.

easier. *See also* it is easier to PULL down than to build up; it is easier to RAISE the Devil than to lay him

east. east, west, home's best (English) No matter how far you may go, you will never find a place preferable to home. W. K. Kelly, *Proverbs of all Nations*, 1859.

east. *See also* when the WIND is in the east, 'tis neither good for man nor beast

Easter. at Easter let your clothes be new, or else be sure you will it rue (English) Always wear new clothes at Easter, or suffer the consequences. William Shakespeare, *Romeo and Juliet*, c.1593. Superstition claims that ill luck will befall any person who does not wear some new item of clothing on Easter Sunday. Those who fail to observe this tradition will suffer, among possible misfortunes, birds' droppings falling on them. It was said in Hampshire that even the dogs would spit at someone who did not wear new clothing on Easter Sunday; in Ireland it was believed that crows would peck out the person's eyes.

Didst thou not fall out with a tailor for
wearing his new doublet before Easter?
William Shakespeare, *Romeo and Juliet*, c. 1593

**when Easter falls in Our Lady's lap,
then let England beware of a rap**
(English) It is ominous for the nation if
Good Friday happens to fall on the
same date as Lady Day. 1648, quoted
in Rollins, *Cavalier and Puritan*, 1923.

easy. easy come, easy go (English) What
has been acquired without much
trouble is easily parted with (usually
quoted in relation to money). John
Arbuthnot, *John Bull*, 1712. Also
encountered in former times with
'easy' replaced by 'lightly' or 'quickly'.
See also a FOOL and his money are soon
parted.

A thriftless wretch, spending the goods
and gear that his forefathers won with the
sweat of their brows; light come, light go.
John Arbuthnot, *John Bull*, 1712

easy does it (English) A reminder that
some tasks require gentle, unhurried
handling. Tom Taylor, *The Ticket-of-
Leave Man*, 1863. Also found as 'gently
does it'.

Important to build bridges ... between the
faiths. Gently does it.
Salman Rushdie, *Midnight's Children*, 1981

easy. *See also* it is easy to find a STICK to
beat a dog; it is easy to be WISE after
the event

**eat. he that would eat the fruit must
climb the tree** (English) Those who
hope to enjoy benefits must work for
them. James Kelly, *A Complete Collection of
Scotish Proverbs*, 1721.

**we must eat to live and not live to
eat** (Greek) A person should eat
enough to maintain his physical
health, without surrendering himself
to gluttony. J. Trevisa, *Higden's*

Polychronicon, 1387. The saying is
attributed to Socrates, who is said to
have uttered it on declining an invitation to live in luxury at the Athenian
court of King Archelaus. According to
Plutarch, Socrates actually said 'bad
men live that they may eat and drink,
whereas good men eat and drink that
they may live'. Related proverbs
include 'eat enough and it will make
you wise', 'eat when you're hungry
and drink when you're dry' and 'eat at
pleasure, drink by measure'. Anyone
who fails to follow the advice of such
proverbs and over-indulges in the
pleasures of the table may consult
another saying to aid recovery: 'he that
eats till he is sick must fast till he is
well'. *See also* the EYE is bigger than the
belly.

I shall eat sufficient ... But I eat to live; I
don't live to eat.
A. W. Pinero, *Preserving Mr Panmure*, 1912

you are what you eat (German/
French/English) The state of a person's
character and physical being is closely
associated with their diet. Anthelme
Brillat-Savarin, *La Physiologie du goût*,
1825. The saying was revived in
the 1960s, when it became a slogan
of a new health-conscious generation
(it was used as the title of a US
health film shown in 1969).

**you've got to eat a peck of dirt
before you die** (English) Everyone
must expect to suffer a certain amount
of hardship and disappointment in
their lives (just as everyone must
accept that there will be small
amounts of dirt in their food). J.
Clarke, *Paroemiographia Anglo-Latina*,
1639. Also encountered with 'ashes'
or 'salt' in the place of 'dirt'.

eat. *See also* DOG does not eat dog; you

can't HAVE your cake and eat it; if you won't WORK you shan't eat

eaten bread is soon forgotten (English) A consumed meal (or other pleasure or favour) is quickly forgotten when the time for the next meal arrives. J. Minsheu, *A Spanish Grammar*, 1599. *See also* it is HARD to pay for bread that has been eaten.

eating. *See* APPETITE comes with eating; the PROOF of the pudding is in the eating

ebb. *See* every FLOW hath its ebb

edged. it is ill jesting with edged tools (English) It is unwise to fool with things that have the potential to cause great harm. Wager, *The Longer Thou Livest*, c.1568.

Sir Apish, jesting with matrimony is playing with edged tools.
Henry Fielding, *Love in Several Masques*, 1728

egg. better an egg today than a chicken tomorrow (English) A small benefit that can be enjoyed at once is better than the uncertain promise of something better that may be enjoyed at some future date. J. Howell, *Paroemiographia*, 1659. *See also* a BIRD in the hand is worth two in the bush; don't COUNT your chickens before they are hatched.

eggs. don't put all your eggs in one basket (Italian/Spanish) Don't place all your hopes on one thing alone (lest an accident result in the destruction of all of them). Cervantes, *Don Quixote de la Mancha*, 1605. The proverb largely replaced the English equivalent 'don't venture all your goods in one bottom' ('bottom' here meaning 'ship'), which was descended from a much older Greek saying. Other largely

archaic versions include 'do not hang all your bells upon one horse' (usually referring to a decision not to leave all one's riches to just one child). It is often heard in the context of business discussions, recommending the spreading of risk.

It was odd how, with all this ingrained care for moderation and secure investment, Soames never put his emotional eggs into one basket. First Irene – now Fleur.
John Galsworthy, *To Let*, 1921

eggs. *See also* you cannot make an OMELETTE without breaking eggs; there is REASON in the roasting of eggs

Egypt. *See* there is CORN in Egypt

eight. *See* SIX hours' sleep for a man, seven for a woman and eight for a fool

elbow. elbow-grease gives the best polish (English) There is no substitute for application and diligent hard work when it comes to getting a good result. Andrew Marvell, *The Rehearsal Transpros'd*, 1672.

Two or three brawny fellows in a corner with meer ink and elbow-grease, do more harm than ...
Andrew Marvell, *The Rehearsal Transpros'd*, 1672

elbow. *See also* you should never TOUCH your eye but with your elbow

elephant. an elephant never forgets (English) Some people will never forget wrongs or injuries done to them (just as elephants are reputed to do). Saki, *Reginald: Reginald on Besetting Sins*, 1910. The proverb is of ancient origin, being known to the Greeks – except that, until the early twentieth century, it was always the camel rather than the elephant that never forgot: 'the camel never forgets an injury'. Elephants owe their reputation for long memories to the ability of working elephants in India to remember the many varied instructions of their handlers.

only an elephant can bear an elephant's load (Indian) Only someone remarkable can achieve remarkable things. Sometimes given in the form of an apology when finding oneself incapable of doing something.

eleven. See RAIN before seven, fine before eleven

elm. every elm has its man (English) Elm trees, being more likely than other trees to break in a high wind and cause injuries, are supposedly destined by fate to fall on certain people. Rudyard Kipling, *Puck of Pook's Hill*, 1906. See also every BULLET has its billet.

empty. an empty purse fills the face with wrinkles (English) The poor age quickly because of worry about their finances. T. Draxe, *Bibliotheca Scholastica*, 1616. Related proverbs include 'an empty purse causes a full heart', 'an empty purse is the devil' and 'an empty purse frights away friends'.

empty sacks will never stand upright (Italian) Without sustenance it is impossible to function. G. Torriano, *Select Italian Proverbs*, 1642. Often quoted to excuse petty acts of gluttony.

Poverty often deprives a Man of all Spirit and Virtue; 'Tis hard for an empty Bag to stand upright.
Benjamin Franklin, *Poor Richard's Almanack*, 1758

empty vessels make the most sound (English) Those who have least of value to impart often have the loudest voices. John Lydgate, *Pilgrimage of Man*, 1430.

I did never know so full a voice issue from so empty a heart: but the saying is true – The empty vessel makes the greatest sound.
William Shakespeare, *Henry V*, c.1598

enchantment. See DISTANCE lends enchantment to the view

end. the end crowns the work (French/English) It is by the end result that effort should be judged. H. Watson, *The Ship of Fools*, 1509. Another proverb claims that 'the end tries all', similarly suggesting that it is in the result that a course of action will be assessed. See also the PROOF of the pudding is in the eating.

Proof must be built up stone by stone ... As I say, the end crowns the work.
Charles Dickens, *The Mystery of Edwin Drood*, 1870

the end justifies the means (Roman) Any course of action is permissible as long as the desired end is achieved; it is often quoted in defence of morally dubious deeds. G. Babington, *Exposition of the Commandments*, 1583 (also found in Ovid's *Heroides*, first century AD). See also all's WELL that ends well.

The End must justifie the means;
He only sins who Ill intends;
Since therefore 'tis to combat Evil;
'Tis lawful to employ the Devil.
Matthew Prior, 'Hans Carvel', 1701

end. See also EVERYTHING has an end; all GOOD things must come to an end; the LONGEST day must have an end; he who WILLS the end, wills the means

ending. See a GOOD beginning makes a good ending

ends. See all's WELL that ends well

endured. See what can't be CURED must be endured

endures. he that endures is not overcome (Roman) Any person who quietly puts up with hardship or cruelty without breaking is thereby unconquered. George Herbert, *Jacula Prudentum*, 1640 (also quoted by Virgil). Related proverbs include 'he that can quietly endure overcometh' and 'he that will not endure labour in this world, let him not be born'.

Men seyn 'the suffrant overcom'th', parde.
Geoffrey Chaucer, *Troilus and Criseyde, c.1385*

enemy. *See* the BEST is the enemy of the good; it is good to make a BRIDGE of gold to a flying enemy; the GOOD is the enemy of the best; there is no LITTLE enemy

England. England is the paradise of women, the hell of horses and the purgatory of servants (English) The English treat women well, but are cruel both to their animals and especially to their servants. John Florio, *Second Fruits,* 1591.

'England is the paradise of women, hell for horses, purgatory of servants.' For the first, *bilia vera* ... For the next, ... *Ignoramus* ... For the last, ... we cast it forth as full of falsehood.
Thomas Fuller, *The History of the Worthies of England,* 1662

England's difficulty is Ireland's opportunity (Irish) When England is distracted by trouble of some kind, then Ireland has the chance to gain some advantage. *Tribune,* 19 January 1856. Another proverb, identifying Ireland as the vulnerable target for invaders, claims 'he that England will win must with Ireland begin'.

England. *See also* what MANCHESTER says today, the rest of England says tomorrow; TURKEY, heresy, hops and beer came into England all in one year

English. the English are a nation of shopkeepers (French) The English have the character and aspirations of an uncultured and unimaginative middle-class merchant (and should be treated as such). Adam Smith, *The Wealth of Nations,* 1776. The saying is popularly attributed (by the English) to the French Emperor Napoleon, though the idea had been voiced in so many words by several English writers decades before the Napoleonic Wars. Other proverbs allege that the English are 'the swearing nation' and 'the Frenchmen's apes'.

To found a great empire for the sole purpose of raising up a people of customers, may at first sight appear a project fit only for a nation of shopkeepers.
Adam Smith, *The Wealth of Nations,* 1776

Englishman. an Englishman's home is his castle (English) Every Englishman considers himself safe from the law and from interference from his neighbours when safe in his own home. H. Étienne, *Stage of Popish Toys,* 1581. In reality, various authorities are entitled to force entry into an Englishman's home under certain conditions (for instance, in pursuit of arrest or search warrants or to enforce a compulsory purchase order). In the past, some commentators have expanded the terms of reference of the proverb, maintaining that it applies equally to the Englishman's conscience, the home of his soul, as much as to his physical residence.

Some people maintain that an Englishman's house is his castle. That's gammon.
Charles Dickens, *The Pickwick Papers,* 1836–37

an Englishman's word is his bond (English) A promise made by an Englishman will always be kept, as a matter of honour. G. Benham, *Book of Quotations,* 1924. Also encountered centuries earlier in the forms 'a king's word should be a king's word' and 'an honest man's word is his bond'.

O kingis word shuld be o kingis bonde.
Lancelot of the Lake, c.1500

one Englishman can beat three Frenchmen (English) A single Englishman is the equal of three foreigners. William Shakespeare, *Henry V*, c.1598.

My men ... there are three privateers ... It's just a fair match for you – one Englishman can always beat three Frenchmen.
Captain Frederick Marryat, *Peter Simple*, 1834

enjoy. if you would enjoy the fruit, pluck not the flower (English) If you wish to enjoy a particular benefit take care not to stifle or destroy the source from which it may emerge. H. G. Bohn, *A Handbook of Proverbs*, 1855. Another proverb advises 'he that would enjoy the fruit must climb the tree'.

enough. enough is as good as a feast (Greek) Having sufficient of something is as satisfying as over-indulgence in it. John Lydgate, *Assembly of the Gods*, c.1420 (also quoted by Euripides in *Suppliants*, c.421 BC). Originally applied largely to gluttony, but now used in many other contexts. *See also* you can have TOO much of a good thing.

A little dish oft furnishes enough: And sure enough is equal to a feast.
Henry Fielding, *Covent Garden Tragedy*, 1732

enough is enough (Roman) Sufficient of something should be enough for anyone. John Heywood, *A Dialogue containing ... the Proverbs in the English Tongue*, 1546 (also found in various forms in the writings of the Classical authors). Rendered in other European languages as '*assai basta, e troppo guasta*' (Italian), '*mieux vaut assez que trop*' (French) and '*genoeg is meer dan overvloed*' (Dutch). Related proverbs include 'he hath enough who is contented with a little'.

As for money, enough is enough; no man can enjoy more.
Robert Southey, *The Doctor*, 1834

enough. *See also* a WORD to the wise is enough

envied. better be envied than pitied (Greek) It is better to inspire jealousy than have people feeling sorry for you. John Heywood, *A Dialogue containing ... the Proverbs in the English Tongue*, 1546 (also found in the writings of Pindar and Herodotus among other Classical authors).

Men say, and truly, that they better be Which be envyed then pittied.
John Donne, *Poems*, 1631

err. to err is human, to forgive divine (Roman/Greek) One should forgive others for their mistakes, as all men make them. Henry Wotton, *J. Yver's Courtly Controversy*, 1578 (similar sentiments were also expressed by Menander and Seneca).

Good-Nature and Good-Sense must ever join; To Err is Humane; to Forgive, Divine.
Alexander Pope, *Essay on Criticism*, 1711

escape. *See* LITTLE thieves are hanged, but great ones escape

eternal. *See* HOPE springs eternal in the human breast

Eve. *See* when ADAM delved and Eve span, who was then the gentleman?

even. *See* never GIVE a sucker an even break; even a WORM will turn

event. *See* it is easy to be WISE after the event

events. *See* COMING events cast their shadows before

every. *See* every ASS loves to hear himself bray; every CLOUD has a silver lining; every COCK crows on his own dunghill; every COOK praises his own broth; every DOG has his day; every

DOG is a lion at home; every DOG is allowed one bite; every ELM has its man; there is an EXCEPTION to every rule; every FAMILY has a skeleton in the cupboard; every HERRING must hang by its own gill; every JACK has his Jill; every LAND has its own law; every LITTLE helps; every MAN after his fashion; every MAN for himself, and the Devil take the hindmost; every MAN has his price; every MAN is the architect of his own fortune; every MAN to his trade; every PICTURE tells a story; every soldier has the baton of a field-marshal in his knapsack; if every man would SWEEP his own doorstep the city would soon be clean; every TUB must stand on its own bottom; there are TWO sides to every question

everybody. everybody loves a lord (English) All men respect rank. F. J. Furnivall, in *Queen Elizabeth's Academy*, 1869.

everybody's business is nobody's business (English) When something is the responsibility of many people, nobody can be found who is willing to take personal responsibility for it. Randle Cotgrave, *A Dictionary of the French and English Tongues*, 1611. Aristotle voiced similar sentiments in *Politics* and Daniel Defoe wrote an essay under the same title in 1725.

I remember that a wise friend of mine did usually say, 'That which is everybody's business is nobody's business'.
Izaak Walton, *The Compleat Angler*, 1653

what everybody says must be true (English) If something is generally believed, the implication is that it must be accurate. *Legends of the Saints*, 1400. *See also* there's NO smoke without fire.

everyone. everyone to his taste (French) Questions of taste are personal and vary from one person to another. John Lyly, *Euphues and His England*, 1580. Given in French as 'chacun à son goût', which is often quoted by English speakers. Equivalent proverbs include 'everyone after his fashion', 'each to his own' and the English saying 'every man as he loveth, quoth the good man when he kissed his cow'.

I own I never could envy Didius in these kinds of fancies of his: – But every man to his own taste.
Laurence Sterne, *Tristram Shandy*, 1759

everyone. *See also* everyone is INNOCENT until proved guilty; you can't PLEASE everyone; everyone STRETCHES his legs according to the length of his coverlet

everything. everything comes to him who waits (English) Patience will be rewarded in the long run. Alexander Barclay, *Eclogues*, c.1514. *See also* all things COME to those who wait.

All things come round to him who will but wait.
Henry Wadsworth Longfellow, *Tales of a Wayside Inn*, 1863

everything has an end (English) Nothing lasts for ever. Geoffrey Chaucer, *Troilus and Criseyde*, c.1385. In its fullest form the proverb runs 'everything has an end, and a pudding has two'. Other proverbs claim 'everything hath a beginning' and 'everything hath its time'. *See also* all GOOD things must come to an end.

Everything has an end. Even young ladies in love cannot read their letters for ever.
Charles Dickens, *Barnaby Rudge*, 1841

everything is good in its season (English) All things (especially foodstuffs) are best enjoyed when in prime condition. W. Stepney, *The Spanish Schoolmaster*, 1591.

everything. See also MONEY isn't everything; a PLACE for everything and everything in its place; there is a REMEDY for everything except death; there is a TIME for everything

evil. evil be to him who thinks it (English) May ill luck befall those who wish ill on others. Geoffrey Chaucer, *The Canterbury Tales*, c. 1387.

Now the evyl which men wysshe to other cometh to hym whiche wyssheth hit.
William Caxton, *Aesop's Fables*, 1484

evil communications corrupt good manners (Hebrew) The influence of those who hold wicked opinions ruins those of good character. J. Palsgrave, *L'Éclaircissement de la langue française*, 1530 (also found in the Bible, Corinthians 15:33, quoted by Saint Paul – though the same saying is also found in Menander's *Thaïs*). See also the ROTTEN apple injures its neighbours; one SCABBED sheep infects the whole flock; he that TOUCHES pitch shall be defiled.

Gude forgie me for swearing – but evil communication corrupteth good manners.
Walter Scott, *The Pirate*, 1821

evil doers are evil dreaders (English) Those who act wickedly are often those who most fear suffering from wickedness themselves. Roger Ascham, *The Scholemaster*, 1570. See also ILL doers are ill dreaders.

If you were more trustful, it would better befit your time of life ... We have a proverb ... that evil doers are aye evil-dreaders.
Robert Louis Stevenson, *Kidnapped*, 1886

evil. See also a GREAT book is a great evil; IDLENESS is the root of all evil; the LOVE of money is the root of all evil; SEE no evil, hear no evil, speak no evil; SUFFICIENT unto the day is the evil thereof

evils. See of TWO evils choose the lesser

example is better than precept (English) Men learn quicker from practical example than from spoken advice. J. Mirk, *Festial*, c. 1400.

It is a trite but true observation, that examples work more forcibly on the mind than precepts.
Henry Fielding, *The Adventures of Joseph Andrews*, 1742

example. See also a GOOD example is the best sermon

exception. the exception proves the rule (English) If something is described as an exception, then it follows that there is a rule that covers all other cases. G. Watts, *Bacon's Advancement of Learning*, 1640 (also encountered in variant forms in the Bible and in Classical writings). In modern usage, the proverb is usually quoted to justify the exceptional case, though originally the idea was that it was by the exception that a rule might be tested. See also there is an EXCEPTION to every rule.

They serve only as exceptions; which, in the grammarian's phrase, confirm and prove a general canon.
Tobias Smollett, *Humphrey Clinker*, 1771

there is an exception to every rule (English) No rule applies in a hundred per cent of cases. T. F., *News from the North*, 1579. See also the EXCEPTION proves the rule.

exchange. See FAIR exchange is no robbery

excuse. See a BAD excuse is better than none; IGNORANCE of the law is no excuse

excuses. he who excuses himself, accuses himself (French/English) Those who seek to excuse themselves sometimes end up only attracting blame to themselves. Randle Cotgrave, *A*

Dictionary of the French and English Tongues, 1611. Rendered in French as 'qui s'excuse, s'accuse'.

excuses. *See also* IDLE people lack no excuses

excusing. *See* ACCUSING the times is but excusing ourselves

exist. *See* although there exist many thousand subjects for elegant CONVERSATION, there are persons who cannot meet a cripple without talking about feet

expands. *See* WORK expands so as to fill the time available

expect. what can you expect from a pig but a grunt? (*English*) Poor behaviour is only to be expected from someone of no refinement. Benjamin Franklin, *Poor Robin's Almanack*, 1732. Related proverbs include 'what can you expect of a hog but his bristles'.

If he had not ... been but a Dumfriesshire hog ... he would have spoken more like a gentleman, but you cannot have more of a sow than a grumph.
Walter Scott, *The Two Drovers*, 1827

expects. *See* BLESSED is he who expects nothing, for he shall never be disappointed

experience. experience is a comb which nature gives us when we are bald (*Chinese*) By the time a person has acquired a lifetime's knowledge it is too late to use use it.

experience is the best teacher (*Roman*) People learn quickest from practical experience. M. L. Weems, letter, 12 November 1803. Originally known in the form of the Latin tag 'experientia docet' ('experience teaches'). The proverb is known in several languages, including Spanish, in which it is rendered as 'experience is not

always the kindest of teachers, but it is surely the best'. Oscar Wilde's reply to the proverb was 'experience is the name everyone gives to his own mistakes'.

experience is the mother of wisdom (*Greek*) Knowledge comes from experience. R. Taverner, *The Garden of Wisdom*, 1539 (also found in the writings of the seventh-century BC Greek lyric poet Alcman). Sometimes encountered as 'experience is the father of wisdom' and in its fullest form as 'experience is the father of wisdom, and memory the mother'.

experience is the teacher of fools (*Roman*) Stupid people have no option but to learn by making mistakes. Roger Ascham, *The Scholemaster*, 1570 (also found in Livy's *History of Rome*, c. 10 BC). Also encountered in the form 'experience is the mistress of fools' (possibly a reference to sixteenth-century dame schools for English children).

Experience is the mistress of knaves as well as of fools.
Roger L'Estrange, *Aesop*, 1692

experience keeps a dear school (*US*) Learning by one's mistakes may prove very costly and painful. Benjamin Franklin, *Poor Richard's Almanack*, 1743. Another proverb concurs: 'experience is good, if not bought too dear'. Yet another, however, warns 'experience is sometimes dangerous'.

Experience keeps a dear school, but Fools will learn in no other.
Benjamin Franklin, *Poor Richard's Almanack*, 1743

extremes meet (*French*) Similarities may often be identified in apparently opposing standpoints, characters, situations etc. Blaise Pascal, *Pensées*, 1662.

That dead time of the dawn, when (as extremes meet) the rake ... and the hard-handed artizan ... jostle ... for the honours of the pavement.
Charles Lamb, *Essays of Elia*, 1822

extremity. *See* MAN's extremity is God's opportunity

eye. an eye for eye, and a tooth for a tooth (Hebrew) Those who inflict harm on others should have to suffer the same harm themselves. Bible, Exodus 21:24. Leviticus 24:20 confirms divine authority for such revenge-taking: 'breach for breach, eye for eye, tooth for tooth: as he hath caused blemish in a man, so shall it be done to him again', but in the Sermon on the Mount Jesus tempers this, suggesting 'turning the other cheek' when under attack from another.

From the continued existence of the old theory, 'an eye for an eye' condemned to death over nineteen hundred years ago, but still dying very hard in this Christian country.
John Galsworthy, *The Spirit of Punishment*, 1910

the eye is bigger than the belly (English) Greed encourages a person to take more than they will be able to cope with (usually quoted in relation to food). John Lyly, *Euphues and His England*, 1580.

A person is said to have his 'eyes bigger than his belly' who takes more food upon his plate than he can eat.
Thomas Love Peacock, *Manley*, 1889

the eye of the master does more work than both his hands (English) Through the supervision of others, a person may achieve more than he or she could by doing the work personally. Benjamin Franklin, *The Way to Wealth*, 1736.

But continual vigilance, rigorous method, what we call 'the eye of the master', work wonders.
Thomas Carlyle, *Past and Present*, 1843

what the eye does not see, the heart does not grieve over (English) What a person does not know cannot worry him (often said to justify keeping a secret from someone). R. Taverner, *Proverbs or Adages of Erasmus*, 1539. Related proverbs include 'what the eye sees not, the heart craves not', meaning that a person cannot yearn for something of which he is unaware. *See also* IGNORANCE is bliss.

I never desire or find fault with that I see not: that proverb is verifies in me; What eye seeth not, the heart rueth not.
John Florio, *Montaigne*, 1603

eye. *See also* BEAUTY is in the eye of the beholder; the MASTER's eye maketh the horse fat; PLEASE your eye and plague your heart; you should never TOUCH your eye but with your elbow

eyes. the eyes are the window of the soul (Roman) A study of a person's eyes will reveal what they are secretly thinking. T. Phaer, *Regiment of Life*, 1545 (the proverb is also found in the writings of Cicero). There is some practical truth in the notion in so far as the pupils dilate when a person is happy or looking at something of which they approve, but shrink when they are displeased by something. *See also* the FACE is the index of the mind.

eyes. *See also* the BUYER has need of a hundred eyes, the seller of but one; FIELDS have eyes, and woods have ears; FOUR eyes see more than two; HAWKS will not pick out hawks' eyes

f

face. the face is the index of the mind (Roman) A person's character is revealed in his or her face. J. Pilkington, *Nehemiah*, 1575 (also found in the writings of Cicero). The notion that all is revealed in the face was the basis of the pseudo-science of physiognomy, in which examination of every feature allowed an insight into inner character. Short noses, for instance, indicated a lazy nature, while joined eyebrows were a sign that someone was a witch, and fat cheeks suggested greed and sensuality. Also encountered in the variant form 'the face is the index of the heart' and in the contrary version 'The face is no index to the heart'. *See also* the EYES are the window of the soul.

You have not to learn that the face is the outward index of the mind within.
Mrs Henry Wood, *Trevlyn Hold*, 1864

face. *See also* don't CUT off your nose to spite your face

fact is stranger than fiction (English) What happens in real life is often much stranger than anything someone might invent. Lord Byron, *Don Juan*, 1823. *See also* TRUTH is stranger than fiction.

'Tis strange – but true; for truth is always strange, –
Stranger than fiction.
Lord Byron, *Don Juan*, 1823

facts are stubborn things (English) Reality can be inconvenient and hard to control. E. Budgell, *Liberty and Progress*, 1732.

Facts, however, are stubborn things, and will not even make a bow to the sweetest of young ladies.
R. D. Blackmore, *Craddock Nowell*, 1866

fade. *See* OLD soldiers never die, they simply fade away

fails. he who never fails will never grow rich (English) Those who are not prepared when necessary to risk failure and learn from it are unlikely to achieve success. Charles Spurgeon, *John Ploughman's Talk*, 1869. The sentiment is supported by another proverb, which runs 'failure teaches success'.

faint heart ne'er won fair lady (English) There is no place for timidity in romance. R. Taverner, *Proverbs or Adages of Erasmus*, 1546.

But 'faint heart never won fair lady,' so I made bold to speak to Rose.
Maria Edgeworth, *Irish Bulls*, 1802

fair. a fair day in winter is the mother of a storm (English) An unseasonally warm day in winter is a warning of bad weather to come. John Clarke, *Paroemiologia Anglo-Latina*, 1639.

all's fair in love and war (English) All strategies are forgivable in love or war, however underhand or unprincipled. T. Shelton, *Cervantes' Don Quixote*, 1620. *See also* the END justifies the means.

All stratagems in love, and that the sharpest war, are lawful.
Beaumont and Fletcher, *Lovers' Progress*, c.1630

fair and soft goes far in a day (English) Those who take things gently and in even temper will do better than those who allow themselves to be overcome by their emotions. *Douce MS*, c.1350. Related proverbs include the rather cynical 'fair and softly, as lawyers go to heaven'.

Fair and softly goes far in a day ... He that spurs on too fast at first setting out, tires before he comes to his journeys end.
John Ray, *A Collection of English Proverbs*, 1670

fair exchange is no robbery (English) No one is worse off when goods or services of equal value are exchanged. John Heywood, *A Dialogue containing ... the Proverbs in the English Tongue*, 1546.

Fair Exchange is no Rob'ry. Spoken when we take up one Thing, and lay down a nother.
James Kelly, *A Complete Collection of Scotish Proverbs*, 1721

fair face and a foul heart (English) A pretty appearance often conceals a vicious nature. Ben Jonson, *Every Man in His Humour*, 1598. Another proverb, 'a fair face cannot have a crabbed heart' disputes this notion, but others that support it include 'fair and foolish' and 'a fair face may be a foul bargain'. *See also* APPEARANCES are deceptive.

I have known fair hides have foul hearts ere now, sister.
Ben Jonson, *Every Man in His Humour*, 1598

fair play is a jewel (US) Nothing is more precious than honesty in dealings with others. Washington Irving, *The History of New York*, 1809. One historical extension of the proverb, now little heard, runs 'fair play is a jewel – let go my hair' (sometimes, 'Lucy, let go my hair'). Related proverbs include 'fair play is good play'.

Well, fair play's a jewel. But I've got the lead of you, old fellow.
James Fenimore Cooper, *The Pioneers*, 1823

fair words break no bones (English) Those who speak kindly and softly of others run little risk of causing anyone hurt. *How the Good Wyfe*, c.1460. Other proverbs along similar lines include 'fair words cost nothing', 'fair words slake wrath' and 'fair words hurt not the tongue', though a contrasting view is expressed in 'fair words fill not the belly' and 'fair words will not make the pot boil'. Equally cynical are 'he who gives fair words feeds you with an empty spoon' and 'fair words make me look to my purse'. *See also* STICKS and stones may break my bones, but names will never hurt me.

fair. *See also* none but the BRAVE deserve the fair; FAINT heart ne'er won fair lady; GIVE and take is fair play; if SAINT Paul's Day be fair and clear, it will betide a happy year; SAINT Swithin's Day, if thou dost rain, for forty days it will remain; Saint Swithin's Day, if thou be fair, for forty days 'twill rain no more; TURN about is fair play

fairest. the fairest rose at last is withered (English) Even the most beautiful will eventually lose their looks. John Florio, *Second Fruites*, 1591. Related proverbs include 'the finest flower will soonest fade', 'the finest lawn soonest stains' and 'the fairest silk is soonest stained'.

faith will move mountains (Hebrew) Those who have true belief in something (typically in God) will have the confidence to attempt the seemingly impossible. Bible, Matthew 17:20. See also if the MOUNTAIN will not go to Mahomet, Mahomet must go to the mountain.

As faith can move mountains, so nothing was impossible to Holy Church.
John Betjeman, *Ghastly Good Taste*, 1933

fall. See BETWEEN two stools you fall to the ground; the BIGGER they are, the harder they fall; if the BLIND lead the blind, both shall fall into the ditch; PRIDE goes before a fall; a REED before the wind lives on, while mighty oaks do fall; UNITED we stand, divided we fall

falling. the falling out of friends is the renewal of love (Roman) When friends quarrel there is every chance that when they make up their friendship will be all the closer. *Parade of Dainty Devices*, 1576 (also quoted by Terence).

Old Terence has taken notice of that; and observes upon it, That lovers falling-out occasions lovers falling-in.
Samuel Richardson, *Clarissa*, 1748

falling. See also never CATCH at a falling knife or friend

falls. See the APPLE never falls far from the tree; the BREAD never falls but on the buttered side; when all FRUIT falls, welcome haws; if the SKY falls we shall catch larks; as a TREE falls, so shall it lie

fame is but the breath of the people (English) Fame has no substance. Coryat, *Crudities*, 1611. Variants include 'all fame is dangerous', 'fame, like a river, is narrowed at its source and

broadest afar off' and 'fame to infamy is a beaten road'.

familiarity breeds contempt (Roman) Respect for someone or something tends to diminish as familiarity increases. Alanus de Insulis, *Satires*, c.1160 (also found in Livy and in Publilius Syrus, *Sententiae*, c.43 BC). Aesop illustrated the proverb in his fable of 'The Fox and the Lion', in which the fox quickly loses his fear of the lion after several meetings.

Men seyne that 'over-greet hoomlynesse engendreth dispreisynge'.
Geoffrey Chaucer, *Tale of Melibee*, c.1390

families. See ACCIDENTS will happen in the best regulated families

family. every family has a skeleton in the cupboard (English) Every family has shameful secrets that are kept carefully hidden from public view. William Thackeray, *The Newcomes*, 1855.

the family that prays together stays together (US) Families that share acts of religious worship are less likely to disintegrate. Father Patrick Peyton, *All for Her*, 1967. Father Peyton invented the slogan for the Roman Catholic Family Rosary Crusade, and it was first heard in a radio broadcast in 1947. This proverbial phrase is now usually heard in a number of variations, the most common of which include 'the family that plays together stays together'.

family. See also there's a BLACK sheep in every family

far-fetched and dear-bought is good for ladies (English) Women are most likely to be pleased with gifts that are both expensive and difficult to obtain. *Douce MS*, c.1350.

But you know, far-fetch'd and dear-bought

is fit for Ladies. I warrant, this cost your Father Two pence half-penny.
Jonathan Swift, *Polite Conversation*, 1738

fashion. *See* when the GORSE is out of bloom, kissing's out of fashion; better be OUT of the world than out of fashion

fast. fast bind, fast find (English) If things are made secure, there is less chance that they will be lost when the owner returns for them (usually quoted when locking doors). William Caxton, *Aesop's Fables*, 1484.

'Fast bind, safe find,' is an excellent proverb. I'll e'en lock her up with the rest.
Beaumont and Fletcher, *The Spanish Curate*, 1622

fast. *See also* BAD news travels fast; a MONEYLESS man goes fast through the market

fastest. *See* he TRAVELS fastest who travels alone

fasting. *See* it's ILL speaking between a full man and a fasting

fat. *See* a GREEN winter makes a fat churchyard; the OPERA isn't over till the fat lady sings

father. like father, like son (English) Children take after their parents. William Langland, *Piers Plowman*, 1362. Sometimes encountered in its Latin form, 'qualis pater, talis filius'. Variants include 'like hen, like chicken', 'like cow, like calf' and 'like crow, like egg'. *See also* like MOTHER, like daughter.

An olde proverbe hath longe agone be sayde That oft the sone in maners lyke wyll be unto the father.
Alexander Barclay, *The Ship of Fools*, 1509

father. *See also* the CHILD is the father of the man; it is a WISE child that knows its own father; the WISH is father to the thought

fault. a fault confessed is half redressed (English) Admitting one's mistakes is a good step towards atoning for them. *Interlude of Wealth and Health*, 1558. The sentiment is reinforced by another proverb, 'a fault once denied is twice committed'.

A fault confessed is more than half amends, but men of such ill spirite as your selfe Worke crosses and debates twixt man and wife.
Arden of Feversham, 1592

faults. faults are thick where love is thin (English) People who dislike one another are quick to find fault with each other. T. Draxe, *Bibliotheca Scholastica*, 1616.

the first faults are theirs that commit them, the second theirs that permit them (English) Those who do nothing to prevent some offence being committed are almost as guilty of it as the actual perpetrators. Thomas Fuller, *Gnomologia*, 1732.

favour. *See* KISSING goes by favour

favours. *See* FORTUNE favours fools; FORTUNE favours the brave

fear. fear lends wings (English) Through terror a person acquires a new turn of speed when it comes to escaping what they are terrified of. Philip Sidney, *Arcadia*, 1580. Less well-known, but related, proverbs include 'fear causeth a man to cast beyond the moon' and 'fear hath a quick ear'.

Therto fear gave her wings.
Edmund Spenser, *The Faerie Queene*, 1590

fear. *See also* BEWARE of Greeks bearing gifts; DO right and fear no man; FOOLS rush in where angels fear to tread

feast. *See* the COMPANY makes the feast; ENOUGH is as good as a feast

feather. feather by feather the goose is plucked (Italian) Step by step a task is completed. G. Torriano, *Select Italian Proverbs*, 1642.

feather. *See also* BIRDS of a feather flock together

feathers. *See* FINE feathers make fine birds

February. if in February there be no rain, 'tis neither good for hay nor grain (English) A dry February bodes ill for hay and grain harvests later in the year. John Ray, *A Collection of English Proverbs*, 1670. In agreement with this saying, other proverbs claim 'if it rains in February every day, in June you're sure of plenty of hay', 'February's rain fills the barn', 'a February spring is not worth a pin', 'if February give much snow, a fine summer it doth foreshow' and 'February fill ditch, black or white, don't care which' ('black' being rain and 'white' being snow). Yet another runs 'February, if ye be foul, the sheep will die in every pool'. *See also* CANDLEMAS Day, put beans in the clay, put candles and candlesticks away; if CANDLEMAS Day be sunny and bright, winter will have another flight; if Candlemas Day be cloudy with rain, winter is gone, and won't come again.

All the moneths in the year curse a fair Februeer.
John Ray, *A Collection of English Proverbs*, 1670

feed a cold and starve a fever (English) Patients with colds should be encouraged to eat healthily, while those with fevers should be denied sustenance. Edward Fitzgerald, *Polonius: A Collection of Wise Saws and Modern Instances*, 1852. In times gone by superstition offered various things a feverish patient might take. These included rolled-up cobwebs, spiders and live insects eaten in slices of apple or with jam or treacle. It has been suggested that the proverb was originally intended to be a warning to the effect that any person who attempted to control a cold by over-eating could expect to suffer a fever as a consequence. Modern medical opinion agrees that a sensible, healthy diet will help to fight a cold, while those suffering from fevers are best sustained with drinks only (they will in any case be disinclined to eat).

Edwin's cold was now fully developed; and Maggie had told him to feed it.
Arnold Bennett, *Clayhanger*, 1910

feeling hath no fellow (English) Having a gut feeling about something or someone is a more reliable guide than the evidence of the other senses. John Ray, *A Collection of English Proverbs*, 1678.

feels. *See* a MAN is as old as he feels, and a woman as old as she looks; PRIDE feels no pain

fell. *See* LITTLE strokes fell great oaks

fellow. *See* STONE-dead hath no fellow

fellows. all fellows at football (English) All footballers are (or should be) friends on the field of play. *Sir John Oldcastle*, 1600.

female. the female of the species is more deadly than the male (English) Women can prove more ruthless and without mercy than their male counterparts (just as the female spider is more to be feared than its mate). Rudyard Kipling, *Morning Post*, 20 October 1911.

fence. no fence against ill fortune (English) There is no way to protect oneself effectively from bad luck.

W. Camden, *Remains concerning Britain*, 1614.

Some evils and calamities assault so violently, that there is no resisting of them.
John Ray, *A Collection of English Proverbs*, 1670

fence. *See also* the GRASS is always greener on the other side of the fence

fences. *See* GOOD fences make good neighbours

festina lente. *See* make HASTE slowly

fetch. *See* a DOG that will fetch a bone will carry a bone

fever. *See* FEED a cold and starve a fever

few. few words are best (English) A few well-chosen words are better than a long rambling speech. *Roxborough Ballads*, c.1600. Related proverbs include 'few words and many deeds' and 'few words to the wise suffice'.

I wonder what the devil possessed me – but few words are best.
Tobias Smollett, *Humphry Clinker*, 1771

few. *See also* you WIN a few, you lose a few

fiction. *See* FACT is stranger than fiction

fiddle. *See* there's many a GOOD tune played on an old fiddle

fiddler. *See* they that DANCE must pay the fiddler

fields have eyes, and woods have ears (English) Secrets will always leak out, even when there seems to be no one else around. *Trinity MS, c.1225. See also* WALLS have ears.

Woods have their eares, and fields their eyes, everie thing hath some instrument of, or helpe for, discoverie.
Randle Cotgrave, *A Dictionary of the French and English Tongues*, 1611

fight. fight fire with fire (English) Employ the same methods that are used against you when retaliating. William Shakespeare, *Coriolanus*,

c.1608. Another proverb insists 'fire drives out fire'.

fight. *See also* COUNCILS of war never fight

fights. he who fights and runs away, lives to fight another day (Greek) It is sometimes wisest to back down from a fight, so that one may return to the fray at a later date. *The Owl and the Nightingale*, 1250 (also found in the writings of Menander). Legend has it that the line was spoken by Demosthenes as he fled from Philip of Macedon at Chaeronea. *See also* DISCRETION is the better part of valour.

For, those that fly, may fight againe, Which he can never do that's slain.
Samuel Butler, *Hudibras*, 1678

fill. *See* WORK expands so as to fill the time available

find. *See* those who HIDE can find; LOVE will find a way; SAFE bind, safe find; SCRATCH a Russian and you find a Tartar; SEEK and ye shall find; it is easy to find a STICK to beat a dog

finders keepers, losers weepers (Roman) Anyone who finds something is entitled to it, while the person who has lost it must reconcile themselves to their loss. J. T. Brockett, *Glossary of North Country Words*, 1825 (variants are also found in the writings of Plautus). The notion encapsulated in the proverb is supported by the law only in certain very limited circumstances. Also encountered in the form 'finding's keepings'.

finds. *See* the DEVIL finds work for idle hands

fine. fine feathers make fine birds (French) Fine clothes lend distinction to the wearer. G. Delamothe, *French*

Alphabet, 1592. *See also* APPEARANCES are deceptive.

As everybody knows, fine feathers make fine birds.
Thomas Hardy, *Tess of the D'Urbervilles*, 1891

fine words butter no parsnips (English) Nothing is actually achieved by talk alone. J. Clarke, *Paroemiologia Anglo-Latina*, 1639. Parsnips are traditionally served with melted butter (words clearly being a poor substitute). Also encountered in the form 'fair words butter no parsnips'.

Who ... said that 'fine words butter no parsnips'? Half the parsnips of society are served and rendered palatable with no other sauce.
William Thackeray, *Vanity Fair*, 1848

fine. *See also* RAIN before seven, fine before eleven

fingers were made before forks and hands before knives (English) Before the invention of cutlery man used his hands to eat with (quoted as an excuse for using the fingers to eat with). *Loseley MSS*, 1567. The fork was first introduced, in Venetian society, in the early sixteenth century, although John the Good, Duke of Burgundy, allegedly used two forks to eat with as early as the fourteenth century. It was not until the eighteenth century that the use of knives and forks became widespread in British society. The proverb is sometimes quoted in other contexts, in reference to the employment of less refined methods.

Miss Thorne ... was always glad to revert to anything and ... would doubtless in time have reflected that fingers were made before forks, and have reverted accordingly.
Anthony Trollope, *Barchester Towers*, 1857

finish. *See* NICE guys finish last

fire. better a little fire to warm us than a great one to burn us (Scottish) A minor benefit that carries with it no danger is preferable to a much greater one that carries with it much risk. James Kelly, *A Complete Collection of Scotish Proverbs*, 1721.

fire and water are good servants, but bad masters (English) Fire and water are useful in various ways, but dangerous if allowed to get out of control. W. Bullein, *Bulwarke of Defence*, 1562. Also encountered as 'fire is a good friend, but a bad enemy'. Another proverb claims 'water is as dangerous as commodious' and the two elements are brought together in 'fire and water have no mercy'.

Fire, the saying goes, is a good servant but a bad master.
Charles Dickens, *Barnaby Rudge*, 1841

fire drives out fire (English) One passion or sensation will be eclipsed by another. William Shakespeare, *Romeo and Juliet*, c.1593.

Tut, man, one fire burns out another's burning.
William Shakespeare, *Romeo and Juliet*, c.1593

fire. *See also* a BURNT child dreads the fire; he CARRIES fire in one hand and water in the other; take the CHESTNUTS out of the fire with the cat's paw; DIRTY water will quench fire; FIGHT fire with fire; you should KNOW a man seven years before you stir his fire; there's NO smoke without fire; if you PLAY with fire you get burnt; THREE removals are as bad as a fire

first. better be first in a village than second at Rome (Roman) It is better to be in a position to exercise unchallenged power in a small community or organization than to play second fiddle to someone else in a grander situation. Nicholas Udall, *Erasmus*, 1542 (also found in Plutarch's *Caesar*). Tradition has it that Julius Caesar quoted the proverb when opting to rule Gaul rather than share power in Rome.

Caesar, when he went first into Gaul, made no scruple to profess *That he had rather be first in a village than second at Rome*.
Francis Bacon, *The Advancement of Learning*, 1605

first catch your hare (English) Do not forget to take the essential first step before embarking upon some project or enterprise (often said as a word of warning to those whose enthusiasm for a project tempts them to forget what they must do first before they can proceed). William Thackeray, *The Rose and the Ring*, 1855. The proverb is often inaccurately attributed to Hannah Glasse, in her *The Art of Cookery made Plain and Easy*, 1747, or else to Mrs Beeton, in her *Book of Household Management*, 1851, in neither of which does it appear in precisely this form (Hannah Glasse's authorship of *The Art of Cookery* itself is also open to question). Though Glasse's apparent use of the phrase made it famous, it had in fact been in common parlance for many years beforehand, a variant of it (mentioning deer rather than hares) being quoted, for instance, by Henry de Bracton in his *De Legibus Angliae* in the thirteenth century: 'it is a common saying that it is best first to catch the stag, and afterwards, when he has been caught, to skin him'. Equivalent proverbs to much the same effect include 'catch your bear before you sell its skin'. *See also* don't COUNT your chickens before they are hatched; don't HALLOO till you are out of the wood.

Take your hare when it is cased [skinned], and make a pudding ...
Hannah Glasse, *The Art of Cookery made Plain and Easy*, 1747

first come, first served (English/French) Those who arrive promptly will get first choice of what is on offer and have the least time to wait. Geoffrey Chaucer, *The Canterbury Tales*, c.1387.

He found the sexton ... making nine graves ... and whoso dies next, first comes, first served.
Robert Armin, *A Nest of Ninnies*, 1608

first impressions are the most lasting (English) The impression a person makes on first acquaintance has a lasting impact. William Congreve, *The Way of the World*, 1700. Jane Austen's classic novel *Pride and Prejudice*, 1796–97, was originally entitled *First Impressions*.

First impressions, you know, often go a long way, and last a long time.
Charles Dickens, *Martin Chuzzlewit*, 1843–44

first things first (English) Tackle things in the correct order (typically in order of importance). G. Jackson, *First Things First*, 1894.

if at first you don't succeed, try, try, try again (English) Do not be discouraged by early failure at something. T. H. Palmer, *Teacher's Manual*, 1840. The proverb was popularized on both sides of the Atlantic in a poem, 'Try (try) again', part of W. E. Hickson's *Moral Songs*, 1857.

it is the first step that is difficult (French) In many enterprises, it is the first stage that presents the biggest challenge. A. Munday and others, *Sir Thomas More*, c.1596. The proverb has its origins in the legend of Saint Denys, who was beheaded by his enemies, but then picked up his head and walked six miles with it. A wise man commented of the story 'the distance ... is not important. It was the first step that was difficult'. *See also* Ce n'est que le PREMIER pas qui coûte.

on the first of March, the crows begin to search (English) The first day of March signals the start of the mating season for crows. M. A. Denham, *Proverbs Relating to the Seasons*, 1846. Medieval superstition placed the beginning of the mating season for birds on 14 February, Saint Valentine's Day.

By the first of March the crows begin to search, By the first of April they are sitting still, By the first of May they are flown away, Creeping greedy back again With October wind and rain.
Edith Holden, *The Country Diary of an Edwardian Lady*, 1906

the first blow is half the battle (Greek) He who begins well will find half his work already done. George Herbert, *Jacula Prudentum*, 1640 (also quoted by Pythagoras, sixth century BC). *See also* WELL begun is half done.

The beginning is half the whole.
Pythagoras, sixth century BC

the first duty of a soldier is obedience (English) Above all else, a soldier is required to obey the orders of his superiors. J. Grant, *The Romance of War*, 1847.

the first seven years are the hardest (English) Things get easier after the difficult initial stages (usually quoted in reference to marriages and new jobs). The saying probably arose during World War I, when service in the regular army was set at seven years. As far back as the fourteenth century, however, a seven-year period was regarded as significant (superstition,

for instance, claimed that children's characters changed every seven years).

first. *See also* the BEST go first, the bad remain to mend; whom the GODS would destroy they first make mad; SELF-preservation is the first law of nature; THINK first and speak afterwards; he that will THRIVE must first ask his wife

fish. all fish are not caught with flies (English) Sometimes different methods from the obvious must be used to acheive a particular end. John Lyly, *Euphues and His England*, 1580.

all is fish that comes to the net (English) The best should be made of any benefit that happens to fall into a person's hands, regardless of what it is (sometimes heard in sarcastic reference to another's unscrupulous readiness to make use of any opportunity). c.1520, published in *Ballads from MSS*, 1868–72. *See also* all is GRIST that comes to the mill.

Black, brown, fair, or tawny, 'tis all fish that comes in your net.
Richard Cumberland, *The Brothers*, 1769

do not make fish of one and flesh of another (English) Treat others equally, with impartiality. J. Clarke, *Paroemiologia Anglo-Latina*, 1639. Also encountered as 'do not make fish of one and fowl of another'.

The complaints alleged against the maids are ... very applicable to our gentleman's gentlemen; I would, therefore, have them under the very same regulations, and ... would not make fish of one and flesh of the other.
Daniel Defoe, *Everybody's Business*, 1725

fish and guests stink after three days (English) Three days are enough to make the presence of any guest irksome (just as a fish will start to go off in that time). John Lyly, *Euphues and His England*, 1580 (a variant may also be found in the writings of Plautus). Also found as 'fish and company stink in three days'. See also a constant GUEST is never welcome.

Fish and visitors smell in three days.
Benjamin Franklin, *Works*, c. 1736

the best fish swim near the bottom (English) The most valuable things can be gained only through the taking of some trouble or effort. Nicholas Breton, *Proverbs*, 1616.

The best fish swim deep.
Thomas Fuller, *Gnomologia*, 1732

the fish always stinks from the head downwards (Greek) Corruption always starts at the top (often quoted in discussion of political corruption). George Pettie, *Guazzo's Civil Conversation*, 1581.

Teste, Fish ever begins to taint at the head; the first thing that's deprav'd in man's his wit.
Randle Cotgrave, *A Dictionary of the French and English Tongues*, 1611

the fish will soon be caught that nibbles at every bait (English) Those who recklessly accept any offer that is presented to them without considering the possible pitfalls will soon find themselves in trouble. Thomas Fuller, *Gnomologia*, 1732.

there are plenty more fish in the sea (English) If one opening fails to meet one's expectations, there are many more opportunities waiting to be seized instead (usually quoted with reference to potential partners as consolation for disappointed lovers). G. Harvey, *Letter-Book*, c. 1573. Originally encountered in the form 'there are as good fish in the sea as ever came out of it' and also found as 'the sea hath

fish for every man'.

There's fish in the sea, no doubt of it, As good as ever came out of it.
W. S. Gilbert, *Patience*, 1881

fish. See also BIG fish eat little fish; it is in vain to CAST your net where there is no fish; CATCHING fish is not the whole of fishing; all CATS love fish but fear to wet their paws; LITTLE fish are sweet; NO man cries stinking fish

fishing. it is good fishing in troubled waters (English) There are plentiful opportunities for advantage when confusion and conflict abound. Richard Grafton, *Chronicles*, 1568.

Thinking it (as the proverb saith) best fishing in troubled waters.
Sir John Harington, *Orlando Furioso*, 1591

fishing. See also CATCHING fish is not the whole of fishing

fit. See you can't fit a QUART into a pint pot

fits. See if the CAP fits, wear it

fix. See if it ain't BROKE, don't fix it

flag. See TRADE follows the flag

flattery. See IMITATION is the sincerest form of flattery

flea. See NOTHING should be done in haste but gripping a flea

fleas. See BIG fleas have little fleas upon their backs to bite them, and little fleas have lesser fleas, and so *ad infinitum*; if you LIE down with dogs, you will get up with fleas

flesh. all flesh is not venison (English) There are many different kinds of meat, some better than others. Wodroephe, *Spared Houres*, 1623.

flesh. See also what's BRED in the bone will come out in the flesh; the NEARER the bone, the sweeter the flesh; the SPIRIT is willing but the flesh is weak

flew. See a BIRD never flew on one wing

flies. flies come to feasts unasked (English) Parasites and other undesirables gather where there is hope of some benefit, regardless of whether their presence has been requested. *Sphere*, 27 September 1924.

flies. See also a CLOSE mouth catches no flies; EAGLES don't catch flies; HONEY catches more flies than vinegar; TIME flies

flight. See BLESSINGS brighten as they take their flight

fling enough dirt and some will stick (Roman) Heaping allegations of misdoings and so forth upon an opponent is a good policy, as some at least are bound to be believed. Francis Bacon, *De Dignitate et Augmentis Scientiarum*, 1623 (quoting Latin sources). The practice was originally associated with Medius, a courtier in the time of Alexander the Great, who favoured such tactics against his enemies. The word 'mud' often replaces 'dirt' (hence the coinage 'mud-slinging'). See also GIVE a dog a bad name and hang him; SLANDER leaves a scar behind it.

Scurrility's a useful trick,
Approv'd by the most politic;
Fling dirt enough, and some will stick.
Edward Ward, *Hudibras Redivivus*, 1706

flock. See BIRDS of a feather flock together

flow. every flow hath its ebb (English) After things reach a climactic peak, however great and unprecedented, sooner or later they inevitably fall back (just as the tide turns after reaching its high point). John Lydgate, *Troy Book*, c.1420.

There is a time when families, and single persons thrive, and there is a time when they go backward.
James Kelly, *A Complete Collection of Scotish Proverbs*, 1721

flowers. See APRIL showers bring forth May flowers

fly. See do not REMOVE a fly from your friend's forehead with a hatchet

flying. See it is good to make a BRIDGE of gold to a flying enemy

foe. a foe is better than a dissembling friend (Greek) An open enemy is less of a threat than a friend of whose devotion you are not entirely sure. Briant, *Dispraise of the Life of a Courtier*, 1548. The proverb is attributed originally to Alexander the Great.

folk. See there's NOWT so queer as folk

folks. See YOUNG folks think old folks to be fools, but old folks know young folks to be fools

follows. See TRADE follows the flag

folly. See where IGNORANCE is bliss, 'tis folly to be wise

fonder. See ABSENCE makes the heart grow fonder

fool. a fool and his money are soon parted (English) Those who are incapable of looking after their own money will soon be deprived of it by sharper minds. Thomas Tusser, *Five Hundred Pointes of Good Husbandrie*, 1573. The story goes that the proverb was first quoted by the historian George Buchanan, a tutor to James VI of Scotland, who easily won a wager with another courtier as to which of them could produce the coarsest passage of verse. Centuries later Carolyn Wells came up with a humorous variant on the old original: 'a fool and his money are soon married'.

She tossed her nose in distain, saying, she supposed her brother had taken him into favour ... : that a fool and his money were soon parted.
Tobias Smollett, Humphry Clinker, 1771

a fool at forty is a fool indeed (English) By the time a person reaches the age of forty, he should possess some knowledge of the way the world works; if he does not he must be irredeemably stupid. Edward Young, The Love of Fame, the Universal Passion, 1725. Another proverb claims 'every man is a fool or a physician at forty' (sometimes 'thirty'), meaning that by that age a man of any sense has a fairly clear idea of his own constitution. According to Plutarch, this last proverb was a favourite saying of the Emperor Tiberius. See also there's no FOOL like an old fool.

Be wise with speed; A fool at forty is a fool indeed.
Edward Young, The Love of Fame, the Universal Passion, 1725

a fool may give a wise man counsel (Greek) Even the wisest person may learn something they did not know from a fool (sometimes spoken in self-deprecation by a person offering another supposedly cleverer person advice). Ywain and Gawain, 1350. Another proverb reminds that 'a fool may sometimes speak to the purpose'.

A Fool may give a wise Man counsel by a time. An Apology of those who offer their Advice to them, who may be supposed to excel them in Parts and Sense.
James Kelly, A Complete Collection of Scotish Proverbs, 1721

a fool thinks himself wise (English) Foolish people have an inflated idea of themselves. Sir Thomas North, The Diall of Princes, 1557.

I do now remember a saying, 'the fool doth think he is wise, but the wise man knows himself to be a fool'.
William Shakespeare, As You Like It, c.1599

a fool will laugh when he is drowning (English) Fools may behave with inappropriate optimism when they are in fact in the deepest trouble. Misogonus, 1577.

a fool's bolt is soon shot (English) Those who act without taking the time to think first waste their efforts (just as a marksman who fires his crossbow too quickly is liable to miss his target). Proverbs of Alfred, c.1320. Another proverb, however, cautions that 'a fool's bolt may sometimes hit the mark'.

'Zounds, I have done,' said he. 'Your bolt is soon shot, according to the old proverb,' said she.
Tobias Smollett, Roderick Random, 1748

better be a fool than a knave (English) It is more defensible to be naturally stupid than it is to be deliberately wicked. T. Lodge, A Fig for Momus, 1595.

'Tis better be a foole then be a fox.
T. Lodge, A Fig for Momus, 1595

send a fool to market and a fool he'll return (English) A fool will never thrive in business, or any other dealings. G. Whitney, Emblems, 1586.

You may go back again, like a fool as you came.
Jonathan Swift, Polite Conversation, 1738

there's no fool like an old fool (English) Those who demonstrate foolishness even though they are of advanced years are doubly culpable. John Heywood, A Dialogue containing ... the Proverbs in the English Tongue, 1546.

And troth he might hae ta'en warning, but there's nae fule like an ould fule.
Walter Scott, Waverley, 1814

you may fool all of the people some of the time, some of the people all of the time, but not all of the people all of the time (US) No one is clever enough to succeed in deceiving everyone consistently without eventually being discovered. Abraham Lincoln, speech, Bloomington, Illinois, 29 May 1856. Another source alleges that Lincoln coined the slogan while in conference with a visitor at the White House. In either event, Lincoln's version echoed similar statements by, among others, Pliny the Younger, Benjamin Franklin, La Rochefoucauld and English essayist John Sterling.

One may be more clever than another, but not more clever than all the others.
La Rochefoucauld, *Maximes*, 1665

fool. *See also* it is better to be BORN a beggar than a fool; a man who is his own LAWYER has a fool for a client; MORE people know Tom Fool than Tom Fool knows; SIX hours' sleep for a man, seven for a woman, and eight for a fool

foolish. *See* PENNY wise, pound foolish

fools. fools and bairns should never see half-done work (Scottish) Fools and children should not be shown incomplete work, as they will be tempted to judge the finished article from what they are shown. Richard Burton, *The Anatomy of Melancholy*, 1621.

It is not fit to be shown to 'bairns and fools,' who, according to our old canny proverb, should never see half done work.
Walter Scott, quoted in Lockhart's *Life*, 1818

fools ask questions that wise men cannot answer (English) Sometimes the slow-witted ask so many questions, or ones of such insight, that even the most intelligent are unable to

answer. G. Torriano, *Italian Proverbs*, 1666. Also encountered in the form 'a fool may ask more questions in an hour than a wise man can answer in seven years'.

Bryce Snaelsfoot is a cautious man ... He knows a fool may ask more questions than a wise man cares to answer.
Walter Scott, *The Pirate*, 1821

fools build houses, and wise men live in them (English) Stupid people do all the work, while the more intelligent enjoy the results. John Ray, *A Collection of English Proverbs*, 1670. Equivalent sayings include 'fools make feasts and wise men eat them' and 'fools may invent fashions that wise men will wear'.

Fools Big [build] Houses and wise Men buy them. I knew a Gentleman buy 2000 l. worth of Land, build a House upon it, and sell both House and Land to pay the Expences of his building.
James Kelly, *A Complete Collection of Scotish Proverbs*, 1721

fools for luck (English) Stupid or mentally retarded people are often held to be the luckiest. Ben Jonson, *Bartholomew Fair*, 1631. The fullest version of the proverb runs 'a fool for luck, and a poor man for children'. Fools and the mad have always been considered lucky, and time was when communities took special care of such people in order to benefit from the luck they brought with them. Fishermen believed that meeting a madman in the street guaranteed a good catch that day, while others insisted that the saliva of a madman had special healing powers. *See also* FORTUNE favours fools.

fools rush in where angels fear to tread (English) Where the more intelligent hesitate to venture, some reckless souls rush in regardless of the risks. Alexander Pope, *Essay on Criticism*, 1711. In Pope's essay, from which the proverb arose, the poet was discussing those critics who express views more thoughtful readers would hesitate to share.

fools. See also CHILDREN and fools tell the truth; EXPERIENCE is the teacher of fools; FORTUNE favours fools; YOUNG folks think old folks to be fools, but old folks know young folks to be fools

foot. See it is not SPRING until you can plant your foot upon twelve daisies

football. See all FELLOWS at football

forbear. See BEAR and forbear

forbidden fruit tastes sweetest (English) There is more enjoyment, allegedly, to be had from something one is not entitled to than from those things one has a legitimate claim to. T. Adams, *The Devil's Banquet*, 1614. The popularity of the proverb was doubtless much reinforced by the tale of the forbidden fruit in the Garden of Eden and a passage in the Old Testament book of Proverbs further advises that 'stolen waters are sweet and bread eaten in secret is pleasant'. Variants include 'stolen fruit is sweet'. See also the GRASS is always greener on the other side of the fence.

Stolen sweets are sweeter;
Stolen kisses much completer;
Stolen looks are nice in chapels;
Stolen, stolen be your apples.
Thomas Randolph, *Song of Fairies*, c.1635

forelock. See TAKE time by the forelock

foretold. See LONG foretold long last, short notice soon past

forewarned is forearmed (Roman) Having foreknowledge of something puts a person at a big advantage. J.

Arderne, *Treatises of Fistula*, c.1425 (also quoted by Plautus).

I now knew the ground which I stood upon; and forewarned was being fore-armed.
Captain Frederick Marryat, *Peter Simple*, 1834

forget. See FORGIVE and forget

forgets. See a BELLOWING cow soon forgets her calf; an ELEPHANT never forgets

forgive. forgive and forget (English) Do not harbour resentment against those who have committed offences against you. *Ancrene Riwle*, c.1200 (also found in the writings of Philo De Josepho around AD 40). Another proverb advises 'revenge a wrong by forgiving it', but another consoles the naturally resentful thus: 'if we are bound to forgive an enemy, we are not bound to trust him'. See also let BYGONES be bygones.

All our great fraie ... Is forgiven and forgotten betwene us quight.
John Heywood, *A Dialogue containing ... the Proverbs in the English Tongue*, 1546

forgive. See also to ERR is human, to forgive divine

forgotten. See LONG absent, soon forgotten

fork. See though you CAST out nature with a fork, it will still return

forks. See FINGERS were made before forks and hands before knives

fortune. fortune favours fools (Roman) The simple-minded often seem to be protected by their own streak of luck. L. Wager, *The Longer thou Livest*, c.1560. See also FOOLS for luck.

'Tis a gross error, held in schools, that Fortune always favours fools.
John Gay, *Fables*, 1737

fortune favours the brave (Roman) The courageous and bold may often enjoy the best luck. Geoffrey Chaucer, *Troilus and Criseyde*, c.1385 (the phrase is also found in Terence and Virgil).

Who had been often told That fortune still assists the bold.
Jonathan Swift, *Strephon and Chloe*, 1731

fortune helps those who help themselves (English) Luck attends those who work at promoting their own interests. Randle Cotgrave, *A Dictionary of the French and English Tongues*, 1611.

when fortune smiles, embrace her (English) When luck turns your way, take full advantage of it. John Ray, *A Collection of English Proverbs*, 1670.

fortune. See also every MAN is the architect of his own fortune

forty. See a FOOL at forty is a fool indeed; LIFE begins at forty; SAINT Swithin's Day, if thou dost rain, for forty days it will remain

fouls. See it's an ILL bird that fouls its own nest

four. four eyes see more than two (Roman) Some things can be done better by two people than by one alone. A. Colynet, *True History of the Civil Wars in France*, 1591. See also TWO heads are better than one.

Matters of inferiour consequence he will communicate to a fast friend, and crave his advice; for two eyes see more than one.
Thomas Fuller, *Holy State*, 1642

four. See also there goes more to MARRIAGE than four bare legs in a bed

fox. the fox preys furthest from his hole (English) Anyone who engages in criminal or otherwise dubious business is best advised to pursue it away from his home territory, so as not to be easily identified as the perpetrator. T. Adams, *Sermons*, 1629. J. Clarke, in *Paroemiologia Anglo-Latina* in 1639, quoted it in the form 'a crafty fox never preyeth neare his den'. Another proverb to the same effect insists 'a wise fox will never rob his neighbour's henroost'.

the more the fox is cursed, the better he fares (English) The greater the volume of complaint against someone or something, the greater it must be assumed has been that person or thing's success. Spelman, *Dialogue*, c.1580.

foxholes. See there are no ATHEISTS in foxholes

free. there is no such thing as a free lunch (US) No favour or benefit comes free of some obligation in return. Mid-nineteenth century. The saying was formerly widely heard in saloon bars in reference to the snacks that were served free of charge to anyone who bought a drink. From the 1970s the phrase has been voiced frequently in discussion of economic affairs (particularly since economist Milton Friedman used it for the title of a book on the subject).

free. See also the BEST things in life are free; THOUGHT is free

Frenchmen. See one ENGLISHMAN can beat three Frenchmen

fresh. See don't throw out your DIRTY water until you get in fresh

Friday. as the Friday, so the Sunday (English) Whatever the weather is like on a Friday dictates what it will be like on the Sunday. *Notes & Queries*, 1853. An extension of the proverb indicates that whatever the weather is like on the Sunday dictates what the rest of the week will be like: 'as the Friday, so the Sunday, As the Sunday, so the week'. Another version runs 'if on Friday it rain, 'twill on Sunday again; if Friday be clear, have for Sunday no fear'.

Friday night's dream on the Saturday told, is sure to come true be it never so old (English) Anyone who shares a Friday night's dream the following day is sure to see it come to pass. Thomas Overbury, *Characters*, 1626.

A Frydayes dreame is all her superstition: that shee conceales for feare of anger.
Sir Thomas Overbury, *Characters*, 1626

Friday's hair and Sunday's horn go to the Devil on Monday morn (English) It is unlucky to cut the hair on a Friday (the day of the Crucifixion) or to trim the fingernails on a Sunday (also a sacred day to Christians). Thomas Middleton, *Any Thing for a Quiet Life*, 1621.

friend. a friend in court is better than a penny in purse (English) Personal contacts within the law will prove more beneficial than mere wealth. *Romance of the Rose*, c.1400.

I shouldn't wonder – friends at court you know ...
Charles Dickens, *Dombey and Son*, 1848

a friend in need is a friend indeed (Roman) A friend who remains constant in time of trouble may be considered true. *Durham Proverbs*, c.1035 (variants may be found in Ennius and in *Epidicus*, written by Plautus in 200 BC). Alternative versions include 'a good friend is never known till a man have need'. A French equivalent runs 'prosperity gives friends, adversity proves them'. A Swedish proverb states 'one should go invited to a friend in good fortune, and uninvited in misfortune'. Lord Samuel rather cynically advised 'a friend in need is a friend to be avoided', while another proverb insists 'if you have one true friend, you have more than your share'. *See also* never CATCH at a falling knife or friend.

A freende is never knowen tyll a man have neede. Before I had neede, my most present foes Semed my most freends, but thus the world goes.
John Heywood, *A Dialogue containing ... the Proverbs in the English Tongue*, 1546

a friend to all is a friend to none (Greek) A person who makes friends with all and sundry will find no one values his or her friendship. Wodroephe, *Spared Houres*, 1623 (also quoted by Diogenes Laertius and attributed ultimately to Aristotle). The notion that it is best to restrict the number of your friends is supported by another proverb, which runs 'have but few friends though much acquaintance'. An extreme viewpoint is represented by the saying 'if you have one true friend, you have more than your share'.

friend. *See also* never CATCH at a falling knife or friend; a MAN's best friend is his dog

friends. *See* the BEST of friends must part; the CAT and dog may kiss, yet are none the better friends; GOD defend me from my friends; from my enemies I can defend myself; SHORT reckonings make long friends

from. *See* from CLOGS to clogs is only three generations; from the SUBLIME to the ridiculous is but a step

frost. *See* so many MISTS in March, so many frosts in May

fruit. when all fruit falls, welcome haws (English) When nothing better is available, what is less than perfect will be warmly welcomed. James Kelly, *A Complete Collection of Scotish Proverbs*, 1721. Often quoted in relation to what may be judged less than ideal partners in love.

When all Fruit's fa's welcome ha's … Spoken when we take up with what's coarse, when the good is spent.
James Kelly, *A Complete Collection of Scotish Proverbs*, 1721

fruit. *See also* he that would EAT the fruit must climb the tree; FORBIDDEN fruit tastes sweetest; SEPTEMBER blow soft, till the fruit's in the loft; the TREE is known by its fruit

frying-pan. out of the frying-pan into the fire (Greek) Escaping one danger only to be exposed to an even worse one. Alexander Barclay, *Eclogues*, 1514 (also found in the writings of Plato and Lucian). The original Greek saying was 'out of the smoke into the flame', while the French render it as '*tomber de la poêle dans la braise*'. The fuller, little heard, version of the proverb runs 'like the flounder, out of the frying-pan into the fire'.

But I was sav'd, as is the flounder, when He leapeth from the dish into the fire.
Sir John Harington, *Orlando Furioso*, 1591

full. full bellies make empty skulls (English) Those who are well fed are less inclined to enterprising thought. Thomas Fuller, *Gnomologia*, 1732. Further proverbs insist 'full bowls make empty brains' and 'a full belly neither fights nor flies well'. On rather different lines, another proverb runs 'he's so full of himself that he is quite empty'.

full cup, steady hand (English) Those who have much to lose should tread carefully, lest they lose what they have.

Durham Proverbs, c.1025. Variants include 'a full cup must be carried steadily'.

When the Cup's full carry it even. When you have arrived at Power and Wealth, take a care of Insolence, Pride, and Oppression.
James Kelly, *A Complete Collection of Scotish Proverbs*, 1721

full. *See also* it's ILL speaking between a full man and a fasting

funeral. one funeral makes many (English) The death of one person is likely to be followed by the deaths of others (specifically, among the mourners who brave the elements at the funeral). R. D. Blackmore, *Perlycross*, 1894. Superstition insists, incidentally, that deaths (like accidents) tend to happen in threes. In parts of eastern England, the death of a woman was considered particularly ominous, a notion expressed in the saying 'if churchyard opens for a she, it will open for three'. Variants include 'one funeral makes another'.

funeral. *See also* DREAM of a funeral and you hear of a marriage

fury. *See* HELL hath no fury like a woman scorned

furze. when the furze is in bloom, my love's in tune (English) When the gorse is in flower, it is the season for love (gorse, or furze, flowers virtually throughout the year). Benjamin Franklin, *Poor Robin's Almanack*, 1752. Another related proverb runs 'under the furze is hunger and cold; under the broom is silver and gold'. *See also* when the GORSE is out of bloom, kissing's out of fashion.

Dog-days are in he'll say's the reason Why kissing now is out of season: but Joan says furze in bloom still, and she'll be kiss'd if she's her will.
Benjamin Franklin, *Poor Robin's Almanack*, 1752.

g

gain. *See* one man's LOSS is another man's gain; there's no great LOSS without some gain; what you lose on the SWINGS you gain on the roundabouts

gained. *See* NOTHING ventured, nothing gained

gains. no gains without pains (English) Hard work and self-sacrifice are usually necessary to secure some benefit. J. Grange, *Golden Aphroditis*, 1577. The saying has become a slogan of health and fitness experts, usually in the form 'no pain, no gain'. Related proverbs include 'pain if forgotten where gain follows' and 'great pain and little gain make a man soon weary'.

Who will the fruyte that harvest yeeldes, must take the payne.
J. Grange, *Golden Aphroditis*, 1577

game. *See* LOOKERS-ON see most of the game

gamekeeper. *See* an old POACHER makes the best gamekeeper

gander. *See* what's SAUCE for the goose is sauce for the gander

garbage in, garbage out (US) What you get out of something depends upon what you put into it (usually quoted in reference to computers). *CIS Glossary of Automated Typesetting and Related Computer Terms*, 1964. Sometimes encountered in the abbreviated form 'GIGO'.

gardener. as is the gardener, so is the garden (English) The quality of a gardener (or any other worker) may be judged by the results of his or her work. Thomas Fuller, *Gnomologia*, 1732.

garlic makes a man wink, drink and stink (English) The consumption of garlic promotes a tendency to lust, heavy drinking and foul breath. Thomas Nashe, *The Unfortunate Traveller*, 1594.

garment. *See* SILENCE is a woman's best garment

gather ye rosebuds while ye may (English) Make the most of things while they are available to you. Robert Herrick, 'To the Virgins, to Make Much of Time', *Hesperides*, 1648. *See also* make HAY while the sun shines.

Gather ye rosebuds while ye may,
Old time is still a-flying:
And this same flower which smiles today
Tomorrow will be dying.
Robert Herrick, 'To the Virgins, to Make Much of Time', *Hesperides*, 1648

gathered. *See* where the CARCASE is, there shall the eagles be gathered together

gathers. *See* a ROLLING stone gathers no moss

geese. *See* on SAINT Thomas the Divine kill all turkeys, geese and swine

general. he is the best general who makes the fewest mistakes (*English*) The most successful leaders are those who make the fewest errors of judgement. Sir I. Hamilton, *Staff Officer's Scrap-Book*, 1907.

generations. *See* from CLOGS to clogs is only three generations; from SHIRTSLEEVES to shirtsleeves in three generations; it takes THREE generations to make a gentleman

generous. *See* be JUST before you're generous

genius is an infinite capacity for taking pains (*English*) Genius is not a natural gift, but the result of diligent hard work. Thomas Carlyle, *Frederick the Great*, 1858.

'Genius' ... means transcendent capacity of taking trouble, first of all.
Thomas Carlyle, *Frederick the Great*, 1858

gentleman. *See* when ADAM delved and Eve span, who was then the gentleman?; it takes THREE generations to make a gentleman

gently. if you gently touch a nettle it'll sting you for your pains (*English*) In certain circumstances bold action is the only alternative, as anything less will result in harm being suffered. John Lyly, *Euphues: The Anatomy of Wit*, 1578. The fullest version of the proverb runs 'if you gently touch a nettle it'll sting you for your pains; grasp it like a lad of mettle, and it soft as silk remains'. Another proverb relating to nettles advises 'nettles don't sting in the month of May'.

Hee which toucheth the nettle tenderly, is soonest stoung.
John Lyly, *Euphues: The Anatomy of Wit*, 1578

gently. *See also* DRIVE gently over the stones

get. get a name to rise early, and you may lie all day (*English*) Those who enjoy a good reputation may trade on it to enjoy easy benefits. Swetnam, *School of Defence*, 1617.

I would not have a man depend too much upon this proverb; for a good name is soon lost, and hardly to be retrieved.
James Kelly, *A Complete Collection of Scotish Proverbs*, 1721

get. *See also* the MORE you get, the more you want

gift. *See* never LOOK a gift horse in the mouth

gifts. *See* BEWARE of Greeks bearing gifts

gill. *See* every HERRING must hang by its own gill

girls will be girls *See* BOYS will be boys

gist. the gist of a lady's letter is in the postscript (*English*) Female correspondents communicate the most important things in their letters in the postscript, almost as an afterthought. Maria Edgeworth, *Belinda*, 1801.

Watching ... the last communication of the sun, and his postscript (which, like a lady's, is the gist of what he means).
R. D. Blackmore, *Springhaven*, 1887

give. better give a penny than lend twenty (*Italian*) It is preferable to make a gift of a single penny, knowing that it will never be repaid, than to lend a larger amount, as the latter may never be repaid.

give a dog a bad name and hang him (*English*) A person may be damned by a poor reputation, whether or not it is deserved. J.

Stevens, *Spanish and English Dictionary*, 1706. *See also* he that has an ILL name is half hanged.

The Liberal impulse is almost always to give a dog a bad name and hang him: that is, to denounce the menaced proprietors as enemies of mankind, and ruin them in a transport of virtuous indignation.
George Bernard Shaw, *The Intelligent Woman's Guide to Socialism*, 1928

give a man an annuity and he'll live for ever (English) Agree to pay a man an income until he dies, and he will live much longer than originally envisaged. Lord Byron, *Don Juan*, 1824.

'Tis said that persons living on annuities
Are longer lived than others ... Some ... do never die.
Lord Byron, *Don Juan*, 1824

give a man enough rope and he will hang himself (English) Allow people with a wild or criminal character enough opportunity (or freedom) and they will infallibly bring about their own downfall. Thomas Fuller, *Holy War*, 1639 (attributed by some to the French satirical writer Rabelais, in *Pantagruel*, 1532). Variants include 'give a thief enough rope and he'll hang himself', which was first recorded in 1678.

Give you women but rope enough, you'll do your own business.
Samuel Richardson, *Sir Charles Grandison*, 1754

give and take is fair play (English) In dealings with others a person cannot complain if he or she loses some things while gaining others. Fanny Burney, *Evelina*, 1778.

Give and take is fair play. All I say is, let it be a fair stand-up fight.
Frederick Marryat, *Newton Forster*, 1832

give credit where credit is due (Hebrew) Those who deserve recognition for their efforts should be honoured accordingly. Bible, Romans 13:7. Formerly found with 'honour' in the place of 'credit'.

Render therfore to al men their dew: ... to whom honour, honour.
Bible, Romans 13:7

give me a child for the first seven years, and you may do what you like with him afterwards (Spanish/French) What a child learns before the age of seven determines his or her future character, regardless of what is subsequently learnt. V. S. Lean, *Collecteana*, 1902–04. Lean associated it particularly with the Jesuits, who were founded by Saint Ignatius Loyola in 1534. Centuries later the Russian revolutionary leader Lenin coined his own version of it: 'give us a child for eight years and it will be a Bolshevik for ever'. Also found in the form 'give me a child for the first seven years, and he is mine for life'. *See also* the CHILD is the father of the man.

give neither counsel nor salt till you are asked for it (English) It is unlucky to offer advice or salt to anyone else unless it is specifically requested. H. G. Bohn, *A Handbook of Proverbs*, 1855. Superstition insists that it is very unwise to allow salt to be taken out of the house, either as a gift or as a loan, because the luck of the household goes with it. This is especially true if the loan takes place at New Year. If salt is actually borrowed, it is unwise for the borrower to repay the loan, as this is also unlucky. As regards the giving of counsel (sometimes rendered as 'advice'), other proverbs counter with the view 'good counsel never comes amiss' and 'good counsel never comes too late'.

give the Devil his due (English) Even the most wicked people usually have a few redeeming features, which must (albeit reluctantly) be acknowledged. John Lyly, *Pappe with Hatchet*, 1589.

The Cavaliers (to give the Divell his due) fought very valiantly.
Prince Rupert's Declaration, 1642

it is better to give than to receive (Hebrew) Those who give are more blessed in the eyes of Heaven than those who receive. Bible, Acts 20:35. Another, concise, proverb backs up the sentiment with 'give and be blessed'.

never give a sucker an even break (US) Never be tempted to offer a fair chance to anyone, however gullible or stupid they are. *Collier's*, 28 November 1925. This piece of advice has been attributed to, among others, US film and stage comedian W. C. Fields, who is thought to have included it as an ad lib in the musical *Poppy* in 1923, and to playwright Edward Albee.

to give a thing, and take a thing, is to wear the Devil's gold ring (Greek) It is ignoble to give something and then to ask for it back again. J. Bridges, *Sermon at Paul's Cross*, 1571 (also found in essence in the writings of Plato). Often heard as a schoolchildren's playground rhyme.

Give a Thing, and take a Thing, Is the ill Man's Goud Ring. A Cant among Children, when they demand a Thing again, which they had bestowed.
James Kelly, *A Complete Collection of Scotish Proverbs*, 1721

gives. he gives twice who gives quickly (Roman) Those who honour their obligations promptly will be doubly appreciated by their creditors. Geoffrey Chaucer, *The Legend of Good Women*, c.1385 (also recorded in the writings of Publilius Syrus).

I did really ask the favour twice; but you have been even with me by granting it so speedily. *Bis dat qui cito dat.*
James Boswell, *Life of Johnson*, 1791

gladness. a man of gladness seldom falls into madness (English) People who adopt a generally optimistic attitude to life are unlikely to be driven mad by their experiences. J. Howell, *Paroemiographia*, 1659.

glass. people who live in glass houses shouldn't throw stones (English) Those who are themselves in a vulnerable position, open to criticism, should refrain from finding fault with others. Geoffrey Chaucer, *Troilus and Criseyde*, c.1385. One tradition attributed the saying in its modern form to James I, who allegedly quoted it to his favourite, the Duke of Buckingham, who had encouraged mobs to break the windows of his opponents and then complained when his own windows were broken in retaliation. *See also* the POT calls the kettle black.

People who live in glass houses have no right to throw stones.
George Bernard Shaw, *Widowers' Houses*, 1892

glasses and lasses are brittle ware (English) Young girls, like glass, are fragile and easily endangered. G. Torriano, *Italian Proverbs*, 1666.

After all his strife he wan but a Strumpet, that for all his travails he reduced (I cannot say reclaymed) but a straggeler: which was as much in my judgement, as to strive for a broken glasse which is good for nothing.
John Lyly, *Euphues: The Anatomy of Wit*, 1578

glitters. all that glitters is not gold (Roman) Not everything that appears valuable or desirable is in fact worth anything. *Hali Meidenhad*, c.1220. The

gloves

original Latin version was 'non omne quod nitet aurum est' ('not all that shines is gold'). For a long time 'glisters' was the common form, but this was generally replaced by 'glitters' after David Garrick introduced it in the Prologue to Oliver Goldsmith's play *She Stoops to Conquer* in 1773. Equivalents in other European languages include the Italian 'every glow-worm is not a fire'. *See also* APPEARANCES are deceptive.

All that glisters is not gold,
Often have you heard that told.
William Shakespeare, *The Merchant of Venice*, c.1596

gloves. *See* a CAT in gloves catches no mice

gluttony. gluttony kills more than the sword (English) Over-indulgence in the good things in life is responsible for more deaths than the more obvious threats of violence etc. Alexander Barclay, *The Ship of Fools*, 1509. According to another proverb, gluttony is a particular danger to the English: 'gluttony is the sin of England'.

More perish by a surfet then the sword.
John Lyly, *Euphues and His England*, 1580

gluttony. *See also* a BELLY full of gluttony will never study willingly

go. *See* go ABROAD and you'll hear news of home; go to BATTERSEA to get your simples cut; go to BED with the lamb, and rise with the lark; EASY come, easy go; LIGHT come, light go; QUICKLY come, quickly go; he that would go to SEA for pleasure, would go to hell for a pastime; don't go near the WATER until you learn how to swim; the WEAKEST go to the wall; many go out for WOOL and come home shorn

goat. *See* if the BEARD were all, the goat might preach

God. do not blame God for having created the tiger, but thank him for not having given it wings (Indian) Rather than complain about something, it is better to console oneself with the thought that it might have been much worse.

God comes at last when we think he is furthest off (English) Just when it seems God will not intervene in human affairs, His influence is felt. J. Howell, *Paroemiographia*, 1659. Related proverbs include 'God comes with leaden feet but strikes with iron hands'.

God defend me from my friends; from my enemies I can defend myself (English/French) It is easier to protect yourself from your enemies than from your friends, from which quarter it is harder to anticipate an attack. Anthony Rivers, *Dictes or Sayings of the Philosophers*, 1477. In keeping with the theme of traitorous friends, the saying was adopted in 1956 by Gavin Maxwell for the title of his book about Sicilian bandit Salvatore Giuliano. Sometimes encountered in the shortened form 'save us from our friends'.

God gives almonds to those who have no teeth *See* the GODS send nuts to those who have no teeth

God heals and the physician hath the thanks (English) When an illness is successfully treated it is the doctor who gets the patient's gratitude, rather than God, who has ordained his or her recovery. George Herbert, *Jacula Prudentum*, 1640. An Italian equivalent runs 'if the patient dies, the doctor has killed him, but if he gets well, the saints have saved him'.

God heals and the doctor takes the fee.

Benjamin Franklin, *Poor Richard's Almanack*, 1736

God help the poor, for the rich can help themselves (*English*) The poor must rely upon divine aid, as they are unable to defend themselves as the wealthy can. Thomas Dekker, *Work for Armourers*, 1609. Related proverbs include 'God help the rich, the poor can beg'.

God helps those who help themselves (*Greek*) Providence is on the side of the person who works hard in pursuit of his own interests. R. Taverner, *Proverbs or Adages of Erasmus*, 1546 (also found in the writings of Aeschylus, Euripides and Aesop). In Aesop's fable, a cart-driver calls on the help of the god Hercules when his cart gets stuck in the mud, only to be berated by Hercules for not first attempting to free it himself. A French version, found in La Fontaine's *Fables*, runs '*aide-toi, le ciel t'aidera*' ('help yourself, heaven will help you'). This slogan was adopted by a French radical political society in 1824. Another French equivalent includes 'God never builds us bridges, but he gives us hands', while the Spanish have 'while waiting for water from heaven, don't stop irrigating'. The Chinese have 'the gods cannot help those who do not seize opportunities'. A waggish rejoinder of unknown origins runs 'God helps those who helps themselves, but God help those who are caught helping themselves'. *See also* FORTUNE helps those who help themselves.

God likes to assist the man who toils.
Aeschylus, *Fragments*, fifth century BC

God is always on the side of the big battalions (*French*) Good fortune inevitably seems to favour the stronger side in any contest. A. Graydon, *Memoirs*, 1822 (earlier recorded in a letter by Madame de Sévigné, 22 December 1673). Also found in the forms 'Providence is always on the side of the big battalions' and 'God sides with the strongest'. The saying is particularly associated with Napoleon, although it goes back much further and may be found, as 'the gods are on the side of the strongest', in Tacitus. Others to quote it have included the Comte de Bussy and Voltaire.

Someone has observed that Providence is always on the side of the big dividends.
Saki, *Reginald*, 1904

God made man, man made money (*English*) God created mankind, but mankind itself invented most of the ills that beset it. The proverb is attributed to John Oldland, who coined it in the early eighteenth century in response to a lawyer with whom he was involved in a legal suit for debt.

God mead man,
And man mead money,
God mead bees,
And bees mead honey,
But the Devil mead lawyers an' 'tornies,
And pleac'd 'em at U'ston and Doten i' Forness.
John Oldland, quoted in the *Lonsdale Magazine*, 1820

God made the country, and man made the town (*Roman*) God is the source of nature and goodness in the world, but the towns and their accompanying evils were invented by man. Abraham Cowley, quoted in J. Wells, *Poems*, 1667 (also found in Varro's *De Re Rustica*, *c.*35 BC). The saying became better known in its modern form after it was quoted by Cowper in *The Task*, 1785. Variants include 'God the first garden made, and the first city Cain'.

There is a saying that if God made the country, and man the town, the Devil made the little country town.
H. Tennyson, *Memoir*, 25 January 1870

God makes the back to the burden (English) Heaven suits the person for the task in hand, so that they will be able to perform what is asked of them. William Cobbett, *Weekly Register*, 12 January 1822.

Heaven suits the back to the burden.
Charles Dickens, *Nicholas Nickleby*, 1839

God never sends mouths but He sends meat (English) Heaven will always answer the needs of the righteous and deserving and will ensure that no child is born without also providing the means for its sustenance. William Langland, *Piers Plowman*, 1377.

For lente nevere was lyf but lyflode were shapen.
William Langland, *Piers Plowman*, 1377

God sends meat, but the Devil sends cooks (English) Good can easily be perverted by evil (just as a bad cook can readily ruin good ingredients). A. Borde, *Dietary of Health*, 1542. Related proverbs include 'God sends corn and the Devil mars the sack'.

This Goose is quite raw: Well, God sends Meat, but the Devil sends Cooks.
Jonathan Swift, *Polite Conversation*, 1738

God tempers the wind to the shorn lamb (French) Heaven protects the weak and the defenceless. Laurence Sterne, *A Sentimental Journey through France and Italy: Maria*, 1768. The proverb as used by Sterne was a reworking of the older French saying, 'Dieu mesure le froid à la brebis tondue' ('God measures the cold to the shorn sheep', recorded in 1594). In the earlier versions, before Sterne, it was always a

'sheep' rather than a 'lamb' that was shorn (lambs, in fact, are never shorn).

Although we cannot turn away the wind, we can soften it; we can temper it, if I may say so, to the shorn lambs.
Charles Dickens, *The Old Curiosity Shop*, 1841

God's in his heaven; all's right with the world (English) Everything is fine. J. Palsgrave, *L'Éclaircissement de la langue française*, 1530. An older version of the proverb, intended to console others in times of trouble, ran 'God is where he was'.

The snail's on the thorn: God's in his heaven – All's right with the world.
Robert Browning, *Works*, 1841

where God builds a church, the Devil will build a chapel (English) Wickedness will often be found flourishing in close proximity to what is good. T. Becon, *Works*, 1560.

Wherever God erects a House of Prayer,
The Devil always builds a Chapel there:
And 'twill be found upon Examination,
The latter has the largest congregation.
Daniel Defoe, *The True-born Englishman*, 1701

you cannot serve God and Mammon (Hebrew) It is impossible to stay true to high moral principles and at the same time to pursue financial reward. Bible, Matthew 6:24. In the original biblical passage, concerning the Sermon on the Mount, the word 'mammon' is an approximation of the Aramaic word meaning wealth or gain. Later generations personalized Mammon as a demon associated with avarice and the acquisition of money. *See also* NO man can serve two masters.

Lady Lufton ... would say of Miss Dunstable that it was impossible to serve both God and Mammon.
Anthony Trollope, *Framley Parsonage*, 1860

God. See also MAN proposes, but God disposes; MAN's extremity is God's opportunity; the MILLS of God grind slowly, yet they grind exceeding small; the NEARER the church, the further from God; the ROBIN and the hen are God's cock and hen; all THINGS are possible with God; put your TRUST in God and keep your powder dry; the VOICE of the people is the voice of God; a WHISTLING woman and a crowing hen are neither fit for God nor men

godliness. See CLEANLINESS is next to godliness

gods. the gods send nuts to those who have no teeth (French/Spanish/English) All too often, favours and benefits seem to be bestowed upon those who are too old or are otherwise debarred from enjoying them. *American Speech*, 1929. In the French version it is 'bread' rather than 'nuts', while the Spanish complain 'God gives almonds to those who have no teeth'.

whom the gods love die young (Greek) The good and the godly are selected by Heaven to die first. W. Hughe, *Troubled Man's Medicine*, 1546 (also quoted by Plautus). The proverb is supposed to have had its origins in a story told by the Greek historian Herodotus in his *History*, c.445 BC. In this tale, the dutiful Cleobis and Biton help a woman to pull her cart to the temple to celebrate the festival of Here. In her gratitude, the woman begs Here to bestow upon the two lads the greatest blessing in her power – and the two boys die in their sleep. It was left to the poet Menander to coin the proverb itself when he retold the same story over a century later. The proverb has often been inscribed on

the gravestones of those who have died young. Philosophers have pondered the accuracy of the saying and have justified it by explaining that it is the 'young at heart' (whatever their age) who find favour with Heaven. Variant forms include 'God takes soonest those whom he loves best'. See also only the GOOD die young.

I was meant to die young and the gods do not love me.
Robert Louis Stevenson, letter, 1894

whom the gods would destroy, they first make mad (Greek) When Heaven marks someone down for death, it first deprives him of his reason. Ben Jonson, *Catiline*, 1611. Euripides and Publius Syrus also recorded versions of the proverb, the latter as 'he whom Fortune would ruin she robs of his wits'. A modern reworking, introduced by Cyril Connolly in *The Unquiet Grave* (1944), runs 'whom the gods would destroy, they first call promising'.

When God will punish, hee will first take away the understanding.
George Herbert, *Outlandish Proverbs*, 1640

gods. See also TAKE the goods the gods provide

goes. See he that goes A-BORROWING, goes a-sorrowing; there goes more to MARRIAGE than four bare legs in a bed; PRIDE goes before a fall; what goes UP must come down

going. when the going gets tough, the tough get going (US) When the chips are down, people of truly strong character are spurred into action. This slogan is popularly attributed to Joseph P. Kennedy, father of US President J. F. Kennedy. In the 1980s the inspirational intent of the late President's father was lampooned in a slogan for T-shirts, 'when the going gets tough, the tough go shopping'.

gold. gold may be bought too dear (English) Even something very desirable is not worth having at too high a price. John Heywood, *A Dialogue containing … the Proverbs in the English Tongue*, 1546.

The fact is, in my opinion, that we often buy money very much too dear.
William Thackeray, *Barry Lyndon*, 1844

gold. *See also* it is good to make a BRIDGE of gold to a flying enemy; to GIVE a thing, and take a thing, is to wear the Devil's gold ring; all that GLITTERS is not gold; the streets of LONDON are paved with gold

golden. a golden key can open any door (English) Money will gain a person access to any place. John Lyly, *Euphues and His England*, 1580. Another proverb warns that there is in fact one door that will not open to a golden key, however: 'God goes in at any gate except heaven's'.

Who is so ignorant that knoweth not, gold be a key for every locke, chieflye with his Ladye.
John Lyly, *Euphues and His England*, 1580

golden. *See also* SILENCE is golden; SPEECH is silver, silence is golden

good. a good beginning makes a good ending (Roman) Care taken at the start of a task is likely to be rewarded by things turning out well at the end. *Proverbs of Hending*, c.1300 (also quoted by Quintilian). *See also* WELL begun is half done.

But in proverbe I have herd seye That who that wel his werk begynneth The rather a good ende he wynneth.
John Gower, *Confessio Amantis*, c.1390

a good conscience is a continual feast (English) A clear conscience will prove a lasting source of consolation. Francis Bacon, *The Advancement of Learning*, 1605.

A good conscience is a continual Christmas.
Benjamin Franklin, *Works*, c.1736

a good dog deserves a good bone (English) Good conduct deserves a reward. Randle Cotgrave, *A Dictionary of the French and English Tongues*, 1611.

A good dog deserves, sir, a good bone.
Ben Jonson, *A Tale of a Tub*, 1633

a good example is the best sermon (English) Setting a good example by one's own conduct is more effective than simply telling others how to behave. Thomas Fuller, *Gnomologia*, 1732. *See also* PRACTISE what you preach.

a good face is a letter of recommendation (Roman) An honest face says as much about a person's character as any praise from a third party. T. Shelton, translation of *Don Quixote*, 1620 (also found in the writings of Publius Syrus). On much the same lines is 'a good face needs no paint' ('paint' being make-up).

There was a passport in his very looks.
Laurence Sterne, *A Sentimental Journey*, 1768

a good horse cannot be of a bad colour (English/Scottish) The quality of a horse (or anything else) may be judged by its colour. J. Carmichaell, *Proverbs in Scots*, 1628. Superstition harbours particular doubts about horses that are white in colour, though piebald horses are lucky and a wish may be made on meeting one. Another proverb has it that 'a dapple-grey horse will sooner die than tire'. *See also* APPEARANCES are deceptive.

It is observed by some, that there is no good horse of a bad colour.
Izaak Walton, *The Compleat Angler*, 1653

a good Jack makes a good Jill (English) A good example will inspire others (usually, a good husband will have a beneficial influence upon his wife). W. Painter, *Palace of Pleasure*, 1623. Also encountered as 'a good husband makes a good wife', and, to counter the original, 'a good Jill may mend the bad Jack' and 'a bad Jack may have as bad a Jill'. *See also* every JACK has his Jill.

A good Jack makes a good Gill ... Inferiours imitate the manners of superiours ... wives of their husbands.
John Ray, *A Collection of English Proverbs*, 1670

a good name is better than a good girdle (English) It is better to have a good reputation than wealth alone (an allusion to the belt or girdle from which people once suspended their purses). Equivalent proverbs include 'good fame is better than a good face', 'a good name is better than riches' and 'a good name is worth gold'. Another proverb adds 'a good name keeps its lustre in the dark'.

a good tree brings forth good fruit (English) Good breeds good. Berners, *Huon*, c.1534.

all good things must come to an end (English) No pleasure lasts for ever. Originally the proverb, recorded as early as the mid-fifteenth century, omitted the word 'good'.

All things have an end, and a pudden [type of sausage] has two.
Jonathan Swift, *Polite Conversation*, 1738

better a good cow than a cow of a good kind (English/Scottish) A proven good personal reputation is better than a good family background. John Buchan, *Huntingtower*, 1922.

good ale is meat, drink and cloth (English) A good supply of beer will compensate the drinker for any deficiencies in clothing or food. Carew, *Survey of Cornwall*, 1602.

Sheer ale supports him under everything. It is meat, drink, and cloth, bed, board, and washing.
Walter Scott, *Guy Mannering*, 1815

good and quickly seldom meet (English) It is rare for a thing to be done both quickly and well. George Herbert, *Jacula Prudentum*, 1640.

good broth may be made in an old pot (English) It is not necessary to have new or perfect utensils to produce a good result. G. Torriano, *Italian Proverbs*, 1666.

good cheap is dear (English) Something that appears to be a bargain because it is sold cheap may prove expensive in that you would never have bought it in the first place if it had not appeared to be such a good buy. George Herbert, *Jacula Prudentum*, 1640.

good clothes open all doors (English) Those who wear decent clothes will find others more ready to offer them opportunities. Thomas Fuller, *Gnomologia*, 1732.

good fences make good neighbours (English) Clear and strong boundaries help maintain cordial relations between states, neighbours, friends etc. (in the most practical sense by preventing animals straying from one property to another and doing damage). E. Rogers, letter, 1640. *See also* a good LAWYER makes a bad neighbour.

My apple trees will never get across
And eat the cones under his pines, I tell him.
He only says, 'Good fences make good neighbours'.

Robert Frost, 'North of Boston', 1914

good luck never comes too late
(English) Good fortune is always welcome, however late is comes. Michael Drayton, *Mooncalf*, c.1610.

good men are scarce (English) Men of real worth and character are only rarely encountered. D. Tuvill, *Essays Moral and Theological*, 1609. Also encountered in the form 'a good man is hard to find'. US film star Mae West is said to have contributed her own typically suggestive version of this latter variant, 'a hard man is good to find'.

Maids, make much of one; good men are scarce.
Thomas Fuller, *Gnomologia*, 1732

good riding at two anchors (Greek) There is safety in having two skills, jobs or other sources of security. John Heywood, *A Dialogue containing ... the Proverbs in the English Tongue*, 1546 (also quoted by Pindar).

Have more strings to thy bow then one, it is safe riding at two ankers.
John Lyly, *Euphues: The Anatomy of Wit*, 1578

good wine engendreth good blood
(English) The drinking of wine promotes healthy blood and emotional strength. G. B. Gelli, *Fearful Fancies of the Florentine Cooper*, 1568.

This same young sober-blooded boy doth not love me; ... but that's no marvel, he drinks no wine.
William Shakespeare, *Henry IV, Part 2*, c.1598

good wine needs no bush (English) If something is of high enough quality, it needs no recommendation but may stand by its own merits. John Lydgate, *Pilgrimage of Man*, 1430. Bacchus, the Roman god of wine, was often depicted with garlands of vine and ivy leaves and ever since Roman times taverns and vintners' shops have been distinguished by bushy displays (or pictures) of vines and ivy. The significance of ivy in vintners' signs was that ivy was reputed to counter the effects of over-indulgence in alcohol (thus implying that the wine being offered was good). Equivalent sentiments may be found in a number of European languages, including French, German and Italian.

If it be true that good wine needs no bush, 'tis true that a good play needs no epilogue.
William Shakespeare, *As You Like It*, c.1599

he is a good dog who goes to church (English) A person might make the effort to appear good and to behave as expected, even if he is not really as worthy as he might seem (just as a dog attending church yet remains a dog). Walter Scott, *Woodstock*, 1826.

Bevis ... fell under the proverb which avers, 'He is a good dog which goes to church'; for ... he behaved himself ... decorously.
Walter Scott, *Woodstock*, 1826

he is a good physician who cures himself (English) Doctors are quick to offer cures to others, but should be judged by how they treat themselves. John Lydgate, *Daunce of Machabree*, c.1430.

if you can't be good, be careful
(US/English) If you cannot resist misbehaving, make sure you don't land yourself in trouble (typically, of a sexual nature). A. M. Binstead, *Pitcher in Paradise*, 1903. The saying was popularized in the USA as early as 1907 through the song 'Be Good! If You Can't Be Good, be Careful!' Wags have added their own versions, including 'if you can't be careful, have fun', 'if

you can't be careful, name it after me' and 'if you can't be careful, buy a pram'.

it is a good horse that never stumbles (English) Even the best horses (and, by extension, people) make mistakes sometimes. J. Palsgrave, *L'Éclaircissement de la langue française*, 1530. One fuller variant of the proverb runs 'it is a good horse that never stumbles, and a good wife that never grumbles'. *See also* even HOMER sometimes nods.

He's a good horse that never stumbled, and a better wife that never grumbled. Both so rare, that I never met with either.
James Kelly, *A Complete Collection of Scotish Proverbs*, 1721

many a good cow hath an evil calf (English) Good character in parents is no guarantee of good character in their offspring. John Heywood, *A Dialogue containing … the Proverbs in the English Tongue*, 1546. *See also* like FATHER, like son.

no good building without a good foundation (English) No project will prosper if the initial work on which it is based is not sound. R. Percyvall, *A Spanish Grammar*, 1599.

on a good bargain, think twice (English) If something is offered at what appears to be a very reasonable price, caution should be exercised as it may have some hidden flaw. George Herbert, *Jacula Prudentum*, 1640.

one good turn deserves another (English) Favours should always be repaid. *Bulletin of John Rylands Library*, c.1400. Parallel, now archaic, sayings with the same meaning included 'giffe gaffe is one good turn for another'. *See also* KA me, ka thee; you SCRATCH my back and I'll scratch yours.

If you'll be so kind to ka me one good

turn, I'll be so courteous to kob you anot her.
Dekker and Ford, *The Witch of Edmonton*, c.1623

only the good die young (Greek) The virtuous and the innocent always seem to die before their time. Daniel Defoe, *Character of Dr S. Annesley*, 1697. *See also* whom the GODS love die young.

Heaven gives its favourites early death.
Lord Byron, *Childe Harolde's Pilgrimage*, 1812

the good is the enemy of the best (English) The temptation to settle for what is good detracts from the willingness to strive for what is even better. J. Kelman, *Thoughts on Things Eternal*, 1912. *See also* the BEST is the enemy of the good.

the only good Indian is a dead one (US) Red Indians are so dangerous and so evil that only when they are dead can they be trusted. J. M. Cavanaugh, *Congressional Globe*, 1868. This saying dates from the days of the Indian Wars in the USA, but has since been adapted to attack many other nationalities (for instance, the Germans and the Japanese during the Second World War).

She did not know why the government made treaties with Indians. The only good Indian was a dead Indian.
Laura Ingalls Wilder, *Little House on the Prairie*, 1935

there's many a good cock come out of a tattered bag (English) Many good things emerge from unpromising situations. C. S. Burne, *Shropshire Folklore*, 1883. The proverb had its origins in cockfighting.

there's many a good tune played on an old fiddle (English) Old age is not necessarily a bar to worthwhile achievement. Samuel Butler, *The Way of All Flesh*, 1902. Equivalent proverbs include 'good broth may be made in an old pot'.

Beyond a haricot vein in one of my legs I'm as young as ever I was. Old indeed! There's many a good tune played on an old fiddle.
Samuel Butler, The Way of All Flesh, 1902

there's one good wife in the country, and every man thinks he hath her (English) Good wives are scarce, but their cunning is such that every married man is fooled into thinking his own spouse is perfect. T. Shelton, Cervantes' Don Quixote, 1620.

They say, that every married man should believe there's but one good wife in the world, and that's his own.
Jonathan Swift, Dialogues, 1738

good. See also BAD money drives out good; the good BERNARD does not see everything; the BEST is the enemy of the good; BRAG is a good dog, but Holdfast is better; it is good to make a BRIDGE of gold to a flying enemy; a CHANGE is as good as a rest; ENOUGH is as good as a feast; EVIL communications corrupt good manners; FAR-fetched and dear bought is good for ladies; it is good FISHING in troubled waters; HOPE is a good breakfast but a bad supper; it's an ILL wind that blows nobody any good; JACK is as good as his master; a LIAR ought to have a good memory; LISTENERS never hear any good of themselves; a MISS is as good as a mile; NO news is good news; a NOD is as good as a wink to a blind horse; there is NOTHING so good for the inside of a man as the outside of a horse; OPEN confession is good for the soul; see a PIN and pick it up, all the day you'll have good luck; all PUBLICITY is good publicity; the ROAD to Hell is paved with good intentions; good SEED makes a good crop; a good SURGEON

must have an eagles's eye, a lion's heart and a lady's hand; you can have TOO much of a good thing; when the WIND is in the east, 'tis neither good for man nor beast

goodness is not tied to greatness (Greek) Goodness and greatness do not necessarily go together. J. Clarke, Paroemiologia Anglo-Latina, 1639.

goods. See TAKE the goods the gods provide

goose. a goose-quill is more dangerous than a lion's claw (English) More harm may be done with a pen than with a more obvious weapon. Thomas Fuller, Gnomologia, 1732. See also the PEN is mightier than the sword.

goose. See also KILL not the goose that lays the golden egg; what's SAUCE for the goose is sauce for the gander

gorse. when the gorse is out of bloom, kissing's out of fashion (English) When the gorse flowers, it is the season for romance (gorse remains in bloom for much of the year). M. A. Denham, Proverbs relating to Seasons, etc., 1846. See also when the FURZE is in bloom, my love's in tune.

got. if you've got it, flaunt it (US) Do not be shy about your good points (typically sexually attractive physical features). Among other instances, the slogan was heard in the 1967 Mel Brooks film comedy The Producers.

what is got over the Devil's back is spent under his belly (English) Money acquired dishonestly is fated to be squandered on the pursuit of debauched pleasure. Gosson, Plays Confuted, 1582.

What's got over the devil's back (that's by

knavery), must be spent under his belly (that's by lechery).
Thomas Middleton, *Michaelmas Term*, 1607

grace will last, beauty will blast (English) Good character will long outlast physical attractiveness. *Proverbis of Wysdom*, c.1450. Also encountered as 'grace will last, favour will blast'.

grain. grain by grain the hen fills her belly (English) Little by little the desired result is achieved. Middleton and Rowley, *The Spanish Gipsy*, 1653.

grain. *See also* if in FEBRUARY there be no rain, 'tis neither good for hay nor grain

grandmother. *See* don't TEACH your grandmother to suck eggs

grass. the grass is always greener on the other side of the fence (English) What others have always seems more attractive than what you have yourself. H. and M. Williams, *Plays of the Year*, 1959. Though known in this form only from the twentieth century, earlier versions of the proverb may be found as far back as the sixteenth century – for instance, as 'the corne in an other mans ground semeth ever more fertyll and plentifull then doth oure owne'. Variants include 'the grass is always greener on the other side of the hill', 'the other side of the road always looks cleanest' and, in the USA, 'the grass is always greener in the next man's yard'. *See also* FORBIDDEN fruit tastes sweetest.

The apples on the other side of the wall are the sweetest.
George Herbert, *Jacula Prudentum*, 1640

while the grass grows, the steed starves (English) Some things come too late to do any good (just as a horse might starve while the grass to feed him is still growing). *Douce MS*, c.1350.

Rosencrantz How can that be when you have the voice of the king himself for your succession in Denmark?
Hamlet Ay, sir, but 'While the grass grows,' – the proverb is something musty.
William Shakespeare, *Hamlet*, c.1600

grease. *See* the SQUEAKING wheel gets the grease

great. a great book is a great evil (Greek) Large books may impress because of their great size, though they may lack any greatness in content and thus exert an undesirable influence. Callimachus, *Fragments*, third century BC. An English variant runs 'a wicked book is the wickeder because it cannot repent'.

Oftentimes it falls out … a great Booke is a great mischiefe.
Richard Burton, *The Anatomy of Melancholy*, 1628

a great fortune is a great slavery (English) Great wealth brings with it great responsibilities. Thomas Fuller, *Gnomologia*, 1732. Related proverbs include 'great honours are great burdens'.

a truly great man never puts away the simplicity of a child (Chinese) The wise man preserves the inquiring innocence of the young.

great men have great faults (English) Remarkable men often have serious flaws in their character. T. Draxe, *Bibliotheca Scholastica*, 1616.

great minds think alike (English) People of distinction share a similar viewpoint (often said when two people congratulate themselves on separately thinking of something or doing something at the same moment). D. Belchier, *Hans Beer-Pot*, 1618. *See also* GREAT wits jump.

great oaks from little acorns grow

(English) Big things can develop from small beginnings. Geoffrey Chaucer, *Troilus and Criseyde*, *c*.1385. Much the same sentiment was voiced in various forms as far back as Classical times, the most famous versions including 'magnum in parvo' ('a lot in a little').

The greatest Oaks have been little Acorns.
Thomas Fuller, *Gnomologia*, 1732

great wits jump (English) People of strong intellect will reach the same conclusion at much the same time. *Wit for Money*, 1691. *See also* GREAT minds think alike.

Great wits jump: – for the moment Dr Slop cast his eyes upon his bag ... the very same thought occurred.
Laurence Sterne, *Tristram Shandy*, 1767

great. *See also* DEATH is the great leveller; LITTLE strokes fell great oaks; LITTLE thieves are hanged, but great ones escape; there's no great LOSS without some gain; POVERTY is no disgrace, but it is a great inconvenience; THRIFT is a great revenue

greater. the greater the right, the greater the wrong (English) Justice taken to the extreme can become an extreme wrong. Richard Grafton, *Chronicle*, 1569. Sometimes encountered, particularly in the legal context, as the Latin tag 'summus jus, summa injuria'.

the greater the sinner, the greater the saint (English) The more wicked a person's past, the more remarkable is their subsequent reformation. Richard Graves, *The Spiritual Quixote*, 1772.

the greater the truth, the greater the libel (English) If something is undeniably true then any attempt to refute it is doubly damnable. Robert Burns, *The Reproof*, 1787. The maxim is often quoted in discussion of libel actions and is particularly associated with William Murray, First Earl of Mansfield, who was a leading judge of the King's Bench in the eighteenth century.

'The greater the truth, the greater the libel', said Warburton, with a sneer.
Edward Bulwer-Lytton, *Pelham*, 1828

greatness. *See* GOODNESS is not tied to greatness

Greek. when Greek meets Greek, then comes the tug of war (English/Dutch) When two people of the same calibre or courage engage, the contest that ensues will be fierce. Nathaniel Lee, *The Rival Queens*, 1677. The proverb has its origins in the spirited resistance that was put up by Greek cities to attacks by Philip of Macedon and Alexander the Great. Nathaniel Lee's original line actually ran 'when Greeks join'd Greeks then was the tug of war'. Another proverb that casts a more dubious light upon the Greek national character runs 'after shaking hands with a Greek, count your fingers'.

Meantime ... Greek was meeting Greek only a few yards off. Mr Hardie was being undermined by a man of his own calibre.
Charles Reade, *Hard Cash*, 1863

Greeks. *See* BEWARE of Greeks bearing gifts

green. a green winter makes a fat churchyard (English) A mild winter promises many deaths to come. J. Swan, *Speculum Mundi*, 1635. Scientists have been known to accept the truth of this proverb, explaining that a mild winter fosters epidemics that might not flourish in colder weather. Variants include 'a green Yule makes a fat churchyard' and 'green Christmas, full churchyard'.

A green yule makes a fat Church-yard. This, and a great many proverbial Observations, upon the Seasons of the Year, are groundless.
James Kelly, *A Complete Collection of Scotish Proverbs*, 1721

greener. *See* the GRASS is always greener on the other side of the fence

grey. grey hairs are death's blossoms (*English*) The appearance of grey hairs are a warning of life passing. R. C. Trench, *On the Lessons in Proverbs*, 1853. Sometimes heard with reference to white rather than grey hairs.

This whyte top wryteth myne olde yeres.
Geoffrey Chaucer, *The Canterbury Tales*, c.1387

the grey mare is the better horse (*English*) The wife is superior (either in character or in terms of running the marriage) to the husband. John Heywood, *A Dialogue containing … the Proverbs in the English Tongue*, 1546.

The vulgar proverb, that the grey mare is the better horse, originated, I suspect, in the preference generally given to the grey mares of Flanders over the finest coach horses of England.
Thomas Macaulay, *The History of England from the Accession of James II*, 1849

grey. *See also* all CATS are grey in the dark

grief. one grief drives out another (*English*) New sorrows expel old ones. James Mabbe, *Celestina*, 1631.

grieve. *See* what the EYE does not see, the heart does not grieve over

grind. *See* the MILL cannot grind with the water that is past; the MILLS of God grind slowly, yet they grind exceeding small

gripping. *See* NOTHING should be done in haste but gripping a flea

grist. all is grist that comes to the mill (*English*) Anything that comes along can be made use of. Thomas Fuller, *Church History of Britain*, 1655. Grist, incidentally, was the name formerly given to corn when it is first brought to the mill for grinding. The proverb appears to have developed from the earlier phrase 'to bring grist to the mill', which signified the getting of some benefit or other. *See also* all is FISH that comes to the net.

Well, let them go on, it brings grist to our mill: for whilst both the sexes stick firm to their honour, we shall never want business.
Samuel Foote, *The Lame Lover*, 1770

ground. *See* BETWEEN two stools you fall to the ground

grow. *See* GREAT oaks from little acorns grow

growing. a growing youth has a wolf in his belly (*English*) The young have a voracious appetite. Benjamin Jowett, *Life*, 1886.

grows. *See* while the GRASS grows, the steed starves

grunt. *See* what can you EXPECT from a pig but a grunt?

guest. a constant guest is never welcome (*English*) A visitor who keeps on returning will soon outstay his welcome. Thomas Fuller, *Gnomologia*, 1732. Similar sentiments may be found in many other languages, including the Indian 'the first day a guest, the second day a guest, the third day a calamity' and the Chinese 'the guest who outstays his fellow-guests loses his overcoat'. *See also* FISH and guests stink after three days.

guilty. a guilty conscience needs no accuser (*English*) Those who are conscious that they have committed offence need not be reminded of it. Geoffrey Chaucer, *The Canterbury Tales*, c. 1387. Variants include 'a guilty conscience is a thousand witnesses'.

A guilty Conscience self accuses. A Man that has done ill ... shews his Guilt.
James Kelly, *A Complete Collection of Scotish Proverbs*, 1721

guys. *See* NICE guys finish last

h

---

habit. the habit does not make the monk See the COWL does not make the monk

habits. See OLD habits die hard

hail brings frost in the tail (English) Hail is usually followed by a period of very cold weather, with frost. J. Clarke, *Paroemiologia Anglo-Latina*, 1639. Another proverb claims 'a hailstorm by day denotes a frost at night'.

hair. one hair of a woman draws more than a team of oxen (English) A woman may use her influence on others to achieve far more than may otherwise be achieved by brute strength. John Florio, *Second Fruites*, 1591.

> And beauty draws us with a single hair.
> Alexander Pope, *The Rape of the Lock*, 1712

hair. See also TAKE the hair of the dog that bit you

half. half a loaf is better than no bread (English) A meagre amount of something is better than nothing at all. John Heywood, *A Dialogue containing ... the Proverbs in the English Tongue*, 1546. Variants include 'half an egg is better than an empty shell'.

> You know the Proverb of the half Loaf, Ariadne, a Husband that will deal thee some Love is better than one who can give thee none.
> Aphra Behn, *The Rover*, 1681

half the truth is often a whole lie (English/US) A person may be more seriously misled by a partial truth than by an outright untruth. Benjamin Franklin, *Poor Richard's Almanack*, 1758.

> That a lie which is half a truth is ever the blackest of lies,
> That a lie which is all a lie may be met and fought with outright,
> But a lie which is part a truth is a harder matter to fight.
> Alfred, Lord Tennyson, 'The Grandmother', *Poems*, 1859

half the world doesn't know how the other half lives (French) Much of humanity lives in ignorance of the radically different existences led by their fellows. J. Hall, *Holy Observations*, 1607 (also quoted by Philippe de Commines in his *Memoires*, 1509, and by Rabelais in *Pantagruel*, 1532).

> It is a common saying, that One Half of the World does not know how the other Half lives.
> Benjamin Franklin, *Poor Richard's Almanack*, 1755

the half is better than the whole (Greek) In some circumstances, it is best to settle for something less, as ultimately this means one will be better off. Hugh Latimer, *Sermon before King's Majesty*, 1550. The proverb is also to be found in the Greek poet Hesiod's *Works and Days*, eighth century BC. Hesiod quoted the saying to his brother Perseus in order to settle a legal dispute between them without having to go to court, implying that it was better to accept half of an estate than press on in the hope of getting the whole estate, only to find it much reduced after court proceedings due to legal costs.

Unhappy they to whom God has not revealed,
By a strong light which must their sense control,
That half a great estate's more than the whole.
Abraham Cowley, *Essays in Verse and Prose*, 1668

half. See also BELIEVE nothing of what you hear, and only half of what you see; two BOYS are half a boy, and three boys are no boy at all; a DANGER foreseen is half avoided; a DISEASE known is half cured; a FAULT confessed is half redressed; the FIRST blow is half the battle; FOOLS and bairns should never see half-done work; he that has an ILL name is half hanged; do not MEET troubles half-way; WELL begun is half done

Halifax. See from HELL, Hull and Halifax, good Lord deliver us

hall. See DO on the hill as you would do in the hall; 'tis MERRY in hall when beards wag all

halloo. don't halloo till you are out of the wood (English/US) Don't expose yourself until all threat of danger is removed. Benjamin Franklin, *Papers*, 1770 (variants may be found in

the writings of Sophocles and Cicero). To 'halloo' (to shout aloud or whistle) while in a wood and thus attract attention to oneself was formerly considered unwise, as woods could harbour all manner of hidden danger. Also encountered in the form 'don't shout till you are out of the wood'. *See also* don't COUNT your chickens before they are hatched.

Don't holla till you are out of the wood. This is a night for praying rather than boasting.
Charles Kingsley, *Hereward the Wake*, 1866

halved. See a TROUBLE shared is a trouble halved

halves. See never DO things by halves

hammer. See the CHURCH is an anvil which has worn out many hammers

hand. one hand for oneself and one for the ship (English) Divide your attentions between serving others and looking after your own interests. *Port Folio*, 1799. The proverb has nautical origins, coming from the English shipyards where workers on new vessels were taught to secure themselves with one hand and keep the other free to do their work.

The maxim, which says, 'one hand for the owner, and t'other for yourself,' ... has saved many a hearty fellow from a fall that would have balanced the purser's books.
James Fenimore Cooper, *The Pilot*, 1822

one hand washes the other (Greek) Favours are bestowed in the expectation of being rewarded. J. Sanforde, *Garden of Pleasure*, 1573 (also quoted by Epicharmus and Seneca). Also encountered in the fuller version, 'one hand washes the other, and both the face'. Variant forms include 'one hand claweth another' and 'one hand will not wash the other for nothing'. See *also* one GOOD turn deserves another; you SCRATCH my back and I'll scratch yours.

Hand washes hand.

Seneca, *Apocolocyntosis divi Claudii*, first century AD

put not thy hand between the bark and the tree (English) Do not interfere in an argument between close relatives. John Heywood, *A Dialogue containing ... the Proverbs in the English Tongue*, 1546. The danger is that the person interfering will find himself 'pinched' between the two parties.

It were a foly for mee, to put hande betweene the barke and the tree.

John Heywood, *A Dialogue containing ... the Proverbs in the English Tongue*, 1546

the hand that rocks the cradle rules the world (US) Those who have influence over children (or at an early stage in the development of something) ultimately have the greatest influence of all. William Ross Wallace, 'The Hand that Rules the World', 1865. *See also* GIVE me a child for the first seven years, and you may do what you like with him afterwards.

They say that man is mighty,
He governs land and sea,
He wields a mighty sceptre
O'er lesser powers that be;
But a mightier power and stronger
Man from his throne has hurled,
And the hand that rocks the cradle
Is the hand that rules the world.

William Ross Wallace, 'The Hand that Rules the World', 1865

hand. *See also* a BIRD in the hand is worth two in the bush; don't BITE the hand that feeds you; FULL cup, steady hand

hands. *See* COLD hands, warm heart; the DEVIL finds work for idle hands; the EYE of the master does more work than both his hands; FINGERS were made before forks and hands before knives; IF ifs and ands were pots and pans, there'd be no work for tinkers' hands; MANY hands make light work

handsome. handsome is as handsome does (English) Good character is proved more through deeds than through mere good looks or promises etc. Geoffrey Chaucer, *The Canterbury Tales*, c.1387. Originally 'handsome' referred to refined or gentlemanly behaviour rather than physical appearance alone. A variant form more usually directed at women runs 'pretty is as pretty does'. *See also* BEAUTY is only skin deep; GRACE will last, beauty will blast.

By my troth, he is a proper man; but he is proper that proper doth.

Thomas Dekker, *The Shoemaker's Holiday*, 1600

he that is not handsome at twenty, wise at forty and rich at fifty, will never be rich, wise or handsome (English) There comes a time in life when it becomes clear that if not already attained, good looks, wisdom and wealth are unlikely ever to be enjoyed. George Herbert, *Jacula Prudentum*, 1640.

hang. hang a thief when he's young and he'll no' steal when he's old (Scottish) Take drastic action at an early stage and any threat of trouble will be nipped in the bud. A. Henderson, *Scottish Proverbs*, 1832.

Hang a thief when he's young, and he'll no' steal when he's auld.

A. Henderson, *Scottish Proverbs*, 1832

he that would hang his dog gives out first that he is mad (English) Those about to commit some wicked or disgraceful deed will often protect themselves in advance by some pretence designed to justify it. J. Palsgrave, *L'Éclaircissement de la langue française*, 1530

hang. *See also* CREAKING doors hang the longest; GIVE a dog a bad name and hang him; GIVE a man enough rope and he will hang himself; every HERRING must hang by its own gill

hanged. he was hanged that left his drink behind (English) Ill luck will attend any person who leaves without first finishing his drink. *Roxborough Ballads*, c.1640. One north of England variant runs 'he will be hanged for leaving his liquor, like the saddler of Bawtry'. The aforesaid saddler of Bawtry was sentenced to be hanged in York and, as was customary, was offered the chance to take a last drink at a local tavern before being taken to the gallows and executed: the saddler, however, turned down the drink and was accordingly dispatched by the hangman without further delay – only for a reprieve to arrive moments later. If the saddler had agreed to slake his thirst, he would have been saved – hence the proverb.

you might as well be hanged for a sheep as for a lamb (English) If you are going to transgress the rules you might as well aim for the highest possible prize, as the penalty if you are caught will be the same (as was true of sheep-stealing in former times). John Ray, *A Collection of English Proverbs*, 1678. *See also* IN for a penny, in for a pound.

So in for the lamb, as the saying is, in for the sheep.
Samuel Richardson, *Clarissa*, 1748

hanged. *See also* if you're BORN to be hanged then you'll never be drowned; CONFESS and be hanged; he that has an

ILL name is half hanged; LITTLE thieves are hanged, but great ones escape

hanging. hanging and wiving go by destiny (English) A person's choice of marriage partner is decided by fate (as is their own ultimate end). John Heywood, *A Dialogue containing … the Proverbs in the English Tongue*, 1546.

The ancient saying is no heresy,
Hanging and wiving goes by destiny.
William Shakespeare, *The Merchant of Venice*, c.1596

hanging. *See also* there are more WAYS of killing a dog than hanging it

ha'porth. *See* don't SPOIL the ship for a ha'porth of tar

happen. *See* ACCIDENTS will happen in the best regulated families

happens. *See* the UNEXPECTED always happens

happy. happy is he that is happy in his children (English) Contented and well-behaved children bring their parents much pleasure. Thomas Fuller, *Gnomologia*, 1732. Representing the child's view, another proverb runs 'happy is the child whose father goes to the Devil'.

happy is the bride the sun shines on (English) It is a good omen for the future of a marriage if the sun shines on a bride on her wedding day. Robert Herrick, *Hesperides*, 1648. *See also* BLESSED are the dead the rain rains on.

The four old bells rang out merrily, and 'Blessed is the bride whom the sun shines on.' 'I have had a great deal of sunshine today,' she said. 'I hope it is a good omen,' I said. 'I hope so,' she said, sweetly and seriously.
Francis Kilvert, *Diary*, 1 January 1873

happy is the country which has no history (English) The history of a nation may prove as much a hindrance as a help, and thus young countries lacking a long history may be considered freer agents. Thomas Carlyle, *Frederick the Great*, 1858–65.

History, which is, indeed, little more than the register of the crimes, follies and misfortunes of mankind.
Edward Gibbon, *The History of the Decline and Fall of the Roman Empire*, 1766–88

if you would be happy for a week take a wife; if you would be happy for a month kill a pig; but if you would be happy all your life plant a garden (English) No pleasure is as lasting as a garden. Thomas Fuller, *The History of the Worthies of England*, 1661. Variants suggest the recipe for a happy life lies in honesty, rather than gardening. A related proverb advises 'he that marries a wife is happy a month, but he that gets a fat benefice lives merrily all his life'.

I say the Italian-humor, who have a merry Proverb, Let him that would be happy for a Day, go to the Barber; for a Week, marry a Wife; for a Month, buy him a New-horse; for a Year, build him a New-house; for all his Life-time, be an Honest man.
Thomas Fuller, *The History of the Worthies of England*, 1661

happy. *See also* CALL no man happy till he dies; a DEAF husband and a blind wife are always a happy couple

hard. hard cases make bad law (Roman) Complicated or exceptional legal cases tend to confuse understanding of the law. G. Hayes, 1854, quoted in W. S. Holdsworth, *The History of English Law*, 1926 (the proverb may also be found in essence as far back as the writings of Sallust in the first century BC).

hard words break no bones (English) Verbal criticism may be resented but cannot cause a person actual physical

harm. *Towneley Play of Noah*, c.1450. *See also* STICKS and stones may break my bones, but names will never hurt me.

I often tell 'em how wrong folks are to say that soft words butter no parsnips, and hard words break no bones.
Anthony Trollope, *The Last Chronicle of Barsetshire*, 1867

it is hard to pay for bread that has been eaten (Danish) A person will rue having to pay retrospectively for something that they have already consumed or enjoyed. *See also* EATEN bread is soon forgotten.

hard. *See also* OLD habits die hard

harder. *See* the BIGGER they are, the harder they fall

hare. *See* FIRST catch your hare; you cannot RUN with the hare and hunt with the hounds

hares. hares may pull dead lions by the beard (English) The most humble and timid may taunt the powerful with impunity after the latter have been brought down. G. Pettie, *Guazzo's Civil Conversation*, 1581.

You are the hare of whom the proverb goes, whose valour plucks dead lions by the beard.
William Shakespeare, *King John*, c.1595

hares. *See also* if you RUN after two hares you will catch neither

harm watch, harm catch (English) A person who is always anxious about coming to harm will attract harm. William Caxton, *Reynard the Fox*, 1481.

Harm watch, harm catch, he says.
Ben Jonson, *Bartholomew Fair*, 1614

haste. haste is from the Devil (English) Those who fail to take enough time over something invite ill results. J. Howell, *Familiar Letters*, 1633. Also found as 'haste is from hell'. A related proverb warns 'a hasty man never wants woe'. See also HASTY climbers have sudden falls.

haste makes waste (English) Doing things too quickly may result in wasted effort and materials. Geoffrey Chaucer, *The Canterbury Tales*, c.1387. A fuller version, recorded in 1678, runs 'haste makes waste, and waste makes want, and want makes strife between the good man and his wife'.

The proverbe seith … in wikked haste is no profit.
Geoffrey Chaucer, *The Canterbury Tales*, c.1387

make haste slowly (Greek/Roman) Going slowly but steadily is often the quickest way to get something done. Geoffrey Chaucer, *Troilus and Criseyde*, c.1385 (also quoted by Suetonius). The proverb was a favourite saying of Emperor Caesar Augustus, who popularized it in its Latin version 'festina lente' (which is still heard). Plutarch expressed the same sentiment as 'hair by hair you will pull out the horse's tail', and quoted a story about the general Sertorius to illustrate it. According to him, Sertorius felt the need to impress upon his troops the effectiveness of slow, patient effort over thoughtless haste. He commanded two of his men, one strong and one weak, to pluck all the hairs from the tails of two horses. The strong man tried to pull out all the hairs at once and could make little impression, but the weak man pulled out hair after single hair until at length the job was successfully done. See also more HASTE, less speed.

He hasteth wel that wisly kan abyde.
Geoffrey Chaucer, *Troilus and Criseyde*, c.1385

more haste, less speed (English) Doing something too quickly may ultimately mean it takes longer to accomplish than if it is done at a steadier pace. *Douce MS*, c.1350. A longer version, recorded in 1721, runs 'the more haste, the worse speed, quoth the tailor to his long thread'. Equivalents include 'haste trips up its own heels'. See also make HASTE slowly; SLOW but sure wins the race.

A mod'rate pace is best indeed.
The greater hurry, the worse speed.
Edward Ward, *Hudibras Redivivus*, 1705

haste. See also MARRY in haste and repent at leisure; NOTHING should be done in haste but gripping a flea

hasty. hasty climbers have sudden falls (English) Those who ascend rapidly in the world are just as likely to fall to earth without warning. *Digby Plays*, c.1480.

Great clymbers fall unsoft.
Edmund Spenser, *The Shepheardes Calendar*, 1579

the hasty bitch bringeth forth blind whelps (Roman) Things done in haste are liable to turn out badly. R. Robinson, translation of Thomas More's *Utopia*, 1556 (also quoted by Livy).

But as the latin proverbe sayeth: the hastye bitche bringeth furth blind whelpes. For when this my worke was finished, the rudeness therof shewed it to be done in poste haste.
R. Robinson, translation of Thomas More's *Utopia*, 1556

the hasty man never wants woe (English) Those who act in haste are likely to regret their actions. Geoffrey Chaucer, *Troilus and Criseyde*, c.1385.

'The hastie person never wants woe,' they say.
George Chapman and others, *Eastward Hoe*, 1605

hatched. See don't COUNT your chickens before they are hatched

hatchet. See do not REMOVE a fly from your friend's forehead with a hatchet

hate. See better a DINNER of herbs than a stalled ox where hate is

have. what you have, hold (English) Defend what is yours, rather than yearn for what belongs to others. *Towneley Play of the Killing of Abel*, c. 1450. Variants include 'hold fast when you have it'. Another proverb warns 'he that will have all, loseth all'.

It is better hold that I have then go from doore to doore and crave.
Towneley Play of the Killing of Abel, c. 1450

you can't have your cake and eat it (English) In certain circumstances one must make a choice between two benefits, as they are mutually incompatible (for example, saving one's money and at the same time spending it). John Heywood, *A Dialogue containing ... the Proverbs in the English Tongue*, 1546. Variants in other languages include the French proverb 'you can't have the cloth and keep the money' and the Italian proverb 'do you want to eat your cake and still have it in your pocket?' See also you can't have it BOTH ways.

She was handsome in her Time; but she cannot eat her Cake, and have her Cake.
Jonathan Swift, *Polite Conversation*, 1738

have. See also what you SPEND, you have; you can have TOO much of a good thing

hawks will not pick out hawks' eyes (English) Those engaged in the same profession (typically, criminal or dependent upon profiting by the loss of others) will not prey on one another. J. Sanforde, *The Garden of Pleasure*, 1573. The proverb is sometimes encountered with reference to crows rather than hawks.

I wadna ... rest my main dependence on the Hielandmen – hawks winna pike out hawks' een. – They quarrel amang themsells ... but they are sure to join ... against a' civilized folk.
Walter Scott, *Rob Roy*, 1817

haws. many haws, many snows (Scottish) If plants produce many haws then the winter that follows will be severe. Robinson, *Whitby Glossary*, 1855. Variants include 'many haws, cold toes'. See also many HIPS and haws, many frosts and snaws.

haws. See also when all FRUIT falls, welcome haws

hay. make hay while the sun shines (German) Make the most of any opportunity when it is presented. John Heywood, *A Dialogue containing ... the Proverbs in the English Tongue*, 1546 (though also recorded in German satirist Sebastian Brant's *Das Narrenschiff* as early as 1494). In farming, ripe hay should be harvested at the first opportunity, in case it is lost through bad weather (a particular threat given the changeable nature of English weather patterns). See also GATHER ye rosebuds while ye may; PROCRASTINATION is the thief of time; never PUT off till tomorrow what you can do today; STRIKE while the iron is hot; TAKE time by the forelock.

We must lose no time; we must make our hay while shines the sun.
Charles Reade, *The Cloister and the Hearth*, 1861

hay. See also if in FEBRUARY there be no rain, 'tis neither good for hay nor grain; a SWARM of bees in May is worth a load of hay

he that will not when he may, when he will he shall have nay (Roman) The person who does not seize an opportunity when it is offered will find no opportunity presents itself when he or she needs it. *Anglo-Saxon Homily*, tenth century AD (also quoted by Saint Augustine). Related proverbs include 'he that doth what he should not shall feel what he would not'.

head. he that hath a head of wax must not walk in the sun (Roman) Those in potentially vulnerable positions should not take unnecessary risks. George Herbert, *Jacula Prudentum*, 1640. *See also* people who live in GLASS houses shouldn't throw stones.

If your head is wax, don't walk in the Sun. Benjamin Franklin, *Poor Richard's Almanack*, 1749

when the head acheth all the body is the worse (English) A person with a sore head feels infirm in all his or her limbs. Wright, *Political Songs from John to Edward II, c.1230*.

head. *See also* the FISH always stinks from the head downwards; where MACGREGOR sits is the head of the table; you cannot put an OLD head on young shoulders; a STILL tongue makes a wise head; there are many WAYS of dressing a calf's head; YORKSHIRE born and Yorkshire bred, strong in the arm and weak in the head

heads. *See* TWO heads are better than one

heal. *See* PHYSICIAN, heal thyself

heals. *See* TIME heals all wounds

health. health is better than wealth (Hebrew) Good health is more valuable than mere riches. Bible, Ecclesiasticus 30. Variants include 'health is great riches', 'the first wealth is health', 'good health is above wealth' and 'a healthy man is a successful man'. Another proverb counters this view, alleging that 'health without money is half an ague'. A Yiddish saying runs

'your health comes first; you can always hang yourself later'. Ideally, of course, a person will possess both health and wealth together, in which case they will allegedly enjoy a third benefit, according to another old proverb: 'health and wealth create beauty'.

Health and strength is above all gold. Bible, Ecclesiasticus 30

health. *See also* POVERTY is the mother of health; WEALTH is enemy to health

healthy. *See* EARLY to bed and early to rise, makes a man healthy, wealthy and wise

hear. hear all, see all, say nowt (English) It is good policy to be vigilant, but also to keep your observations to yourself. *Proverbs of Wisdom*, 1400. A proverb of Yorkshire origins. The fullest version runs 'hear all, see all, say nowt, tak' all, keep all, gie nowt, and if tha ever does owt for nowt do it for thysen'. *See also* SEE no evil, hear no evil, speak no evil.

It seems queer, that you do it and get no profit. I should think you've forgotten the Yorkshire proverb, 'An' if tha does owt for nowt, do it for thysen.' D. H. Lawrence, letter, 1 February 1913

hear. *See also* go ABROAD and you'll hear news of home; ASK no questions and hear no lies; BELIEVE nothing of what you hear, and only half of what you see; there are none SO DEAF as those who will not hear; DREAM of a funeral and you hear of a marriage; LISTENERS never hear any good of themselves

heard. *See* CHILDREN should be seen and not heard

heart. what comes from the heart goes to the heart (English) Anything that is born of real emotion will stir emotion in others when they hear of it. J. Platt, *Morality*, 1878.

heart. *See also* ABSENCE makes the heart grow fonder; COLD hands, warm heart; what the EYE does not see, the heart does not grieve over; FAINT heart ne'er won fair lady; HOME is where the heart is; HOPE deferred makes the heart sick; if it were not for HOPE, the heart would break; PLEASE your eye and plague your heart; it is a POOR heart that never rejoices; put a STOUT heart to a stey brae; the WAY to a man's heart is through his stomach

heat. *See* if you can't STAND the heat, get out of the kitchen

heaven. heaven protects children, sailors and drunken men (English) The young, seafarers and drunkards, being variously exposed to danger through innocence, occupation or incapacity, often seem to survive the worst perils unscathed, as though blessed with divine protection. T. Hughes, *Tom Brown at Oxford*, 1861.

Heaven, they say, protects children, sailors, and drunken men; and whatever answers to Heaven in the academical system protects freshmen.
T. Hughes, *Tom Brown at Oxford*, 1861

heaven. *See also* CROSSES are ladders that lead to heaven; it is EASIER for a camel to go through the eye of a needle than it is for a rich man to enter into the kingdom of heaven; GOD's in his heaven, all's right with the world; MARRIAGES are made in heaven; NO coming to heaven with dry eyes; who SPITS against heaven it falls in his face

heavy. a heavy purse makes a light heart (English) A rich man is a happy man. Alexander Barclay, *Eclogues*,

c.1510. *See also* a LIGHT purse makes a heavy heart.

A heavy purse makes a light heart. There 'tis exprest.
Ben Jonson, *The New Inn*, 1631

hedge. a hedge between keeps friendship green (English) Maintaining some privacy even from one's closest friends helps to keep relationships on a healthy footing. J. Mapletoft, *Select Proverbs*, 1707. *See also* GOOD fences make good neighbours; LOVE your neighbour, yet pull not down your hedge.

hedge. *See also* one man may STEAL a horse, while another may not look over a hedge

heirs. *See* WALNUTS and pears you plant for your heirs

Hell. from Hell, Hull and Halifax, Good Lord deliver us (English) May we never find ourselves in Hell, Hull or Halifax. A. Copley, *Wits, Fits, etc.*, 1594. Hull formerly had a reputation for strict government and harsh treatment of vagrants and beggars, while Halifax reputedly had its own notorious 'Gibbet Law', which made possible the summary execution of anyone found guilty of stealing cloth. It has been suggested that 'Hell' was originally intended to signify Elland, another clothmaking town in the same area.

Hell and Chancery are always open (English) Lawyers, like demons, are always ready to do mischief. Thomas Fuller, *Gnomologia*, 1732.

Hell hath no fury like a woman scorned (English) A woman's anger is more to be feared than anything else on Earth. Beaumont and Fletcher, *The Knight of Malta*, 1625.

Heav'n has no Rage, like Love to Hatred turn'd, Nor Hell a Fury, like a Woman scorn'd.
William Congreve, *The Mourning Bride*, 1697

Hell. *See also* the ROAD to Hell is paved with good intentions; he that would go to SEA for pleasure, would go to Hell for a pastime

help. help you to salt, help you to sorrow (English) At table, it is unlucky to pass the salt to another person. G. Torriano, *Italian Proverbs*, 1666.

No one would at table spoon salt on to another person's plate, for 'Help you to salt, help you to sorrow'.
Flora Thompson, *Lark Rise to Candleford*, 1945

help. *See also* a MOUSE may help a lion

helps. he helps little that helps not himself (English) Those who wish to help others should first help themselves. J. Sandford, *The Garden of Pleasure*, 1573.

helps. *See also* GOD helps those who help themselves; every LITTLE helps

hen. *See* the ROBIN and the wren are God's cock and hen; a WHISTLING woman and a crowing hen are neither fit for God nor men

herbs. *See* better a DINNER of herbs than a stalled ox where hate is

here today, gone tomorrow (English) Some things disappear almost as quickly as they come (often heard in reference to money). T. Draxe, *Bibliotheca Scholastica*, 1616. *See also* EASY come, easy go.

heresy. *See* TURKEY, heresy, hops and beer came into England all in one year

hero. *See* NO man is a hero to his valet

herring. every herring must hang by its own gill (English) It is up to each individual to account for his own actions. S. Harward, MS, 1609.

Another saying connected with herrings claims 'of all the fish in the sea, the herring is the king'.

Na, na! let every herring hing by its ain head, and every sheep by its ain shank.
Walter Scott, *Rob Roy*, 1817

hesitates. he who hesitates is lost (English) In certain circumstances the taking of an immediate decision is of paramount importance. Joseph Addison, *Cato*, 1713.

It has often been said of woman that she who doubts is lost ... never thinking whether or no there be any truth in the proverb.
Anthony Trollope, *Can You Forgive Her?*, 1865

hid. *See* LOVE and a cough cannot be hid

hide. don't hide your light under a bushel (Hebrew) Don't conceal your talents or good qualities from others. Edward Lytton, *Kenelm*, 1873 (based on a passage in the Bible, Matthew 5:15). 'Bushel' in this case signifies the wooden or earthenware vessel that was formerly used for the purposes of measurement.

Neither do men lyght a candell, and put it under a busshell, but on a candlestick, and it lighteth all them which are in the house.
William Tyndale, Bible, Matthew 5:15, 1526–34

hide nothing from thy minister, physician and lawyer (English) It is foolish to keep anything secret from those who may influence your spiritual, corporeal or legal state. John Florio, *First Fruites*, 1578.

To friend, lawyer, doctor, tell plain your whole case;
Nor think on bad matters to put a good face.
Benjamin Franklin, *Poor Richard's Almanack*, 1748

those who hide can find (English) Those who hide things are the most likely to be able to find them again. *Seven Sages of Rome, c.* 1400.

higher. the higher the monkey climbs the more he shows his tail (*Hebrew*) The more a person enjoys advancement the more his weaknesses reveal themselves. John Wycliffe, Bible, Proverbs 3:35, *c.* 1395.

The higher you climb, the more you shew your A—. Verified in no instance more than in Dulness aspiring. Emblematized also by an Ape climbing and exposing his posteriors.
Alexander Pope, *Dunciad*, 1743

highest. the highest flood has the lowest ebb (*English*) Extreme events are accompanied by equally extreme lulls or reversals. Wright, *Songs, c.* 1555.

hill. *See* DO on the hill as you would do in the hall

hills. *See* BLUE are the hills that are far away

hindered. *See* MEAT and mass never hindered man

hindmost. *See* every MAN for himself and the Devil take the hindmost

hips. many hips and haws, many frosts and snaws (*English*) The more hips and haws in the autumn, the more severe the winter will be. M. A. Denham, *A Collection of Proverbs ... relating to the Weather,* 1846. *See also* many HAWS, many snows.

hire. *See* the LABOURER is worthy of his hire

hires. he who hires the horse must ride before (*English*) A person who pays for something is entitled to enjoy it to the full, before all others. J. Clarke, *Paroemiographia Anglo-Latina,* 1639.

history. history repeats itself (*English*)

History goes in cycles. George Eliot, *Scenes of Clerical Life,* 1858.

History, we know, is apt to repeat itself.
George Eliot, *Scenes of Clerical Life,* 1858

history. *See also* HAPPY is the country which has no history

hits. he that once hits will be ever shooting (*English*) A person who once tastes success at something will be tempted to try to repeat this success over and over again. T. Wilson, *Rhetorique,* 1560.

He that once hits, is ever bending.
George Herbert, *Jacula Prudentum,* 1640

hobby-horse. every man has his hobby-horse (*English*) Every person has his or her own pet passion, interest or line of argument. Sir Matthew Hale, *Contemplations,* 1676. A hobbyhorse, in Middle English, signified a small or medium-sized horse.

Nay, if you come to that, Sir, have not the wisest of men in all ages, not excepting Solomon himself, – have they not had their Hobby Horses; – their running horses, – their coins and their cockle-shells, their drums and their trumpets, their fiddles, their pallets, – their maggots and their butterflies? – and so long as a man rides his Hobby-Horse peaceably and quietly along the King's highway, and neither compels you or me to get up behind him, – pray, Sir, what have either you or I to do with it?
Laurence Sterne, *Tristram Shandy,* 1759–67

hoist your sail when the wind is fair (*English*) Embark on new enterprises when conditions are ideal. B. Melbancke, *Philotimus,* 1583. *See also* make HAY while the sun shines; STRIKE while the iron is hot.

A man should strike while the iron is hot, and hoist sail while the wind is fair.
Walter Scott, *The Fortunes of Nigel,* 1822

hold. *See* what you HAVE, hold

Holdfast. *See* BRAG is a good dog, but Holdfast is better

home. home is home, as the Devil said when he found himself in the Court of Session (*Scottish*) The law is crooked and unjust, and thus a natural home for the Devil. W. Motherwell, quoted in A. Henderson, *Scottish Proverbs*, 1832. The Scottish Court of Session, founded in 1532, is the senior civil tribunal in Scotland.

home is home, though it be never so homely (*English*) A person always feels most relaxed in his or her own home, no matter how humble it may be. John Heywood, *A Dialogue containing ... the Proverbs in the English Tongue*, 1546.

The saying is, that home is home, be it never so homely.
Charles Dickens, *Dombey and Son*, 1848

home is where the heart is (*Roman*) The emotions of most people are rooted in their homes, however widely they might travel from it. J. J. McCloskey, 1870, quoted in Goldberg and Heffner, *Davy Crockett and Other Plays*, 1940 (also recorded in various forms as far back as Pliny, who may have coined it).

home, sweet home (*English*) The greatest contentment and solace is to be found at home (often quoted on returning home after a hard day). John Howard Payne, 'Home, Sweet Home', 1823. The proverb was a favourite subject for needlework samplers in the nineteenth century, when the US-born lyricist John Howard Payne's rather sentimental song, set to the music of Sir Henry Bishop, was hugely popular on both sides of the Atlantic. Payne may well have derived his inspiration from a variety of earli-

er proverbial phrases along similar lines, including 'home is home, though it be never so homely' and 'for home though homely twere, yet it is sweet', a line from an English translation of Ariosto's *Orlando Furioso*, 1591.

home. *See also* go ABROAD and you'll hear news of home; CHARITY begins at home; CURSES, like chickens, come home to roost; EAST, west, home's best; an ENGLISHMAN's home is his castle; the LONGEST way round is the shortest way home; there's no PLACE like home; a WOMAN's place is in the home; many go out for WOOL and come home shorn

Homer. even Homer sometimes nods (*Greek*) Even the great have their lapses. Horace, *De Arte Poetica*, c.20 BC. *See also* to ERR is human, to forgive divine; it is a GOOD horse that never stumbles.

I think it shame when the worthy Homer nods; but in so long a work it is allowable if drowsiness comes on.
Horace, *De Arte Poetica*, c.20 BC

honest. an honest man's word is as good as his bond *See* an ENGLISHMAN's word is his bond

honest men marry quickly, wise men not at all (*English*) Good men see no threat in marriage and enter into it willingly, but wise men know better and remain single. James Howell, *Epistolae Ho-Elianae; or Familiar Letters*, 1645–55.

you cannot make people honest by Act of Parliament (*English*) It is impossible to persuade a person to be honest unless they choose to be so themselves. Ben Jonson, *The Devil is an Ass*, 1631. Also encountered with the word 'sober' replacing 'honest'.

If he were to be made honest by an act of

parliament, I should not alter in my faith of him.
Ben Jonson, *The Devil is an Ass*, 1631

honest. *See also* every honest MILLER has a thumb of gold

honesty. honesty is the best policy (*Greek*) The wise man chooses to be honest in all his dealings. Edwin Sandys, *Europae Speculum*, 1599. The proverb is common to several European languages and was quoted by Cervantes in *Don Quixote* in 1615.

My policy was chosen from the proverb, Random; I thought honesty the best.
George Colman the Younger, *Ways and Means*, 1788

honesty. *See also* BEAUTY and honesty seldom agree

honey. honey catches more flies than vinegar (*English*) A kindly, soft-voiced approach is likely to get better results than aggression. G. Torriano, *Italian Proverbs*, 1666. Along similar lines is the proverb 'cover yourself with honey and the flies will eat you'.

Tart Words make no Friends: spoonful of honey will catch more flies than Gallon of Vinegar.
Benjamin Franklin, *Poor Richard's Almanack*, 1744

honey is dear bought if licked off thorns (*English*) Something desirable may come at such a cost as to make it not worth having. *Old English Homilies*, c.1175. Equivalent proverbs include 'honey is sweet, but the bee stings' and 'no honey without gall'.

He that licks honey from a nettle pays too dear for it.
Thomas Fuller, *Gnomologia*, 1732

honour. honour buys no beef (*English*) A good reputation does not in itself bring any tangible benefit.

Thomas Shadwell, *The Sullen Lover*, 1668. Also encountered in the form 'honour buys no beef in the market'. *See also* VIRTUE is its own reward.

I am not ambitious of that. As the excellent proverb says, 'Honour will buy no beef'.
Thomas Shadwell, *The Sullen Lover*, 1668

there is honour among thieves (*English*) Criminals observe their own code of honour between themselves. P. A. Motteux, *Don Quixote*, 1703 (much the same sentiment was expressed in Classical times by Cicero and Publilius Syrus among others). *See also* DOG does not eat dog; HAWKS will not pick out hawks' eyes.

A plague on it when thieves cannot be true one to another.
William Shakespeare, *Henry IV, Part 1*, c.1597

honour. *See also* the more COST the more honour; he that DESIRES honour is not worthy; the POST of honour is the post of danger; a PROPHET is not without honour save in his own country

honours change manners (*Roman*) Those who receive honours and accolades are all too prone to adopt a superior, arrogant attitude to others around them. John Lydgate, *Chaucer*, c.1430.

How I have offended the Lord of Lindesay I know not, unless honours have changed manners.
Walter Scott, *The Abbot*, 1820

hood. the hood does not make the monk *See* the COWL does not make the monk

hook. a hook is well lost to catch a salmon (*English*) Sometimes it is desirable to accept a small sacrifice in order to gain a much greater prize. T. Draxe, *Bibliotheca Scholastica*, 1633.

hook. *See also* the BAIT hides the hook

hope. hope deferred makes the

heart sick (*Hebrew*) The postponement of expected benefit is singularly galling. John Wycliffe, *Bible*, Proverbs 13:13.

And felt what kind of sickness of the heart it was which arises from hope deferred.
Laurence Sterne, *A Sentimental Journey*, 1768

hope for the best and prepare for the worst (*English*) It is good policy to strive for the best possible outcome, but at the same time to guard against things going awry. Norton and Sackville, *Gorboduc*, 1565.

It's best to hope the best, though of the worst affrayd.
Edmund Spenser, *The Faerie Queene*, 1590

hope is a good breakfast but a bad supper (*English*) Hope at the beginning of an enterprise is fine, but it is less healthy if only hope is left at the end. W. Rawley, *Resuscitatio*, 1661. Related proverbs include 'he that lives on hope will die fasting' and 'hope is the poor man's bread'.

hope springs eternal in the human breast (*English*) Mankind is incurably optimistic, however bad things might get. Alexander Pope, *Essay on Man*, 1732. *See also* every CLOUD has a silver lining; the DARKEST hour is just before the dawn; NEVER say die; TOMORROW is another day.

Hope springs eternal in the human breast:
Man never is, but always to be, blest.
The soul, uneasy and confin'd from home,
Rests and expatiates in a life to come.
Alexander Pope, *Essay on Man*, 1732

if it were not for hope, the heart would break (*English*) When everything else goes wrong, hope alone staves off despair. *Ancrene Wisse*, 1250. Related proverbs include 'he that wants hope is the poorest man alive'

and 'he that hopes not for good, fears not evil'.

No harm in hoping, Jack! My uncle says, Were it not for hope, the heart would break.
Samuel Richardson, *Clarissa*, 1748

hope. *See also* where there's LIFE there's hope; he that LIVES in hope dances to an ill tune

hopefully. *See* it is better to TRAVEL hopefully than to arrive

hops. *See* TURKEY, heresy, hops and beer came into England all in one year

horse. have a horse of your own and then you may borrow another's (*Welsh*) If you have a horse of your own, there is more chance that you will be able to persuade another person to lend you theirs. J. Howell, *Paroemiographia*, 1659.

you can lead a horse to water, but you can't make him drink (*English*) A person may be engineered into a position to do something, but it may prove more difficult to persuade them actually to do it. *Old English Homilies*, c.1175. Related proverbs include 'let a horse drink when he will, not what he will'.

'Well,' said she ... 'one man can take a horse to water but a thousand can't make him drink.'
Anthony Trollope, *Barchester Towers*, 1857

horse. *See also* don't put the CART before the horse; a GOOD horse cannot be of a bad colour; it is a GOOD horse that never stumbles; the GREY mare is the better horse; it is too LATE to shut the stable-door after the horse has bolted; all lay LOADS on a willing horse; never LOOK a gift horse in the mouth; the MAN who is born in a stable is a horse; for want of a NAIL the shoe was lost; a NOD is as good as a wink to a blind horse; there is NOTHING so good for the inside of a man as the outside of a horse; a SHORT horse is soon curried; one man may STEAL a horse, while another may not look over a hedge; if TWO ride on a horse, one must ride behind; he that hath a WHITE horse and a fair wife is never without trouble

horseback. *See* set a BEGGAR on horseback, and he'll ride to the Devil

horses. horses for courses (English) Some personalities are better suited to particular enterprises, situations, interests and so on, than others. A. E. T. Watson, *Turf*, 1891. The saying is derived from the world of horseracing, and it refers to the fact that different courses suit particular mounts. *See also* there is no ACCOUNTING for tastes.

the horses of hope gallop, but the asses of experience go slowly (Russian) One's hopes may run on unchecked, but the person who knows better from past experience will exercise caution.

horses. *See also* don't CHANGE horses in mid-stream; if you can't RIDE two horses at once, you shouldn't be in the circus; if WISHES were horses, beggars would ride

hot. hot love is soon cold (English) Over-passionate love soon dies. R. Whitford, *Werke for Housholders*, 1537. Related proverbs include 'hot love, hasty vengeance'.

I hope that such hot love cannot be so soone colde.
John Lyly, *Euphues: The Anatomy of Wit*, 1578

hot. *See also* a LITTLE pot is soon hot; STRIKE while the iron is hot

hounds. *See* you cannot RUN with the hare and hunt with the hounds

hour. an hour in the morning is worth two in the evening (English) Work is best done in the morning, when a person is fresh and willing. William Hone, *Every-day Book*, 1827. A variant of the proverb recommends an hour's work before breakfast, as this is worth two hours at any later time.

one hour's sleep before midnight is worth two after (English) Sleep taken before midnight will bring much more benefit than sleep taken after that hour. George Herbert, *Outlandish Proverbs*, 1640. Herbert, in fact, claims that an hour's sleep before midnight is worth no less than three hours' sleep later. *See also* EARLY to bed and early to rise, makes a man healthy, wealthy and wise.

there is but an hour in a day between a good housewife and a bad (English) It only takes an hour a day for a conscientious housekeeper to keep things in good order. William Hone, *Every-day Book*, 1827.

hour. *See also* the DARKEST hour is just before the dawn; LOSE an hour in the morning, chase it all day

hours. *See* SIX hours' sleep for a man, seven for a woman and eight for a fool

house. a house divided against itself cannot stand (Hebrew) Internal dissension will quickly result in the disintegration of any organization or enterprise. Bible, Mark 3:23–26 (also found in the fables of Aesop). *See also* DIVIDE and rule; UNITED we stand, divided we fall.

How can Satan cast out Satan? And if a kingdom be divided against itself, that kingdom cannot stand. And if a house be divided against itself, that house cannot stand. And if Satan rise up against himself,

and be divided, he cannot stand, but hath an end.
Bible, Mark 3:23–26.

better one house spoiled than two (English) It is preferable for two argumentative or otherwise undesirable people to be married to each other than for them to marry elsewhere and thus blight the lives of other partners. T. B. de la Primaudaye's *French Academy*, 1586. Also encountered in the form 'better one house troubled than two' and 'better one house filled than two spilled'.

Where the old proverb is fulfild, better one house troubled then two.
Robert Greene, *Penelope's Web*, 1587

house. *See also* BY the street of by and by one arrives at the house of never; LEARNING is better than house and land

houses. *See* FOOLS build houses, and wise men live in them; people who live in GLASS houses shouldn't throw stones

Hull. *See* from HELL, Hull and Halifax, good Lord deliver us

human. *See* to ERR is human, to forgive divine

hundred. a hundred pounds of sorrow pays not one ounce of debt (English) Remorse does nothing to repay one's financial obligations to others. George Herbert, *Outlandish Proverbs*, 1640. The version that Herbert quotes runs 'a hundred loade of thought will not pay one ounce of debts'.

hundred. *See also* the BUYER has need of a hundred eyes, the seller of but one

hunger. hunger breaks through stone walls (English) Hunger will drive men to desperate measures, overwhelming any obstacles in the way. John Heywood, *A Dialogue*

containing ... the Proverbs in the English Tongue, 1546.

They said they were an-hungry; sigh'd forth proverbs: That hunger broke stone walls.
William Shakespeare, *Coriolanus*, c.1608

hunger drives the wolf out of the wood (English/French) Necessity will force things previously concealed into the open. William Caxton, *Cato*, 1483.

This one ... I own is the child of necessity. Hunger, thou knowest, brings the wolf out of the wood.
Tobias Smollett, *Gil Blas*, 1748

hunger is the best sauce (Roman) All food tastes good to a person who is very hungry. Cicero, *De Finibus*, first century BC. Related proverbs include 'hunger finds no fault with the cookery', 'hunger makes hard beans sweet' and 'hungry dogs will eat dirty puddings', which was quoted by Horace. A US equivalent runs 'hunger finds no fault with mouldy corn'.

Nor do you Find fault with the sauce, keen hunger being the best.
Philip Massinger, *Unnatural Combat*, 1639

hungry. a hungry man is an angry man (English) Hunger makes men irascible and liable to fight. D. Fergusson, *Scottish Proverbs*, c.1641.

hunt. *See* you cannot RUN with the hare and hunt with the hounds

hurt. *See* no man is ANGRY that feels not himself hurt; what you don't KNOW can't hurt you ; STICKS and stones may break my bones, but names will never hurt me

hurts. he that hurts another hurts himself (English) A person who harms another harms himself, as his conscience will give him no peace and his own reputation will be indelibly stained. John Florio, *First Fruites*, 1578.

husband. the husband is always the last to know (*English*) In cases of marital or other domestic discord it is always the husband (or alternatively the wife) who is the last to hear about it. John Marston, *What you Will*, 1604.

'It is with love as with cuckoldom' – the suffering party is at least the third, but generally the last who knows anything about the matter.
Laurence Sterne, *Tristram Shandy*, 1756

husband. *See also* a DEAF husband and a blind wife are always a happy couple

i

ice. if the ice will bear a man before Christmas, it will not bear a duck after (English) If the ice is thick on the water at Christmas, it is unlikely to be strong enough to stand on in the weeks to follow. M. A. Denham, *A Collection of Proverbs … relating to the Weather*, 1846. Also encountered in the form 'if the ice will bear a goose before Christmas, it will not bear a duck after' (and sometimes heard with a mouse replacing the duck). Variants include 'when November's ice will bear a duck winter will be all slush and muck'.

ice. *See also* the RICH man has his ice in the summer and the poor man gets his in the winter

idle. an idle brain is the Devil's workshop (English) Those who have little to think about easily fall into bad ways. W. Perkins, *Works*, 1602. Variants on the same theme include 'an idle head is a box for the wind', 'an idle person is the Devil's cushion' and 'the Devil tempts all, but the idle man tempts the Devil'. *See also* the DEVIL finds work for idle hands; IDLENESS is the root of all evil.

an idle youth a needy age (English) Those who do not work hard in their youth will find they have nothing laid by to help them in old age. Randle Cotgrave, *A Dictionary of the French and English Tongues*, 1611. Other versions include 'be not idle and you shall not be longing'.

idle people have the least leisure (English) It is those with the most time on their hands who always seem to complain the most about not having enough time to do what they want to do. John Ray, *A Collection of English Proverbs*, 1678. Another proverb observes, 'idle people take the most pains'. *See also* the BUSIEST men have the most leisure.

'Got a great deal to do,' retorted Jog, who, like all thoroughly idle men, was always dreadfully busy.
R. S. Surtees, *Sponge's Sporting Tour*, 1853

idle people lack no excuses (English) Lazy people always have excuses for not doing something. J. Withals, *A Short Dictionary in Latin and English*, 1616.

idle. *See also* it is idle to SWALLOW the cow and choke on the tail

idleness. idleness is the root of all evil (English) Those who have nothing to do are vulnerable to temptation.

Geoffrey Chaucer, *The Canterbury Tales*, *c*.1387. Variants include 'idleness is the parent of all vice', 'of idleness comes no goodness', 'idleness is the key of beggary', 'idleness is the mother of poverty' and 'idleness must thank itself if it go barefoot'. *See also* the DEVIL finds work for idle hands; an IDLE brain is the Devil's workshop; the LOVE of money is the root of all evil.

Idleness is the Root of all Evil; the World's wide enough, let 'em bustle.
George Farquhar, *The Beaux' Strategem*, 1707

idleness turns the edge of wit (*English*) Sloth makes the mind dull and blunts a person's wits. Bodenham, *Belvedere*, 1600. Also encountered as 'idleness makes the wit rust' and 'idleness is the canker of the mind'.

Sloth tourneth the edge of wit, study sharpeneth the mind.
John Lyly, *Euphues: The Anatomy of Wit*, 1578

if. if ifs and ands were pots and pans, there'd be no work for tinkers' hands (*English*) Optimistic views of future possibilities must be tempered by a salutary reminder that these are dependent on other (probably unlikely) things happening first. Charles Kingsley, *Alton Locke*, 1850. Sir Thomas More quoted much the same proverb, in a truncated form, *c*.1535: 'what quod the protectour thou servest me I wene with iffes and with andes'.

Then he came with his If's and And's.
Samuel Richardson, *Clarissa*, 1748

if. *See also* if ANYTHING can go wrong, it will; if the BEARD were all, the goat might preach; if you can't BEAT 'em, join 'em; if the BLIND lead the blind, both shall fall into the ditch; if at FIRST you don't succeed, try, try, try again; if you can't be GOOD, be careful; if a JOB's worth doing, it's worth doing well; if

the MOUNTAIN will not go to Mahomet, Mahomet must go to the mountain; if you can't RIDE two horses at once, you shouldn't be in the circus; if you can't STAND the heat, get out of the kitchen

ignorance. ignorance is a voluntary misfortune (*English*) The ignorant have only themselves to blame for not paying more attention to getting a good education. *Politeuphuia*, 1669.

ignorance is bliss (*Roman*) Sometimes it is better not to know. Thomas Gray, 'Ode on a Distant Prospect of Eton College', 1742 (also found in various forms in the writings of Sophocles and Erasmus). Also encountered in its fuller form 'where ignorance is bliss, 'tis folly to be wise', a direct quotation from Gray's poem. Other proverbs on similar themes include 'ignorance is the peace of life' and 'ignorance and incuriosity are two very soft pillows'. An old Roman proverb runs 'what one knows it is sometimes useful to forget'. Among other diverse comments upon the nature of ignorance are 'ignorance is the mother of devotion' and 'ignorance is the mother of impudence'. *See also* what the EYE does not see, the heart does not grieve over; KNOWLEDGE is power; he that KNOWS nothing, doubts nothing.

Thought would destroy their paradise.
No more; where ignorance is bliss,
'Tis folly to be wise.
Thomas Gray, 'Ode on a Distant Prospect of Eton College', 1742

ignorance of the law is no excuse (*English*) It is no defence to claim that one did not know that what one has done was illegal. Thomas Hoccleve, *The Regiment of Princes*, *c*.1412. This principle has been enshrined in a legal maxim, rendered in Latin as 'ignorantia iuris neminem excusat'.

Ignorance of the Law excuses no man; not that all Men know the Law, but because 'tis an excuse every man will plead, and no man can tell how to confute him.
John Selden, Table-Talk, 1654

ignorance. See also ART has no enemy but ignorance; it is better to CONCEAL one's knowledge than to reveal one's ignorance

ill. an ill agreement is better than a good judgement (English) There is more to be gained by reaching an out-of-court settlement with a rival, however unsatisfactory, than there is by pursuing what may be a good case in law. George Herbert, Jacula Prudentum, 1640.

an ill bird lays an ill egg (English) Bad things must be expected of bad people or organizations. G. Pettie, Guazzo's Civil Conversation, 1581. Equivalent proverbs include 'ill seed, ill weed'.

an ill master makes an ill servant (English) Those who behave badly must expect their servants or employees to do likewise, following their example. G. Torriano, Italian Proverbs, 1666. Among related proverbs is 'an ill servant will never be a good master'.

he that has an ill name is half hanged (English) Those with bad reputations are much more likely to be condemned when suspected of some crime. 1400, quoted in C. Brown, Religious Lyrics of the XIVth Century, 1957.

Your hero makes laws to get rid of your thief, and gives him an ill name that he may hang him.
Thomas Love Peacock, Maid Marian, 1822

ill comes in by ells and goes out by inches (English) Misfortunes accumu-late faster than they go. George Herbert, Jacula Prudentum, 1640.

ill doers are ill dreaders (Roman) Those who do evil are often those who fear evil the most. Alexander Barclay, The Ship of Fools, 1509 (also quoted by Plautus). Also encountered in the form 'ill doers are ill deemers'. See also EVIL doers are evil dreaders.

Put me not to quote the old saw, that evil doers are evil dreaders.
Walter Scott, The Fair Maid of Perth, 1828

ill egging makes ill begging (English) Through enticement and flattery a person may be persuaded to act in an evil manner. William Camden, Remains concerning Britain, 1605.

ill-gotten gains seldom prosper (Greek) Dishonestly acquired goods rarely bring any real benefit with them. Edmund Spenser, Mother Hubbard's Tale, 1591 (also quoted by Hesiod in Opera et Dies in the eighth century BC). Also found as 'ill-gotten goods thrive not' and 'ill-gotten goods thrive not to the third heir'. Equivalent proverbs include 'ill gotten, ill spent', which was quoted by Plautus and Cicero.

Ill-gotten goods ne'er thrive; I played the thief, and now am robbed myself.
Ben Jonson, The Case is Altered, 1609

ill weeds grow apace (English/French) Evil accumulates much faster than good (just as rank weeds grow faster than flowers and herbs). c.1470, quoted in Anglia, 1918.

'Ay,' quoth my uncle Gloucester, 'Small herbs have grace: great weeds do grow apace' ... I would not grow so fast, Because sweet flow'rs are slow and weeds make haste.
William Shakespeare, Richard III, c.1592

it's an ill bird that fouls its own nest (English) Those who commit some crime or act against their own fellows are particularly deserving of condemnation. *The Owl and the Nightingale*, 1250. Variants include 'it's a foul bird that defiles its own nest' and, on a slightly different tack, 'it's an ill bird that pecks out the dam's eyes'. *See also* there is HONOUR among thieves; the JAY bird don't rob his own nest.

An olde proverbe seyde ys in englyssh: men seyn 'that brid or foule ys dyshonest, what that he be and holden ful chirlyssh, that useth to defoule his oone nest.
Thomas Hoccleve, *Minor Poems*, 1402

it's an ill dog that deserves not a crust (Greek) There is a spark of goodness in even the most evil persons, making them deserving of modest acts of kindness. John Ray, *A Collection of English Proverbs*, 1670.

it's an ill wind that blows nobody any good (English) It is rare indeed that someone somewhere does not enjoy benefit from even the worst of situations. John Heywood, *A Dialogue containing ... the Proverbs in the English Tongue*, 1546. The proverb is of nautical origins, referring to the fact that the wind that is blowing in the wrong direction for one ship is probably blowing another ship where it wants to go. *See also* every CLOUD has a silver lining.

Ill blows the wind that profits nobody.
William Shakespeare, *Henry VI, Part 3*, c.1591

it's ill putting a naked sword in a madman's hand (English) It is reckless to give a weapon of any kind to a person who is in a mood to use it. John Heywood, *A Dialogue containing ... the Proverbs in the English Tongue*, 1546.

it's ill speaking between a full man and a fasting (Scottish) There is little

chance of two parties agreeing when one has what the other has not (specifically, when one has eaten and the other is hungry). D. Fergusson, *Scottish Proverbs*, 1641.

Ye maun eat and drink, Steenie ... for we do little else here, and it's ill speaking between a fou man a fasting.
Walter Scott, *Redgauntlet*, 1824

it's ill waiting for dead men's shoes (English) Those who hope to benefit through promotion and so forth on the death of others may have a very long (and bitter) time to wait. J. Palsgrave, *L'Éclaircissement de la langue française*, 1530.

That's but sma' gear, puir thing; she had a sair time o't with the auld leddy. But it's ill waiting for dead folk's shoon.
Walter Scott, *Guy Mannering*, 1815

ill. *See also* when CHILDREN stand still they have done some ill; he that LIVES in hope dances to an ill tune; it is ill SITTING at Rome and striving with the Pope; a SOW may whistle, though it has an ill mouth for it; never SPEAK ill of the dead

imitation is the sincerest form of flattery (English) Attempts made to imitate someone or something should be accepted as a compliment. Charles Caleb Colton, *Lacon*, 1820. The proverb was usually originally encountered without the words 'form of'.

impossible. *See* the DIFFICULT we do at once, the impossible takes a little longer

impressions. *See* FIRST impressions are the most lasting

in. in for a penny, in for a pound (English) If you are going to do something, you might as well commit yourself to it fully. E. Ravenscroft, *Canterbury Guests*, 1695. *See also* you might as well be HANGED for a sheep as for a lamb.

Now, gentlemen, I am not a man who does things by halves. Being in for a penny, I am ready as the saying is to be in for a pound.
Charles Dickens, *The Old Curiosity Shop*, 1841

in. *See also* in the COUNTRY of the blind, the one-eyed man is king

inch. an inch is as good as a mile (English) It makes little difference in the long run whether a man is defeated by a narrow margin or a large one. John Heywood, *A Dialogue containing ... the Proverbs in the English Tongue*, 1546. The proverb was originally often rendered with 'yard' or 'ell' (about 45 inches, based on the length of a person's forearm) in the place of 'mile'. *See also* a MISS is as good as a mile.

His great surprise was, that so small a pistol could kill so big a man ... an inch was as good as an ell.
Walter Scott, *The Heart of Midlothian*, 1818

inclined. *See* as the TWIG is bent, so is the tree inclined

Indian. *See* the only GOOD Indian is a dead one

Indies. *See* he who would BRING home the wealth of the Indies, must carry the wealth of the Indies with him

industry is fortune's right hand, and frugality her left (English) Hard work and thrift will be rewarded. *Havelok the Dane*, c.1300.

... a proverb which has been worth ten times more to me than all my little purse contained.
Maria Edgeworth, *Popular Tales*, 1799

infinite. *See* GENIUS is an infinite capacity for taking pains

innocent. everyone is innocent until proved guilty (English) No one should be presumed guilty until actually proved to be so. *Spectator*, 6 August 1910. Another proverb, however, warns that 'innocence is no protection'.

inside. *See* there is NOTHING so good for the inside of a man as the outside of a horse

intentions. *See* the ROAD to hell is paved with good intentions

interest will not lie (English) Interest in something will persuade a person to do what he or she would not otherwise venture to do. John Bunyan, *Work of Jesus Christ*, 1688.

Our English proverb is, Interest will not lie; interest will make a man do that which otherwise he would not do.
John Bunyan, *Work of Jesus Christ*, 1688

invention. *See* NECESSITY is the mother of invention

Ireland. *See* ENGLAND's difficulty is Ireland's opportunity

iron. *See* STRIKE while the iron is hot

irons. many irons in the fire, some must cool (English) A person who tries to pursue several projects at once will find that some at least fail to prosper or hold their interest. W. Paget, *Letter to Somerset*, c.1549.

Make haste, then; for I have more irons in the fire.
John Dryden, *An Evening's Love*, 1671

j

Jack. every Jack has his Jill (English)
For every man there is a woman
who will be for him an ideal match.
John Skelton, *Magnyfycence*, 1529.
Often quoted to reassure those
who despair of ever finding a mate.
Also found as 'never a Jack but there's
a Jill'. Equivalents include 'every pot
has its lid'. *See also* a GOOD Jack makes
a good Jill; MARRIAGES are made in
heaven.

Jack shall have Jill;
Nought shall go ill.
William Shakespeare, *A Midsummer Night's
Dream*, c.1596

Jack is as good as his master
(English) All men are equal, though
some be servants and others masters. J.
Stevens, *Spanish and English Dictionary*,
1706.

Is it the general opinion of seamen before
the mast? Come, tell us. Jack's as good as
his master in these matters.
Charles Reade and Dion Boucicault, *Foul Play*,
1868

Jack of all trades is master of none
(English) Those who claim mastery of
a wide range of skills are unlikely
in reality to be really adept at
anything. Maria Edgeworth, *Popular
Tales*, 1800. Also encountered in the

form 'Jack of all trades is of no
trade'. Equivalents in other languages
include the French saying 'when one
is good at everything, one is good at
nothing' and the German proverb 'the
master of one trade will support a
wife and seven children: the master
of seven trades will not support
himself'.

Old Lewis Baboon was a sort of Jack of all
trades, which made the rest of the trades-
men jealous.
John Arbuthnot, *John Bull*, 1712

Jack. *See also* a GOOD Jack makes a good
Jill; all WORK and no play makes Jack a
dull boy

**jade. a jade eats as much as a good
horse** (English) It costs just as much to
keep a poor quality horse (or by
extension, a wife, etc.) as it does to
keep a good one. George Herbert,
Jacula Prudentum, 1640.

**jam tomorrow and jam yesterday,
but never jam today** (English)
Promises may be made of good times
to come, or references made to good
times past, but only rarely are these
promises realized in the present. Lewis
Carroll, *Through the Looking-Glass*, 1871.

'The rule is, jam to-morrow and jam yesterday – but never jam to-day.' 'It must come

sometimes to "jam to-day",' Alice objected. 'No, it can't,' said the Queen.
Lewis Carroll, *Through the Looking-Glass*, 1871

January. a January spring is worth nothing (English) Mild weather in January is no guarantee that there will be mild weather in the months to follow. M. A. Denham, *Proverbs relating to the Weather*, 1846. Another proverb is more explicit: 'a summerish January, a winterish spring', while another exclaims 'January warm, the Lord have mercy!' Other ominous signs for the months to come that may be detected in January include the first signs of growing grass.

jaundiced. to the jaundiced eye all things look yellow (English) Those with a cynical view of life will see the bad in everything. Geoffrey Chaucer, *The Canterbury Tales*, c.1387. It was formerly widely believed that all people with jaundice saw the world in a yellow tint.

All looks yellow to the jaundic'd eye.
Alexander Pope, *Essay on Criticism*, 1709

jaw. *See* JOUK and let the jaw go by

jay. the jay bird don't rob his own nest (West Indian) Thieves do not steal from their own fellows. *See also* there is HONOUR among thieves; it's an ILL bird that fouls its own nest.

jest. *See* there's many a TRUE word spoken in jest

jewel. *See* FAIR play is a jewel

Jill. *See* a GOOD Jack makes a good Jill; every JACK has his Jill

Joan is as good as my lady in the dark (English) Matters of rank are unimportant in certain circumstances. Anthony Munday, *The Downfall of the Earl of Huntingdon*, 1601.

Much also we shall omit about confusion of Ranks, and Joan and My Lady.
Thomas Carlyle, *Sartor Resartus*, 1838

job. if a job's worth doing, it's worth doing well (English) Having decided to do something, it is worth making the extra effort to do the job well, rather than leaving things slipshod. Lord Chesterfield, letter, 10 March 1746. Often encountered with the word 'thing' replacing 'job'. Charles Dickens often quoted the proverb, while G. K. Chesterton offered comfort to those who make the extra effort but find the results do not match their expectations: 'if a thing is worth doing, it is worth doing badly'. *See also* don't SPOIL the ship for a ha'-porth of tar.

'If a thing's worth doing at all,' said the Professor ... 'it's worth doing well.'
H. G. Wells, *Bealby*, 1915

join. *See* if you can't BEAT 'em, join 'em

jouk and let the jaw go by (Scottish) Act with caution to avoid trouble. James Kelly, *A Complete Collection of Scotish Proverbs*, 1721. 'Jouk' is a Scottish dialect word for 'stoop', while 'jaw' signifies a torrent of water.

Gang your ways hame, like a gude bairn – jouk and let the jaw gae by.
Walter Scott, *Rob Roy*, 1817

Jove but laughs at lovers' perjury (Roman) Promises between lovers' are rarely kept. William Shakespeare, *Romeo and Juliet*, c.1593 (also quoted by Tibullus in *Elegies* in the first century BC). Also encountered in the form 'Jove laughs at lovers' lies'.

Love endures no Tie, And Jove but laughs at Lovers Perjury!
John Dryden, *Poems*, 1700

judge. a judge knows nothing unless it has been explained to him three times (English) Only after constant repetition will a judge understand anything. Another proverb, quoted by Geoffrey Chaucer in the fourteenth century, claims 'a good judge conceives quickly, judges slowly'.

don't judge a man by the words of his mother, listen to the comments of his neighbours (Yiddish) To find out what a man is really like do not rely on what his mother says, as her views will be biased, but talk to his neighbours.

judge not, that ye be not judged (Hebrew) Do not condemn others for their failings, in case you find yourself similarly condemned. Bible, Matthew 7:1. Related proverbs include 'who judges others, condemns himself'.

Deme ye noman, and ye shal not be demed.
William Caxton, *Reynard the Fox*, 1481

never judge by appearances (Hebrew) Do not rely upon physical appearance as a guide to character. Bible, John 7:24. One of many proverbs with biblical origins – though many centuries later, in 1891, the wit Oscar Wilde, in *The Picture of Dorian Gray*, observed 'it is only the shallow people who do not judge by appearances'. Variants include 'you cannot judge a tree by its bark'. *See also* APPEARANCES are deceptive; the COWL does not make the monk; FINE feathers make fine birds.

Judge not according to the appearance, but judge righteous judgement.
Bible, John 7:24

no one should be judge in his own cause (English) All judges should be impartial and have no personal interest in the cases they hear. R. Pecock, *Repressor of Blaming of Clergy*, c.1449. The principle is enshrined in a legal maxim, rendered in Latin as '*nemo debet esse iudex in propria causa*'.

No man is a good judge in his own cause. I believe I am tolerably impartial.
John Wesley, letter, 3 November 1775

judge. *See also* you can't judge a BOOK by its cover

June. *See* a DRIPPING June sets all in tune

just. a just war is better than an unjust peace (Roman) A war fought for good reasons is preferable to a peace founded on injustice. Samuel Daniel, *A History of the Civil Wars between York and Lancaster*, 1595 (also found in the writings of Tacitus).

For oft we see a wicked peace
To be well chang'd for war.
Samuel Daniel, *Ulysses and Siren*, 1605

be just before you're generous (English) Bear in mind your existing obligations to others before acting generously to third parties. E. Haywood, *Female Spectator*, 1745.

I owe every farthing of my money ... There's an old proverb – be just before you're generous.
Frederick Marryat, *Peter Simple*, 1834

justice. *See* the CLERK makes the justice

justifies. *See* the END justifies the means

k

ka me, ka thee (English) You do me a favour and I will do you a favour in return. John Heywood, *A Dialogue containing ... the Proverbs in the English Tongue*, 1546. *See also* you SCRATCH my back and I'll scratch yours.

Ka me, ka thee – it is a proverb all over the world.
Walter Scott, *Kenilworth*, 1821

keep. keep a thing seven years and you'll always find a use for it (English) Never assume a thing is useless, as time will reveal how it may be usefully employed. W. Painter, *Palace of Pleasure*, 1623.

According to the Proverb; Keep a thing seven years, and then if thou hast no use on't throw't away.
Thomas Killigrew, *Parson's Wedding*, 1663

keep bad men company and you'll soon be of their number (English) Those who mix with bad company will inevitably be influenced by them. George Herbert, *Jacula Prudentum*, 1640.

keep no more cats than will catch mice (English) Only keep what is useful. J. Dare, *Counsellor Manners*, 1673. This is often quoted with reference to employees or family members who fail to earn their keep.

Keep no more Cats than will Catch Mice. Ecquipage and Attendance ... must be agreeable to Character, Dignity and Fortune.
S. Palmer, *Moral Essays on Proverbs*, 1710

keep something for the sore foot (English) Save something for when one is old, ill or otherwise hard-pressed. James Kelly, *A Complete Collection of Scotish Proverbs*, 1721. *See also* SAVE something for a rainy day.

Preserve something for age, distress, and necessity.
James Kelly, *A Complete Collection of Scotish Proverbs*, 1721

keep your mouth shut and your eyes open (English) It is good policy to say little but remain vigilant to what goes on around you. S. Palmer, *Moral Essays on Proverbs*, 1710. Variants include the US proverb 'keep your eyes wide open before marriage, and half shut afterwards'.

Keep your mouth close an' your een open.
A. Ramsay, *A Collection of Scots Proverbs*, 1737

keep your shop and your shop will keep you (English) Look after your business and you will prosper by it. George Chapman and others, *Eastward Hoe*, 1605. Variants include 'keep your house and your house will keep you'.

I would earnestly recommend this adage to every mechanic in London, 'Keep your shop, and your shop will keep you.'
Oliver Goldsmith, in *The Bee*, 17 November 1759

keep your weather-eye open (English) Keep a good lookout for changes in the weather (or for trouble of any kind). Admiral Smyth, *Sailor's Word-Book*, 1867. Originally a nautical proverb: lookouts on ships were supposed to keep their 'weather-eye' towards the wind, watching for sudden squalls.

why keep a dog and bark yourself? (English) It is senseless to do something yourself when you are paying someone else to do it. B. Melbancke, *Philotimus*, 1583.

What? keep a dog and bark my self. That is, must I keep servants, and do my work my self.
John Ray, *A Collection of English Proverbs*, 1670

keep. *See also* THREE may keep a secret, if two of them are dead; put your TRUST in God, and keep your powder dry

keepers. *See* FINDERS keepers, losers weepers

keeps. *See* EXPERIENCE keeps a dear school; a MAN is known by the company he keeps

kettle. *See* the POT calls the kettle black

key. *See* a GOLDEN key can open any door

kill not the goose that lays the golden egg (Greek) Do not make changes that will result in the loss of some benefit to yourself. William Caxton, *Aesop's Fables*, 1484. *See also* don't throw the BABY out with the bathwater.

A man ... had a goose, which everie daie laid him a golden egge, hee ... kild his goose, thinking to have a mine of golde in

her bellie, and finding nothing but dung, ... wisht his goose alive.
John Lyly, *Pappe with Hatchet*, c.1589

killed. *See* CARE killed the cat; CURIOSITY killed the cat

killing. killing no murder (English) In certain circumstances killing someone should be regarded as no crime. Sexby and Titus, *Killing Noe Murder*, 1657 (a notorious Royalist-backed pamphlet, published in Holland, that called for the assassination of the Lord Protector, Oliver Cromwell). Colonel Edward Sexby, one of the authors of the celebrated pamphlet, was a Leveller who in 1657 narrowly failed to kill Cromwell himself. Sometimes attributed to Irish origins.

In Ireland, not only cowards, but the brave 'die many times before their death'. There killing is no murder.
Maria Edgeworth, *Castle Rackrent*, 1800

killing. *See also* there are more WAYS of killing a cat than choking it with cream; there are more WAYS of killing a dog than choking it with butter

kills. *See* it is the PACE that kills; it is not WORK that kills, but worry

kind. *See* you've got to CRUEL to be kind; better a GOOD cow than a cow of a good kind

kindle not a fire that you cannot extinguish (English) Do not start trouble that might overwhelm you. B. R., *Euterpe*, 1584.

kindness is lost that is bestowed on children and old folks (Greek) The young and the very old will soon forget any kindness showed them. Alexander Barclay, *The Ship of Fools*, 1509 (originally attributed to Aristotle).

king. a king without learning is but a crowned ass (English) A monarch who lacks education is a fool, despite the fact that he is of high status in society. John Berners, *Huon of Bordeaux*, c. 1534.

the king can do no wrong (English) An absolute monarch is the source of ultimate legal authority, and is thus technically above the law, being immune to the actions of the courts. John Selden, *Table-Talk*, 1689. The principle is enshrined in the legal maxim 'rex non potest peccare'. The proverb may be applied to anybody who occupies a position of supreme influence. In 1977 disgraced US president Richard Nixon quoted it in an attempt to justify his actions during the 'Watergate' scandal prior to his resignation: 'When the President does it, that means it is not illegal.'

The King can do no wrong ... The prerogative of the crown extends not to do any injury: it is created for the benefit of the people, and therefore cannot be exerted to their prejudice.
William Blackstone, *Commentaries on the Laws of England*, 1765

the king can make a knight, but not a gentleman (English) Aristocratic fine manners are inbred and cannot be acquired by virtue of rank or bestowed by others, even by monarchs. John Selden, *Table-Talk*, 1689.

king. *See also* a CAT may look at a king; in the COUNTRY of the blind, the one-eyed man is king; a PECK of March dust is worth a king's ransom

kings have long arms (Greek) The influence of the powerful may extend a considerable distance. R. Taverner, *Proverbs or Adages of Erasmus*, 1539 (also quoted by Ovid in *Heroides*, AD 166). Related proverbs include 'kings have many ears and many eyes', which may be found in the writings of Lucian. The notion of long-armed influence is most familiar in the UK in the phrase 'the long arm of the law'.

Kings have long Arms, but misfortune longer.
Benjamin Franklin, *Poor Richard's Almanack*, 1752

kiss. many kiss the child for the nurse's sake (English) In certain circumstances kindness or favours may be shown to someone in order to impress a third party. John Heywood, *A Dialogue containing ... the Proverbs in the English Tongue*, 1546 (also recorded in thirteenth-century manuscripts). *See also* PRAISE the child and you make love to the mother.

Many one kisses the bairn for love of the nurrish. That is, shows their kindness to the companions, friends, or relations, of those upon whom they have a design, which they hope by their influence to effect.
James Kelly, *A Complete Collection of Scotish Proverbs*, 1721

kissing goes by favour (English) People are free to bestow their favours (as they do their kisses) on whoever they choose. William Camden, *Remainings concerning Britain*, 1605.

Kissing goes by Favour. Men shew Regard, or do Service, to People as they affect.
James Kelly, *A Complete Collection of Scotish Proverbs*, 1721

kissing. *See also* when the GORSE is out of bloom, kissing's out of fashion

kitchen. kitchen physic is the best physic (English) The best remedies are to be found in the kitchen. W. Bullein, *Bulwarke of Defence*, 1562.

kitchen. *See also* if you can't STAND the heat, get out of the kitchen

kittens. *See* WANTON kittens make sober cats

knapsack. *See* every SOLDIER has the baton of a field-marshal in his knapsack

knaves and fools divide the world (English) The entire population of the world is either wicked or stupid. John Ray, *A Collection of English Proverbs*, 1670.

knife. *See* never CATCH at a falling knife or friend

knocks. *See* OPPORTUNITY seldom knocks twice at any man's door

know. know thyself (Greek) Self-knowledge should be the goal of everyone. J. Trevisa, *Higden's Polychronicon*, 1387 (also attributed to Solon and found in the writings of Pausanias and Juvenal, among other Classical writers). The proverb was originally inscribed at the temple of Apollo at Delphi.

Know then thyself, presume not God to scan; The proper study of Mankind is Man. Alexander Pope, *Essay on Man*, 1732

what you don't know can't hurt you (English) Some secrets are best left undisclosed, as knowledge of them would only cause trouble. G. Pettie, *Petite Pallace*, 1576. *See also* IGNORANCE is bliss.

So long as I know it not, it hurteth mee not. G. Pettie, *Petite Pallace*, 1576

you never know what you can do till you try (English) Lack of confidence that you can do something should not hold you back from at least attempting to do it. William Cobbett, *A Year's Residence in the USA*, 1818.

I have often heard my poor old uncle say that no man knows what he can do till he tries.

Captain Frederick Marryat, *Frank Mildmay*, 1829

you should know a man seven years before you stir his fire (English) You should wait until you know someone very thoroughly before you assume you are entitled to interfere in his or her private life. Charles Dibdin, *Professional Life*, 1803.

know. *See also* better the DEVIL you know than the devil you don't know; HALF the world doesn't know how the other half lives; the HUSBAND is always the last to know; come LIVE with me and you'll know me; MORE people know Tom Fool than Tom Fool knows

knowledge. knowledge is power (English) Those who have knowledge of something are automatically put at an advantage. Francis Bacon, *Meditationes Sacrae: De Haeresibus*, c.1626. Another proverb supports this view, stating that at the very least 'knowledge is no burden'. *See also* FOREWARNED is forearmed; IGNORANCE is bliss; MONEY is power.

A man of knowledge encreaseth strength. Bible, Proverbs 24:5

knowledge. *See also* it is better to CONCEAL one's knowledge than to reveal one's ignorance

known. *See* a MAN is known by the company he keeps; the TREE is known by its fruit

knows. he knows best what good is that has endured evil (English) Only a person who has personal experience of evil can really distinguish what is genuinely good. H. G. Bohn, *A Handbook of Proverbs*, 1855.

he knows how many beans make five (English) He is no fool and is not easily deceived. John Galt, *Laurie Todd*, 1830. This proverb refers to an ancient trick question, in which a person is first asked how many beans make five (five) and is then asked how many blue beans make five white ones. The answer is five, peeled.

he that knows little, often repeats it (English) Those who possess only a few facts or stories take every opportunity to repeat them. J. Mapletoft, *Select Proverbs*, 1707. Another, rather contradictory, proverb claims 'who knows most, speaks least'.

he that knows nothing, doubts nothing (French) Those who know no better have no reason to question anything. Randle Cotgrave, *A Dictionary of the French and English Tongues*, 1611.

knows. *See also* NECESSITY knows no law; it is a WISE child that knows its own father

1

labour is light where love doth pay
(English) Work goes easily when it is done for reasons of love. Thomas Drayton, *Ideas*, 1594.

labourer. the labourer is worthy of his hire (Hebrew) A good workman is entitled to payment for his service. Bible, Luke 10:7.

Your service will not be altogether gratuitous, my old friend – the labourer is worthy of his hire.
Walter Scott, St Ronan's Well, 1824

ladders. *See* CROSSES are ladders that lead to heaven

ladies. *See* FAR-fetched and dear-bought is good for ladies

lady. *See* FAINT heart ne'er won fair lady; the GIST of a lady's letter is in the postscript; the OPERA isn't over till the fat lady sings

lamb. *See* GOD tempers the wind to the shorn lamb; you might as well be HANGED for a sheep as for a lamb; MARCH comes in like a lion and goes out like a lamb

lame. the lame tongue gets nothing (English) Those who are incapable or unwilling to put their case verbally are unlikely to gain any reward.

William Camden, *Remains concerning Britain*, 1605.

land. every land has its own law (Scottish) Each nation has it own legal codes, with its own peculiar emphases. J. Carmichaell, *Proverbs in Scots*, 1628.

Every land hath its own Laugh, and every Corn its own Caff. Every Country hath its own Laws, Customs and Usages.
James Kelly, A Complete Collection of Scotish Proverbs, 1721

he that hath land hath quarrels (English) Anyone who owns land has to accept that it is likely to lead to contention of some kind in the future. George Herbert, *Jacula Prudentum*, 1640. Also found as 'he that hath land hath war'. Another proverb warns 'he that hath some land, must have some labour'.

land was never lost for want of an heir (Italian) There is never any shortage of heirs when it comes to the estates of the rich. John Ray, *A Collection of English Proverbs*, 1678.

land. *See also* you BUY land you buy stones, you buy meat you buy bones; LEARNING is better than house and land

lane. *See* it is a LONG lane that has no turning

lapwing. the lapwing cries farthest from her nest (English) To deceive predators, lapwings attempt to draw attention away from their nest by making as much noise as they can from a distance. John Lyly, *Euphues and His England*, 1580.

Far from her nest the lapwing cries away: My heart prays for him, though my tongue do curse.
William Shakespeare, *The Comedy of Errors*, c.1593

larks. *See* if the SKY falls we shall catch larks

last. it is the last straw that breaks the camel's back (Roman) When things are at breaking point it takes very little to swing the balance. J. Bramhall, *The Defence of True Liberty of Human Actions*, 1655 (also quoted by Seneca). Variants over the years have included 'it is the last feather that breaks the horse's back'.

As the last straw breaks the laden camel's back, this piece of underground information crushed the sinking spirits of Mr Dombey.
Charles Dickens, *Dombey and Son*, 1848

last make fast (English) The last person to come through a door or gate should close it behind him. *Douce MS*, c.1350.

our last garment is made without pockets (Italian) All men are fated to die and thus to be deprived of all their earthly possessions. R. C. Trench, *On the Lessons in Proverbs*, 1853. The last garment in question is a shroud.

the last drop makes the cup run over (English) When things are on the brink it only requires the smallest additional thing or event to tip the scales. Thomas Fuller, *The Church History of Britain*, 1655. *See also* it is the LAST straw that breaks the camel's back.

last. *See also* there are NO BIRDS in last year's nest; let the COBBLER stick to his last; the HUSBAND is always the last to know; he who LAUGHS last laughs longest; NICE guys finish last

lasting. *See* FIRST impressions are the most lasting

late. better late than never (Roman) Doing something late is better than not doing it at all. *Ancrene Riwle*, c.1200 (also quoted by Livy c.10 BC). Ambrose Bierce added his own light-hearted version of the proverb, writing 'better late than before anybody has invited you'.

Oh, Mr Dexter, we have been so anxious, but better late than never. Let me introduce you to Miss Wilbraham and Gräfin von Meyersdorf.
Graham Greene, *The Third Man*, 1950

he that riseth late must trot all day (US) A person who gets up late must spend the rest of the day working at top speed in order to catch up. Coined by Benjamin Franklin. *See also* an HOUR in the morning is worth two in the evening.

it is never too late to learn (English) Age is no bar to learning. Roger L'Estrange, *Seneca's Morals*, 1678. *See also* you're never too OLD to learn; you can't TEACH an old dog new tricks.

it is never too late to mend (English) Things can still be put right, however much time has passed. Robert Greene, *Never Too Late*, 1590. *See also* a STITCH in time saves nine.

it is too late to shut the stable-door after the horse has bolted (Roman) It is useless taking precautions to prevent something that has already happened. *Douce MS, c.* 1350 (also quoted by Plautus). Alternative versions of the proverb include 'when your daughter is stolen, close Pepper Gate' – Pepper Gate being a gate on the road leading out of Chester that on one occasion was belatedly ordered to be closed on the mayor's orders after the mayor's own daughter eloped with her lover.

It was only shutting the Stable Door after the Stead was stoln.
Daniel Defoe, *Robinson Crusoe*, 1719

late children, early orphans (English) Children who are born to elderly parents are likely to be orphaned at a relatively early age. Benjamin Franklin, *Poor Richard's Almanack*, 1742.

late. *See also* the EARLY man never borrows from the late man

laugh. laugh and grow fat (English) A person with a jovial, jolly nature grows fat on the comforts of a carefree life. John Harington, *The Metamorphosis of Ajax*, 1596.

He seems to have reversed the old proverb of 'laugh and be fat'.
Walter Scott, *Peveril of the Peak*, 1823

laugh and the world laughs with you; weep and you weep alone (Greek) Others are always ready to keep company with those who approach the world in a confident frame of mind, but those who are gloomy and troubled will find themselves shunned. Ella Wheeler Wilcox, 'Solitude', 1883 (the same sentiments were expressed by Horace many centuries before).

Rejoyce with them that doe rejoice, and weepe with them that weepe.
Bible, Romans 12:15

laugh before breakfast, you'll cry before supper (English) Those who rejoice too early (perhaps literally before breakfast) may find their premature joy reversed later on. James Kelly, *A Complete Collection of Scotish Proverbs*, 1721. Sometimes encountered with 'sing' in the place of 'laugh'. Equivalent proverbs include 'laugh at leisure, you may weep before night'.

let them laugh that win (English) Those who come out on top are entitled to congratulate themselves. John Heywood, *A Dialogue containing ... the Proverbs in the English Tongue*, 1546.

So, so, so, so. They laugh that win.
William Shakespeare, *Othello*, c.1602

laughed. he is not laughed at that laughs at himself first (English) Making fun at your own expense is a way of forestalling the gibes of others. Thomas Fuller, *Gnomologia*, 1732.

laughs. he who laughs last laughs longest (English) He who finishes up on top at the end of something enjoys the most lasting victory. John Masefield, *The Widow in the Bye-Street*, 1912. The proverb in its modern form is closely related to the more old-fashioned 'he laughs best who laughs last', which was first recorded in both French and Italian and was being heard in English as early as 1706, when Sir John Vanbrugh quoted it in his play *The Country House*. Archaic equivalents include 'better the last smile than the first laughter'.

In this life he laughs longest who laughs last.
John Masefield, *The Widow in the Bye-Street*, 1912

laughs. *See also* JOVE but laughs at lovers' perjury; LOVE laughs at locksmiths

laughter is the best medicine (English)
A good laugh is the best remedy for
most ills. Opinions about the effica-
cious effects of laughter are not unan-
imous: another proverb warns 'laugh
till you cry, sorrow till you die'.

**law. he that goes to law holds a wolf
by the ears** (English) Any person who
takes a complaint to the courts risks
bringing down the wrath of the law
upon himself. Richard Burton, *The
Anatomy of Melancholy*, 1621.

**in a thousand pounds of law
there's not an ounce of love** (English)
There is no place in the law for sentiment or sympathy. Randle Cotgrave, *A
Dictionary of the French and English Tongues*,
1611.

**law governs man, and reason the
law** (English) Man is bound by the law,
which in turn (at least in theory) is
governed by logic and reason. Thomas
Fuller, *Gnomologia*, 1732.

the law is a bottomless pit (English)
Pursuing a case through the courts
will exhaust the richest purse. John
Arbuthnot, *John Bull*, 1712. Archaic
equivalents include 'law is a lickpen-
ny' and 'law is a pickpurse'. Another
proverb warns 'lawsuits consume
time, and money, and rest, and
friends'.

Law is a bottomless pit; it is a cormorant, a
harpy, that devours everything.
John Arbuthnot, *John Bull*, 1712

the law is an ass (English) Laws are not
always wise, just or sensible. George
Chapman, *Revenge for Honour*, 1634.

'If the law supposes that,' said Mr Bumble
... 'the law is a ass – an idiot.'
Charles Dickens, *Oliver Twist*, 1838

**there's one law for the rich and
another for the poor** (English) The
rich get more lenient treatment from

the legal establishment than the poor
do. Captain Frederick Marryat, *The
King's Own*, 1830. Related proverbs
include 'laws catch flies, but let the
hornets go free', recorded in the early
fifteenth century, and 'laws are like
cobwebs: while the small flies are
caught the great break through'.
Another takes a broader approach:
'rich men have no faults'. Much the
same sentiment is expressed in the
traditional rhyme: 'the law doth punish man or woman that steals the
goose from off the common, but lets
the greater felon loose that steals the
common from the goose'.

Is there nothing smuggled besides gin?
Now, if the husbands and fathers of
these ladies – those who have themselves
enacted the laws – wink at their infringe-
ment, why should not others do so? ...
There cannot be one law for the rich and
another for the poor.
Captain Frederick Marryat, *King's Own*, 1830

law. *See also* AGREE, for the law is costly;
HARD cases make bad law; IGNORANCE of
the law is no excuse; every LAND has its
own law; NECESSITY knows no law; POS-
SESSION is nine points of the law; SELF-
preservation is the first law of nature

laws. *See* where DRUMS beat, laws are
silent; NEW lords, new laws

**lawyer. a good lawyer makes a bad
neighbour** (English) Lawyers make
bad neighbours, because they are in a
position to use their knowledge of the
law to their own advantage. Randle
Cotgrave, *A Dictionary of the French and
English Tongues*, 1611. Also found as 'a
good lawyer, an evil neighbour'.

a good lawyer must be a great liar
(English/French) To succeed in the law a
man must be an accomplished liar. J.
Smith, *Grammatica Quadrilinguis*, 1674.

a lawyer's opinion is worth nothing unless paid for (English) A lawyer gives good advice only when he has been paid. William Shakespeare, *King Lear*, 1605.

Then 'tis like the breath of an unfee'd lawyer, you gave me nothing for't.
William Shakespeare, *King Lear*, 1605

a man who is his own lawyer has a fool for a client (English) Anyone who relies upon his own judgement in the courts rather than employ someone with relevant specialist knowledge is a fool. Philadelphia Port Folio, 1809.

a wise lawyer never goes to law himself (English) Those who practise the law and thereby know its limitations and the costs involved never make the mistake of taking their own cases to court. G. Torriano, *Select Italian Proverbs*, 1642.

lawyers' houses are built on the heads of fools (English) Lawyers earn their salaries through the foolishness of their clients, who in the course of pursuing frequently hopeless cases run up huge legal bills. George Herbert, *Jacula Prudentum*, 1640. Related proverbs to much the same effect include 'lawyers' gowns are lined with the wilfulness of their clients'.

lay. *See* all lay LOADS on a willing horse; it is easier to RAISE the Devil than to lay him

lay-overs for meddlers (English/US) Those who meddle in matters that do not concern them will be punished ('lay-overs' – or 'layers' – being smacks). F. Grose, *Classical Dictionary of the Vulgar Tongue*, 1785. Quoted as a threat to over-inquisitive or impertinent children.

lazy. *See* LONG and lazy, little and loud

lead. *See* if the BLIND lead the blind, both shall fall into the ditch; CROSSES are ladders that lead to heaven; you can lead a HORSE to water, but you can't make him drink; all ROADS lead to Rome

leak. *See* a LITTLE leak will sink a great ship

leap. a leap year is never a good sheep year (English) Livestock never prosper in leap years. J. Chamber, *Treatise against Judicial Astrology*, 1601.

men leap over where the hedge is lowest (English) Those in the weakest position make the easiest targets for others. John Heywood, *A Dialogue containing ... the Proverbs in the English Tongue*, 1546. Variants include 'everyone leaps over the dyke where it is lowest'.

Men loup the dike where it is leaghest. That is, oppress and over-run those who are least able to resist them.
James Kelly, *A Complete Collection of Scotish Proverbs*, 1721

leap. *See also* LOOK before you leap

leaping. there's no leaping from Delilah's lap into Abraham's bosom (English) Those who live lives of sin and debauchery on Earth cannot expect to enter Heaven, the abode of Abraham, when they die.

learn. *See* it is never too LATE to learn; LIVE and learn; you're never too OLD to learn; we must learn to WALK before we can run; don't go near the WATER until you learn how to swim

learning. a little learning is a dangerous thing (English) Incomplete knowledge of something can be more dangerous than no knowledge of it at all. Alexander Pope, *Essay on Criticism*, 1711. Also encountered as 'a little knowledge is a dangerous thing'.

Other proverbs warning of the potential dangers of education include 'learning in a prince is like a knife in the hand of a madman'. Ambrose Bierce, meanwhile, dismissed learning as 'the kind of ignorance distinguishing the studious'. *See also* IGNORANCE is bliss.

A little learning is a dang'rous thing;
Drink deep, or taste not the Pierian spring:
There shallow draughts intoxicate the brain,
And drinking largely sobers us again.
Alexander Pope, *Essay on Criticism*, 1711

learning is better than house and land (English) A good education is more valuable than the possession of property. Samuel Foote, *Taste*, 1752. Variants include 'when house and land are gone and spent, then learning is most excellent'.

When ign'rance enters, folly is at hand;
Learning is better far than house and land.
David Garrick, prologue to Oliver Goldsmith, *She Stoops to Conquer*, 1773

learning. *See also* there is no ROYAL road to learning

least said, soonest mended (English) The less one says after committing some lapse of good behaviour the less time it will take to repair relationships with those thus offended. *The Parlement of Byrdes*, c.1460. Formerly usually encountered in the form 'little said soon amended'.

I should be angry if I proceed in my guesses – and little said is soon amended.
Samuel Richardson, *Clarissa*, 1748

least. *See also* IDLE people have the least leisure

leather. there is nothing like leather (English) Those with vested interests in or specialist knowledge of something are first to recommend their own

wares, services, and so on. Roger L'Estrange, *Aesop*, 1692. The proverb is also heard in a literal context, usually applauding the hardwearing qualities of leather. The story goes that when a certain town was threatened by a siege the town council called a meeting to discuss how best to fortify their defences. A shipbuilder immediately recommended wooden walls and the stonemason spoke up in favour of stone, but the local currier had no doubts: 'there is nothing like leather'.

'I dare say, my remark came from the professional feeling of there being nothing like leather,' replied Mr Hale.
Elizabeth Gaskell, *North and South*, 1855

leave. leave no stone unturned (Greek) Spare no effort or neglect no possibility when looking for something or undertaking some task. *Dice-Play*, c.1550 (also quoted by Euripides and Pliny).

leave off while the play is good (English) Quit while you are ahead. *Douce MS*, c.1350.

When I saw our host break ranks ... I e'en pricked off with myself while the play was good.
Walter Scott, *The Monastery*, 1820

leave well alone (Roman) If something is more or less satisfactory as it stands it is best not to interfere with it. Geoffrey Chaucer, *Envoy to Bukton*, c.1386 (also quoted by Terence in the second century BC). Often encountered as 'let well alone'. The saying was adopted as a maxim by the British prime minister Lord Melbourne in the mid-nineteenth century. *See also* if it ain't BROKE, don't fix it; LET well alone; let SLEEPING dogs lie.

He knew when to let well alone, a knowledge which is more precious than a

knowledge of geography.
Arnold Bennett, *The Card*, 1911

leaves. if on the trees the leaves still hold, the coming winter will be cold (English) If leaves remain on the trees late into the autumn this is a sure sign of a severe winter to come. M. Stevenson, *Twelve Moneths*, 1661. Another proverb insists that if leaves show their undersides rain should be expected shortly.

legs. *See* he is like a CAT; fling him which way you will, he'll light on his legs; there goes more to MARRIAGE than four bare legs in a bed; everyone STRETCHES his legs according to the length of his coverlet

leisure. *See* the BUSIEST men have the most leisure; IDLE people have the least leisure; there is LUCK in leisure; MARRY in haste and repent at leisure

lend. he that doth lend doth lose his money and friend (English) The person who agrees to lend money to a friend risks losing both his money and the friendship. William Shakespeare, *Hamlet*, c.1600.

Neither a borrower or lender be;
For loan oft loses both itself and friend.
William Shakespeare, *Hamlet*, c.1600

lend not horse, nor wife, nor sword (English) Never lend out your horse, your wife or your sword (formerly many people's most valuable possessions). E. Hellowes, *Guevara's Epistles*, 1574. The order in which the three are listed varies: sometimes the horse and the sword are ranked before the wife.

lend only that which you can afford to lose (English) When you lend money, lend it on the assumption that it will never be returned and ensure that you will be able to bear

the loss. Rowland Hill, *Commonplace Book*, c.1500. Variants include 'lend never that thing thou needest most'.

lend your money and lose your friend (English) If you lend money to your friends, your friendship is sure to suffer. William Shakespeare, *Hamlet*, c.1600. *See also* neither a BORROWER nor a lender be.

It is not the lending of our money that loses our friend; but the demanding it again.
James Kelly, *A Complete Collection of Scotish Proverbs*, 1721

lender. *See* neither a BORROWER nor a lender be

lends. *See* DISTANCE lends enchantment to the view

length begets loathing (English) Anything that goes on too long will be resented by those upon whom it is inflicted. C. Jarvis, *Don Quixote*, 1742.

length. *See also* everyone STRETCHES his legs according to the length of his coverlet

lengthens. *See* as the DAY lengthens, so the cold strengthens

leopard. a leopard can't change its spots (Hebrew) It is impossible for a person (or animal) to transform their inherited nature. Bible, Jeremiah 13:23. An Ashanti variant runs 'the rain beats a leopard's skin, but it does not wash off the spots'.

Can the Ethiopian change his skin, or the leopard his spots?
Bible, Jeremiah 13:23

less. *See* more HASTE, less speed

lesser. *See* of TWO evils choose the lesser

let. let well alone (English) If things are satisfactory as they are, then it is best not to interfere with them. *Scoggin's Jests*, c.1570 (also quoted by Terence).

See also LEAVE well alone; let SLEEPING dogs lie.

This immortal work ... will stand for centuries ... It is well: it works well: let well alone.
Thomas Love Peacock, *The Misfortunes of Elphin*, 1829

let. See also let the BUYER beware; let BYGONES be bygones; let the COBBLER stick to his last; let the DEAD bury the dead; let them LAUGH that win; LIVE and let live; let SLEEPING dogs lie; SPARE at the spigot, and let out at the bung-hole

letter. See the GIST of a lady's letter is in the postscript

leveller. See DEATH is the great leveller

liar. a liar is not believed when he speaks the truth (Roman) Those who have a reputation for telling lies will be ignored when they attempt to tell the truth. Anthony Rivers, *Dictes or Sayings of the Philosophers*, 1477 (also quoted by Cicero).

a liar is worse than a thief (English) It is morally less defensible to be a liar than it is to be a thief. W. Painter, *Chaucer New Painted*, 1623. See also SHOW me a liar and I will show you a thief.

But sure the proverbe is as true as briefe,
A lyer's ever worse then a thiefe.
John Taylor, *All the Workes of John Taylor, the Water Poet*, 1630

a liar ought to have a good memory (Roman) Those who tell lies must make sure they remember what they have said, as they may easily be caught out in their lies. Thomas Wyatt, *Poetical Works*, 1542 (also quoted by Quintilian and Saint Jerome).

A Lyar should have a good Memory. Lest he tell the same Lye different ways.
James Kelly, *A Complete Collection of Scotish Proverbs*, 1721

liar. See also COMMON fame is a common liar

libel. See the GREATER the truth, the greater the libel

liberty is not licence (English) Freedom is not the same as licence to do whatever you want. John Milton, sonnet, 1645. Often quoted in discussions of the nature of democracy.

Licence they mean when they cry liberty.
John Milton, sonnet, 1645

liberty. See also the PRICE of liberty is eternal vigilance

lie. a lie travels around the world while truth is putting on her boots (English) Lies, being frequently more salacious and interesting, spread much faster than truths. Charles Haddon Spurgeon, *John Ploughman's Talk*, 1869 (also attributed tentatively to Mark Twain). The saying enjoyed new currency after it was quoted by British prime minister James Callaghan in the House of Commons in 1976.

if you lie down with dogs, you will get up with fleas (Roman) Those who mix with undesirable company will pick up undesirable habits. J. Sandford, *The Garden of Pleasure*, 1573 (also quoted by Seneca).

They have a certain spice of the disease; For they that sleep with dogs shall rise with fleas.
John Webster, *The White Devil*, 1612

one lie makes many (English) A person who lies once will be obliged to back up his story with many more lies. Nicholas Udall, *Flowers out of Terence*, 1533. Variants include 'a lie begets a lie' and 'one trick needs another trick to back it up'.

lie. See also a BLISTER will rise upon one's tongue that tells a lie; HALF the truth is often a whole lie; as you MAKE your bed, so you must lie in it; as a TREE falls, so shall it lie

lies. lies have short legs (English) Lies are easily unmasked and are rarely believed for long. J. Sandford, *The Garden of Pleasure*, 1573. Also encountered in the form 'lies have short wings'.

lies. *See also* ASK no questions and hear no lies; TRUTH lies at the bottom of a well

life. life begins at forty (English) People enjoy new zest for life when they reach the age of forty. William B. Pitkin, *Life Begins at Forty*, 1932. Professor Pitkin's book tackled the challenge offered by the increasing amount of leisure time that was becoming available to the middle-aged. Subsequently the phrase became the title of a popular hit song by Jack Yellen and Ted Shapiro, memorably recorded by Sophie Tucker in 1937.

life is just a bowl of cherries (US) Life is full of delights and pleasures (intended sarcastically). Ray Henderson, 'Life is just a bowl of cherries', 1931. Henderson's song, with lyrics by Lew Brown, was written for the Broadway musical show *George White's Scandals of 1931*. Related proverbs include 'life would be too smooth if it had no rubs in it' ('rubs' being 'obstacles') and 'life wasn't meant to be easy', a line from George Bernard Shaw's *Back to Methuselah*, which was also a favourite catchphrase of Australian prime minister Malcolm Fraser in the late 1970s.

life is sweet (English) It is good to be alive. *Patience*, c.1350.

All this is very true; but life is sweet for all that.
Henry Fielding, *Jonathan Wild*, 1743

life isn't all beer and skittles (English) No one can expect to lead a completely carefree existence. Charles Dickens, *The Pickwick Papers*, 1836.

The men ... fell in for their first march, when they began to realize that a soldier's life was not all beer and skittles.
Rudyard Kipling, *Drums Fore and Aft*, 1888

where there's life there's hope (Greek) Hope cannot be extinguished as long as a person clings to life. R. Taverner, *Proverbs or Adages of Erasmus*, 1539 (also quoted by Cicero and Terence). Also encountered as 'while there's life there's hope'.

While there's life, there's hope, he cry'd;
Then why such haste? so groan'd and dy'd.
John Ray, *A Collection of English Proverbs*, 1670

life. *See also* ART is long, life is short; the BEST things in life are free; if you would be HAPPY for a week take a wife; if you would be happy for a month kill a pig; but if you would be happy all your life plant a garden; my SON is my son till he gets him a wife, but my daughter's my daughter all the days of her life; VARIETY is the spice of life

light. a light purse makes a heavy heart (English) Lack of money will depress the spirits. H. Chettle, *Piers Plainnes*, 1595. *See also* a HEAVY purse makes a light heart.

light come, light go (English) What comes easily, goes just as easily. Geoffrey Chaucer, *The Canterbury Tales*, c.1387. Also found as 'lightly gained, quickly lost'. *See also* EASY come, easy go.

Our honestest customers are the thieves ... with them and with their purses 'tis

lightly come, and lightly go.
Charles Reade, *The Cloister and the Hearth*, 1861

light gains make heavy purses
(English) Small but swift financial gains
can quickly multiply. John Heywood,
*A Dialogue containing ... the Proverbs in the
English Tongue*, 1546. Not unrelated is
the proverb 'a light purse makes a
heavy heart'. *See also* look after the PEN-
NIES and the pounds will look after
themselves.

light. *See also* don't HIDE your light
under a bushel; MANY hands make
light work

**lightning never strikes the same
place twice** (US) If a particular
spot has been struck by lightning it
is highly unlikely to be struck by
a second bolt at a later date. P. H.
Myers, *Prisoner of the Border*, 1857. In
fact there is no factual justification
for the notion of lightning never
striking the same plot twice: certain
high buildings, including the Empire
State Building in New York, have
been hit hundreds of times over the
years. There are also several unlucky
individuals who claim to have been
struck by lightning on more than one
occasion.

like. like breeds like (English)
Offspring take after their parents. R.
Edgeworth, *Sermons*, 1557. *See also* like
FATHER, like son.

Like men, like manners:
Like breeds like, they say.
Alfred, Lord Tennyson, *Poems*, 1842

like cures like (Roman) Treat a problem by employing its characteristics
against itself. C. Bede, *Verdant Green*,
1853. The approach has become one
of the guiding principles of homoe-
opathic medicine, although it might
also be quoted in many other con-

texts. *See* TAKE the hair of the dog that
bit you.

like it or lump it (English) Accept
what is offered with good grace, however unsatisfactory, as it is all that is on
offer. John Neal, *The Down-Easters*, 1833.

Well, what I always say is, people must take
me as they find me, and if they don't like it
they can lump it.
W. Somerset Maugham, *Of Human Bondage*,
1915

like will to like (Greek) Those with
similar backgrounds or characters will
tend to flock together. *Scottish Legendary*,
c.1375 (also quoted by Homer and
Cicero). Also found in the fuller form
'like will to like, quoth the Devil to the
collier'. Equivalent sayings include
'like loves like'. *See also* BIRDS of a feather flock together.

Like will to like, each Creature loves his
kind.
Robert Herrick, *Hesperides*, 1648

like. *See also* like FATHER, like son; like
MASTER, like man; like MOTHER, like
daughter; like PEOPLE, like priest

likes. *See* who likes not his BUSINESS, his
business likes not him

linen. *See* never CHOOSE your women or
your linen by candlelight; don't WASH
your dirty linen in public

lining. *See* every CLOUD has a silver lining

link. *See* a CHAIN is no stronger than its
weakest link

lion. *See* as a BEAR has no tail, for a lion
he'll fail; every DOG is a lion at home;
a LIVE dog is better than a dead lion; a
MAN is a lion in his own cause; MARCH
comes in like a lion and goes out like
a lamb; a MOUSE may help a lion

lip. *See* there's MANY a slip 'twixt cup and
lip

lips. *See* the CAT knows whose lips she licks

listeners never hear any good of themselves (English) Those who listen in to other people's conversations will only hear things about themselves they would rather not hear. *Mercurius Elencticus*, 1647. A related saying runs 'men love to hear well of themselves'.

'If it is fated that listeners are never to hear any good of themselves,' said Mrs Browdie, 'I can't help it, and I am very sorry for it.' Charles Dickens, *Nicholas Nickleby*, 1839

little. a little leak will sink a great ship (English) It can take only a minor problem to bring about the demise of a major enterprise. Thomas Fuller, *The Holy State*, 1642.

Beware of little expenses, a small leak will sink a great ship.
Benjamin Franklin, *Poor Richard's Almanack*, 1745

a little of what you fancy does you good (English) A little self-indulgence now and then can only be good for you. Fred W. Leigh and George Arthurs, 'A little of what you fancy does you good', c.1890. This song title acquired proverbial status after it was taken up by music hall singer Marie Lloyd and became one of her most celebrated hits. When Lloyd sang it the inference was that the self-indulgence in question was sexual in nature, but the line has since been quoted in reference to a much wider range of pleasures, including the consumption of chocolates and alcohol.

a little pot is soon hot (English) People small of stature are often more irascible than those who are somewhat larger. John Heywood, *A Dialogue containing ... the Proverbs in the English Tongue*, 1546.

Now were I not a little pot and soon hot, my very lips might freeze to my teeth.
William Shakespeare, *The Taming of the Shrew*, c.1592

by little and little the bird makes his nest (English) Through small repeated efforts the final aim is achieved. T. Wright, *Essays on the Middle Ages*, 1846. The same sentiment is voiced in such parallel sayings as 'little and often fills the purse' and 'little and good fills the trencher'.

every little helps (French) Even the smallest contributions help to increase the total. *See also* MANY a mickle makes a muckle; look after the PENNIES and the pounds will look after themselves.

Every little helps, said the ant, weeing in the sea at the height of midday.
Gabriel Meurier, *Trésor des Sentences*, 1590

little birds that can sing and won't sing must be made to sing (English) Those who unreasonably refuse to co-operate must expect to be pressured to do as required. John Ray, *A Collection of English Proverbs*, 1678.

The bird that can sing, and will not sing, should be gar'd sing. Spoken when we use rough means to perverse people.
James Kelly, *A Complete Collection of Scotish Proverbs*, 1721

little fish are sweet (English) Small treats or gifts may be enjoyed just as much as larger ones. R. Forby, *Vocabulary of East Anglia*, 1830.

little pitchers have big ears (English) Children overhear many things that they are not intended to hear (usually quoted as a warning not to discuss adult matters in front of the young). John Heywood, *A Dialogue containing ... the Proverbs in the English Tongue*, 1546. The 'ears' of a pitcher are its handles.

Archbishop Good madam, be not angry with the child.
Queen Elizabeth Pitchers have ears.
William Shakespeare, *Richard III*, c.1592

little strokes fell great oaks (Roman) Repeated small efforts will finally overcome great obstacles. Geoffrey Chaucer, *Romaunt of the Rose*, c.1400 (also quoted by Diogenianus in the second century AD). Variants include 'an oak is not felled at a single stroke'.

And many strokes, though with a little axe, Hews down and fells the hardest-timber'd oak.
By many hands your father was subdued.
William Shakespeare, *Henry VI, Part 3*, c.1591

little thieves are hanged, but great ones escape (English) Those who are guilty of petty offences tend to be hounded by the authorities, while those guilty of much more serious crimes often seem to escape notice. J. Clarke, *Paroemiologia Anglo-Latina*, 1639.

little things please little minds (Roman) Trivial people are satisfied with trivial things. G. Pettie, *Petite Pallace*, 1576 (also quoted by Ovid). Another proverb bluntly states 'little things are pretty'.

Little things affect little minds.
Benjamin Disraeli, *Sybil*, 1845

there is no little enemy (English) All enemies are dangerous, however tempting it may be to dismiss them as harmless. J. Howell, *Paroemiographia*, 1659.

little. *See also* BIG fish eat little fish; BIG fleas have little fleas upon their backs to bite them; BIRDS in their little nests agree; GREAT oaks from little acorns grow; a little LEARNING is a dangerous thing; LONG and lazy, little and loud;

LOVE me little, love me long; MUCH cry and little wool

live (adj). **a live dog is better than a dead lion** (Hebrew) Something alive or active, however imperfect, is preferable to something that has more qualities, but is dead or otherwise useless. Bible, Ecclesiastes 9:4.

When the lion is shot, the dog gets the spoil. So he had come in for Katherine, Alan's lioness. A live dog is better than a dead lion.
D. H. Lawrence, *The Woman Who Rode Away*, 1928

live (verb). **come live with me and you'll know me** (English) In order to know someone really well you must live with them. Sean O'Casey, *Juno and the Paycock*, 1925.

I only seen him twice; if you want to know me, come an' live with me.
Sean O'Casey, *Juno and the Paycock*, 1925

live and learn (English) Learn the lessons offered by experience (often said of bitter or disappointing experiences). G. Gascoigne, *Glass of Government*, 1575. A Yiddish variant runs 'as we live, so we learn'.

I was innocent myself once, but *live and learn* is an old saying, and a true one.
David Garrick, *Miss in her Teens*, 1747

live and let live (Dutch) Act with tolerance to others, as you would wish them to do to you. Gerard de Malynes, *Ancient Law-Merchant*, 1622. The proverb is found in several European languages. *See also* DO as you would be done by; it takes all SORTS to make a world.

You knows, master, one must live and let live, as the saying is.
Tobias Smollett, *Sir Launcelot Greaves*, 1762

they that live longest, see most (English) Those who live to an advanced age have the benefit of the greatest experience. T. Shelton, *Cervantes' Don Quixote*, 1620.

live. *See also* we must EAT to live and not live to eat; people who live in GLASS houses shouldn't throw stones; MAN cannot live by bread alone; THREATENED men live long

lived. *See* BRAVE men lived before Agamemnon

lives. he lives long who lives well (*English*) Those who pursue full, worthwhile lives may be thought of as long-lived, whatever age they are when they die. T. Wilson, *The Art of Rhetoric*, 1553. Variants include 'he lives long that lives till all are weary of him'.

he that lives in hope dances to an ill tune (*English*) Those who have only hope to rely upon for the future find themselves in a far from satisfactory position. John Florio, *Second Fruites*, 1591. Other proverbs warn 'he that lives on hope hath a slender diet' and 'who lives by hope will die by hunger'.

He that liveth in Hope, danceth without a Fiddle.
Thomas Fuller, *Gnomologia*, 1732

he that lives long suffers much (*English*) A long life brings with it a proportionate amount of suffering. T. Shelton, *Cervantes' Don Quixote*, 1620.

he who lives by the sword dies by the sword (*Hebrew*) Those who adopt violent methods shall in all probability meet a violent end themselves. Bible, Matthew 26:52.

All they that take the sword shall perish with the sword.
Bible, Matthew 26:52

who lives well dies well (*English*)

Those who have lived full, worthwhile lives can die in peace. Richard Pynson, *Kalendar of Shepherds*, 1506.

lives. *See also* a CAT has nine lives; he who FIGHTS and runs away, lives to fight another day; HALF the world doesn't know how the other half lives; a REED before the wind lives on, while mighty oaks do fall

load. *See* a SWARM of bees in May is worth a load of hay

loads. all lay loads on a willing horse (*English*) The gullible and acquiescent will always be taken advantage of. John Heywood, *A Dialogue containing ... the Proverbs in the English Tongue*, 1546. Variants include 'the willing horse is always most ridden'.

loaf. *See* HALF a loaf is better than no bread; a SLICE off a cut loaf isn't missed

loan. *See* SELDOM comes a loan laughing home

loathing. *See* LENGTH begets loathing

lock. no lock will hold against the power of gold (*English*) Money will open all doors. John Lyly, *Euphues and His England*, 1580. *See also* a GOLDEN key can open any door.

And who is so ignorant that knoweth not, gold be a Key for every locke?
John Lyly, *Euphues and His England*, 1580

locksmiths. *See* LOVE laughs at locksmiths

loft. *See* SEPTEMBER blow soft, till the fruit's in the loft

London. the streets of London are paved with gold (*English*) London, with its wealth of easy opportunities, is the place to go to if you want to make your fortune. *A New Account of Compliments; or, The Complete English Secretary, with a Collection of Playhouse Songs*,

1789. The proverb is associated by many people with the legend of Dick Whittington, the penniless youth destined to become Lord Mayor, who was lured to London by the the rumour of streets paved with gold.

long. it is a long lane that has no turning (English) Runs of bad fortune do not last forever. *Stationers' Register*, 1633.

It is a long lane that has no turning – Do not despise me for my proverbs.
Samuel Richardson, *Clarissa*, 1748

long absent, soon forgotten (English) People or things not constantly present are soon forgotten about. Randle Cotgrave, *A Dictionary of the French and English Tongues*, 1611. *See also* OUT of sight, out of mind.

long and lazy, little and loud (English) Those who are tall tend to be idle, while those who are short make up for their lack of stature by making as much noise as possible. T. Whytehorne, *Autobiography*, c.1576. The fullest form of the proverb runs 'long and lazy, little and loud; fat and fulsome, pretty and proud'. Variants include 'long and lazy, little and loud, fair and sluttish, foul and proud'.

Long and lazie. That was the Proverb. Let my mistress be Lasie to others, but be long to me.
Robert Herrick, *Hesperides*, 1648

long foretold long last, short notice soon past (English) If a barometer gives long advance warning of weather to come, that weather will remain for a long time, but if there is little warning then it will come and go very quickly. A. Steinmetz, *Manual of Weathercasts*, 1866.

The barometer is … misleading … Boots … read a poem which was printed over the top of the oracle, about 'Long foretold, long last; Short notice, soon past'.
Jerome K. Jerome, *Three Men in a Boat*, 1889

long. *See also* ART is long, life is short; KINGS have long arms; he LIVES long who lives well; LOVE me little, love me long; NEVER is a long time; OLD sins cast long shadows; SHORT reckonings make long friends; a STERN chase is a long chase; he who SUPS with the Devil should have a long spoon; THREATENED men live long

longest. the longest day must have an end (English) Even the worst and most disappointing days will come to an end after twenty-four hours. John Lyly, *Euphues and His England*, 1580. Variants include 'the longest night will have an end'.

But it sufficeth that the day will end.
William Shakespeare, *Julius Caesar*, 1599

the longest way round is the shortest way home (English) Sometimes it is quicker to avoid short cuts and take the longer route. John Lyly, *Euphues and His England*, 1580. Another English proverb supports this contention: 'he that leaves the highway, to cut short, commonly goes about'.

longest. *See also* BARNABY bright, Barnaby bright, the longest day and the shortest night; CREAKING doors hang the longest; he who LAUGHS last laughs longest; they that LIVE longest, see most

look. always look on the bright side (English) Always maintain an optimistic outlook, even when things seem to be going against you. James Payn, *Lost Sir Massingberd*, 1864. *See also* where there's LIFE there's hope.

look before you leap (Greek) Carefully assess the risks before committing yourself to some course of action. *Douce MS*, c.1350. Also encoutered in the form 'look ere you leap'. *See also* RECULER pour mieux sauter.

When you feel tempted to marry, think of our four sons and two daughters, and look twice before you leap.
Charlotte Brontë, *Shirley*, 1849

look for your money where you lost it (English) If you lose money in business or at gambling the best policy is to try to reclaim it by the same means. V S Lean, *Collectanea*, 1902–04.

never look a gift horse in the mouth (English/European) Those who receive presents or favours should not examine them too carefully for faults in case they should appear ungrateful. Saint Jerome, fifth century AD. Looking a horse in the mouth is a recognized procedure in buying and selling horses, as a check of its teeth gives a reliable indication of the animal's age (in times gone by some unscrupulous dealers filed down the teeth of their horses in order to make them seem younger). National variants include the Italian 'don't worry about the colour of a gift horse'. *See also* BEGGARS can't be choosers.

look. *See also* a CAT may look at a king; look after the PENNIES and the pounds will look after themselves; those who PLAY at bowls must look out for rubbers; one man may STEAL a horse, while another may not look over a hedge

lookers-on see most of the game (Roman) Those who watch while others act see more of the action than they do and so their advice should be taken seriously. J. Palsgrave, in *Acolastus*,

1529 (also quoted by Seneca).

A stander-by, sir, sees more than a gamester.
John Vanbrugh, *The Mistake*, 1706

looks. looks breed love (English) It is through visual impressions that love is inspired. R. Taverner, *Proverbs or Adages of Erasmus*, 1539. Variants include 'loving comes by looks'.

Tell me where is fancy bred? ... It is engender'd in the eyes,
With gazing fed.
William Shakespeare, *The Merchant of Venice*, c.1596

looks. *See also* the DEVIL looks after his own; if it looks like a DUCK, walks like a duck and quacks like a duck, it's a duck; a MAN is as old as he feels, and a woman as old as she looks

lord. *See* EVERYBODY loves a lord

lords. *See* NEW lords, new laws

lose. lose an hour in the morning, chase it all day (English) An hour's work lost in the morning will never be made up. Samuel Smiles, *Self-Help*, 1859. Variants include 'lost time is never found again'. *See also* he that riseth LATE must trot all day.

you cannot lose what you never had (English) You should not lament what is lost if it was never yours to call your own in the first place. Christopher Marlowe, *Hero and Leander*, 1593.

'He has broke all; there's half a line and a good hook lost.' 'I and a good Trout too.' 'Nay, the Trout is not lost, for ... no man can lose what he never had.'
Izaak Walton, *The Compleat Angler*, 1676

lose. *See also* what you lose on the SWINGS you gain on the roundabouts

loses. *See* a BLEATING sheep loses a bite; a TALE never loses in the telling; the SUN loses nothing by shining into a puddle; you WIN a few, you lose a few

losers. *See* FINDERS keepers, losers weepers

loss. one man's loss is another man's gain (English) What is a loss to one man may result in profit to another. T. Berthelet, *Erasmus' Sayings of Wise Men*, c.1527.

Doubtless one man's loss is another man's gain.
Walter Scott, *The Pirate*, 1821

there's no great loss without some gain (English) Disappointments or other losses often bring with them some compensatory benefit. David Fergusson, *Scottish Proverbs*, 1641. *See also* every CLOUD has a silver lining; what you lose on the SWINGS you gain on the roundabouts.

lost. better lost than found (English) Sometimes it is better to have mislaid something or someone that will only be a source of greater grief if found again. G. Pettie, *Petite Pallace*, 1576.

He is gone to seek my young mistress; and I think she is better lost than found.
Porter, *The Angry Woman of Abingdon*, 1599

lost. *See also* he who HESITATES is lost; 'tis better to have LOVED and lost, than never to have loved at all; for want of a NAIL the shoe was lost; what a NEIGHBOUR gets is not lost

lottery. *See* MARRIAGE is a lottery

loud. *See* LONG and lazy, little and loud

louder. *See* ACTIONS speak louder than words

louse. better a louse in the pot than no flesh at all (English) It is better to have something, however negligible, than nothing whatsoever. J. Clarke, *Paroemiologia Anglo-Latina*, 1639.

love. love and a cough cannot be hid (English) There is no keeping love secret, just as a cough cannot be suppressed. *Cursor Mundi*, 1325.

If there are two things not to be hidden – love and a cough – I say there is a third, and that is ignorance.
George Eliot, *Romola*, 1863

love begets love (English) Love promotes love in others. Robert Herrick, *Hesperides*, 1648. Sometimes encountered in the Latin version '*amor gignit amorem*' ('love produces love'). Related proverbs include 'likeness begets love'.

Love love begets, then never be Unsoft to him who's smooth to thee.
Robert Herrick, *Hesperides*, 1648

love cannot be compelled (English) It is impossible to command love against its inclination. Geoffrey Chaucer, *The Canterbury Tales*, c.1387.

Ne may love be compeld by maisterie.
Edmund Spenser, *The Faerie Queene*, 1590

love conquers all (Roman) Love will triumph over all obstacles. Also encountered in the Latin form '*amor vincit omnia*'.

love is blind (Greek) Those who are in love are blinded to things that they would otherwise notice (typically faults in the object of their desire). Geoffrey Chaucer, *The Canterbury Tales*, c.1387 (also quoted by Theocritus and Plautus). Perhaps significantly, in Classical Rome it was customary for sculptors to depict the god of love Cupid blindfolded. A rather cynical proverb adds 'love is blind – and when you get married you get your eyesight back'.

If love is blind, love cannot hit the mark.
William Shakespeare, *Romeo and Juliet*, c.1593

love laughs at locksmiths (English) Love will triumph, despite all attempts to hinder it. George Colman the Younger, *Love Laughs at Locksmiths*, 1803. *See also* LOVE will find a way.

Were beauty under twenty locks kept fast,
Yet love breaks through and picks them all at last.
William Shakespeare, *Venus and Adonis*, c.1592

love makes the world go round (French/Italian) Human affairs are motivated by love. Lewis Carroll, *Alice's Adventures in Wonderland*, 1865 (also quoted by Jacopone da Todi and Dante). *See also* MONEY makes the world go round.

In for a penny, in for a pound,
'Tis love that makes the world go round.
W. S. Gilbert, *Iolanthe*, 1882

love me little, love me long (English) The best love is bestowed in a spirit of moderation and constancy, rather than precipitately and passionately. *Archiv*, 1500.

Love me little, love me long. A Dissuasive from shewing too much, and too sudden Kindness.
James Kelly, *A Complete Collection of Scotish Proverbs*, 1721

love me, love my dog (English) If you love me, you must also undertake to love everything about me. *Early Miscellany*, c.1480. The saying is associated with Saint Bernard of Clairvaux (not to be confused with Saint Bernard of Menthon, the twelfth-century French Benedictine monk who founded two hospices in the Alps and after whom Saint Bernard dogs were named).

That you must love me, and love my dog … we could never yet form a friendship … without the intervention of some third anomaly … the understood dog in the proverb.
Charles Lamb, *Popular Fallacies*, 1826

love will creep where it can not go (English) Where love may not proceed openly it is pursued with stealth and caution. *Towneley Plays*, c.1400.

love will find a way (English) Love cannot be denied and will find a way through all obstacles in the end. T. Deloney, *The Gentle Craft*, 1607. Also encountered in the form 'love will find out the way'.

love your neighbour, yet pull not down your hedge (English) By all means maintain close relations with your neighbours, but for your friendship to prosper ensure there remains some guarantee to protect your privacy. George Herbert, *Jacula Prudentum*, 1640. *See also* a HEDGE between keeps friendship green.

one cannot love and be wise (Roman) Any person who falls in love will find their good sense deserting them. T. Berthelet, *Erasmus' Sayings of Wise Men*, c.1527 (also quoted by Publilius Syrus). Other proverbs along the same lines run 'love and knowledge live not together' and 'love is without reason'. On the other hand, another proverb advises 'love makes a wit of a fool'.

If a man could not love and be wise, surely he could flirt and be wise at the same time.
George Eliot, *Middlemarch*, 1872

the love of money is the root of all evil (Hebrew) The desire for money leads men into all manner of selfishness and wickedness. Bible, 1 Timothy 6:7–10. Sometimes encountered in the truncated form 'money is the root of all evil', which has a somewhat altered meaning. Twentieth-century reworkings of the ancient proverb have included 'the lack of money is the root of all evil'. *See also* you cannot serve GOD and Mammon.

For the love of money is the root of all evil,

leading men to flounder in their Christian faith and fall into deep unhappiness.
Bible, 1 Timothy 6:7–10

love. *See also* the COURSE of true love never did run smooth; all's FAIR in love and war; when the FURZE is in bloom, my love's in tune; whom the GODS love die young; LUCKY at cards, unlucky in love; be OFF with the old love before you are on with the new; PITY is akin to love; when POVERTY comes in at the door, love flies out of the window; PRAISE the child and you make love to the mother; the QUARREL of lovers is the renewal of love

loved. 'tis better to have loved and lost, than never to have loved at all (English) Any experience of love, whether happy or not, is better than no experience of it at all. William Congreve, *The Way of the World*, 1700.

Say what you will, 'tis better to be left, than never to have lov'd.
William Congreve, *The Way of the World*, 1700

lovers. *See* JOVE but laughs at lovers' perjury; the QUARREL of lovers is the renewal of love

loves. *See* EVERYBODY loves a lord

luck. there is luck in leisure (English) It is sometimes sensible not to consider carefully before taking action. G. Meriton, *Yorkshire Dialogue*, 1683. *See also* more HASTE, less speed; LOOK before you leap.

there is luck in odd numbers (Roman) Odd numbers are luckier than even numbers. William Shakespeare,

The Merry Wives of Windsor, c.1598 (also quoted by Virgil). In the ancient world odd numbers were considered the fundamental numbers of nature, with nine, for instance, representing the Deity (according to Pythagoras), and it was probably thus that they acquired a reputation for being lucky. *See also* THIRD time lucky.

Good luck lies in odd numbers ... They say there is divinity in odd numbers, either in nativity, chance or death.
William Shakespeare, *The Merry Wives of Windsor*, c.1598

luck. *See also* CARE and diligence bring luck; the DEVIL's children have the Devil's luck; FOOLS for luck; see a PIN and pick it up, all the day you'll have good luck

lucky. it is better to be born lucky than rich (English) Good luck is of more value than mere riches. J. Clarke, *Paroemiologia Anglo-Latina*, 1639.

lucky at cards, unlucky in love (English) Those who are lucky in gambling will enjoy less luck in love affairs (usually quoted as compensation to someone who has just lost a gambling stake of some kind). T. W. Robertson, *Society*, 1866. Variants include 'lucky in life, unlucky in love'.

Well, Miss, you'll have a sad Husband, you have such good Luck at Cards.
Jonathan Swift, *Polite Conversation*, 1738

lucky. *See also* THIRD time lucky

lump. *See* LIKE it or lump it

lunch. *See* there is no such thing as a FREE lunch

m

MacGregor. where MacGregor sits is the head of the table (English) Wherever an influential person settles, there power settles also. R. W. Emerson, *American Scholar*, 1837. The name concerned varies; the MacGregor sometimes quoted is thought by some to be the Scottish outlaw hero 'Rob Roy' MacGregor.

mackerel. mackerel sky and mares' tails make lofty ships carry low sails (English) Dappled white clouds high in the sky are a sign of troubled, rainy weather in the offing. R. Inwards, *Weather Lore*, 1869. Variants include 'mackerel scales, furl your sails'.

mackerel. *See also* throw out a SPRAT to catch a mackerel

mad. one mad action is not enough to prove a man mad (English) It takes more than an isolated instance of aberrant behaviour for a person to be declared mad. Thomas Fuller, *Gnomologia*, 1732.

mad. *See also* BUTTER is mad twice a year; whom the GODS would destroy, they first make mad

made. *See* GOD made the country, and man made the town; PROMISES, like pie-crust, are made to be broken

Mahomet. *See* if the MOUNTAIN will not go to Mahomet, Mahomet must go to the mountain

maids. *See* OLD maids lead apes in hell

maintains. what maintains one vice would bring up two children (English) The pursuit of vice is costly. Benjamin Franklin, in Arber's *English Garner*, 1758.

make. as you make your bed, so you must lie in it (English) A person must bear the consequences of his or her own actions. G. Harvey, *Marginalia*, c.1590. Similar sentiments were expressed in the Classical world, Terence, for instance, observing in his *Phormio* (161 BC) that 'you have mixed the mess and you must eat it'. *See also* as you SOW, so shall you reap.

As you make your bed, so you lye down. According to your Conditions you have your Bargain.
c.1590, quoted in James Kelly, *A Complete Collection of Scotish Proverbs*, 1721

make. *See also* do not make FISH of one and flesh of another; make HASTE slowly; make HAY while the sun shines; if you don't make MISTAKES you don't make anything; you cannot make an OMELETTE without breaking eggs; you can't make a SILK purse out of a sow's ear

male. *See* the FEMALE of the species is more deadly than the male

malice hurts itself most (English) Ill feeling towards others eats away at the person who harbours it. John Clarke, *Paroemiologia Anglo-Latina*, c.1639. Other proverbs add 'malice hath a sharp sight and strong memory' and 'malice seldom wants a mark to shoot at'.

Malice drinketh up the greatest part of its own poison.
Thomas Fuller, *Gnomologia*, 1732

Mammon. *See* you cannot serve GOD and Mammon

man. a man can die but once (English) Mortals need suffer death only once. William Shakespeare, *Henry IV, Part 2*, c.1598.

Death of one person can be paid but once.
William Shakespeare, *Antony and Cleopatra*, c.1606

a man can do no more than he can (English) It is futile asking someone to do more than they are capable of. J. Palsgrave, *L'Éclaircissement de la langue française*, 1530.

a man is a lion in his own cause (English) When a person has a vested interest in something he or she will work at it more assiduously than would be the case otherwise. David Fergusson, *Scottish Proverbs*, 1641.

a man is as old as he feels, and a woman as old as she looks (English) The age of a woman may be judged from her appearance, while a man may decide it from his inner condition. Mortimer Collins, 'How Old Are You?', 1855. Wags have since varied

the proverb as follows, 'a man is as old as the woman he feels'. Also encountered in Italian.

O wherefore our age be revealing?
Leave that to the registry books!
A man is as old as he's feeling,
A woman as old as she looks.
Mortimer Collins, 'How Old Are You?', 1855

a man is known by the company he keeps (English) A person's character may be judged by the quality of his friends and associates. M. Coverdale, *H. Bullinger's Christian State of Matrimony*, 1541 (it may also be found in various forms in the writings of Euripides and Aesop). Formerly usually quoted in discussing a woman's choice of marriage partners. Less-often heard English equivalents include 'bad company is the ruin of a good character' and 'as a man is, so is his'. The proverb is also found in other European languages. An Italian variant, recorded in 1574, goes 'Tel me with whom thou doest goe, and I shall know what thou doest', while a Spanish version, quoted by Cervantes in *Don Quixote* in 1615, runs 'Tell me what company you keep, and I'll tell you what you are'.

There is a proverb, Mrs Joyner, 'You may know him by his company'.
William Wycherley, *Love in a Wood*, 1672

a man of straw is worth a woman of gold (English/French) A feeble and relatively ineffective man is, by virtue of his sex, still the equal of the most accomplished woman. John Florio, *Second Fruites*, 1591.

a man of words and not of deeds is like a garden full of weeds (English) A man who is unwilling to back his promises with action is of little worth. J. Howell, *Paroemiographia*, 1659.

a man without religion is like a

horse without a bridle (Roman) A person who has no religious faith lacks a direction in life. Richard Burton, *The Anatomy of Melancholy*, 1621.

Justice and religion are the two chief props ... of a ... commonwealth: ... as Sabellicus delivers, a man without religion is like an horse without a bridle.
Richard Burton, *The Anatomy of Melancholy*, 1621

a man's best friend is his dog (English) The one companion a man can rely on to be faithful is his dog. Alexander Pope, *Letters*, 1737. Another proverb advises 'a man, a horse and a dog are never weary of each other's company'.

Histories are more full of examples of the fidelity of dogs than of men.
Alexander Pope, *Letters*, 1737

as a man lives so shall he die (Hebrew) The character of a man's life will be reflected in the manner in which he meets his death, when it is too late for him to change the pattern of his existence. Bible, Ecclesiastes 11:3. In its fullest form the proverb is sometimes given as 'as a man lives so shall he die, as a tree falls, so shall it lie'.

as soon as man is born he begins to die (Roman) Every minute of life brings a person closer to death. *King Edward III*, 1596.

While man is growing, life is in decrease,
And cradles rock us nearer to our tomb.
Our birth is nothing but our death
   begun.
Edward Young, *Night Thoughts*, 1742

every man after his fashion (English) Each individual must follow his or her own inclination. John Heywood, *A Dialogue containing ... the Proverbs in the English Tongue*, 1546.

Every man after his fashen.
Francis Bacon, *Promus*, c.1594

every man for himself and the Devil take the hindmost (Spanish) Those who finish last must look after themselves. Beaumont and Fletcher, *Philaster*, 1620 (also recorded in variant forms in the writings of Horace). Legend has it that devotees of the Devil at Toledo, or Salamanca, were forced to run the length of a subterranean hall, the Devil snatching the man who came last and making him his imp. The line is shouted out in a traditional children's chasing game. Originally found in the shorter form 'Devil take the hindmost'.

every man has his price (English) Every person will betray his principles if offered a big enough reward. The proverb is often attributed to Sir Robert Walpole, though it seems that in reality it was his political rival Sir William Wyndham who coined it in the course of a speech attacking Walpole that he gave in the House of Commons on 13 March 1734. Sir William himself denied he had originated the phrase and claimed it was already old when he used it (it may tentatively be derived from the writings of Epictetus as far back as the first century AD).

every man is the architect of his own fortune (Roman) It is up to each individual to create their own good fortune in life. R. Taverner, *Proverbs or Adages of Erasmus*, 1539 (also quoted by Juvenal and others).

Architects of their own happiness.
John Milton, *Eikonoklastes*, 1649

every man to his trade (English) Each individual should be allowed to practise the trade to which they have been brought up. R. Taverner, *Proverbs or Adages of Erasmus*, 1539.

Every man to his craft, says the proverb, the parson to the prayer-book, and the groom to the curry-comb.
Walter Scott, *Kenilworth*, 1821

if a man once fall, all will tread on him (English) Any man brought low by scandal or some other setback will find everyone bands together to join in criticism of him. J. Palsgrave, *L'Éclaircissement de la langue française*, 1530.

man cannot live by bread alone (Hebrew) There is more to life than the maintenance of mere bodily existence alone. Bible, Deuteronomy 8:3 and Matthew 4:4.

Man canna live by bread alone, but he assuredly canna live without it.
John Buchan, *Witch Wood*, 1927

man is a bubble (Greek) The life of a man does not last long and leaves as little impression. R. Taverner, *Proverbs or Adages of Erasmus*, 1539.

man is the measure of all things (Greek) Man is capable of subjugating all things to his will. George Chapman, *Caesar and Pompey*, 1631 (also quoted by Plato).

As of all things man is said the measure,
So your full merits measure forth a man.
George Chapman, *Caesar and Pompey*, 1631

man is to man a wolf (Roman) Men can behave with animal viciousness to those perceived to be their rivals. Cornelius Agrippa, *The Vanity of Arts and Sciences*, 1569 (also quoted by Plautus). A contrasting view is offered by the proverb 'man is to man a god' and the more equivocal 'man is to man either a god or a wolf'.

I mourn the pride and avarice that make man a wolf to man.
William Cowper, *The Task*, 1785

man proposes, but God disposes (Hebrew) Men may initiate enterprises, but it is God who decides how they turn out. Bible, Proverbs 16:9 (also quoted by William Langland, *Piers Plowman*, in 1377, by Thomas à Kempis in 1420 and before him in variant forms by Plato). It is also found in most other European languages and has equivalents elsewhere in the world, the Chinese for instance having 'man may plan, but Heaven executes'. Related proverbs in English include 'man doth what he can and God what He will'.

A man's heart deviseth the way: but the Lord directeth his steps.
Bible, Proverbs 16:9

man's extremity is God's opportunity (English) It is when life is at its least bearable that people are most likely to turn to religious faith to keep them going. T. Adams, *Works*, 1629.

the man who is born in a stable is a horse (English) A person will acquire the manners and characteristics of his upbringing. M. Scott, *Tom Cringle's Log*, 1833. Also encountered in the contrasting form 'a man is not a horse because he was born in a stable'.

whatever man has done, man may do (English) It stands to reason that anything one man can do can be done by others. Charles Reade, *Hard Cash*, 1863. Another proverb on contrasting lines runs 'a man that does what no other man does is wondered at by all'.

man. *See also* a BLIND man's wife needs no paint; the CHILD is the father of the man; in the COUNTRY of the blind, the one-eyed man is king; DO right and fear no man; a DROWNING man will clutch at a straw; EARLY to bed and early to rise makes a man healthy, wealthy and wise; the EARLY man never borrows from the late man; every ELM has its man; GIVE a man enough rope and he will hang himself; GOD made man, man made money; a HUNGRY man is an angry man; it's ILL speaking between a full man and a fasting; you should KNOW a man seven years before you stir his fire; a man who is his own LAWYER has a fool for a client; one man's LOSS is another man's gain; MANNERS maketh man; like MASTER, like man; one man's MEAT is another man's poison; MONEY makes a man; a MONEY-LESS man goes fast through the market; NINE tailors make a man; NO man can serve two masters; NO man is a hero to his own valet; NO man is wise at all times; NO moon, NO man; there is NOTHING so good for the inside of a man as the outside of a horse; better be an OLD man's darling than a young man's slave; the RICH man has his ice in the summer and the poor man gets his in the winter; SIX hours' sleep for a man, seven for a woman and eight for a fool; one man may STEAL a horse, while another may not look over a hedge; the STYLE is the man; TIME and tide wait for no man; the WAY to a man's heart is through his stomach; a WILFUL man must have his way; when the WIND is in the east, 'tis neither good for man nor beast

Manchester. what Manchester says today, the rest of England says tomorrow (English) Radical thinking may originate not in capitals or at the heads of organizations but in more remote areas. Rudyard Kipling, *A Day's Work*, 1898. The proverb is often encountered with other cities (both British and US) usurping the place of Manchester, which owed its claim to

original thought to its reputation as a champion of free trade in the 1840s.

manners maketh man (English) It is by a person's standards of civilized behaviour that he may be judged. *Douce MS*, c.1350. Also found as 'manners maketh the man'.

The difference is, that in days of old Men made the manners; manners now make men.
Lord Byron, Don Juan, 1824

manners. See also EVIL communications corrupt good manners; OTHER times, other manners

manure. See the BEST manure is under the farmer's foot

many. many a mickle makes a muckle (English) A lot of small amounts amassed together will amount to a considerable total. *Ancrene Wisse*, 1250. The original form of the proverb ran 'many a little makes a mickle' ('mickle' signifying a considerable amount), or alternatively 'many a pickle makes a mickle'. 'Muckle', a mock-dialect nonsense word suggesting a large quantity of something, first appeared in the late eighteenth century.

A Scotch addage, than which nothing in nature is more true ... 'many mickles make a muckle'.
George Washington, Writings, 1793

many hands make light work (Greek) The more people help the less work each will have to do. *Sir Beves*, c.1330 (also quoted in variant forms by Hesiod and other writers in Classical times). One variant in which the Romans knew the proverb ran 'by the hands of many a great load is lightened'.

Most Hands dispatch apace,
And make light work, (the proverb says).
Samuel Butler, Hudibras, 1678

there's many a slip 'twixt cup and lip (English) Things can go amiss even at the very last moment before they are finally made secure (just as a drink may be dropped or slopped before the cup reaches the mouth). R. Taverner, *Proverbs or Adages of Erasmus*, 1539 (also quoted by Erasmus).

many. *See also* too many COOKS spoil the broth; many DROPS make a shower; there's many a GOOD tune played on an old fiddle; many HAWS, many snows; many HIPS and haws, many frosts and snaws; many IRONS in the fire, some must cool; so many MEN, so many opinions; there's many a TRUE word spoken in jest; many go out for WOOL and come home shorn

March. March comes in like a lion and goes out like a lamb (English) The month of March usually begins with severe weather, which calms and becomes mild by the end. J. Fletcher, *Wife for a Month*, 1625. Occasionally heard with the lion and the lamb reversed. Variants include 'March comes in with an adder's head and goes out with a peacock's tail'.

Charming and fascinating he resolved to be. Like March, having come in like a lion, he purposed to go out like a lamb.
Charlotte Brontë, *Shirley*, 1849

March. *See also* APRIL showers bring forth May flowers; on the FIRST of March, the crows begin to search; so many MISTS in March, so many frosts in May; a PECK of March dust is worth a king's ransom

marches. *See* an ARMY marches on its stomach

mare. *See* the GREY mare is the better horse; MONEY makes the mare to go

market. *See* BUY in the cheapest market and sell in the dearest; a MONEYLESS man goes fast through the market

marriage. marriage is a lottery (English) The achievement of a successful marriage with an ideal partner is more a matter of chance than of choice and all who enter into it are taking a risk. Ben Jonson, *The Tale of a Tub*, 1633. *See also* MARRIAGES are made in heaven.

I smile to think how like a lottery
These weddings are.
Ben Jonson, *The Tale of a Tub*, 1633

marriage makes or mars a man (English) Marriage to the right partner will seal a man's happiness, while marriage to the wrong partner will break him. J. Howell, letter, 1625.

there goes more to marriage than four bare legs in a bed (English) There is more to achieving happiness in marriage than compatibility in sexual matters (the challenges of parenthood being one of the consequences thus implied). John Heywood, *A Dialogue containing ... the Proverbs in the English Tongue, c.* 1549.

A sort of penny-wedding it will prove, where all men contribute to the young folks' maintenance, that they may not have must four bare legs in a bed thegether.
Walter Scott, *The Fortunes of Nigel*, 1822

marriage. *See also* DREAM of a funeral and you hear of a marriage

marriages are made in heaven (Hebrew) The choice of marital partners is directed by God. W. Painter, *The Palace of Pleasure*, 1567 (also quoted in the Midrash in AD 550). The sentiment may also be found in French. Variants include 'wedding is destiny, and hanging likewise'. *See also* HANGING and wiving go by destiny; MARRIAGE is a lottery.

House and riches are the inheritance of fathers: and a prudent wife is from the Lord.
Bible, Proverbs 19:14

marries. he that marries a widow and three children marries four thieves (English) The man who marries a widow with children will find they rob him of all his wealth. John Ray, *A Collection of English Proverbs*, 1670. On not dissimilar lines is 'he that marries a widow and two daughters has three back doors to his house'. Husbands of widows are further warned that 'he who marries a widow will often have a dead man's head thrown in his dish' (meaning that the second husband will have to withstand constant comparison with the first), 'never marry a widow unless her first husband was hanged' and also that 'it's dangerous marrying a widow, because she hath cast her rider'. On a more positive, if cynical, note another proverb observes that 'it is easy to marry a widow as to put a halter on a dead horse'. Another encourages the man thinking of marrying a widow not to delay: 'marry a widow before she leaves mourning'.

he that marries late marries ill (English) People who marry late are unlikely to enjoy a happy married life. Thomas Nashe, *Works*, 1589. Equivalent proverbs include 'he that marries ere he be wise will die ere he thrive'.

marry. marry in haste and repent at leisure (French/Italian) Those who get married without taking time to question the wisdom of it will live to regret it in the years to come. W. Painter, *The Palace of Pleasure*, 1566 (also quoted in variant forms centuries

earlier by Socrates and Philemon among others).
He who would marry is on the road to repentance.
Philemon, *Fragments*, c.300 BC

marry in Lent, and you'll live to repent (English) It is unlucky to marry during the season of Lent, as marriages contracted then offend heaven and will not prosper. Mrs G. L. Banks, *Manchester Man*, 1876.

marry in May and rue the day (Roman) May is the unluckiest month of the year and thus the one month to avoid when choosing a wedding date. *Poor Robin's Almanack*, 1675 (also quoted by Ovid). Also encountered in the form 'marry in May, rue for aye'. Less well known equivalents include 'married in May will soon decay' and 'to wed in May is to wed poverty'.

marry with your match (Roman) When seeking a partner in marriage, it is best to choose someone from the same rank and station as yourself. John Clarke, *Paroemiologia Anglo-Latina*, 1639 (also quoted by Ovid). Variants include 'marry a wife of thine own degree'.

martyrs. See the BLOOD of the martyrs is the seed of the Church

mass. See MEAT and mass never hindered man

master. like master, like man (Roman) The character of a man is reflected in that of his servants or employees. J. Palsgrave, *L'Éclaircissement de la langue française*, 1530 (also quoted by Cicero).
The Proverbe be true that sayes, like master, like man', and I may add, 'like lady, like maid'. Lady Hercules was fine, but her maid was still finer.
T. Shelton, *Cervantes' Don Quixote*, 1620

the master's eye maketh the horse fat (Greek) A person takes special care to nurture what belongs to him (and is also prone to see what belongs to him as being perhaps better than it really is). Hugh Latimer, *Sermons*, 1552 (also quoted by Aristotle).

It is the eye of the master that fatteth the horse, and the love of the woeman, that maketh the man.
John Lyly, *Euphues: The Anatomy of Wit*, 1578

master. *See also* the EYE of a master does more work than both his hands; JACK is as good as his master; JACK of all trades is master of none; he that TEACHES himself has a fool for his master

masters. masters should be sometimes blind, and sometimes deaf (English) There are occasions when a master is best advised to turn a blind eye to the misdemeanours of his underlings. Thomas Fuller, *Gnomologia*, 1732.

masters. *See also* NO man can serve two masters

May. May chickens come cheeping (English) As May is the unluckiest month of the year, when evil spirits roam abroad, any young born in that month are unlikely to be worth keeping. A. Hislop, *Proverbs of Scotland*, 1868. In times gone by this superstition was so firmly believed that litters of kittens and other young animals were routinely destroyed. It was also supposed that human children born in May were unlikely to prosper and would probably die before reaching maturity — thus the Cornish proverb 'May chets bad luck begets' ('chets' being 'children'). Variants include 'May birds are aye cheeping'. *See also* MARRY in May and rue the day.

May. *See also* APRIL showers bring forth May flowers; he who BATHES in May will soon be laid in clay; ne'er CAST a clout till May be out; so many MISTS in March, so many frosts in May; a SWARM of bees in May is worth a load of hay; a WET May brings plenty of hay

means. *See* he who WILLS the end, wills the means; the END justifies the means

measure. don't measure other people's corn by one's own bushel (English) Refrain from judging other's behaviour or efforts and so forth by one's own standards. W. Saltonstall, *Picturae Loquentes*, 1631.

Pray do not measure my corn with your bushel, old Drybones!
John Gay, *The Wife of Bath*, 1713

there is a measure in all things (Greek) Moderation should be exercised in all circumstances. Geoffrey Chaucer, *Troilus and Criseyde*, c.1385 (also quoted by Horace). *See also* MODERATION in all things.

If the prince be too important, tell him there is measure in every thing.
William Shakespeare, *Much Ado About Nothing*, c.1598

measure. *See also* MAN is the measure of all things

meat. meat and mass never hindered man (Scottish) A man should give time to the eating of meat and the taking of mass, as these can only give him new strength to tackle his work. J. Carmichaell, *Proverbs in Scots*, 1628. Variants include 'meat and matins hinder no man's journey' and 'prayers and provender hinder no man's journey'.

I beg to remind you of an old musty saw, that meat and mass never hindered man.
Robert Louis Stevenson, *Catriona*, 1893

one man's meat is another man's poison (Roman) What one person values and enjoys another man will detest or complain of. John Heywood, *A Dialogue containing ... the Proverbs in the English Tongue*, 1546 (also quoted by Lucretius in *De Rerum Natura* in 45 BC). *See also* BEAUTY is in the eye of the beholder.

It is more true of novels than perhaps of anything else, that one man's food is another man's poison.
Anthony Trollope, *Autobiography*, 1883

meat. *See also* you BUY land you buy stones, you buy meat you buy bones; GOD never sends mouths but He sends meat; GOD sends meat, but the Devil sends cooks

meddlers. *See* LAY-overs for meddlers

medicine. there is no medicine against death (English) The one incurable disease is death. William Cowper, *Yearly Bill of Mortality*, 1787. *See also* there is a REMEDY for everything except death.

No medicine, though it oft can cure,
Can always balk the tomb.
William Cowper, *Yearly Bill of Mortality*, 1787

medicine. *See also* LAUGHTER is the best medicine

meet. do not meet troubles half-way (Roman) There is no point exposing yourself to trouble before you need to. J. C. Hutcheson, *Crown and Anchor*, 1896 (also quoted by Seneca). *See also* never TROUBLE trouble till trouble troubles you.

Are you come to meet your trouble? The fashion of the world is to avoid cost, and you encounter it.
William Shakespeare, *Much Ado About Nothing*, c.1598

meet on the stairs and you won't meet in heaven (English) Bad luck will befall those who pass each other on the same set of stairs. R. Hunt, *West of*

England, 1865. The superstition that it is unlucky to pass on the stairs is thought to date from rougher times: people were deemed particularly vulnerable to attack from assassins when climbing or descending stairs because it was more difficult to draw their swords to defend themselves from any sudden attack. To avoid bad luck that might be provoked by crossing on the stairs, tradition suggests either waiting until the other person has passed on their way or undertaking such precautions as crossing the fingers.

meet. *See also* EXTREMES meet

meets. *See* when GREEK meets Greek then comes the tug of war

memory. *See* he is an ill COMPANION that has a good memory; a LIAR ought to have a good memory

men. all men are mortal (English) All men must die. Geoffrey Chaucer, *The Canterbury Tales*, c.1387.

it is the men who make a city (Greek) The character of a city depends more upon its inhabitants than upon the physical realities of bricks and mortar. Thomas Fuller, *Gnomologia*, 1732 (also quoted by Thucydides).

It is men who make a city, not walls, or ships without crews.
Thucydides, *History of the Peloponnesian War*, fifth century BC

so many men, so many opinions (Roman) Every man has his own unique set of opinions and individual outlook on the world. Geoffrey Chaucer, *The Canterbury Tales*, c.1387 (also quoted by Terence). Also found as 'so many men, so many minds'. *See also* so many COUNTRIES, so many customs.

Doctors differ. So many persons, so many minds.
Samuel Richardson, *Sir Charles Grandison*, 1754

men. *See also* the BEST laid schemes of mice and men gang oft agley; the BEST of men are but men at best; men are BLIND in their own cause; BRAVE men lived before Agamemnon; the BUSIEST men have the most leisure; DEAD men don't bite; DEAD men tell no tales; GOOD men are scarce; THREATENED men live long; one VOLUNTEER is worth two pressed men; YOUNG men may die, but old men must die

mend. either mend or end (English) If something is imperfect and cannot be improved, it is best to dispense with it altogether. John Florio, *Montaigne*, dedication, 1603.
I would set my life on any chance,
To mend it or be rid on't.
William Shakespeare, *Macbeth*, c.1604

mend. *See also* it is never TOO LATE to mend; when THINGS are at the worst they soon begin to mend

mended. *See* LEAST said, soonest mended

mending. *See* a WOMAN and a ship ever want mending

mercy. mercy surpasses justice (English) The demands of justice can be swayed by the impulse to show mercy. Geoffrey Chaucer, *Troilus and Criseyde*, c.1385.
Here may men see that mercy passeth right.
Geoffrey Chaucer, *Troilus and Criseyde*, c.1385

mercy to the criminal may be cruelty to the people (English) In showing leniency to a criminal it is possible that a court is exposing the general populace to future harm. Joseph Addison, *Spectator*, 1711.
In the public administration of justice, mercy to one may be cruelty to others.

Joseph Addison, *Spectator*, 1711

merrier. *See* the MORE the merrier

merry. all are not merry that dance (English) Appearances of jollity on the dance floor can be deceptive. Geoffrey Chaucer, *The Parlement of Fowls*, 1380. Also found as 'all are not merry that dance lightly'.
Daunseth he murye that is myrtheles?
Geoffrey Chaucer, *The Parlement of Fowls*, 1380

it is good to be merry and wise (English) It is good policy to remain sensible even when greatly enjoying yourself. Nicholas Udall, *Roister Doister*, c.1540.
Come, come, George, let's be merry and wise.
Beaumont and Fletcher, *The Knight of the Burning Pestle*, 1611

'tis merry in hall when beards wag all (English) It is a sure sign, during a feast, that everyone is enjoying themselves when their beards are seen to wag (with laughter). *King Alisaunder*, c.1310.
Be merry, be merry, my wife has all ... 'Tis merry in hall when beards wag all.
William Shakespeare, *Henry IV, Part 2*, c.1598

merry. *See also* a CHERRY year, a merry year; a plum year, a dumb year

Merryman. *See* the best DOCTORS are Dr Diet, Dr Quiet and Dr Merryman

mice. *See* the BEST laid schemes of mice and men gang oft agley; a CAT in gloves catches no mice; when the CAT's away, the mice will play; KEEP no more cats than will catch mice

mickle. *See* MANY a mickle makes a muckle

midge. *See* the MOTHER of mischief is no bigger than a midge's wing

midnight. *See* one HOUR's sleep before midnight is worth two after

mid-stream. See don't CHANGE horses in mid-stream

might is right (*Greek*) Usual standards of justice can be overwhelmed by the influence of the powerful. 1327, quoted in T. Wright, *Political Songs*, 1839 (also quoted in Plato's *Republic*, by Plautus and by Lucan in *Pharsalia*).

O, that right should thus overcome might!
William Shakespeare, *Henry IV, Part 2, c.*1598

mightier. See the PEN is mightier than the sword

mighty. See a REED before the wind lives on, while mighty oaks do fall

mile. See an INCH is as good as a mile; a MISS is as good as a mile

milk. See why BUY a cow when milk is so cheap?; it's no use CRYING over spilt milk

mill. the mill cannot grind with the water that is past (*English*) It is impossible to make anything of times or opportunities that have already passed. T. Draxe, *Adages*, 1616.

mill. See also all is GRIST that comes to the mill; much WATER goes by the mill that the miller knows not of

miller. every honest miller has a thumb of gold (*English*) Even the most honest millers make illegal money by cheating their customers by virtue of the flour that sticks to their thumb. Geoffrey Chaucer, *The Canterbury Tales*, c.1387. If thus accused of having a 'golden thumb', many a miller in former times would retort that only a cuckold could see it. Other proverbs questioning the honesty of millers include 'many a miller many a thief' and 'put a miller, a tailor and a weaver into one bag, and shake them, the first that comes out will be a thief'.

Wel koude he stelen corn and tollen thries,
And yet he hadde a thombe of gold pardee.
Geoffrey Chaucer, *The Canterbury Tales, c.*1387

miller. See also much WATER goes by the mill that the miller knows not of

mills. the mills of God grind slowly, yet they grind exceeding small (*English*) It may take a long time to get your revenge on someone, but when you do it is sure to be doubly crushing. George Herbert, *Outlandish Proverbs*, 1640.

Though the mills of God grind slowly, yet they grind exceeding small;
Though with patience He stands waiting, with exactness grinds He all.
Henry Wadsworth Longfellow, 'Retribution', 1870

mind. mind your own business (*English*) Do not pay unwarranted interest in the affairs of others, but concentrate instead on your own. J. Clarke, *Paroemiologia Anglo-Latina*, 1639.

mind. See also the FACE is the index of the mind; OUT of sight, out of mind; TRAVEL broadens the mind

minds. See GREAT minds think alike; LITTLE things please little minds

miracles. the age of miracles is past (*English*) Miracles are unlikely to happen and belong to the long-distant, legendary, past. William Shakespeare, *Henry V, c.*1598. In more recent years the proverb has been reworked into the facetious 'the age of miracles is not past', often quoted sarcastically when something unexpected (but long overdue) actually happens.

It must be so; for miracles are ceas'd;
And therefore we must needs admit the means
How things are perfected.
William Shakespeare, *Henry V, c.*1598

mirror. the best mirror is an old

friend (Spanish) Old friends can be relied upon to give flattering accounts of how you look. George Herbert, *Outlandish Proverbs*, 1640.

mischief. better a mischief than an inconvenience (English) It is better to put up with some small nuisance in order to avoid some greater problem. T. Wilson, *Discourse upon Usury*, 1572.

mischief. *See also* the MOTHER of mischief is no bigger than a midge's wing

misery. it is misery enough to have been once happy (English) For those who have fallen on bad times it is particularly painful to be reminded of how happy they once were. Bullein, *Bulwark of Defence*, 1562.

Miserum est fuisse felicem ... it is a great miserie to have beene happy.
Richard Burton, *The Anatomy of Melancholy*, 1624

misery loves company (English) Those who feel depressed find consolation in the company of others, particularly if they are similarly afflicted. John Lyly, *Euphues: The Anatomy of Wit*, 1578. *See also* ADVERSITY makes strange bedfellows.

If misery loves company, misery has company enough.
Henry David Thoreau, *Journal*, 1 September 1851

misfortunes never come singly (English) If something goes wrong the chances are something else will too. *King Alisaunder*, c. 1300. Also found in the form 'misfortunes never come alone'. *See also* it never RAINS but it pours.

When sorrows come, they come not single spies, but in battalions.
William Shakespeare, *Hamlet*, c. 1600

misreckoning is no payment (English) Paying someone less than is due to them is little better than paying them

nothing at all. John Heywood, *A Dialogue containing ... the Proverbs in the English Tongue*, 1546.

miss. a miss is as good as a mile (English) Failing by a narrow margin is in the final analysis no better than failing by a wider margin. William Camden, *Remains concerning Britain*, 1614. The proverb was originally given as 'an inch in a miss is as good as an ell' (an ell being an archaic measurement equivalent to forty-five inches). *See also* an INCH is as good as a mile.

A narrow shave; but a miss is as good as a mile.
George Bernard Shaw, *Arms and the Man*, 1894

you never miss the water till the well runs dry (English/Scottish) It is only when something is no longer available that you start to miss it and value it. J. Carmichaell, *Proverbs in Scots*, 1628.

missed. *See* a SLICE off a cut loaf isn't missed

mist from the hill brings water to the mill (English) Mist on high ground warns of wet weather to come. R. P. Chope, *Hartland Dialect*, 1891. Variants include 'when the mist comes from the hill, then good weather it doth spill; when the mist comes from the sea, then good weather it will be'. Another version is specific to anglers: 'when the mist creeps up the hill, fisherman out and try your skill; when the mist begins to nod, fisherman then put up your rod'.

mistakes. if you don't make mistakes you don't make anything (English) Those who are not prepared to risk making mistakes will never achieve anything. Joseph Conrad, *The Outcast of the Islands*, 1896. *See also* NOTHING ventured, nothing gained.

It's only those who do nothing that make no mistakes, I suppose.
Joseph Conrad, *The Outcasts of the Islands*, 1896

mistress. when the mistress is the master, parsley grows the faster (English) Parsley grows best in a garden where the woman rules the household. Charlotte Burne, *Shropshire Folk-Lore*, 1883.

mists. so many mists in March, so many frosts in May (English) The prevalence of mist in March is an indication of how much frost will lie on the ground in May. A. Hopton, *Concordancy of Years*, 1612.

mixen. See better WED over the mixen than over the moor

mocking is catching (English) Those who scorn others for their faults may well find they have fallen prey to the same faults themselves. J. Heywood, *Play of Love*, 1533.

moderation in all things (Greek) It is sensible to be moderate in everything you do. Herman Melville, *Mardi*, 1849 (also quoted by Hesiod in *Works and Days*). See also there is a MEASURE in all things.

molehill. See don't make a MOUNTAIN out of a molehill

Monday's child is fair of face, Tuesday's child is full of grace; Wednesday's child is full of woe, Thursday's child has far to go; Friday's child is loving and giving, Saturday's child works hard for its living; and the child that's born on the Sabbath day, is fair and wise and good and gay (English) The day upon which a person is born gives an indication of their underlying character. A. E. Bray, *Traditions of Devon*, 1838. A related proverbial rhyme suggests which are the best days of the week for getting married: 'Monday for wealth, Tuesday for health, Wednesday the best day of all; Thursday for crosses, Friday for losses, Saturday no luck at all'.

money. all things are obedient to money (Roman) There is no limit to the influence of money in earthly affairs. Geoffrey Chaucer, *The Canterbury Tales*, c.1387 (also quoted by Horace). Related proverbs include 'what will not money do?' and 'money answers all things'.

All the world to gold obeieth.
John Gower, *Confessio Amantis*, c.1390

money begets money (English) Money, once obtained, attracts more money to it. T. Wilson, *Discourse upon Usury*, 1572. Also found as 'money draws money'. See also MONEY makes money.

We have got to recollect that money makes money, as well as makes everything else.
Charles Dickens, *Our Mutual Friend*, 1865

money has no smell (Roman) Money carries with it no taint of wherever it might have come from. Arnold Bennett, *Mr Prohack*, 1922. The proverb arose from a comment by the Roman emperor Vespasian, responding to his son Titus's reservations about raising money via a tax imposed on public lavatories: 'and yet it comes from urine'. Another proverb with the same meaning is the English 'money is welcome though it come in a dirty clout', first recorded in the mid-sixteenth century.

He understood in a flash the deep wisdom of that old proverb ... that money has no smell.
Arnold Bennett, *Mr Prohack*, 1922

money is power (English) Wealth

brings with it influence. N. Ames, *Almanack*, 1741. Much the same sentiment is expressed in the proverb 'all things are obedient to money' (which was quoted in Classical times by Horace among others).

money isn't everything (English/US) The getting of money is not the only consideration in life. Eugene O'Neill, *Marco Millions*, 1927. Another proverb, though, warns 'he that wants money wants all things'.

money makes a man (English) A man with money is taken more seriously by the world at large, regardless of his other qualities or flaws. R. L. Greene, *Early English Carols*, 1500. A fuller version of the proverb runs 'money makes a man free everywhere'.

Money most truly and fearfully 'makes the man'. A difference in income, as you go lower, makes more and more difference … in all which polishes the man.
Charles Kingsley, *Alton Locke*, 1850

money makes money (English) Money can be used to make more money. T. Wilson, *Discourse upon Usury*, 1572. A less well-known proverb advises 'if thou wouldst keep money, save money; if thou wouldst reap money, sow money'. *See also* MONEY begets money.

Money, says the proverb, makes money. When you have got a little, it is often easy to get more.
Adam Smith, *The Wealth of Nations*, 1776

money makes the mare to go (English) Anything can be accomplished with money. 1500, quoted in R. L. Greene, *Early English Carols*, 1935. Equivalent proverbs include 'money makes the old wife trot'.

money makes the world go round (US) It is money that motivates all the

world's important activities. Fred Ebb and John Kander, song title, *Cabaret*, 1966. A related proverb runs 'money governs the world'. Centuries before the phrase was made famous as the song from *Cabaret* it had been voiced elsewhere in various disguised forms, including a seventeenth-century Dutch version. *See also* LOVE makes the world go round.

money talks (English) The promise of money buys any favour or influence that a person may desire. G. Torriano, *Italian Proverbs*, 1666. Though it is only in the twentieth century that the proverb has appeared in its modern form, the same sentiment has been voiced in various forms many centuries previously and equivalents may be found in many European languages. Examples from elsewhere include 'money answers all things' and the Italian 'the tongue hath no force when golde speaketh'.

Money will say more in one moment than the most eloquent lover can in years.
Henry Fielding, *The Miser*, 1733

money. *See also* BAD money drives out good; BEAUTY is potent, but money is omnipotent; a FOOL and his money are soon parted; GOD made man, man made money; the LOVE of money is the root of all evil; where there's MUCK, there's money; you PAYS your money and you takes your choice; TIME is money

moneyless. a moneyless man goes fast through the market (English) A person with no money to spend has no reason to linger where things might be purchased. James Kelly, *A Complete Collection of Scotish Proverbs*, 1721. The proverb is sometimes quoted to convey the idea that those who are in need of something will hurry to where it might be obtained.

monk. *See* the COWL does not make the monk; the DEVIL sick would be a monk

monkey. *See* the HIGHER the monkey climbs the more he shows his tail; SOFTLY, softly, catchee monkey

monkeys. *See* if you PAY peanuts, you get monkeys

moon. the moon does not heed the barking of dogs (Roman) It is futile to rant against nature or against other things or persons that are incapable of change. John Lyly, *Euphues and His England*, 1580.

Doth the moon care for the barking of a dog? They detract, scoffe, and raile (saith one), and bark at me on every side; but I ... vindicate myself by contempt alone. Richard Burton, *The Anatomy of Melancholy*, 1621

moon. *See also* NO moon, no man

moor. *See* better WED over the mixen than over the moor

more. more people know Tom Fool than Tom Fool knows (English) People in the public eye are known by more people than they know themselves. S. Holland, *Wit and Fancy in a Maze*, 1656. The name Tom Fool was traditionally applied both to simpletons and to the Fools of historical drama. Also encountered with 'Jack' in the place of 'Tom Fool'.

It was no satisfaction to me that I knew not their faces, for they might know mine ... according to the old English proverb, 'that more knows Tom Fool, than Tom Fool knows'. Daniel Defoe, *Colonel Jack*, 1723

the more knave, the better luck (English) The more unprincipled a person is, the more they seem to benefit

by strokes of good fortune. Hugh Latimer, *Sermons*, 1550.

the more laws, the more offenders (English) The more rules there are to break, the more offences will be committed. J. Palsgrave, *L'Éclaircissement de la langue française*, 1530.

the more the merrier (English) The greater the number the better the end result. *The Pearl*, c.1380. A fuller version of the proverb points out the contrasting advantages of a smaller number of people at a party or meal: 'the more the merrier; the fewer the better fare'. *See also* too many COOKS spoil the broth.

The old proverb comes true — 'the more the merrier: but the fewer the better fare'. Charles Kingsley, *Westward Ho!*, 1855

the more you get, the more you want (Greek) A little of something good only feeds the appetite for more. R. Rolle, *Psalter*, c.1340 (also quoted by Horace in his *Epistles*). Variants in other languages include the French 'plus il en a, plus il en veut'.

My more having would be a source To make me hunger more. William Shakespeare, *Macbeth*, c.1604

the more you stir, the worse it will stink (English) The more you probe into others' secrets the greater trouble you will provoke. John Heywood, *A Dialogue containing ... the Proverbs in the English Tongue*, 1546.

Pray let Grub-street alone, for the more you stir the more it will stink. Henry Fielding, *Covent Garden Journal*, 1752

more. *See also* the more COST the more honour; more HASTE, less speed; MUCH would have more; there are more WAYS of killing a cat than choking it with cream; there are more WAYS of killing a dog than choking it with butter; there are more WAYS of killing a dog than hanging it

morning dreams come true (*Greek*) Things dreamt after midnight are sure to come true. J. Palsgrave, *Acolastus*, 1540 (also quoted by Horace in *Satires*).

And all the morning dreams are true.
Ben Jonson, *Love Restored*, 1616

morning. *See also* LOSE an hour in the morning, chase it all day; RED sky at night, shepherd's delight; red sky in the morning, sailor's warning

mortal. *See* all MEN are mortal

moss. *See* a ROLLING stone gathers no moss

mother. like mother, like daughter (*Hebrew*) Daughters take after their mothers both in character and mannerisms. Bible, Ezekiel 16:44. Variants include 'like mistress, like maid'. *See also* like FATHER, like son.

Every one that useth proverbs shall use this proverb against thee, saying, As is the mother, so is her daughter.
Bible, Ezekiel 16:44

the mother of mischief is no bigger than a midge's wing (*English/Scottish*) Grave consequences can result from the smallest item of gossip or unsubstantiated rumour. J. Carmichaell, *Proverbs in Scots*, 1628.

mother. *See also* NECESSITY is the mother of invention; POVERTY is the mother of health; PRAISE the child, and you make love to the mother

mother-in-law. there is but one good mother-in-law, and she is dead (*English*) There is no such thing as a good mother-in-law. Wise, *New Forest*, 1863. Equivalents include 'the best mother-in-law wears a green overcoat' (in other words, is dead and

buried). Other proverbs concerning mothers-in-law include 'the mother-in-law remembers not that she was a daughter-in-law'. *See also* NEVER rely on the glory of the morning or on the smile of your mother-in-law.

mountain. don't make a mountain out of a molehill (*Greek*) Don't exaggerate minor problems so that they become major ones. William Roper, *Life of More*, 1557. Equivalents in other European languages, all descended from an ancient Greek saying, include the French 'to make an elephant out of a fly'.

Those people are ever swelling mole hills to mountains.
Samuel Foote, *The Lame Lover*, c.1760

if the mountain will not go to Mahomet, Mahomet must go to the mountain (*Arabic*) If it is impossible to do something the easy way then it must be done the hard way. Francis Bacon, *Essays*, 1597. According to Bacon, in his essay 'Of Boldness', Mahomet promised the faithful that he would call a mountain to him and preach from the top of it — but when he called the mountain did not come. Mahomet calmly explained that this was a sign of God's mercy, for had the mountain moved to where they stood they would all have been crushed. He then announced that as the mountain would not come to him, he would have to go to the mountain. The mountain has since been identified as Mount Safa near Mecca. Bacon may have produced his English version of the proverb after reading the Arabic *Anecdotes of Chodja Nas'reddin Dschocha er Rumi*: 'if the palm tree does not come to Dschocha, Dschocha will go to the palm tree'.

Neither Kitty nor I can change our habits,
even for friendship ... Mountains cannot
stir ... but Mahomet can come to the
mountain as often as he likes.
Edward Bulwer-Lytton, *The Caxtons*, 1849

mountains. *See* FAITH will move mountains

mouse. a mouse may help a lion
(English) The small and insignificant
may still provide invaluable service
to the great and powerful. *Mirror
for Magistrates*, 1563. The proverb has
its origins in Aesop's fable about the
lion and the rat, which was first printed in English by William Caxton in
1484.

**the mouse that has only one hole is
easily taken** (Roman) The fugitive who
has only one place of safety to shelter
in will soon be located. Geoffrey
Chaucer, *The Canterbury Tales*, c.1387
(also quoted by Plautus). Also found
in several other European languages.

The house that always trusts to one poor
hole,
Can never be a mouse of any soul.
Alexander Pope, *The Wife of Bath*, 1717

mouse. *See also* it is a BOLD mouse that
breeds in the cat's ear; ONE for the
mouse, one for the crow, one to rot,
one to grow; don't pour WATER on a
drowned mouse

mouth. *See* never LOOK a gift horse in the
mouth; a SOW may whistle, though it
has an ill mouth for it

**mouths. out of the mouths of babes
and sucklings** (Hebrew) The young
may, however unwittingly, voice great
truths or perceptive insights. Bible,
Psalms 8:2 and Matthew 21:16.

Jesus saith unto them, Yea, have yee never
read, Out of the mouth of babes and sucklings thou hast perfected praise.
Bible, Matthew 21:16

mouths. *See also* GOD never sends
mouths but He sends meat

move. *See* FAITH will move mountains

much. much coin, much care (Greek)
Great riches bring with them the cares
of responsibility and the anxiety that
they will be lost. J. Clarke, *Paroemiologia
Anglo-Latina*, 1639 (also quoted by
Horace).

Care follows increasing wealth.
Horace, *Odes*, first century BC

much cry and little wool (English)
Those who boast much of what they
have to offer often turn out to have the
least to offer in reality. J. Fortescue, *On
the Governance of England*, 1475. *See also*
EMPTY vessels make the most sound.

Thou wilt at best but suck a bull,
Or shear swine, all cry and no wool.
Samuel Butler, *Hudibras*, 1663

much would have more (Greek)
Those who enjoy something find they
can never have enough of it. *Douce MS*,
c.1350 (also quoted by Horace). *See
also* the MORE you get, the more you
want.

Much would have more; but often meets
with less.
Thomas Fuller, *Gnomologia*, 1732

much. *See also* you can have TOO much
of a good thing

**muck. where's there's muck, there's
money** (English) Where there is muck
– be it in the form of soil, dirt, dung
or industrial grime – there is money
to be made. John Ray, *A Collection of
English Proverbs*, 1678. The saying was
coined in the late sixteenth century
when farmers first learned that
spreading dung and other 'muck' on
their land would promote their crops
and enjoyed new currency after the
Industrial Revolution when factories,
a source of new wealth, belched out

soot and smoke. Also found, in northern England especially, as 'where there's muck, there's brass' and 'where there's muck, there's luck'. Other variants include 'muck and money go together'.

muckle. *See* MANY a mickle makes a muckle

multitude. *See* CHARITY covers a multitude of sins

murder. murder will out (English) It is impossible to keep terrible crimes such as murder secret. *Cursor Mundi*, c.1325. *See also* TRUTH will out.

O blisful god, that art so just and trewe!
Lo, how that thou biwreyest mordre alway,
Mordre wol out, that see we day by day.
Geoffrey Chaucer, *The Canterbury Tales*, c.1387

murder. *See also* KILLING no murder

music. music hath charms (English) One of the properties of music is the soothing of a troubled mind. William Congreve, *The Mourning Bride*, 1697. A contrasting proverb, however, runs 'all music jars when the soul's out of tune'.

Music hath charms to soothe the savage breast,
To soften rocks or bend a knotted oak.
William Congreve, *The Mourning Bride*, 1697

music helps not the toothache (English) Music may have many qualities, but has its limitations and cannot ease physical pain. George Herbert, *Jacula Prudentum*, 1640.

must. what must be, must be (English) What is fated to happen will happen. Geoffrey Chaucer, *The Canterbury Tales*, c.1387. Variants include 'what shall be, shall be'. The same sentiment is encountered in many other languages, including the oft-quoted Italian: 'che sarà sarà'.

I must kiss you ... What must be, must be.
Beaumont and Fletcher, *The Scornful Lady*, 1616

n

---

nail. for want of a nail the shoe was lost (English) All might be lost if some minor flaw is not remedied in time. T. Adams, *Works*, 1629. The full version of the proverb runs, 'for want of a nail the shoe was lost; for want of a shoe the horse was lost; and for want of a horse the man was lost'. *See also* don't SPOIL the ship for a ha'porth of tar; a STITCH in time saves nine.

For want of a nail the shoe was lost, for want of a shoe the horse was lost, an' for want of a horse the man was lost — aw, that's a darlin' proverb, a daarlin'.
Sean O'Casey, *Juno and the Paycock*, 1925

nail drives out nail (Greek) The old is often inevitably replaced by the new. *Ancrene Wisse*, 1250 (also found in the writings of Aristotle). Also found as 'one nail drives out another'. The origins of the proverb lie in the practice of using a new nail as a punch to dislodge an old one.

As one nail by strength drives out another,
So the remembrance of my former love
Is by a newer object quite forgotten.
William Shakespeare, *The Two Gentlemen of Verona*, c.1594

naked. See ANYTHING will fit a naked man

name. See GET a name to rise early, and you may lie all day; GIVE a dog a bad name and hang him; he that has an ILL name is half hanged; a ROSE by any other name would smell as sweet

names. See NO names, no pack drill; STICKS and stones may break my bones, but names will never hurt me

Naples. See SEE Naples and die

nation. See the ENGLISH are a nation of shopkeepers

nature. nature abhors a vacuum (Roman) An empty space of any kind runs contrary to the natural order of things. Thomas Cranmer, *Answer to Gardiner*, 1551 (derived ultimately from Plutarch).

Whatever philosophy may determine of material nature, it is certainly true of intellectual nature, that it abhors a vacuum: our minds cannot be empty.
Samuel Johnson, letter, 20 June 1771

nature does nothing in vain (Greek) There is a purpose behind all the workings of nature. G. Harvey, *Marginalia*, c.1580 (also found in the writings of Aristotle).

Nature which doth nothing in vain.
Francis Bacon, *The Advancement of Learning*, 1605

nature passes nurture (English) A person's inbred character will always have more influence than what they are taught. Stapylton, *Juvenal*, 1647. Sometimes quoted in reference to art, supporting the view that art can be but a pale imitation of nature. *See also* NURTURE passes nature.

nature will have its course (English) Natural processes cannot be denied. *Beryn*, c.1400.

nature. *See also* though you CAST out nature with a fork, it will still return; you can DRIVE out nature with a pitchfork, but she keeps on coming back; *also* SELF-preservation is the first law of nature

nay. *See* he that WILL not when he may, when he will he shall have nay

near is my coat but nearer my skin (English) In the last resort a person will, however reluctantly, put his own interests (represented by his own skin) above all other concerns. *Ballads*, c.1579 (also found in the writings of Plautus). Variant forms include 'near is my kirtle, but nearer is my smock', 'the smock is nearer than the petticoat' and 'near is my shirt but nearer my skin'.

And though to fortune near be her petticoat,
Yet nearer is her smock, the queen doth note.
Ben Jonson, *The Alchemist*, 1612

nearer. the nearer the bone, the sweeter the flesh (English) The choicest portions of something are often to be found in close proximity to the poorest. Bartholomew, *On the Properties of Things*, 1398. Another proverb with a rather different viewpoint has it that 'flesh is aye fairest that is farthest from the bone', a saying formerly often applied to those who are plump but healthy looking.

The nearer the bane the sweeter, as your

honours weel ken.
Walter Scott, *The Bride of Lammermoor*, 1819

the nearer the church, the further from God (English/French/German) Those who live nearest the church and make a show of following its tenets in public often turn out to be the least sincere in their faith. Robert Manning of Brunne, *Handlyng Synne*, c.1303. Variants include 'the nearer Rome, the worse Christian' and 'the nearer the Pope, the worse Christian', which both date from the Reformation.

For the nearer the church – the proverb is somewhat musty.
Walter Scott, *Redgauntlet*, 1824

necessity. necessity is the mother of invention (English) Need prompts all manner of ingenuity. Roger Ascham, *Toxophilus*, 1545. *See also* NEEDS must when the Devil drives.

I soaled my Shoes with wood, which I cut from a Tree ... No man could more verify the Truth ... That, Necessity is the Mother of Invention.
Jonathan Swift, *Gulliver's Travels*, 1726

necessity knows no law (Roman) All rules are cast aside when circumstances dictate action. William Langland, *Piers Plowman*, 1377 (also quoted by Publilius Syrus and other Classical authors). German Chancellor Bethmann-Hollweg quoted the proverb in the Reichstag on 4 August 1914 in justification of his country's invasion of Belgian territory. *See also* NEEDS must when the Devil drives.

So spake the Fiend, and with necessitie,
The Tyrant's plea, excus'd his devilish deeds.
John Milton, *Paradise Lost*, 1667

need. *See* a FRIEND in need is a friend indeed

needs. needs must when the Devil

drives (English) One must do whatever is necessary when circumstances leave no other choice. John Lydgate, *Assembly of the Gods*, c.1450. Sometimes shortened to 'needs must'. Related proverbs include 'need makes the old wife trot' and 'need will have its course'.

He must needs go that the devil drives.
William Shakespeare, *All's Well that Ends Well*, c.1602

needs. *See also* GOOD wine needs no bush; a GUILTY conscience needs no accuser

ne'er. *See* ne'er CAST a clout till May be out

neighbour. look to thyself when thy neighbour's house is on fire (Roman) When disaster strikes those close to you it is wise to take steps to safeguard your own interests. Horman, *Vulgaria*, 1519 (also found in Virgil and Horace).

what a neighbour gets is not lost (English) Favours won by friends or neighbours may also indirectly bring benefit to you. L. Wager, *Mary Magdalene*, 1567.

neighbour. *See also* a good LAWYER makes a bad neighbour

neighbours. *See* GOOD fences make good neighbours

nest. *See* there are NO BIRDS in last year's nest; it's an ILL bird that fouls its own nest

nests. *See* BIRDS in their little nests agree

net. in vain the net is spread in the sight of the bird (Hebrew) It is futile setting a trap in sight of the proposed victim. Bible, Proverbs 1:17.

the net fills though the fisherman sleeps (Greek) Good things may still come to those who do nothing to help

themselves. White-Kennett, *Erasmus' In Praise of Folly*, 1683. The Greeks derived the proverb from the Athenian general Timotheus, who enjoyed great good fortune in his campaigns despite not being an outstanding thinker. Another Greek proverb employing similar imagery runs 'the net of the sleeper catches fish'.

net. *See also* it is in vain to CAST your net where there is no fish; all is FISH that comes to the net

nettle. *See* if you GENTLY touch a nettle it'll sting you for your pains

never. never is a long time (English) Given enough time, most things are possible (usually quoted in response to someone who claims something will never happen). Geoffrey Chaucer, *The Canterbury Tales*, c.1387. Variants include 'never is a long day'.

Nevere to thryve were to long a date.
Geoffrey Chaucer, *The Canterbury Tales*, c.1387

never rely on the glory of the morning or on the smile of your mother-in-law (English) Good weather in the morning and the good-heartedness of your mother-in-law are not to be trusted. J. W. R. Scott, *The Foundations of Japan*, 1922.

never say die (English) Never give up hope. Charles Dickens, *The Pickwick Papers*, 1837.

never work with children or animals (US) Those who enter business partnerships (especially in the sphere of showbusiness) with children or animals are sure to experience difficult times. Often attributed to US comedian W. C. Fields.

never. *See also* BY the street of by and by one arrives at the house of never; never CATCH at a falling knife or friend;

never CHOOSE your women or your linen by candlelight; never DO things by halves; never GIVE a sucker an even break; never JUDGE by appearances; better LATE than never; it is never too LATE to learn; it is never too LATE to mend; never LOOK a gift horse in the mouth; never PUT off till tomorrow what you can do today; never SPEAK ill of the dead; you should never TOUCH your eye but with your elbow; a WISE man is never less alone than when he is alone

new. always something new out of Africa (Greek) Africa may be depended upon as a rich source of new sights and discoveries. Aristotle, *De Anima*, fourth century BC. The original Greek proverb was quoted in Pliny's *Natural History*, in the form '*Africa semper aliquid novi afferre*', and was probably inspired by the commonly held notion that Africa was the haunt of monsters.

Out of Africa.
Film title, 1985

new lords, new laws (English) When new people take control changes in the law are inevitable. E. Hall, *Chronicle*, 1547.

'I was lately married to a woman, and she's my vocation now.' … 'New lords new laws, as the saying is.'
Thomas Hardy, *Far From the Madding Crowd*, 1874

new things are fair (English) Anything new is thereby attractive. Geoffrey Chaucer, *The Legend of Good Women*, c.1380. Also encountered as 'everything new is fine'. *See also* what is NEW cannot be true.

Men loven of propre kynde newefangelnesse.
Geoffrey Chaucer, *The Canterbury Tales*, c.1387

what is new cannot be true (English) Never trust a novelty. J. Clarke, *Paroemiologia Anglo-Latina*, 1639. The fuller form of the proverb is 'what is new cannot be true, and what is true cannot be new'. The proverb is countered by another ancient saying, 'newer is truer'. *See also* NEW things are fair.

I found that generally what was new was false.
James Boswell, *Life of Johnson*, 1791

when a new book appears, read an old one (English) Stick to what you know you will enjoy, or have already found yourself to be content with. A. C. Benson, *From A College Window*, 1907. Benson attributed this quip, often sarcastically directed at anyone rooted in their own prejudices, to Charles Lamb.

you can't put new wine in old bottles (Hebrew) You can't always marry new ideas or innovations with old contexts. Bible, Matthew, 9:17. Because new wine expands as it matures, it is inadvisable to put it in old bottles (formerly made of skin) as the old skin will not stretch as new skin does, and therefore bursts and the wine is lost. *See also* you can't TEACH an old dog new tricks.

new. *See also* a new BROOM sweeps clean; there is NOTHING new under the sun; be OFF with the old love before you are on with the new

news. *See* go ABROAD and you'll hear news of home; BAD news travels fast; NO news is good news

nice. a nice wife and a back door will soon make a rich man poor (English) A wealthy man will soon find his riches gone if he has an extravagant wife and dishonest servants (who come and go by the back door). *Proverbs of Good Counsel*, c.1450.

nice guys finish last (US) It takes a certain degree of ruthlessness to succeed in life. c.1946 (commonly attributed to Leo Durocher, manager of the Brooklyn Dodgers baseball team, 1951–54). Usually quoted in justification for some unscrupulous act.

night. night is the mother of counsel (Greek) Night-time is the best time for thinking and making plans. J. Sandford, *The Garden of Pleasure*, 1573 (also found in the writings of Menander).

Untroubled night, they say, gives counsell best.
Edmund Spenser, *The Faerie Queene*, 1590.

the night is no man's friend (German) No man is safe during the hours of darkness, when evil spirits roam. R. C. Trench, *On the Lessons in Proverbs*, 1853.

night. *See also* BARNABY bright, Barnaby bright, the longest day and the shortest night; RED sky at night, shepherd's delight; red sky in the morning, sailor's warning

nine. nine tailors make a man (French) It takes the work of nine tailors – or nine tailors themselves – to make a man. Thomas Dekker and John Webster, *Northward Hoe*, 1605. The origins of the proverb are disputed, with some authorities suggesting a real man may be distinguished by his possession of sets of clothes from nine different tailors, while others claim that tailors are physically feeble as a consequence of their work and thus it takes nine (or, sometimes, two or three) of them to amount to a man. Yet others claim a link with the 'nine tailors' rung by bell-ringers – an allusion

to the tradition of ringing a funeral bell nine times for a man, six for a woman and three for a child. Another proverb casting tailors in a dubious light runs 'a hundred tailors, a hundred weavers and a hundred millers make three hundred thieves'.

Does it not stand on record that the English Queen Elizabeth, receiving a deputation of Eighteen Tailors, addressed them with 'Good morning, gentlemen both!'
Thomas Carlyle, *Sartor Resartus*, 1838

nine. *See also* a CAT has nine lives; PARSLEY seed goes nine times to the Devil; POSSESSION is nine points of the law; it is not SPRING until you can plant your foot upon twelve daisies; a STITCH in time saves nine

no. no bad deed goes unpunished (English) Anyone guilty of an evil act will get their comeuppance eventually. A cynical modern reworking of this rather moralistic proverb runs 'no good deed goes unpunished'.

no coming to heaven with dry eyes (English) Those aspiring to sainthood, or simply a place in heaven, must expect to suffer while on earth. T. Adams, *Sermons*, 1629.

no cross, no crown (English) There is no enjoying the prize without some effort or sacrifice first. Francis Quarles, *Ester*, 1621.

no man can serve two masters (Hebrew) It is impossible to be faithful to more than one master or ideal simultaneously. Bible, Matthew 6:24. The proverb made its first appearance in English literature in a collection of political songs around 1330. *See also* you cannot serve GOD and Mammon.

Men cannot serve two masters.
George Bernard Shaw, *Saint Joan*, 1924

no man cries stinking fish (English)

No one speaks ill of their own wares or attributes (including fishmongers advertising their fish). L. Price, *A Map of Merry Conceits*, 1656.

I replied that I was a young gentleman of large fortune (this was not true; but what is the use of crying bad fish?).
William Thackeray, *Barry Lyndon*, 1844

no man is a hero to his valet (French) The aura of mystique is much reduced with intimate knowledge of a person's personal character. John Florio, *Montaigne's Essays*, 1603. The saying is most commonly attributed to the seventeenth-century Frenchwoman Madame Cornuel, though much the same may be found in the writings of Plutarch and Montaigne. *See also* FAMIL-IARITY breeds contempt.

And to his very valet seemed a hero.
Lord Byron, *Beppo*, 1818

no man is wise at all times (Roman) Even those who are very wise make mistakes. J. Clarke, *Paroemiologia Anglo-Latina*, 1639 (also quoted by Pliny). *See also* even HOMER sometimes nods.

I was tired of being always wise, and could not help gratifying their request, because I loved to see them happy.
Oliver Goldsmith, *The Vicar of Wakefield*, 1766

no mischief but a woman or a priest is at the bottom of it (Roman) Women and the clergy are at the root of most disputes to beset mankind. Hugh Latimer, *Second Sermon before Edward VI*, 1549 (also quoted by Juvenal).

Such a plot must have a woman in it.
Samuel Richardson, *Sir Charles Grandison*, 1754

no moon, no man (English) Babies born at the time when there is no moon (in other words, when it is between cycles) are unlikely to prosper. Thomas Hardy, *The Return of the Native*, 1878. Superstition claims that

babies born at this time are unlikely to live beyond puberty. The ideal time for childbirth is during the waxing of a new moon.

'No moon, no man.' 'Tis one of the truest sayings ever spit out. The boy never comes to anything that's born at new moon.
Thomas Hardy, *The Return of the Native*, 1878

no names, no pack drill (English) By keeping the names of guilty parties secret no one can be punished (pack drill – drilling at length while carrying a heavy backpack – being a standard punishment for minor transgressions in the armed forces). O. Onions, *Peace in our Time*, 1923.

I know some as are as sweet as the blossoms that bloom in the May – oh, no names, no pack drill.
Sean O'Casey, *Juno and the Paycock*, 1925

no news is good news (English/Italian) When no news about something is to be had this may be accepted as a good sign, as bad news would be communicated soon enough. James I, letter, 1616 (though also attributed to Italian sources of an earlier date).

no pain, no gain *See* no GAINS without pains

no penny, no paternoster (English) If no fee is forthcoming, no service will be performed. William Tyndale, *The Obedience of a Christian Man*, 1528. The proverb derives from the practice of priests demanding payment before carrying out religious services.

Who at a dead lift,
Can't send for a gift
A pig to the priest for a roster,
Shall heare his clarke say ...
No pennie, no Pater Noster.
Robert Herrick, *Hesperides*, 1648

no silver, no servant (English) No one

will work for someone who has no money. T. Draxe, *Bibliotheca Scholastica*, 1633.

no time like the present (*English*) Don't put things off, but do them straight away. G. Legh, *Accidence of Armoury*, 1562. *See also* PROCRASTINATION is the thief of time.

there's no smoke without fire (*Roman*) When rumours about something spread there is sure to be some nugget of truth at the bottom of it. Thomas Hoccleve, *Works*, c.1422 (also quoted by Plautus).

There can no great smoke arise, but there must be some fire, no great reporte without great suspition.
John Lyly, *Euphues: The Anatomy of Wit*, 1578

you can have no more of a fox than the skin (*English*) You cannot get more from someone or something than there is to be had. Alexander Barclay, *Eclogues*, c.1514. Variants include 'you can have no more of a cat but her skin'. *See also* you cannot get BLOOD from a stone.

no. *See also* there's no such thing as a FREE lunch; HALF a loaf is better than no bread; no one should be JUDGE in his own cause; there is no LEAPING from Delilah's lap into Abraham's bosom; there's no great LOSS without some gain; there's no PLACE like home; no PLEASURE without pain; if there were no RECEIVERS, there would be no thieves; there is no ROYAL road to learning; SEE no evil, hear no evil, speak no evil; SHROUDS have no pockets; TIME and tide wait for no man

noblesse oblige (*French*) The aristocracy, or those who occupy positions of high standing, have responsibilities as well as rights. Duc de Levis, *Maximes et Preceptes*, 1808 (though similar

sentiments were expressed centuries before by Aeschylus and Euripides).

nobody. *See* EVERYBODY's business is nobody's business; it's an ILL wind that blows nobody any good

nod. a nod is as good as a wink to a blind horse (*English*) The smallest hint conveys a wealth of meaning, though only if the other person is capable of registering it. William Godwin, *Caleb Williams*, 1794. The phrase enjoyed a revival in the early 1970s when it was repeated, as 'nudge, nudge, say no more' in a famous *Monty Python* television comedy sketch, in which it was used to suggest all manner of sexual innuendo.

A wink's as good as a nod with some folks.
Dorothy Wordsworth, *Journal*, 1802

nods. *See* even HOMER sometimes nods

none. *See* a BAD excuse is better than none; there are none so BLIND as those who will not see; none but the BRAVE deserve the fair; there are none so DEAF as those who will not hear

north. out of the north all ill comes forth (*English*) The north of the British Isles is the source of great trouble. Michael Drayton, *England's Heroical Epistles*, 1597. A less well-known proverb goes into more detail: 'the north for greatness, the east for health, the south for neatness, the west for wealth', while another runs 'the north of England for an ox, the south for a sheep and the middle part for a man'.

Three ills come from the North, a cold wind, a shrinking cloth and a dissembling man.
John Ray, *A Collection of English Proverbs*, 1670

the north wind doth blow and we shall have snow (*English*) When the wind blows from the north it brings cold weather with it. Ralph Inwards,

Weather Lore, 1893. Related proverbs advise 'when the wind is in the north, the skilful fisher goes not forth' and 'when the wind's in the north you mustn't go forth'. By way of contrast, though, another proverb runs 'a northern air brings weather fair'.

nose. he that has a great nose thinks everybody is speaking of it (English) It is easy for someone who fancies they have some defect or weakness to imagine everyone else is talking about it. Thomas Fuller, *Gnomologia*, 1732. Related sayings include 'his nose will abide no jests'.

I went to the Court for the first time to-day, and, like the man with the large nose, thought everybody was thinking of me and my mishaps.
Walter Scott, *Journal*, 24 January 1826

nose. *See also* don't CUT off your nose to spite your face

nothing. he that has nothing is frightened of nothing (English) He who has nothing to lose cannot be frightened. William Roper, *Life of More*, c.1557.

nothing comes of nothing (Greek) Nothing can happen if one has nothing to start with. Geoffrey Chaucer, *Boethius*, c.1374. Related proverbs include 'where nothing is, nothing can be had'. The philosopher Xenophanes quoted the proverb as the founding principle upon which his theory of the eternity of matter was based. According to Persius, in *Satires*, 'from nothing nothing, and into nothing can nothing return'.

Nothing will come of nothing. Speak again.
William Shakespeare, *King Lear*, 1605

nothing dries sooner than a tear (Roman) Public demonstrations of sorrow or grief are often shortlived, suggesting insincerity. T. Wilson, *The Arte of Rhetorique*, 1560 (also found in the writings of Cicero). Sometimes found in the form 'nothing dries sooner than a woman's tears'.

These are but moonish shades of griefs or fears;
There's nothing sooner dries than women's tears.
John Webster, *The White Devil*, 1612

nothing for nothing (English) Everything must be paid for. T. Brown, *Works*, 1704. Another proverb runs, 'nothing for nothing, and very little for a halfpenny'. *See also* you don't get SOMETHING for nothing.

Nothing for nothing, young man.
George Eliot, *Romola*, 1863

nothing is burdensome as a secret (French) Keeping a secret is the most difficult thing in the world.

nothing is certain but death and taxes (English) The only things that can be relied upon to happen are the coming of death and the arrival of tax demands. Daniel Defoe, *History of the Devil*, 1726. Formerly also encountered as 'nothing is certain but death and quarter day' (quarter days being the days upon which taxes were due).

In this world nothing can be said to be certain, except death and taxes.
Benjamin Franklin, letter, 13 November 1789

nothing is certain but the unforeseen (English) What has not been envisaged is always the one thing that actually happens. J. A. Froude, *Oceana*, 1886. *See also* the UNEXPECTED always happens.

nothing is impossible (English) All things can be acheived. J. C. Bridge, *Cheshire Proverbs*, 1917. One variant form runs 'naught's impossible, as the old woman said when they told her her cauf [calf] had swallowed the grindstone'. Related proverbs include 'nothing is impossible to a willing heart'. *See also* NEVER say die.

nothing should be done in haste but gripping a flea (English) Nothing should be done without careful thought beforehand, with the exception of killing a flea (which must be done immediately before it can escape). N. L'Estrange, *Anecdotes and Traditions*, 1655.

Nothing to be done in haste, but gripping of Fleas … Spoken when we are unreasonably urged to make haste.
James Kelly, *A Complete Collection of Scotish Proverbs*, 1721

nothing so bad but it might have been worse (English) However bad things might appear, there is consolation in the fact that they are still not as bad as they might be. Walter Scott, *Rob Roy*, 1817. *See also* always LOOK on the bright side.

nothing so bold as a blind mare (Scottish) A person unaware of the true state of things will venture where others will not. J. Carmichaell, *Proverbs in Scots*, 1628.

nothing succeeds like success (French) Success breeds success. A. D. Richardson, *Beyond Mississippi*, 1867.

nothing ventured, nothing gained (English) Only by making an attempt to do something is there any chance of achieving it. John Heywood, *A Dialogue containing … the Proverbs in the English Tongue*, 1546. Also found in French, Spanish and other European languages. Variants in English include 'nothing venture, nothing have', the form in which it

was quoted by Geoffrey Chaucer in *Troilus and Criseyde*, c.1385, 'nothing venture, nothing win' and 'nothing seek, nothing find'. The French and Spanish have 'he who will not risk himself will never go to the Indies' – a reference to the trading links those countries had with the West Indies in former times. *See also* FAINT heart ne'er won fair lady.

I'm sorry the gentleman's daunted – nothing venture, nothing have – but the gentleman knows best.
Charles Dickens, *The Old Curiosity Shop*, 1841

there is nothing lost by civility (English) Good manners cost nothing. G. and W. Grossmith, *Diary of a Nobody*, 1892. *See also* CIVILITY costs nothing.

there is nothing new under the sun (Hebrew) Every supposedly new idea or feat has in reality been conceived or performed somewhere, sometime before. Bible, Ecclesiastes 1:9. Sometimes found in the abbreviated form 'nothing new'. Proverbs expressing similar sentiments include 'there's never a new fashion but it's old'.

My dear fellow! There is nothing new under the sun.
George Orwell, *Coming Up for Air*, 1939

there is nothing so good for the inside of a man as the outside of a horse (English) Horse-riding is superlative for promoting the well-being of man. G. W. E. Russell, *Social Silhouettes*, 1906. The saying enjoyed revived attention in 1987 when it was quoted by President Ronald Reagan and described as one of his favourite proverbs. Before him it had also been heard on the lips of Rear Admiral Grayson, personal physician to President Woodrow Wilson, and allegedly on those of British prime minister Lord Palmerston.

nothing. *See also* BELIEVE nothing of what you hear, and only half of what you see; BLESSED is he who expects nothing, for he shall never be disappointed; there is nothing like LEATHER; the SUN loses nothing by shining into a puddle

notice. *See* LONG foretold long last, short notice soon past

nowt. there's nowt so queer as folk (English) People are infinitely unpredictable. *English Dialect Dictionary*, 1905.

nowt. *See also* when in DOUBT, do nowt; HEAR all, see all, say nowt

numbers. *See* there is LUCK in odd numbers; there is SAFETY in numbers

nurture passes nature (French) Education and upbringing outweigh a person's inbred character. Randle Cotgrave, *A Dictionary of the French and English Tongues*, 1611. *See also* NATURE passes nurture.

But you see how Education altereth Nature. John Lyly, *Euphues: The Anatomy of Wit*, 1578

nuts. *See* the GODS send nuts to those who have no teeth

O

oak. beware of the oak, it draws the stroke; avoid the ash, it courts the flash (English) To evade lightning during a thunderstorm, it is best not to seek shelter under oak or ash trees. *Folk-Lore Record*, 1878. In its fullest form, the proverb advises: 'creep under the thorn, it can save you from harm'. Other trees and plants recommended by superstition as places of safety during storms include the beech, walnut, bay, laurel, elder, holly and mistletoe. Somewhat perversely, many householders in past centuries kept boughs of oak in the house in the belief that they would protect the building from lightning strike (to this day window-blinds and lights often have pulls in the shape of an oak acorn). *See also* LIGHTNING never strikes the same place twice.

when the oak is before the ash, then you will get only a splash (English) If the oak trees produce leaves before the ash, then the coming months will see little rain and the summer (and consequently the harvest) will be a fine one. *Notes & Queries*, 1852. The proverb further advises, 'when the ash is before the oak, then you may expect a soak'. Curiously, in Cornwall and other parts of Europe if the oak comes into leaf before the ash this is treated as a sign of a poor summer in store.

oaks. *See* GREAT oaks from little acorns grow; LITTLE strokes fell great oaks; a REED before the wind lives on, while mighty oaks do fall

oaths. *See* CHILDREN are to be deceived with comfits and men with oaths

obedience. *See* the FIRST duty of a soldier is obedience

odd. *See* there is LUCK in odd numbers

odious. *See* COMPARISONS are odious

off. be off with the old love before you are on with the new (English) It is advisable to end old relationships before embarking on new ones. R. Edwards, *Damon and Pithias*, 1571.

It is best to be off wi' the old love Before you be on wi' the new.
Walter Scott, *The Bride of Lammermoor*, 1819

offenders never pardon (Roman) It is not for those who have committed some offence to pardon themselves. George Herbert, *Outlandish Proverbs*, 1640 (also found in Tacitus).

Forgiveness to the Injur'd does belong;
But they ne'r pardon who have done the wrong.
John Dryden, *The Conquest of Granada*, 1672

old. better be an old man's darling

than a young man's slave (English) The wife of an old man enjoys an easier life than the wife of a younger man, who will make more demands on her. John Heywood, *A Dialogue containing ... the Proverbs in the English Tongue*, 1546.

he that would be well old must be old betimes (English) Those who hope for a lengthy old age must become old early in life. R. Taverner, *Proverbs or Adages of Erasmus*, 1539.

if the old year goes out like a lion, the new year will come in like a lamb (English) If the year ends with bad weather, the new year will see an improvement in prevailing weather conditions. R. Inwards, *Weather Lore*, 1893.

old bees yield no honey (English) The elderly are poor workers and bring in little of worth. John Ray, *A Collection of English Proverbs*, 1670. Not unrelated is 'old cattle breed not'.

old fish and young flesh feed men best (English) The meat of mature fish and the company of young women are the best possible fare for a man. John Heywood, *A Dialogue containing ... the Proverbs in the English Tongue*, 1546.

There goes a saying, and 'twas shrewdly said,
Old fish at table, but young flesh in bed.
Alexander Pope, 'January and May', 1717

old friends and old wine are best (English) Friendships that have been tried and tested over the years should be cherished most, as should vintage wines. T. Draxe, *Bibliotheca Scholastica*, 1633. Variants include 'old friends and old wine and old gold are best' and 'old fish, old oil and an old friend are the best'. Another

proverb insists 'old love will not be forgotten'.

old habits die hard (English/US) It is difficult to break old habits, however undesirable they may be. Benjamin Franklin, quoted in the *London Chronicle*, 1758. *See also* you can't TEACH an old dog new tricks.

old maids lead apes in hell (English) Old women who die unmarried are fated in punishment to keep the company of apes in the underworld. George Gascoigne, *Posies*, 1575.

Therefore I will ... lead his apes into hell ... and there will the devil meet me ... and say, Get you to heaven, Beatrice, get you to heaven; here's no place for you maids: so deliver I up my apes.
William Shakespeare, *Much Ado About Nothing*, c.1598

old men are twice children (Greek) In old age men and women return to the simple innocence of their infancy, as though children once more. R. Taverner, *Proverbs or Adages of Erasmus*, 1539 (also found in the writings of Aristophanes).

They say an old man is twice a child.
William Shakespeare, *Hamlet*, c.1600

old men go to death, death comes to young men (English) The aged seek death as a release, but the young have to be actively sought out by death. Francis Bacon, *Apophthegms*, 1625. Related proverbs include 'the old man has his death before his eyes; the young man behind his back'. *See also* YOUNG men may die, but old men must die.

old men will die and children soon forget (English) It is in the nature of things that the old die and are forgotten by those they leave behind. *Black Letter Ballads*, c.1567.

old sins cast long shadows (English) Offences committed in one's youth come back to provoke guilt in one's old age. Agatha Christie, *Sad Cypress*, 1940. Related proverbs include 'old sin makes new shame'.

old soldiers never die, they simply fade away (English) Veteran soldiers, having proved that they have discovered how to survive all the risks and hardships of life in the armed forces, seem as a rule to live to an advanced age, as though they do not recognize death's dominion over them. J. Foley, 'Old Soldiers Never Die', 1920. Foley's song, which originated the proverb, was written in the wake of the First World War and remained lastingly popular. It began as a parody of the gospel hymn 'Kind Words Never Die'.

there are more old drunkards than old doctors (French) Medical men may criticize the habits of habitual drunkards, but there is no guarantee that they will live as long.

'tis an old rat that won't eat cheese (English) Men or women who are immune to the lure of flattery or luxury are rare indeed. *Brewer's Phrase and Fable*, 1958. The notion is that an old rat has learned from experience not to be tempted by the cheese that is placed in a trap.

where old age is evil, youth can learn no good (English) If adults set a bad example, it must be expected that youth will follow it. T. Draxe, *Bibliotheca Scholastica*, 1633.

you cannot put an old head on young shoulders (English) It is useless to expect the young to behave with the wisdom of their elders. H. Smith, *Preparative to Marriage*, 1591.

We should not expect to find old heads upon young shoulders.
Charles Dickens, *Martin Chuzzlewit*, 1850

you're never too old to learn (Roman) Age is no bar to learning. Alexander Barclay, *Eclogues*, 1530 (also found in the writings of Seneca). See also it is never too LATE to learn.

old. See also you cannot CATCH old birds with chaff; there's no FOOL like an old fool; there's many a GOOD tune played on an old fiddle; HANG a thief when he's young and he'll no' steal when he's old; a MAN is as old as he feels, and a woman as old as she looks; you can't put NEW wine in old bottles; be OFF with the old love before you are on with the new; an old POACHER makes the best gamekeeper; you cannot SHIFT an old tree without it dying; you can't TEACH an old dog new tricks; YOUNG folks think old folks to be fools, but old folks know young folks to be fools; YOUNG men may die, but old men must die

older. the older the wiser (English) Wisdom comes with age. J. Clarke, *Paroemiologia Anglo-Latina*, 1639. Contrasting proverbs include 'the older the worse'. See also there's no FOOL like an old fool.

omelette. you cannot make an omelette without breaking eggs (French) Sometimes it is necessary to accept some minor loss in order to achieve one's aim (usually directed at someone who hopes to get something for nothing). T. P. Thompson, *Audi Alteram Partem*, 1859 (also cited in the *Dictionnaire de l'Académie*, 1878). This saying has been variously attributed to Robespierre and Napoleon.

'My dear Flora, you cannot make an omelette without breaking eggs,' said I.
Robert Louis Stevenson, *Saint Ives*, 1897

once. See once BITTEN, twice shy; once a PRIEST, always a priest; once a THIEF, always a thief; once a WHORE, always a whore

one. it will all be one in a hundred years' time (English) Nothing we do now will make any difference to how things are in a hundred years' time. Randle Cotgrave, *A Dictionary of the French and English Tongues*, 1611.

one for sorrow, two for joy; three for a girl, four for a boy; five for silver, six for gold; seven for a secret, never to be told; eight for heaven, nine for hell; and ten for the devil's own self (English) Seeing one magpie is unlucky, according to superstition, though various interpretations may be attached to the sightings of two or more. T. Park, note in Brand's *Antiquities*, c.1780. The reputation of the magpie as an ill-starred bird is derived from Christian mythology, the magpie allegedly refusing to enter Noah's Ark and subsequently declining to wear full mourning black at the Crucifixion. The popular rhyme is known in a number of variations. One recorded in Lancashire in the middle of the nineteenth century runs, 'one for anger, two for mirth, three for a wedding, four for a birth, five for rich, six for poor, seven for a bitch, eight for a whore, nine for a burying, ten for a dance, eleven for England, twelve for France'.

one for the mouse, one for the crow, one to rot, one to grow (English) When sowing it is advisable to give up three seeds for lost for every one that will take root. *Notes & Queries*, 1850.

one year's seeding means seven years' weeding (English) Allow weeds or other undesirable things to go unchecked just once and you will find it takes much more time to retrieve the situation later. Harland and Wilkinson, *Lancashire Legends*, 1873.

one. See also a BIRD never flew on one wing; one BUSINESS begets another; the BUYER has need of a hundred eyes, the seller of but one; every DOG is allowed one bite; when one DOOR shuts, another opens; don't put all your EGGS in one basket; one ENGLISHMAN can beat three Frenchman; one FUNERAL makes many; one GOOD turn deserves another; one GRIEF drives out another; one HAIR of a woman draws more than a team of oxen; one HAND for oneself and one for the ship; one HAND washes the other; one HOUR's sleep before midnight is worth two after; better one HOUSE spoiled than two; one LIE makes many; one man's LOSS is another man's gain; one man's MEAT is another man's poison; NAIL drives out nail; one PICTURE is worth ten thousand words; one man may STEAL a horse, while another may not look over a hedge; one STEP at a time; one SWALLOW does not make a summer; if TWO ride on a horse, one must ride behind; TWO heads are better than one; one VOLUNTEER is worth two pressed men; one WEDDING brings another

one-eyed. See in the COUNTRY of the blind, the one-eyed man in king

open. open confession is good for the soul (Scottish) Making a clean breast of things promotes spiritual health. c.1641, quoted in E. Beveridge, *D. Fergusson's Scottish Proverbs*, 1924. Sometimes spoken sarcastically when someone boasts of wrongs they have committed.

open. *See also* a DOOR must either be shut or open; a GOLDEN key can open any door

opens. *See* when one DOOR shuts, another opens

opera. the opera isn't over till the fat lady sings (US) A situation is not resolved until a particular event occurs. *Washington Post*, 13 June 1978. The phrase is thought to have arisen through the clichéd notion that all grand operas culminate in an oversized prima donna delivering an aria, typically clad in Nordic horned helmet and costume. In fact, few operas end like this (with the notable exception of *Tristan and Isolde*). Alternatively, in the 1970s US opera singer Kate Smith was often called upon to sing 'God Bless America' before home games of the Philadelphia Flyers ice hockey team: every time she sang, the team won and consequently games were deemed a foregone conclusion before play had even started. A third suggested origin relates to steam engines. In former times ships' boilers were commonly dubbed 'fat ladies' and it was only when a sufficient head of steam had been raised, signalled by a safety whistle sounding, that an engine could be operated. In recent years the phrase has been enthusiastically taken up by football commentators to communicate the fact that changes in a final scoreline are possible right up to the last whistle.

opera. *See also* BED is the poor man's opera

opinion. opinion rules the world (English) The world is much influenced by opinions and reputations. Markham, *The English House-wife*, 1615.

opinion. *See also* he that COMPLIES against his will is of his own opinion still

opinions. *See* so many MEN, so many opinions

opportunity. opportunity makes a thief (English) The realization that it is possible to make easy gains through an act of dishonesty will tempt many an otherwise honest person. *Hali Meidenhad*, c.1220. One variant applies the same idea to love, 'oppotunity makes a lover' and yet another insists 'opportunity is whoredom's bawd'. Other related proverbs include 'an open door may tempt a saint'.

Opportunity makes the thief ... Therefore, masters ... ought to secure their moneys and goods under lock and key, that they do not give ... a temptation to steal.
John Ray, *A Collection of English Proverbs*, 1670

opportunity seldom knocks twice at any man's door (English) Opportunities should be grasped whenever they present themselves, as it is unlikely they will come again. G. Fenton, *Bandello*, 1567. Another proverb with much the same message runs, 'occasion is bald behind'. Also related is 'an occasion lost cannot be redeemed'. In the form 'opportunity knocks (but once)' the proverb provided the title for a celebrated British television talent show that ran from the mid-1950s to 1977.

opportunity. *See also* ENGLAND's difficulty is Ireland's opportunity; MAN's extremity is God's opportunity

order is heaven's first law (English) Self-discipline is the first requisite for the person who hopes to win divine approval (or harmony of any kind). Alexander Pope, *Essay on Man*, 1734.

orphans. *See* LATE children, early orphans

other. other times, other manners
(*Greek*) Different standards of behaviour are appropriate in different eras. G. Pettie, *Petite Pallace*, 1576 (also found in the writings of Pindar). *See also* when in ROME, do as the Romans do.

other. *See also* the GRASS is always greener on the other side of the fence; HALF the world doesn't know how the other half lives; one HAND washes the other

ounce. an ounce of mirth is worth a pound of sorrow (*English*) A little wit or humour balances out a great deal of sadness. G. Pettie, *Petite Pallace*, 1576.

an ounce of practice is worth a pound of precept (*English*) A little practical experience is better than any amount of theoretical study. T. Whythorne, *Autobiography*, c.1576. Variants include 'an ounce of discretion is worth a pound of learning', 'discretion' here signifying ingrained wit.

ounce. *See also* a POUND of care will not pay an ounce of debt

our. *See* our COUNTRY, right or wrong

out. better be out of the world than out of fashion (*English*) It is preferable to be dead than to be seen to be out of touch with what is modish or fashionable. J. Clarke, *Paroemiologia Anglo-Latina*, 1639.
'Why, Tom, you are high in the Mode.' ... 'It is better to be out of the World, than out of the Fashion.'
Jonathan Swift, *Polite Conversation*, 1738

out of debt, out of danger (*English*) Those who owe nothing to anyone may be judged safe from all threat. J. Clarke, *Paroemiologia Anglo-Latina*, 1639. Related proverbs include 'out of debt out of deadly sin' and 'he that gets out of debt grows rich'.
Out of Debt out of Danger ... A Man in Debt is a Slave, and can't act with Liberty. S. Palmer, *Proverbs*, 1710

out of office, out of danger (*English*) Losing a particular post or job might at the same time deliver a person from threats that came with it. Philip Massinger, *A New Way to Pay Old Debts*, 1633.

out of sight, out of mind (*English*) Anything (or anyone) that is not constantly in view is quickly forgotten. *Proverbs of Alfred*, c.1250. *See also* IGNORANCE is bliss.
Sir John and the rest saw no more of her; and out of sight was out of mind.
Charles Kingsley, *The Water Babies*, 1863

out. *See also* when the GORSE is out of bloom, kissing's out of fashion; don't HALLOO till you are out of the wood; out of the MOUTHS of babes and sucklings; MURDER will out; never tell TALES out of school; TRUTH will out

outside. *See* there is NOTHING so good for the inside of a man as the outside of a horse

over. *See* the OPERA isn't over till the fat lady sings; the SHARPER the storm, the sooner it's over

owl. the owl was a baker's daughter
(*English*) A person's knowledge of their own inner character is not lost, even if circumstances change. William Shakespeare, *Hamlet*, c.1600. The proverb alludes to a Gloucestershire legend that a baker's daughter was turned into an owl in punishment after she objected to the generous size of a loaf that her mother was preparing for Christ when he begged for something to eat.

Well, God 'ield you! They say the owl was a baker's daughter.
William Shakespeare, *Hamlet*, c.1600

own. *See* the DEVIL looks after his own

owt. *See* HEAR all, see all, say nowt

ox. *See* better a DINNER of herbs than a stalled ox where hate is

oyster. *See* he was a BOLD man that first ate an oyster

oysters. never eat an oyster unless there is an R in the month (*English*) Oysters should only be eaten in months that are spelt with an R in them, as they are unpalatable at other times. W. Harrison, *Description of England*, 1577. In fact, this proverb is based on good sense, as the months between May and August are the breeding season for English oysters (though in practice imported oysters are now available at any time of the year). The legal close season for oysters in England, however, runs from 15 June to 4 August. In connection with the scarcity of native English oysters on menus during the close season comes another proverb, 'who eats oysters on Saint James's Day will never want'. Saint James's Day falls on 25 July, well into the close season, and thus anyone who could arrange for such a luxury as oysters on such a date could be presumed to be immensely rich. Another, largely archaic, saying runs, 'oysters are ungodly, because they are eaten without grace; uncharitable because we leave nought but shells; and unprofitable because they must swim in wine'.

P

pace. it is the pace that kills (English)
Going about something too energeti-
cally for too long can have fatal consequences. William Thackeray, *Pendennis*,
1850. The ideal pace to tackle something was formerly alleged to be that
of the average alderman, and those
who approached things in a sensible,
leisurely manner were said to be
'paced like an alderman'. *See also* it is
not WORK that kills, but worry.

You're going too fast, and can't keep up the
pace ... it will kill you.
William Thackeray, *Pendennis*, 1850

pack. *See* NO names, no pack drill

packages. *See* the BEST things come in
small packages

paddle your own canoe (US) Rely
upon yourself. Captain Frederick
Marryat, *Settlers in Canada*, 1844. It was
popularized by a poem by Sarah
Bolton in 1854 and was also quoted
by President Abraham Lincoln.

Voyage upon life's sea,
To yourself be true,
And, whatever your lot may be,
Paddle your own canoe.
Sarah Bolton, in *Harper's Magazine*, May 1854

pain. pain past is pleasure (English)
There is satisfaction to be gained from
remembering past suffering, and a
person may be judged to be richer
for the experience. G. Fenton,
Bandello, 1567. Another proverb along
similar lines runs 'past labour is
pleasant'.

**pains. pains to get, care to keep, fear
to lose** (English) Wealth is hard to
acquire, and once attained creates in
the possessor anxiety that it will be
lost. T. Draxe, *Bibliotheca Scholastica*,
1633.

pains. *See also* no GAINS without pains;
GENIUS is an infinite capacity for taking
pains

paint. *See* a BLIND man's wife needs no
paint

painted. *See* the DEVIL is not as black as
he is painted

**pair. one pair of heels is often worth
two pairs of hands** (English)
Sometimes it is preferable to be able to
run away from a situation than to
attempt to grapple with it. *Gammer
Gurton's Needle*, 1575. *See also* DISCRETION is
the better part of valour.

I ... made two pair of legs (and these were
not mine, but my mare's) worth one pair
of hands ... I e'en pricked off with myself.
Walter Scott, *The Monastery*, 1820

pans. *See* IF ifs and ands were pots and pans, there'd be no work for tinkers' hands

pardon. pardon all but thyself (English) Forgive others who do wrong, but be highly critical of your own misdeeds. Randle Cotgrave, *A Dictionary of the French and English Tongues*, 1611.

pardon. *See also* OFFENDERS never pardon

parsley seed goes nine times to the Devil (English) Parsley must go nine times to Hell before it will start to grow. R. Barnsley, in *Wit Restored*, 1658. Tradition insists that the Devil will claim the first eight sowings (presumably an attempt to explain why parsley takes so long to germinate) and that only really wicked people can grow it in abundance.

People say parsley seed goes seven times (some are moderate, discarding the holy number as unfit, and say five) to the Old Lad, it is so long a-germinating.
D. H. Lawrence, letter, 4 May 1908

parsley. *See also* the BABY comes out of the parsley-bed; when the MISTRESS is the master, parsley grows the faster

parsnips. *See* FINE words butter no parsnips

part. *See* the BEST of friends must part ; DISCRETION is the better part of valour; if you're not part of the SOLUTION, you're part of the problem

parted. *See* a FOOL and his money are soon parted

passion. when passion entereth at the foregate, wisdom goeth out of the postern (English) Passion overrules good sense. Thomas Fuller, *Gnomologia*, 1732. Another proverb

warns 'passion will master you, if you do not master your passion'.

past. past cure, past care (English) When something has gone beyond the point where anything can be done there is no point worrying about it. William Shakespeare, *Love's Labour's Lost*, c.1594.

Things past redress are now with me past care.
William Shakespeare, *Richard II*, c.1595

things past cannot be recalled (English) It is too late to change what has already been done. H. Medwall, *Nature*, 1500. *See also* what's DONE cannot be undone.

Since a thing past can't be recalled … we may be content.
Maria Edgeworth, *Popular Tales*, 1804

pastime. *See* he that would go to SEA for pleasure, would go to Hell for a pastime

paternoster. *See* NO penny, no paternoster

path. every path hath a puddle (English) There is no easy path to success. George Herbert, *Jacula Prudentum*, 1640.

But ilka bean has its black, and ilka path has its puddle.
Walter Scott, *Rob Roy*, 1817

patience. he that hath no patience hath nothing (English) Patience is the one essential quality, without which a person has nothing. Randle Cotgrave, *A Dictionary of the French and English Tongues*, 1611. Another proverb adds 'he that hath patience, hath fat thrushes for a farthing'.

patience is a virtue (English) Those who await things with patience are to be admired. William Langland, *Piers Plowman*, 1377. Other proverbs celebrating patience include 'patience is the best remedy', 'patient men win the day' and 'patience is a plaster for all sores'.

Pacience is an heigh vertue, certeyn.
Geoffrey Chaucer, The Canterbury Tales, c.1387

patriotism is the last refuge of a scoundrel (English) Calling on patriotic feeling is the last resort of the man who has no better argument to offer. Samuel Johnson, quoted in James Boswell, Life of Johnson, 1791.

Paul. See if SAINT Paul's Day be fair and clear, it will betide a happy year

paved. See the ROAD to Hell is paved with good intentions

pay. if you pay not a servant his wages, he will pay himself (English) Servants or employees who are not paid as promised will help themselves to what they think they are entitled. Thomas Fuller, Gnomologia, 1732.

if you pay peanuts, you get monkeys (English) Those who pay low wages cannot expect good work from their staff. L. Coulthard, in Director, August 1966.

pay beforehand was never well served (English) The person who pays for work in advance will find that the work proceeds slowly and not to their satisfaction. John Florio, Second Fruites, 1591.

pay. See also they that DANCE must pay the fiddler; the DEVIL to pay and no pitch hot; SPEAK not of my debts unless you mean to pay them

pays. he who pays the piper calls the tune (English) The person who provides the money for something is entitled to dictate how things should proceed. James Kelly, A Complete Collection of Scotish Proverbs, 1721. The saying derives from the hiring of musicians for public and private celebrations. Also related is the saying 'as you pipe, I must dance', which signifies the need to do what another person pays you to do. See also they that DANCE must pay the fiddler.

you pays your money and you takes your choice (English) Once you have paid over your money you are free to choose (though usually with the implication that you are faced with two equally uninspiring alternatives). Punch, 1846.

pays. See also it pays to ADVERTISE; DEATH pays all debts; the THIRD time pays for all

peace. if you want peace, prepare for war (Roman) The best way to preserve peace is to maintain strong armed forces as a deterrent. David Lyndsay, The Satyre of the Thrie Estaitis, 1540 (also quoted by Vegetius in Epitoma Rei Militaris). Occasionally encountered in the original Latin, 'si vis pacem, para bellum'. Related proverbs include ''tis safest making peace with sword in hand'.

The Commonwealth of Venice in their Armory have this inscription, Happy is that Citty which in time of peace thinkes of warre, a fit Motto for every mans private house.
Richard Burton, The Anatomy of Melancholy, 1624

peace makes plenty (English/French) Prosperity comes with peace. Reliquae Antiquae, fifteenth century. The fuller version of the proverb, known in several variant forms, runs 'peace maketh plenty, plenty maketh pride, pride maketh war, war maketh poverty,

poverty maketh peace'.

> Peace, dear nurse of arts, plenties, and joyful births.
> William Shakespeare, *Henry V*, c.1598

peacock. the peacock hath fair feathers, but foul feet (English) Even the most magnificent and beautiful people or animals have some flaw, of which they are very conscious. T. Draxe, *Bibliotheca Scholastica*, 1616. Other proverbs relating to peacocks include 'when the peacock loudly calls, look out for storms and squalls', 'no peacock envies another peacock his tail' and the Burmese 'the sparrow is sorry for the peacock at the burden of its tail'.

pearls. *See* don't CAST your pearls before swine

pears. *See* WALNUTS and pears you plant for your heirs

peck. a peck of March dust is worth a king's ransom (English) A dry March is unusual and therefore much to be valued. John Heywood, *Play of Weather*, 1533.

peck. *See also* you've got to EAT a peck of dirt before you die

pen. the pen is mightier than the sword (Roman) The writer wields more power than the soldier. Claus Petri, 1520 (also quoted by Cicero). According to William Shakespeare, in *Hamlet*, 'many wearing rapiers are afraid of goose-quills'. *See also* a GOOSE-quill is more dangerous than a lion's claw.

> Beneath the rule of men entirely great,
> The pen is mightier than the sword.
> Edward Bulwer-Lytton, *Richelieu*, 1839

pennies. look after the pennies and the pounds will look after themselves (English) Take care about gathering in the smallest amounts of money and soon you will find you have a considerable amount. Lord Chesterfield, letter, 5 February 1750. Chesterfield attributed the proverb to William Lowndes, Secretary to the Treasury under William and Mary, Queen Anne and George I. *See also* every LITTLE helps.

> Take care of the pence and the pounds will take care of themselves is as true of personal habits as of money.
> George Bernard Shaw, *Pygmalion*, 1912

penny. a penny saved is a penny earned (English) By saving a penny you end up a penny better off, just as if you had actually earned it. George Herbert, *Jacula Prudentum*, 1640. Also found as 'a penny saved is a penny got'.

> I saved five pounds out of the brickmaker's affair ... It's a very good thing to save one, let me tell you: a penny saved, is a penny got!
> Charles Dickens, *Bleak House*, 1853

penny wise, pound foolish (English) A person who is niggardly in parting with small amounts of money but careless when it comes to larger sums is a fool. E. Topsell, *Four-footed Beasts*, 1607.

> He never would insure his ricks ... Miss Diana has often told him he deserved to have his ricks take fire for being penny wise and pound foolish.
> Mrs Henry Wood, *Trevlyn Hold*, 1864

penny. *See also* a BAD penny always turns up; better GIVE a penny than lend twenty; IN for a penny, in for a pound; NO penny, no paternoster

people. like people, like priest (Hebrew) The common masses ape the views of their priest (or other leader), whether they be right or wrong. *Bible*,

Hosea 4:9. A variant form is 'like prince, like people'.

Like priest, like people ...Always taken in the worse sense.
John Ray, *A Collection of English Proverbs*, 1670

people. *See also* you may FOOL all of the people some of the time, some of the people all of the time, but not all of the people all of the time; people who live in GLASS houses shouldn't throw stones; IDLE people have the least leisure; MORE people know Tom Fool than Tom Fool knows; the VOICE of the people is the voice of God

perfect. *See* PRACTICE makes perfect

perjury. *See* JOVE but laughs at lovers' perjury

philosopher. *See* it is not the BEARD that makes the philosopher

physician, heal thyself (Hebrew) Sort out your own problems before venturing to advise others who suffer from the same failings. Bible, Luke 4:23.

Ye will surely say to me this proverb, Physician, heal thyself; whatever we have heard done in Capernaum, do also here in thy country.
Bible, Luke 4:23

pick. *See* HAWKS will not pick out hawks' eyes; see a PIN and pick it up, all the day you'll have good luck

picture. every picture tells a story (English) Much may be read into even the smallest incidents or images. Charlotte Brontë, *Jane Eyre*, 1847. The phrase enjoyed a revival in the early twentieth century when it was adopted as a slogan for Doane's Backache Kidney Pills.

one picture is worth ten thousand words (US) More may be said in a picture than in any amount of words.

Frederick R. Barnard, in *Printers' Ink*, 8 December 1921. Barnard claimed a Chinese origin for the proverb, but it seems more likely that he actually coined it himself.

pictures are the books of the unlearned (English) Pictures may convey depths of meaning to those who cannot read and are thus unable to glean the same information from books. Thomas Fuller, *The History of the Worthies of England*, 1660.

piece. a piece of churchyard fits everybody (English) No one is immortal. George Herbert, *Jacula Prudentum*, 1640.

pie-crust. *See* PROMISES, like pie-crust, are made to be broken

pig. *See* CHILD's pig but father's bacon; what can you EXPECT from a pig but a grunt?

pigs might fly, if they had wings (English) Something is as unlikely to come to pass as pigs are to fly. Thomas Fuller, *Gnomologia*, 1732. Often heard in the shortened form 'pigs might fly'. An alternative runs 'pigs may fly, but they are very unlikely birds'. According to a lesser known saying, 'pigs fly in the air with their tails forward'.

pilot. *See* in a CALM sea every man is a pilot

pin. see a pin and let it lie, you'll want a pin before you die (English) It is bad luck not to pick up a pin lying on the ground. James Halliwell-Phillipps, *Nursery Rhymes and Tales of England*, 1845. Variants on the usual proverb run 'he that will not stoop for a pin, will never be worth a pound' and 'he that takes not up a pin, slights his wife'. *See also* see a PIN and pick it up, all the day you'll have good luck.

see a pin and pick it up, all the day you'll have good luck (English) It is good luck to pick up a pin lying on the ground. Samuel Pepys, *Diary*, 2 January 1668. One superstition suggests that much depends upon which way the pin is pointing before is picked up: if it points away from the finder it brings good luck, but it threatens bad luck if it points towards the finder. An entirely different viewpoint, however, is expressed by the rival proverb 'pick up pins pick up sorrow'. James Joyce, in *Ulysses*, published in 1922, reports the belief among women that it is unlucky to pick up a pin, because it 'cuts' love. *See also* see a PIN and let it lie, you'll want a pin before you die.

pin. *See also* it is a SIN to steal a pin

pint. *See* you can't fit a QUART into a pint pot

piper. *See* he who PAYS the piper calls the tune

piss not against the wind (Italian) Do not run contrary to the general flow. G. Torriano, *Select Italian Proverbs*, 1642.

Chi piscia contra il vento si bagna la commiscia. He that pisseth against the wind, wets his shirt. It is to a man's own prejudice, to strive against the stream.
John Ray, *A Collection of English Proverbs*, 1670

pitch. *See* he that TOUCHES pitch shall be defiled

pitcher. the pitcher goes so often to the well that it is broken at last (English) A particular trick or subterfuge, previously lucrative on many occasions, finally fails to achieve the desired result. *Ayenbite of Inwit*, 1340. The proverb is often quoted in refer-

ence to longstanding practices that have been revealed to be dishonest. Also encountered in several other European languages, including French, Dutch and Portuguese.

A pot may goo so longe to water that at the laste it cometh to broken hoom.
William Caxton, *Reynard the Fox*, 1481

pitchers. *See* LITTLE pitchers have big ears

pitchfork. *See* you can DRIVE out nature with a pitchfork, but she keeps on coming back

pitied. *See* better be ENVIED than pitied

pity is akin to love (English) To feel pity for someone requires emotions close to love. William Shakespeare, *Twelfth Night*, c.1601. Variants include 'pity is but one remove from love'.

I pity you – that's a degree to love.
William Shakespeare, *Twelfth Night*, c.1601

place. a place for everything and everything in its place (English) The person who keeps everything neatly in order will enjoy a peaceful and trouble free existence. George Herbert, *Jacula Prudentum*, 1640. It is thought that the proverb resulted from an amalgamation of two earlier sayings, 'there is a place for everything' and 'everything in its place' – though one authority suggests it derives from the necessity recognized by early printers to keep their type in proper order. Related sayings include 'everything is good in its season'. *See also* CLEANLINESS is next to godliness.

there's no place like home (English) Being in one's own home brings a particular pleasure that can be enjoyed nowhere else. John Howard Payne, 'Home, Sweet Home', 1823. The US-born Payne wrote the song for the London musical stage as part of the musical play *Clari, the Maid of Milan*, and it became a great favourite on both sides of the Atlantic in the Victorian era. *See also* EAST, west, home's best; HOME is where the heart is; HOME, sweet home.

Mid pleasures and palaces though we may roam,
Be it ever so humble, there's no place like home!
A charm from the skies seems to hallow us there,
Which, seek through the world, ne'er is met with elsewhere.
John Howard Payne, 'Home, Sweet Home', 1823

place. *See also* LIGHTNING never strikes the same place twice; a WOMAN's place is in the home

plague. *See* PLEASE your eye and plague your heart

plain dealing is a jewel (English) Honesty in all one's dealings with others is an ideal much to be valued. B. Melbancke, *Philotimus*, 1583. The rarity of honesty in everyday dealings is lamented in the proverbial sayings 'plain dealing is dead, and died without issue' and 'plain dealing is praised more than practised'. Another warns 'plain dealing is a jewel, but he that useth it shall die a beggar'.

Plain dealing is a jewel; but they that wear it, are out of fashion.
Thomas Fuller, *Gnomologia*, 1732

plant. *See* it is not SPRING until you can plant your foot upon twelve daisies; WALNUTS and pears you plant for your heirs

play. as good play for nought as work for nought (English) If you are not going to be paid you might as well take things easy doing what you want as engage in harder toil.

Nicholas Udall, *Flowers for Latin Speaking*, 1533.

if you play with fire you get burnt (English) Those who flirt with danger risk coming to harm. H. Vaughan, *Silex Scintillans*, 1655. *See also* FIRE and water are good servants, but bad masters.

those who play at bowls must look out for rubbers (English) While setting about some difficult or perilous task beware of possible obstacles and impediments. William Shakespeare, *Richard II*, c.1595. The origins of the proverb lie in the game of bowls, in which the slightest irregularity in the ground might affect the way in which the bowls run. A 'rubber' denotes the collision of two bowls.

Lady Madam, we'll play at bowls.
Queen 'Twill make me think the world is full of rubs.
William Shakespeare, *Richard II*, c.1595

play. *See also* when the CAT's away, the mice will play; FAIR play is a jewel; GIVE and take is fair play; TURN about is fair play; all WORK and no play makes Jack a dull boy

please. please your eye and plague your heart (English) Those who choose partners (or other things) primarily for their appearances are likely to suffer in the long run. A. Brewer, *The Lovesick King*, c.1617. *See also* APPEARANCES are deceptive.

Many a substantial farmer ... would be glad to marry her; but she was resolved to please her eye, if she should plague her heart.
Tobias Smollett, *Roderick Random*, 1748

you can't please everyone (English) It is impossible to satisfy all sides all the time. E. Paston, letter, 16 May 1472. Other proverbs warn 'he had need rise betimes that would please everybody', 'he that all men will please shall never find ease' and 'he that would please all and himself too, undertakes what he cannot do'.

please. See also LITTLE things please little minds

pleasure. no pleasure without pain (English) Some effort or sacrifice is required before anything can be enjoyed. G. Pettie, *Petite Pallace*, 1576. Also encountered in the form 'no pleasure without repentance'.

His store of pleasure must be sauced with pain.
Christopher Marlowe, *Dr Faustus, c.* 1590

pleasure. See also BUSINESS before pleasure; he that would go to SEA for pleasure would go to Hell for a pastime

pleasures. the pleasures of the rich are bought with the tears of the poor (English) The less privileged often suffer the consequences of the pleasure-seeking activities of the wealthier classes. T. Draxe, *Bibliotheca Scholastica*, 1633. According to the popular music-hall song 'She was Poor, but She was Honest': 'it's the rich what gets the pleasure, it's the poor what gets the blame'.

plenty makes poor (English) Those who enjoy considerably increased wealth may still consider themselves poor, as their needs have also grown at a similar rate. Edmund Spenser, *The Faerie Queene*, 1590.

Abundance makes me poor.
John Fletcher, *The Lover's Progress*, 1623

plough. never let the plough stand to catch a mouse (English) Never let yourself be distracted by trifles from the business in hand. John Ray, *A Collection of English Proverbs*, 1678.

plum. See a CHERRY year, a merry year; a plum year, a dumb year

plus. See plus ça CHANGE, plus c'est la même chose

poacher. an old poacher makes the best gamekeeper (English) It is good policy to employ a former practitioner of some craft (usually criminal) to combat others engaged in the same activities. Geoffrey Chaucer, *The Canterbury Tales, c.* 1387. See also set a THIEF to catch a thief.

pockets. See SHROUDS have no pockets

poet. a poet is born not made (English) The ability to write poetry (or to engage in other artistic activities) depends upon a person's natural talent rather than acquired skills. Philip Sidney, *An Apologie for Poetrie, c.* 1581.

points. See POSSESSION is nine points of the law

poison. poison is poison though it comes in a golden cup (English) Poison is no less effective when served up in a fine vessel. G. Pettie, *Petite Pallace*, 1576.

Doe we not commonly see that in paynted pottes is hidden the deadlyest poyson?
John Lyly, *Euphues: The Anatomy of Wit,* 1578

poison. See also one man's MEAT is another man's poison

policy. See HONESTY is the best policy

politeness. See PUNCTUALITY is the politeness of princes

politics makes strange bedfellows (English) Unlikely alliances are forged in the course of political compromise. P. Hone, *Diary*, 9 July 1839. See also ADVERSITY makes strange bedfellows.

poor. a poor man's table is soon spread (English) When a person has very little, it does not take long to set it out. T. Draxe, *Bibliotheca Scholastica*, 1616.

he is not poor that hath little, but he that desireth much (English) A man will consider himself poor if he has not sufficient wealth to do as he wants. G. Colville, 1556.

it is a poor heart that never rejoices (English) No one should feel guilty for engaging in celebration (often quoted in defence of drinking alcohol or some other indulgence). Captain Frederick Marryat, *Peter Simple*, 1834.

What happened when I reached home you may guess … Ah! Well, it's a poor heart that never rejoices.
Charles Dickens, *Barnaby Rudge*, 1841

poor men seek meat for their stomach; rich men stomach for their meat (English) The poor have to work hard for their food, while the more wealthy engage in work or exercise simply to raise an appetite to eat. A. Copley, *Wits, Fits and Fancies*, 1595.

poor. *See also* CHILDREN are poor men's riches; he is a poor COOK that cannot lick his own fingers; there's one LAW for the rich and another for the poor; the RICH man has his ice in the summer and the poor man gets his in the winter

poorer. the poorer the church, the purer the church (English) Money corrupts, and thus the less a church possesses the closer its congregation is to heaven. W. C. Hazlitt, *English Proverbs*, 1869.

Pope. *See* it is ill SITTING at Rome and striving with the Pope

porridge. *See* SAVE your breath to cool your porridge

port. any port in a storm (English) Any shelter will do if the situation is desperate enough. J. Cleland, *Memoirs of a Woman of Pleasure*, 1749. Occasionally encountered in the form 'sailors have a port in every storm'.

As the Scotsman's howf lies right under your lee, why, take any port in a storm.
Walter Scott, *The Pirate*, 1821

possession is nine points of the law (English) Possession of property or land is tantamount to legal ownership. Edward III, 1595. This time-honoured proverb is not in fact supported by any specific law, though in practice it has some claims to validity. The 'nine points' (sometimes eleven) have been listed as (1) a good deal of money, (2) a good deal of patience, (3) a good cause, (4) a good lawyer, (5) a good counsel, (6) good witnesses, (7) a good jury, (8) a good judge and (9) good luck.

In those days possession was considerably more than eleven points of the Law. The baron was therefore convinced that the earl's outlawry was infallible.
Thomas Love Peacock, *Maid Marian*, 1822

possible. *See* all's for the BEST in the best of all possible worlds; all THINGS are possible with God

post. the post of honour is the post of danger (Roman) The greatest honours come with the greatest risks. Lord Berners, *Huon*, 1533.

For I remembered your old Roman axiom, the more the danger, still the more the honour.
John Fletcher, *Rule a Wife and Have a Wife*, 1624

postscript. *See* the GIST of a lady's letter is in the postscript

postern. a postern door makes a thief (English) Any house with a back door is vulnerable to thieves and other evil-doers. *Proverbs of Good Counsel*, c.1450.

The Postern Door Makes Thief and Whore. Thomas Fuller, *Gnomologia*, 1732

pot. the pot calls the kettle black (*Spanish/Arabic*) It is hypocritical for a person to accuse another of something of which they themselves are equally guilty. Miguel de Cervantes, *Don Quixote*, 1615. Similar proverbs may be found in several other European languages, including German and French — the latter in the form 'dirty-nosed folk always want to wipe other folks' noses'. Equivalents in English include 'the kiln calls the oven burnt house'.

As another old proverb says, do not let the kettle call the pot black-arse! Aphra Behn, *The Feign'd Courtezans*, 1679

pot. *See also* a LITTLE pot is soon hot; you can't fit a QUART into a pint pot; a WATCHED pot never boils

pots. *See* IF ifs and ands were pots and pans, there'd be no work for tinkers' hands

pound. a pound of care will not pay an ounce of debt (*English*) Worrying about one's debts does nothing to reduce them. L. Wright, *Display of Dutie*, 1589.

pound. *See also* IN for a penny, in for a pound; an OUNCE of practice is worth a pound of precept; PENNY wise, pound foolish

pounds. *See* look after the PENNIES and the pounds will look after themselves

pours. *See* it never RAINS but it pours

poverty. poverty breeds strife (*English*) Lack of money engenders quarrels, particularly between man and wife. John Ray, *A Collection of English Proverbs*, 1678. *See also* when POVERTY

comes in at the door, love flies out of the window.

poverty is no disgrace, but it is a great inconvenience (*English*) It is possible to deny that poverty is the fault of the person concerned, but this does not lessen its unwelcome impact. John Florio, *Second Fruites*, 1591. Variants include the Yiddish 'poverty is no disgrace, but no honour either'. Another proverb enlarges on the feelings of shame associated with poverty: 'poverty is not a shame, but the being ashamed of it is'.

'Poverty's no disgrace, but 'tis a great inconvenience' was a common saying among the Lark Rise people ... Flora Thompson, *Lark Rise to Candleford*, 1945

poverty is not a crime (*English*) It is not generally the fault of the poor that they are destitute. John Florio, *Second Fruites*, 1591. Variants include 'poverty is no sin' and the Spanish 'poverty is not perversity'.

Mrs Nickleby ... said through her tears that poverty was not a crime. Charles Dickens, *Nicholas Nickleby*, 1839

poverty is the mother of health (*English*) Those who have no money for more elaborate fare eat more sparingly and sensibly and thus enjoy improved health. William Langland, *Piers Plowman*, 1377. Another proverb, of Japanese origins, claims 'the poor sleep soundly'.

poverty makes strange bedfellows *See* ADVERSITY makes strange bedfellows

when poverty comes in at the door, love flies out of the window (*English*) The strains created by lack of money breaks down loving relationships. William Caxton, *A Game of Chess*, 1474. Also related are 'poverty parteth fellowship' and 'love lasteth as long as the money endureth'. Another proverb warns that love is not only victim of poverty, claiming that 'there is no virtue that poverty destroyeth not'.

poverty. *See also* he who is CONTENT in his poverty is wonderfully rich

powder. *See* put your TRUST in God and keep your powder dry

power. power corrupts (English) When a person gains power the temptation is to misuse it. Anthony Trollope, *The Prime Minister*, 1876. The proverb is often encountered in the fuller form 'power tends to corrupt, and absolute power corrupts absolutely'.

We know that power does corrupt, and that we cannot trust kings to have loving hearts.
Anthony Trollope, *The Prime Minister*, 1876

power. *See also* KNOWLEDGE is power; MONEY is power

practice makes perfect (Greek) To be really good at something you must repeat it over and over again. Thomas Norton, *Ordinall of Alchimy*, 1477 (also quoted in various forms by Publilius Syrus, Periander and Pliny the Younger). Formerly usually encountered in the form 'use maketh mastery'.

Use makes perfect.
Walter Scott, *The Antiquary*, 1816

practice. *See also* an OUNCE of practice is worth a pound of precept

practise what you preach (English) If you tell other people how to behave, you should behave the same way yourself. William Langland, *Piers Plowman*, 1377. Another proverb confirms the notion as follows: 'he preaches well that lives well'. *See also* a GOOD example is the best sermon.

Divines do not always practise what they preach.

Charles Dickens, *The Old Curiosity Shop*, 1840

praise. let every man praise the bridge he goes over (English) All men should acknowledge services done for them by others. John Ray, *A Collection of English Proverbs*, 1678. Sometimes heard in the form 'everyone speaks well of the bridge which carries him over'.

Well, praise the bridge that carried you over.
George Colman the Younger, *The Heir-at-Law*, 1797

praise is not pudding (English) Flattery and praise may be pleasing, but they bring no actual benefit in themselves. Alexander Pope, *The Dunciad*, 1728. A related proverb observes 'praise without profit puts little in the pot'.

Since t'is not improbable, that a Man may receive more solid Satisfaction from Pudding, while he is living, than from Praise, after he is dead.
Benjamin Franklin, *Poor Richard's Almanack*, 1750

praise no man till he is dead (English) Reserve final judgement on a person until they are dead, for only then is it possible to make a definitive statement about their worth. R. Taverner, *Proverbs or Adages of Erasmus*, 1540.

praise the child and you make love to the mother (English) Those who wish to win over a mother can do no better than compliment their offspring. William Cobbett, *Advice to Young Men*, 1829. Variants include 'he that wipes the child's nose kisses the mother's cheek'.

praise the sea but keep on land (English) By all means admire the sea, but do not venture upon it and thus expose yourself to risk. John Florio,

Second Fruites, 1591. A less well-known proverb that similarly warns of the dangers of venturing on the sea ominously advises 'he that would learn to pray, let him go to sea'. See also he that would go to SEA for pleasure, would go to Hell for a pastime.

praise. See also SELF-praise is no recommendation

pray. See also an ANGRY man is not fit to pray

prays. See also the FAMILY that prays together stays together

precept. See EXAMPLE is better than precept; an OUNCE of practice is worth a pound of precept

premier. ce n'est que le premier pas qui coûte (French) It is only the first step that costs anything (meaning, it is the first step that is remarkable). Attributed to Madame du Deffand (1697–1780) when told the miracle of Saint Denys, who is supposed to have walked some distance after he was beheaded. See also it is the FIRST step that is difficult.

prepare. See HOPE for the best and prepare for the worst; if you want PEACE, prepare for war

Presbyterianism is no religion for a gentleman (English) Presbyterianism, being essentially a 'low church' branch of Christianity, is not grand and noble enough for the high born. This inflammatory remark is traditionally attributed to Charles II, who harboured secret Catholic sympathies, and was directed at the Presbyterian Duke of Lauderdale, who promptly switched faiths. In The New Forcers of Conscience John Milton voiced his own proverbial view of the matter, insisting that beyond their names there is little

in reality to choose between such reformed faiths as Presbyterianiam and the older versions: 'New Presbyter is but Old Priest writ large'.

present. See there is no TIME like the present

preservation. See SELF-preservation is the first law of nature

pressed. See one VOLUNTEER is worth two pressed men

prevention is better than cure (English) It is better to forestall a problem before it arises than treat it after it has already become established. Henry de Bracton, De Legibus, c.1240.

price. the price of liberty is eternal vigilance (Irish) Liberty must be carefully guarded against all threats. John Philpot Curran, 1790. The saying was later adopted as a maxim by the US reformer Wendell Phillips in 1852.

price. See also every MAN has his price

pride. pride feels no pain (English) Pride persuades people to accept and ignore pain and difficulty if giving in to it will lead to some loss of face. T. Adams, The Devil's Banquet, 1614. The proverb is usually quoted in reference to clothing, explaining why many people will endure some degree of bodily discomfort in order to look good. Related proverbs include 'pride feels no frost'.

Pride feels no cold. Spoken ... to Beaus with their open Breasts, and Ladies with their extravagant Hoops.
James Kelly, A Complete Collection of Scotish Proverbs, 1721

pride goes before a fall (Hebrew) Displays of arrogance are all too often quickly followed by humiliation. Bible, Proverbs 16:18. Formerly also encountered in the forms 'pride will have a fall' and 'pride never left his master without a fall'.

'Pride shall have a fall, and it always was and will be so!' observes the housemaid.
Charles Dickens, *Dombey and Son*, 1816

pride must abide (English) Those who are arrogant must put up with critical remarks from others. Elizabeth Gaskell, *North and South*, 1855.

I kept myself up with proverbs as long as I could; 'Pride must abide' – and such wholesome pieces of pith!
Elizabeth Gaskell, *North and South*, 1855

priest. once a priest, always a priest (English) Once a person takes holy orders they will always be at heart a priest, even if subsequently defrocked. G. A. Sala, *Twice Round the Clock*, 1859. The proverb had particular reference in Tudor times, when many converts to the newly established Church of England were presumed by their enemies to retain Roman Catholic leanings, despite their disavowals of the Church of Rome. Variants include 'once a bishop, always a bishop'.

You must be quite sure, Stephen, that you have a vocation because it would be terrible if you found afterwards that you had none. Once a priest always a priest, remember.
James Joyce, *A Portrait of the Artist as a Young Man*, 1916

priest. See also like PEOPLE, like priest

prince. See whosoever DRAWS his sword against the prince must throw the scabbard away

princes. See PUNCTUALITY is the politeness of princes

probabilities. a thousand probabilities do not make one truth (English) What is thought probable is not

necessarily accurate. H. G. Bohn, *A Handbook of Proverbs*, 1855.

problem. See if you're not part of the SOLUTION you're part of the problem

procrastination is the thief of time (English) Putting things off results only in time being wasted. Edward Young, 'Night Thoughts', 1742 (similar thoughts were voiced at an earlier date by Seneca and Erasmus, among others). Equivalents in other languages include the Dutch 'stay but a while, you lose a mile' and the Spanish 'when the fool has made up his mind the market has gone by'. In 1891 Oscar Wilde offered a contrasting view of time-wasting in *The Picture of Dorian Gray*: 'he was always late on principle, his principle being that punctuality is the thief of time'. See also never PUT off till tomorrow what you can do today; there is no TIME like the present; TOMORROW never comes.

Procrastination is the thief of time;
Year after year it steals, till all are fled,
And to the mercies of a moment leaves
The vast concerns of an eternal scene.
Edward Young, 'Night Thoughts', 1742

proffered service stinks (English) When a person has a service or product to offer for sale no one seems anxious to acquire it, but when the same person goes out to buy something it always seems impossible to get through demand. Douce MS, c.1350.

When I go to market to sell, my commodity stinks; but when I want to buy ... it can't be had for love or money.
Tobias Smollett, *Humphrey Clinker*, 1771

promise is debt (English) As soon as you make a promise to someone you are under an obligation to them. Geoffrey Chaucer, *The Canterbury Tales*, c.1387.

promises, like pie-crust, are made to be broken (English) It is inevitable that all promises will be broken. *Heraclitus Ridens*, 1681. Another proverb runs 'promises are either broken or kept'.

'Promises like that are mere pie-crust,' said Ralph.
Anthony Trollope, *Ralph the Heir*, 1871

proof. the proof of the pudding is in the eating (English) The true worth of something is revealed when it is put to the test in practice. *King Alisaunder*, c.1300. In the Middle Ages favourite delicacies of the populace included bulky meat puddings enclosed in a length of intestine or in dough – the only sure way to test (or 'prove') them to see if they were cooked all the way through was to taste them.

The thin soft cakes ... were done liberal justice to in the mode which is best proof of cake as well as pudding.
Walter Scott, *The Fair Maid of Perth*, 1828

property has its duties as well as its rights (English) Landowners have obligations as well as privileges. J. E. T. Rogers, *Industrial and Commercial History*, 1891.

prophet. a prophet is not without honour save in his own country (Hebrew) While acknowledged for his gifts and good points further abroad, they may still remain unrecognized by those closer to home. Bible, Matthew 13:58. *See also* FAMILIARITY breeds contempt.

A prophet is not without honour, except in his own country, and in his own house.
Bible, Matthew 13:58

proposes. *See* MAN proposes, but God disposes

prosper. *See* CHEATS never prosper

protects. *See* HEAVEN protects children, sailors and drunken men

proud. a proud heart and a beggar's purse agree not well together (English) Those who have no money cannot afford to be arrogant. John Lydgate, *Minor Poems*, c.1430.

A proud mind and a poor purse are ill met.
Thomas Fuller, *Gnomologia*, 1732

proves. *See* the EXCEPTION proves the rule

provide. *See* TAKE the goods the gods provide

providence is always on the side of the big battalions *See* GOD is always on the side of the big battalions

public. *See* don't WASH your dirty linen in public

publicity. all publicity is good publicity (English) It does not matter what kind of publicity you get, as publicity of any kind gets your name or product known. P. Cave, *The Dirtiest Picture Postcard*, 1974. Also encountered in the form 'any publicity is good publicity'.

pudding. *See* PRAISE is not pudding; the PROOF of the pudding is in the eating

puddle. *See* the SUN loses nothing by shining into a puddle

pull. it is easier to pull down than to build up (English) Destroying things is easier than creating them. R. Stanyhurst, *History of Ireland*, 1577.

pull Devil, pull baker (English) Said to encourage two parties competing over the same prize, and implying that unscrupulous tactics will be employed. George Colman the Elder, *Rolliad*, 1759. Also encountered with 'parson' instead of 'baker'.

Then my mither and her quarrelled, and pu'ed me twa ways at anes, as if ilk had and end o' me, like Punch and the Deevil rugging about the Baker at the fair.
Walter Scott, *Old Mortality*, 1816

pun. he that would make a pun

would pick a pocket (English) Those who are given to making puns are of such low character that they would be quite capable of committing other nefarious acts. Alexander Pope, *The Dunciad*, 1729. Pope was actually quoting critic John Dennis, who had remarked to the composer Purcell, 'any man who would make such an execrable pun would not scruple to pick my pocket' (though the phrase is often attributed to Samuel Johnson). According to Pope, Dennis was inspired to make the remark after Purcell had complained about the lack of service by a waiter (or 'drawer') in a particular tavern and had then likened the tavern in question to a table – because neither had a drawer.

A great Critick formerly … declared He that would pun would pick a Pocket.
Alexander Pope, *The Dunciad*, 1729 (note)

punctuality. punctuality is the politeness of princes (French) It is a sign of good breeding to turn up to meetings and so forth on time. Samuel Smiles, *Self-Help*, 1859 (generally attributed originally to Louis XVIII, who listed it among his favourite sayings). Also encountered in the form 'punctuality is the politeness of kings'.

punctuality is the soul of business (English) Promptness in all things to essential to good business. T. C. Haliburton, *Wise Saws*, 1853.

punished. See CORPORATIONS have neither bodies to be punished nor souls to be damned

pure. to the pure all things are pure (Hebrew) Those who are pure in spirit see all that is good and holy in the world around them. Bible, Titus 1:15.

Unto the pure all things are pure, but unto them that are defiled, and unbeleeving, is nothing pure.
Bible, Titus 1:15

purse. let your purse be your master (English) It is good policy to be guided in your lifestyle by what you can afford. J. Clarke, *Paroemiologia Anglo-Latina*, 1639. Those who fail to pay heed to their purses are warned 'wrinkled purses make wrinkled faces' and also that 'an empty purse frightens away friends'.

purse. See also you can't make a SILK purse out of a sow's ear

put. never put off till tomorrow what you can do today (English) It is good policy to do things right away, instead of putting them off to a later date. Geoffrey Chaucer, *The Canterbury Tales*, c.1387. See also make HAY while the sun shines; PROCRASTINATION is the thief of time; there is no TIME like the present; TOMORROW never comes.

No procrastination; never put off till tomorrow what you can do to-day.
Lord Chesterfield, letter, 26 December 1749

put not your trust in princes (Hebrew) Rulers are but men beneath all their pomp, and no more to be trusted than any other men. Bible, Psalms 46:3.

put off the evil hour as long as you can (English) Try to delay the hour when you must tackle some distasteful task as long as possible. Jonathan Swift, *Dialogues*, 1738.

put. See also don't put the CART before the horse; don't put all your EGGS in one basket; you can't put NEW wine in old bottles; you cannot put an OLD head on young shoulders; put a STOUT heart to a stey brae; put your TRUST in God and keep your powder dry.

q

quarrel. the quarrel of lovers is the renewal of love (Roman) Lovers or friends who have quarrelled and then been reconciled will find their relationship thereby strengthened. R. Edwardes, *Paradise of Dainty Devises*, 1576 (also found in the writings of Terence).

She would ... picke quarrells upon no occasion, because she would be reconciled to him againe ... The falling out of lovers is the renuing of love.
Richard Burton, *The Anatomy of Melancholy*, 1624

quarrel. *See also* a BAD workman blames his tools; it takes TWO to make a quarrel

quart. you can't fit a quart into a pint pot (US/English) Some things are impossible to achieve due to shortage of space, time or other resources. Charlotte Gilman, *The Living of Charlotte Perkins Gilman*, 1935. Also encountered with pint 'bottle', pint 'mug' and pint 'cup'.

Queen Anne is dead (English) What purports to be fresh news is in fact already known by everyone. Ballad, quoted in Lady Pennyman, *Miscellanies*, 1722. This rather sarcastic saying was born in the confusion that surrounded reports of the death of Queen Anne in 1714. The demise of the queen – from erysipelas – was of particular import as she was childless (despite having been pregnant seventeen times) and there was much controversy over the succession, with the rival factions being represented by the Protestant Hanoverians and the Catholic James Edward Stuart. On her deathbed the queen finally nominated the Hanoverian George I to succeed her, thus settling the question: her death some two days later was thus of comparatively little interest and effectively 'old news'. To compound the confusion, rumours of her death circulated from the moment that the announcement concerning the succession was made. A fuller version of the saying runs 'as dead as Queen Anne the day after she died'. Less often heard is another English proverb along similar lines, 'Queen Elizabeth is dead' (again signifying stale news). A French equivalent is 'C'est vieux comme le Pont-Neuf' ('that's as old as the Pont-Neuf') – the Pont-Neuf being the oldest bridge spanning the Seine in Paris.

Lod help you! Tell 'em Queen Anne's dead.
George Colman the Younger, *The Heir-at-Law*,
1797

queer. *See* there's NOWT so queer as folk

quench. *See* DIRTY water will quench fire

question. *See* ASK a silly question and you'll get a silly answer; there are TWO sides to every question

questions. *See* ASK no questions and hear no lies; FOOLS ask questions that wise men cannot answer

quick at meat, quick at work (English) Those who eat their meals fastest are likely also to be the fastest workers. Randle Cotgrave, *A Dictionary of the French and English Tongues*, 1611.

quickly. quickly come, quickly go (English) What is easily obtained may be equally easily lost (often quoted in reference to money). B. Melbancke, *Philotimus*, 1583. *See also* EASY come, easy go.

quickly. *See also* he GIVES twice who gives quickly

quiet. a quiet conscience sleeps in thunder (English) Those who are not troubled by guilty acts sleep soundly. James Kelly, *A Complete Collection of Scotish Proverbs*, 1721. Related proverbs include 'quiet sleep feels no foul weather'.

a quiet tongue makes a wise head (English) Those who know how to keep silent when necessary are the wisest. J. Heywood, *Epigrams*, 1562.

quiet. *See also* the best DOCTORS are Dr Diet, Dr Quiet and Dr Merryman

quit while you are ahead (English) Leave off doing something while you are in a good position, thus avoiding any loss to one's winnings etc. *Douce MS*, c.1350. Historical variants include 'leave off while the play is good'.

quote. *See* the DEVIL can quote scripture for his own purpose

r

**race. the race is not to the swift, nor
the battle to the strong** (Hebrew) It is
not necessarily the fastest and the
strongest who always win. Bible,
Ecclesiastes 9:11. A potential winner
must, however, at least be in the
race, as another less well-known
proverb points out: 'the race is got by
running'.

It is not honesty, learning, worth,
wisdome, that preferres men, The race is
not to the swift, nor the battell to the
stronger.

Richard Burton, *The Anatomy of Melancholy*,
1632

race. *See also* SLOW but sure wins the
race

**ragged. a ragged colt may make a
good horse** (English) A wild youth
may yet turn out to be a reliable and
worthy adult. R. Hill, *Commonplace Book*,
c.1500.

Aft a ragged cowte's been known To mak a
noble aiver.

Robert Burns, *Dream*, 1786

rain. after rain comes sunshine
(English) Fine weather often follows
quickly on a shower. William Caxton,
Aesop's Fables, 1484. Not unrelated are
the proverbs 'a little rain stills a great
wind', 'a sunshiny shower won't last

half an hour', 'plenty rain, plenty sunshine' and the sailors' saying 'more
rain, more rest'. Gardeners are similarly advised that rain will not necessarily last, via the proverb 'although it
rain, throw not away thy watering-
pot'. *See also* every CLOUD has a silver
lining.

**rain before seven, fine before
eleven** (English) Rain early in the
morning presages fine weather from
eleven o'clock. *Notes & Queries*, 1853. A
variant upon the notion has produced
the related proverb, 'if it rains at
eleven, 'twill last till seven'. Also
encountered in the form 'if rain
begins at early morning light, 'Twill
end ere day at noon is bright'.

rain. *See also* BLESSED are the dead that
the rain rains on; if in FEBRUARY there
be no rain, 'tis neither good for
hay nor grain; SAINT Swithin's Day, if
thou dost rain, for forty days it will
remain

**rainbow. a rainbow in the morning
is the shepherd's warning; a rainbow at night is the shepherd's
delight** (English) A rainbow early in
the day threatens bad weather, while
one late in the day promises fine

weather to come. L. Digges, *Prognostication*, 1555. The notion may have some basis in fact as rainbows appear only when there is moisture (such as may suggest approaching rain) in the air. Variants include 'if there be a rainbow at morn, put your hook in the corn; a rainbow at eve, put your head in the sheave', 'if there be a rainbow in the eve, it will rain and leave; but if there be a rainbow in the morrow, it will neither lend nor borrow', 'rainbow at noon, rain comes soon' and 'if the rainbow comes at night, the rain is gone quite'. *See also* RED sky at night, shepherd's delight; red sky in the morning, sailor's warning.

A rainbow in the Eastern sky,
The morrow will be fine and dry.
A rainbow in the West that gleams,
Rain tomorrow falls in streams.
Chinese proverb

rains. if it rains when the sun is shining, the Devil is beating his wife (English) Rain and fine weather mixed are an indication of perverse, evil natures at work. Jonathan Swift, *Dialogues*, 1738. In many versions the Devil uses a leg of mutton to beat his wife with.

if it rains when the wind is in the east, it will rain for twenty-four hours at least (English) An easterly wind is a sure sign of prolonged rain to come. John Aubrey, *Natural History of Wiltshire*, c.1685.

it never rains but it pours (English) Minor misfortunes pile up on one another, as if deliberately to increase the victim's misery. John Arbuthnot, *It Cannot Rain but it Pours*, 1726.

A wife with a large fortune too. It never rains but it pours, does it, Mr Thorne?

Anthony Trollope, *Barchester Towers*, 1857

raise. it is easier to raise the Devil than to lay him (English) It is easier to start trouble than it is to restore peace once more. Thomas Fuller, *The Church History of Britain*, 1655. Related proverbs include 'raise no more spirits than you can conjure down'.

Alas! the Devil's sooner raised than laid.
David Garrick, prologue to Sheridan's *The School for Scandal*, 1777

ransom. *See* a PECK of March dust is worth a king's ransom

rat. *See* 'tis an OLD rat that won't eat cheese

rats desert a sinking ship (English) If an enterprise is about to collapse the first to leave are those with the least interest in what happens to it. T. Lupton, *A Thousand Notable Things*, 1579. Sailors have believed for centuries that rats know long in advance that a particular ship is doomed and will desert it long before it actually founders. By extension it is thought to be a good omen if rats are seen boarding a vessel. A realistic explanation for the belief suggests that rats will desert a ship if a vessel ships water and the bilges where the rats live are flooded. A leaking ship is likely to founder, hence the link between the rats' departure and any catastrophe that then befalls the vessel in question. The proverb is also encountered in the form 'rats desert a falling house': scientists confirm that rats may indeed be more sensitive than humans to minor earth tremors that may be the precursor of major earthquakes (in former times rats were often taken into caves and mines to provide warnings of imminent collapses). Rats are also supposed to vacate premises if someone within is close to death.

A rotten carcass of a boat, ... the very rats instinctively have quit it.
William Shakespeare, *The Tempest*, c.1610

reach. *See* STRETCH your arm no further than your sleeve will reach

reap. *See* as you SOW, so shall you reap; they that SOW the wind shall reap the whirlwind

reason. there is reason in the roasting of eggs (English) There is purpose behind every course of action, however bizarre. J. Howell, *Paroemiographia*, 1659.

But there's reason in the roasting of eggs, and ... money is not so plentiful ... that your uncle can afford to throw it into the Barchester gutters.
Anthony Trollope, *The Last Chronicle of Barset*, 1867

recalled. *See* things PAST cannot be recalled

receive. *See* it is better to GIVE than to receive

receivers. if there were no receivers, there would be no thieves (English) There would be no point in dishonesty if there were not others ready to reward it and profit by it. Geoffrey Chaucer, *The Canterbury Tales*, c.1387. Another proverb insists 'the receiver is as bad as the thief'.

This proverbe preeves, Where be no receyvers, there be no theeves.
John Heywood, *A Dialogue containing ... the Proverbs in the English Tongue*, 1546

reckonings. *See* SHORT reckonings make long friends

recommendation. *See* SELF-praise is no recommendation

reconciled. take heed of reconciled enemies and of meat twice boiled (English) Do not trust former enemies

when they claim to be friends once more. Geoffrey Chaucer, c.1386. Related proverbs include 'a reconciled friend is a double enemy'.

Beware of meat twice boiled and an old foe reconcil'd.
Benjamin Franklin, *Poor Richard's Almanack*, 1733

reculer pour mieux sauter (French) Draw back and consider the situation before committing yourself. Michel de Montaigne, *Essays*, 1580 (also found in essence in the writings of Ovid). Often quoted in the original French, but also encountered in English as 'we must recoil a little, to the end we may leap the better'. *See also* LOOK before you leap.

We must recoil a little, to the end we may leap the better.
George Herbert, *Jacula Prudentum*, 1640

red sky at night, shepherd's delight; red sky in the morning, sailor's warning (English) A red sunset is a prelude of fine weather to come, while a red dawn presages bad weather in store. John Wycliffe, Bible, Matthew 26:2, c.1395. The proverb is based on a vestige of good sense, for the weather systems governing the British climate are generally formed in the Atlantic, to the west, and thus when the sun sets in the west it will appear red if the air approaching the British Isles is dry and warm. A red sun in the morning is less significant, as it rises in the east. The state of the coming weather systems are obviously of particular importance to both shepherds and sailors (shepherds and sailors being more or less interchangeable in the proverb). Related proverbs include 'if red the sun begins his race, expect that rain will flow apace' and 'if the sun in red should set, the next day surely will be wet; if the sun should set in grey, the next will be a rainy day'.

Like a red morn, that ever yet betoken'd Wreck to the seaman ... Sorrow to shepherds.
William Shakespeare, *Venus and Adonis*, c. 1592

redressed. *See* a FAULT confessed is half redressed

reed. a reed before the wind lives on, while mighty oaks do fall (English) In difficult times the humble and insignificant may survive while those who would normally be considered their superiors perish. Geoffrey Chaucer, *Troilus and Criseyde*, c. 1385. Variant forms include 'oaks may fall when reeds stand the storm'.

Though I live obscure, yet I live cleane and honest, and when as the lofty oake is blowne downe, the silly reed may stand.
Richard Burton, *The Anatomy of Melancholy*, 1621

regulated. *See* ACCIDENTS will happen in the best regulated families

rejoices. *See* it is a POOR heart that never rejoices

remedies. *See* DESPERATE diseases call for desperate remedies

remedy. no remedy but patience (Roman) For some complaints or problems there is no solution except to wait for things to come right. *Letter of Muscovy Company*, 1557 (also found in the writings of Horace). *See also* TIME heals all wounds.

the remedy may be worse than the disease (Roman) Countermeasures may be so radical that some may consider them to be worse than the problems they are designed to solve. Francis Bacon, 'Of Sedition and Troubles', 1597 (also found in the writings of Publilius Syrus in the first century BC and in Seneca). This proverb was originally quoted in medical contexts but is now applied in many other situations.

Things will therefore stand as they are; the remedy would be worse than the disease.
Lord Byron, letter, 1807

there is a remedy for everything except death (English) Death is a malady for which there is no cure. John Lydgate, *The Dance of Machabree*, c. 1430. Another proverb ignores the limitation imposed by death, claiming 'there is a remedy for everything, could men but find it'.

There is a remedy for everything but death, said Don Quixote; for 'tis but having a Barke ready at the Sea side, and in spite of all the world we may embarke our selves.
T. Shelton, *Cervantes' Don Quixote*, 1620

removals. *See* THREE removals are as bad as a fire

remove. do not remove a fly from your friend's forehead with a hatchet (Chinese) Taking extreme measures to counter a minor problem may lead to considerably greater harm resulting.

render unto Caesar that which is Caesar's (Hebrew) Hand over what you have to those who claim a stronger title to them. Bible, Matthew 22:21. The proverb is usually quoted in discussion of business affairs, particularly tax revenues demanded by government (echoing the original context – the taxes imposed on all Romans under the rule of Julius Caesar).

Render therefore unto Caesar the things which are Caesar's; and unto God the things that are God's.
Bible, Matthew 22:21

renewal. *See* the QUARREL of lovers is the renewal of love

repairs. he who repairs not his gutter repairs his whole house (English) A person who fails to make timely repairs will find that eventually he or she will have to institute much more extensive repairs to counter damage done. John Ruskin, *The Seven Lamps of Architecture*, 1849. Variants include 'he who repairs not a part builds all'. *See also* a STITCH in time saves nine.

repeats. *See* HISTORY repeats itself

repent. *See* MARRY in haste and repent at leisure

repentance comes too late (English) Repenting after the harm is done does nothing to reduce the effects. John Lydgate, *The Fall of Princes*, c.1440. A contrasting viewpoint is offered by the saying 'it is never too late to repent'.

rest. *See* a CHANGE is as good as a rest; after DINNER rest a while, after supper walk a mile

returns. *See* the DOG returns to its vomit

revenge. revenge is a dish that is best eaten cold (English) Those who take their time over exacting their revenge upon their enemies will find it has added savour. C. Lowe, *Prince Bismarck*, 1885. Also found in the form 'revenge is a dish that should be served cold'.

revenge is sweet (Greek) There is satisfaction to be had in exacting one's revenge upon an enemy. William Painter, *The Palace of Pleasure*, 1566 (also found in essence in Homer's *Iliad* in the ninth century BC).

Revenge, at first, though sweet,
Bitter 'ere long, back on itself recoils.
John Milton, *Paradise Lost*, 1667

revenue. *See* THRIFT is a great revenue

revolutions are not made with rosewater (French) Major changes cannot be made without a certain degree of violence and disruption. 1789, Nicolas Chamfort, quoted in Marmontel, *Oeuvres*, 1818.

On either side harm must be done before good can accrue – revolutions are not to be made with rose water.
Lord Byron, letter, 3 October 1819

reward. *See* VIRTUE is its own reward

rich. he that will be rich before night may be hanged before noon (French) Those who hope for rapid wealth must not be too fastidious about the methods they adopt to achieve their aim, even to the extent of committing crime. H. Estienne, *World of Wonders*, 1607.

the rich man has his ice in the summer and the poor man gets his in the winter (English) The difference between a rich man and a poor man lies not so much in what they can get but in the power the wealthy man has to get it when he wants it. W. B. Masterson, quoted in the *Morning Telegraph*, 27 October 1921. Another proverb suggests another way to judge real wealth, 'he is rich enough that wants nothing', while another runs, 'he is rich enough that needeth neither to flatter nor borrow'.

rich. *See also* he who is CONTENT in his poverty is wonderfully rich; it is EASIER for a camel to go through the eye of a needle than it is for a rich man to enter into the kingdom of heaven; there's one LAW for the rich and another for the poor; it is better to born LUCKY than rich

riches have wings (Hebrew) Wealth is

easily lost. Bible, Proverbs 23:5.

For riches taketh her to her wings, as an eagle, and flieth into the heaven.
Bible, Proverbs 23:5

riches. *See also* CHILDREN are poor men's riches

ride. if you can't ride two horses at once, you shouldn't be in the circus (English) If you cannot meet the expected standard, you should not enter the fray. G. McAllister, *James Maxton*, 1935.

ride. *See also* set a BEGGAR on horseback, and he'll ride to the Devil; if TWO ride on a horse one must ride behind; if WISHES were horses, beggars would ride

rides. he rides well that never falls (English) No one is immune from making mistakes. Thomas Malory, *Morte d'Arthur*, 1485.

He rode sure indeed, that never caught a fall in his life.
Thomas Fuller, *Gnomologia*, 1732

he who rides a tiger is afraid to dismount (Chinese) Those who embark on perilous enterprises may find that it is unsafe to do anything but follow their course to the very end. W. Scarborough, *Collection of Chinese Proverbs*, 1875.

ridiculous. *See* from the SUBLIME to the ridiculous is but a step

right. *See* the CUSTOMER is always right; DO right and fear no man; GOD's in his heaven, all's right with the world; MIGHT is right; TWO wrongs don't make a right

ring. *See* to GIVE a thing, and take a thing, is to wear the Devil's gold ring

ripe. *See* SOON ripe, soon rotten

rise. *See* go to BED with the lamb and rise with the lark; EARLY to bed and early to

rise, makes a man healthy, wealthy and wise; GET a name to rise early, and you may lie all day; a STREAM cannot rise above its source

road. the road to Hell is paved with good intentions (English) Those who mean well often end up doing evil. E. Hellowes, *Guevara's Epistles*, 1574. Also (particularly in former times) encountered in the form 'Hell is paved with good intentions'. Another proverb insists 'the road to Hell is easy'.

Hell is full of good meanings and wishings.
George Herbert, *Jacula Prudentum*, 1633

road. *See also* there is no ROYAL road to learning

roads. all roads lead to Rome (Italian) All alternative courses or lines of thought lead to the same destination or conclusion. Geoffrey Chaucer, *A Treatise on the Astrolabe*, 1391. The saying recalls the prime of Imperial Rome, when much of Europe was linked by the unparalleled Roman road system and when Rome dominated all matters cultural. The idea that Rome was the centre of the human universe was kept alive after the collapse of the Empire through the Roman Catholic Church, which sited its headquarters at the Vatican and thus endowed the city with the claim of being the spiritual centre of the civilized world. Similar proverbs may be found in many other cultures, including Chinese (where all roads lead to Peking) and Japan (where they lead to the palace of the Mikado).

Every one soon or late comes round by Rome.
Robert Browning, *The Ring and the Book*, 1869

roasting. *See* there is REASON in the roasting of eggs

robbery. *See* FAIR exchange is no robbery

robin. the robin and the wren are God's cock and hen (English) The humble robin and the wren are especially loved by Heaven. *Poetical Description of Song Birds*, 1787. The fuller version of the proverb runs, 'the robin and the wren are God's cock and hen; the martin and the swallow are God's mate and marrow'. Sometimes the sparrow takes the place of the robin. Legend has it that the robin acquired its red breast when it was singed while bringing water to souls tormented in the fires of Hell, or alternatively that it was splashed with the blood of Christ as it tried to pull the thorns from his brow. The wren has traditionally been considered the wife of the robin and it is consequently risking the direst misfortune to kill either bird or destroy their eggs or nests. Another proverb warns 'he that hunts robin or wren will never prosper boy nor man'.

In Hampshire we have this couplet, 'Little Cock Robin and Little Jenny Wren, Are God Almighty's little Cock and Hen.' And agreeably to this these birds are held sacred, no boys, however daring, venturing to take their nests or to kill them.
W. Holloway, *Provincialisms*, 1838

Robin Hood. many talk of Robin Hood who never shot with his bow (English) Some people boast of deeds in which they had no role. Geoffrey Chaucer, *Troilus and Criseyde*, c.1385.

Robin Hood could brave all weathers but a thaw wind (English) The least bearable aspect of the weather is a 'thaw wind', a raw and pene-

trating wind that often blows from the south or south-east after a frost or snow. W. Neville, *The Life and Exploits of Robin Hood*, 1855. The proverb is especially well known in Yorkshire, the probable home territory of the semifictional outlaw hero. Inhabitants of the area around Rochdale might refer to a 'Robin Hood wind', a piercing cold wind from the north or east coming off Blackstone Edge.

rocks. *See* the HAND that rocks the cradle rules the world

rod. *See* SPARE the rod and spoil the child

rolling. a rolling stone gathers no moss (English) Those who are always busy consequently keep themselves clear of all unnecessary encumbrances. William Langland, *Piers Plowman*, 1362 (also found in the writings of Erasmus).

Your popular rumour, unlike the rolling stone of the proverb, is one which gathers a deal of moss in its wanderings up and down.
Charles Dickens, *The Old Curiosity Shop*, 1841

Rome. Rome was not built in a day (French) It takes time and effort to achieve the remarkable (just as it took centuries for Imperial Rome to be built). R. Taverner, *Proverbs or Adages of Erasmus*, 1546. The proverb is occasionally heard in reference to other major cities, particularly Paris.

As Rome … had not been built in a day, so neither had Mademoiselle Gerard Moore's education been completed in a week.
Charlotte Brontë, *Shirley*, 1849

when in Rome, do as the Romans do (Roman) When you find yourself in unfamiliar surroundings, it is good policy to compromise one's usual habits and customs and to imitate the manners and way of life of the inhabitants. Saint Ambrose, *Advice to Saint Augustine*, AD 387. The story goes that Saint Ambrose was approached by Saint Augustine for advice when the latter's mother – Saint Monica – arrived in Milan and expressed confusion about whether to fast on a Saturday (as they did in Rome) or to ignore the ruling (as they did in Milan). Saint Ambrose's considered opinion was that she should adapt her practice to whatever was the custom in the place in which she found herself: 'if you are at Rome, live after the Roman fashion; if you are elsewhere, live as they do there'. Much the same advice may be found in varying forms in numerous other cultures around the world. An equivalent, though now archaic, proverb from elsewhere in Europe ran 'never wear a brown hat in Friesland' – an allusion to the extraordinary headwear commonly adopted by inhabitants of that region (a knitted cap surmounted by a silk skull-cap, a metal turban and a high bonnet). Anyone who appeared on the streets wearing humbler head attire would be mocked and jeered.

Rome. *See also* all ROADS lead to Rome; it is ill SITTING at Rome and striving with the Pope

room. there is always room at the top (English) There will always be opportunities for the ambitious to reach the upper echelons. Attributed to the nineteenth-century US politician Daniel Webster. The story goes that Webster quoted the line when it was suggested to him that he should abandon his plans to become a lawyer, as the profession was already overcrowded.

You're the sort of young man we want. There's always room at the top.
John Braine, *Room at the Top*, 1957

roost. *See* CURSES, like chickens, come home to roost

root. *See* IDLENESS is the root of all evil; the LOVE of money is the root of all evil

rope. *See* GIVE a man enough rope and he will hang himself

rose. a rose by any other name would smell as sweet (English) It is not the name of something that distinguishes it, but its intrinsic character. William Shakespeare, *Romeo and Juliet*, c.1593.

What's in a name? that which we call a rose
By any other name would smell as sweet;
So Romeo would, were he not Romeo called.
William Shakespeare, *Romeo and Juliet*, c.1593

no rose without a thorn (English) Many desirable things, like roses, carry their own dangers with them. John Lydgate, *Bochas*, c.1435. Sometimes encountered in the fuller form 'no rose without a thorn, or a love without a rival'.

Hath not thy rose a thorn, Plantagenet?
William Shakespeare, *Henry VI, Part 1*, c.1590

rose. *See also* ANYTHING may be spoken if it be under the rose; the FAIREST rose at last is withered

rosebuds. *See* GATHER ye rosebuds while ye may

rose-water. *See* REVOLUTIONS are not made with rose-water

rot. *See* ONE for the mouse, one for the crow, one to rot, one to grow

rotten. the rotten apple injures its neighbours (English) Evil or corruption is contagious and will infect those close at hand unless quickly isolated. *Ayenbite of Inwit*, 1340.

The rotten apple spoils his companion.
Benjamin Franklin, *Poor Richard's Almanack*,
1736

rotten. *See also* there is SMALL choice in
rotten apples; SOON ripe, soon rotten

**rough. take the rough with the
smooth** (English) Bad times and experiences must be accepted as a necessary accompaniment to the enjoyment
of what is good. *Beryn, c.*1400.

roundabouts. *See* what you lose on the
SWINGS you gain on the roundabouts

**royal. there is no royal road to
learning** (Greek) The acquisition of
knowledge can be acheived only
through study. E. Stone, *Euclid's Elements*,
1745 (quoting Euclid).

There is no royal road to learning; no
short cut to the acquirement of any
valuable art.
Anthony Trollope, *Barchester Towers*, 1857

rubbers. *See* those who PLAY at bowls
must look out for rubbers

rue. *See* MARRY in May and rue the day

rule. *See* DIVIDE and rule; the EXCEPTION
proves the rule; there is an EXCEPTION to
every rule

**ruled. he who will not be ruled
by the rudder must be ruled by
the rock** (English) Those who will
not listen to good advice or pay heed
to changing circumstances must learn
bitter lessons from experience (just
as a ship that does not respond
to the helm will be shipwrecked).
G. Torriano, *Select Italian Proverbs*,
1642.

rules. *See* the HAND that rocks the cradle
rules the world

**run. if you run after two hares you
will catch neither** (English) A person
who divides his attention between
trying to achieve two goals simultaneously is unlikely to attain either.
Alexander Barclay, *The Ship of Fools*,
1509 (also found in the *Adages* of
Erasmus).

I am redie to take potions … yet one thing
maketh to feare, that in running after two
Hares, I catch neither.
John Lyly, *Euphues and His England*, 1580

**you cannot run with the hare and
hunt with the hounds** (English) It is
impossible to align oneself with two
clearly and actively opposed sides.
John Lydgate, *Minor Poems*, 1449. A
hunting proverb that was much quoted from Tudor times onwards.

The whole thing … gave me a look of running with the hare and hunting with the
hounds.
Robert Louis Stevenson, *Catriona*, 1893

run. *See also* the LAST drop makes the
cup run over; STILL waters run deep;
we must learn to WALK before we can
run

runs. *See* he who FIGHTS and runs away,
lives to fight another day

rush. *See* FOOLS rush in where angels fear
to tread

Russian. *See* SCRATCH a Russian and you
find a Tartar

rust. *See* it is better to WEAR out than to
rust out

S

Sabbath. *See* MONDAY's child is fair of face

sack. there comes nought out of the sack but what was there (English) It is impossible to get more out of something than was put in in the first place. L. Evans, *Withals Dictionary Revised*, 1586.

sacks. *See* EMPTY sacks will never stand upright

safe. better safe than sorry (English) Don't take unecessary risks. S. Lover, *Rory O'More*, 1837.

it is best to be on the safe side (English) Caution is the best policy. John Dryden and William Cavendish, Duke of Newcastle, *Sir Martin Mar-all*, 1668. *See also* better SAFE than sorry.

Determining to be on the safe side, he made his apology in form as soon as he could say any thing.
Jane Austen, *Sense and Sensibility*, 1811

safe bind, safe find (English) Keep your valuables secure, so that you may find them again. John Bale, *King Johan*, c.1540.

Safe bind, safe find – it may be once away and aye away.
Walter Scott, *St Ronan's Well*, 1824

safety. there is safety in numbers (Hebrew) If you are one of large number of people, there is less chance that you will be singled out for attention. Bible, Proverbs 11:14.

She determined to call upon them and seek safety in numbers.
Jane Austen, *Emma*, 1815

said. *See* EASIER said than done; LEAST said, soonest mended

sailors. *See* HEAVEN protects children, sailors and drunken men; any PORT in a storm

Saint. if Saint Paul's Day be fair and clear, it will betide a happy year (English) If the weather on Saint Paul's Day – 25 January – is fine, then a good year will follow. Robert of Avesbury, *History*, c.1340. Conversely, if it rains or snows on Saint Paul's Day a poor harvest later in the year is deemed inevitable. If the day turns out windy then warfare must shortly be expected; if it is cloudy then many people are fated to die soon.

on Saint Thomas the Divine kill all turkeys, geese and swine (English) The feast day of Saint Thomas the Apostle – 21 December – is the last day upon which animals should be slaughtered in preparation for Christmas. *An Agreeable Companion*, 1742. Variants include 'the day of Saint Thomas the Divine is good for brewing, baking and killing fat swine'.

Saint Swithin's Day, if thou dost rain, for forty days it will remain; Saint Swithin's Day, if thou be fair, for forty days 'twill rain no more (English) If it rains on Saint Swithin's Day – 15 July – then it will rain consecutively for the next forty days. Ben Jonson, *Every Man Out of His Humour*, 1599. Saint Swithin (sometimes given as Saint Swithun) was bishop of Winchester until his death in 862. At his own request Swithin was buried humbly at a spot he chose himself in the grounds of Winchester cathedral – so that the 'sweet rain of heaven might fall upon his grave' – and there he remained until 15 July 871, when work was set in progress to move his body to a more prestigious location within the building itself. Heavy rain prevented the completion of this enterprise and after forty days' continual downpour the plan was given up altogether, the workers interpreting the deluge as a sign of the saint's disapproval. The tradition that rain that falls on Saint Swithin's Day will continue for another forty days has since become established as one of the best known of all British weather myths (despite the fact that in 963, regardless of the saint's wishes, his remains were sheltered from the elements through the building of a shrine over his grave). The notion has survived regardless of the fact that Saint Swithin's 15 July related to the Julian Calendar, not the Gregorian Calendar adopted several centuries later. Popular tradition has it that Saint Swithin brings rain on 15 July in order to christen the year's apples (an idea supported by the ancient rhyme 'till Saint Swithin's Day be past, the apples be not fit to taste'). Forecasters deny that the tradition can be relied upon, though they concede that mid-July often witnesses a fundamental change in weather patterns. In any case, another proverb insists that any bad weather ushered in by Saint Swithin will be mopped up by 24 August, Saint Bartholomew's Day: 'all the tears that Saint Swithin can cry, Saint Bartlemy's mantle wipes them dry'. Another less well-known proverb, meanwhile, suggests a similar interpretation for rain that falls a clear month earlier, on 15 June: 'if Saint Vitus' Day be rainy weather, it will rain for thirty days together'.

O here, Saint Swithin's, the fifteen day, variable weather, for the most part rain ... why it should rain forty days after, now, more or less, it was rule held afore I was able to hold a plough.
Ben Jonson, *Every Man Out of His Humour*, 1599

saint. *See also* the DEVIL sick would be a monk; the GREATER the sinner, the greater the saint

saints. all are not saints that go to church (English) Those who attend church regularly are not necessarily morally any better than those who do not. L. Evans, *Withals Dictionary Revised*, 1586. Equivalent proverbs include 'all are not saints that use holy water'.

salmon and sermon have both their season in Lent (English) Both salmon-fishing and sermons are at their best leading up to Easter. J. Howell, *Paroemiographia*, 1659.

salt. salt water and absence wash

away love (English) A sea voyage will always dampen one's ardour for lovers left behind. 1805, Horatio Nelson, quoted in Robert Southey's *Life of Nelson*, 1813.

I'm very glad that we're off to-morrow – salt water cures love, they say, sooner than anything else.
Captain Frederick Marryat, *Poor Jack*, 1840

salt. *See also* GIVE neither counsel nor salt till you are asked for it; HELP you to salt, help you to sorrow

salve. there's a salve for every sore (English) There is no ill that cannot be relieved one way or another. *The School House of Women*, 1542. Another proverb suggests 'seek your salve where you get your sore'.

But let us hence, my sovereign, to provide a salve for any sore that may betide.
William Shakespeare, *Henry VI, Part 3*, c.1591

Saturday. Saturday's flit will never sit (English) Servants engaged on a Saturday will never stay for long. Sternberg, *The Dialect of Northamptonshire*, 1851. The proverb expressed an old superstition, and for centuries it was considered very unlucky for a person hopeful of a domestic post to turn up for their first day's work on a Saturday. A fuller version of the proverb runs 'Saturday servants never stay, Sunday servants run away'. Also encountered as 'Saturday's flittings, light sittings'.

there is never a Saturday without some sunshine (English) The sun always shines on Saturdays, if only for a brief moment. Robert Southey, *The Doctor*, 1835.

sauce. what's sauce for the goose is sauce for the gander (English) What is good for one person can be presumed to be good for another (espe-cially if discussing a husband and wife or other members of opposite sexes). John Ray, *A Collection of English Proverbs*, 1670. Some authorities suggest that the original sauce in question, the ideal accompaniment for both goose and gander at the table, was goose-berry sauce (thus, perhaps, the fruit's name). Others suggest that the proverb was derived from an older French saying.

Teach them that 'sauce for goose is sauce for gander'.
Lord Byron, *Don Juan*, 1823

sauce. *See also* HUNGER is the best sauce

sauter. *See* RECULER pour mieux sauter

save. save a thief from the gallows and he shall cut your throat (English) Some people are so evil that gratitude is alien to their natures. William Camden, *Remains Concerning Britain*, 1614. Variants include 'save a thief from the gallows and he shall hate you', 'save a thief from the gal-lows and he will be the first shall do thee a mischief', 'save a thief from the gallows and he will help to hang you' and 'save a stranger from the sea and he'll turn your enemy'.

Whence else came the English proverb, that if you save a thief from the gallows, he shall be the first to cut your throat.
Daniel Defoe, *Colonel Jack*, 1723

save something for a rainy day (English) It is good policy when times are good to save money or other ben-efits for future use when times are hard. Related proverbs include 'save something for the man that rides on the white horse' (in other words, an old man – because of his white hair) and 'save while you may for age and want, no morning sun lasts a whole day'.

save your breath to cool your porridge (English) Do not expend your energy on things that are not important. Deloney, *The Gentle Craft*, c.1598.

Instead of asking riddles ... ye would keep your breath to cool your porridge.
Robert Louis Stevenson, *Kidnapped*, 1886

saved. *See* a PENNY saved is a penny earned

saves. *See* a STITCH in time saves nine

saving is getting (English) Money that is got by saving is just as valuable as money got by any other means. G. Torriano, *Select Italian Proverbs*, 1642. *See also* a PENNY saved is a penny earned.

savours. *See* the CASK savours of the first fill

say. better say nothing, than nothing to the purpose (English) If you have nothing worthwhile to add, then it is better not to say anything at all. J. Chamberlain, *Letters*, 1605. Related proverbs include 'say well or be still'.

say. *See also* DO as I say, not as I do; HEAR all, see all, say nowt

saying is one thing, and doing another (English) It is one thing to say you will do something, but quite another actually to do it. John Heywood, *A Dialogue containing ... the Proverbs in the English Tongue*, 1546. *See also* ACTIONS speak louder than words.

I see that saying and doing are two things, and hereafter I shall better observe this distinction.
John Bunyan, *Pilgrim's Progress*, 1678

says. he who says what he likes shall hear what he does not like (Roman) Those who speak out loud everything they think, without regard for the feelings of others, are likely to attract hostile responses from others. R. Taverner, *Proverbs or Adages of Erasmus*,

1539 (also quoted by Terence). Along the same lines is 'say little but think the more', first recorded in the fifteenth century.

Peace husband ... speake no more than you should, least you heare what you would not.
Robert Greene, *Pandosto*, 1588

says. *See also* what EVERYBODY says must be true; what MANCHESTER says today, the rest of England says tomorrow

scabbard. *See* whosoever DRAWS his sword against the prince must throw the scabbard away

scabbed. one scabbed sheep infects the whole flock (Roman) It takes only one tainted or infected individual to contaminate everyone or everything in the vicinity. *Douce MS*, c.1350 (also quoted by Juvenal). Also encountered in the form 'one scabbed sheep mars a whole flock'.

From one rude Boy that's us'd to mock,
Ten learn the wicked Jest;
One sickly Sheep infects the Flock,
And poysons all the rest.
Isaac Watts, *Divine Songs*, 1728

scalded. a scalded cat fears cold water (English) Everyone learns to avoid what has caused them harm before, even to the extent of fearing what is actually quite harmless. Randle Cotgrave, *A Dictionary of the French and English Tongues*, 1611. Also encountered with 'dog' in the place of 'cat'. Equivalent sayings include 'whom a serpent has bitten, a lizard alarms' and 'he who is bitten by a serpent is afraid of a rope'. *See also* once BITTEN, twice shy; a BURNT child dreads the fire.

scarce. *See* GOOD men are scarce

scarlet. *See* an APE's an ape, a varlet's a varlet, though they be clad in silk or scarlet

schemes. *See* the BEST laid schemes of mice and men gang oft agley

school. *See* EXPERIENCE keeps a dear school; never tell TALES out of school

scorned. *See* HELL hath no fury like a woman scorned

scratch. scratch a Russian and you find a Tartar (*French*) Every Russian at heart has the aggressive and barbarous character of the Tartar. J. Gallatin, *Diary*, 2 January 1823 (often attributed originally to Napoleon). The proverb has since been adapted to refer to other nationalities – including, for instance, Puerto Rican: 'scratch a Puerto Rican and you find a Spaniard'.

scratch an Englishman and you'll find a seaman (*English*) All Englishmen are seafarers at heart.

you scratch my back and I'll scratch yours (*Greek*) You do me a favour, and I will do you a favour in return. Randle Cotgrave, *A Dictionary of the French and English Tongues*, 1611. Historical variants include 'scratch me and I'll scratch thee' and 'scratch my back and I'll claw your elbow'. *See also* KA me, ka thee.

We are all getting liberal now; and (provided you can scratch me if I scratch you) what do I care … whether you are a Dustman or a Duke?
Wilkie Collins, *The Moonstone*, 1868

scripture. *See* the DEVIL can quote scripture for his own purpose

sea. he that would go to sea for pleasure, would go to Hell for a pastime (*English*) The man that would voluntarily go to sea is reckless of his own welfare. A. J. Boyd, *Shellback*, 1899. Heard chiefly among sailors. *See also* PRAISE the sea but keep on land.

the sea and the gallows refuse

none (*English*) No man is immune from the dangers posed by the sea or from death by hanging. T. Gentleman, *England's Way to Win Wealth*, 1614. Other proverbs expressing similar sentiments include the French saying 'the sea has an enormous thirst and an insatiable appetite'.

sea. *See also* in a CALM sea every man is a pilot; there are plenty more FISH in the sea

search. *See* on the FIRST of March, the crows begin to search

second. second thoughts are best (*Greek*) Reappraisal brings better understanding. Ralph Holinshed, *Chronicles*, 1577 (also quoted by Euripides in *Hippolytus*).

Second thoughts, they say, are best: I'll consider of it once again.
John Dryden, *The Spanish Friar*, 1681

the second blow makes the fray (*English*) It takes two to make a fight, so it is only when the second person retaliates that conflict is properly joined. Francis Bacon, *The Colours of Good and Evil*, 1597. Also encountered in the fuller form 'the first blow makes the wrong, the second blow makes the fray'. *See also* it takes TWO to make a quarrel.

secret. wherever there is a secret there must be something wrong (*English*) Secrets are a sure sign that something is being kept hidden that ought to be revealed. Roger North, *Lives*, 1696.

secret. *See also* NOTHING is burdensome as a secret; THREE may keep a secret, if two of them are dead

see. see Naples and die (*Italian*) Naples is the fairest city in the world, so having seen it the traveller might as well die, as he will never see anything better. G. A. Sala, *The American Revolution*, 1882. There is a darker side to this seemingly lighthearted boast, for Naples was once notorious for epidemics of typhoid and cholera, and as a result in former times many visitors did die after seeing the city. Occasionally applied to other cities (often sarcastically).

see no evil, hear no evil, speak no evil *(Japanese)* The proverb is supposed to have had its origins in the sixteenth-century carvings of Three Wise Monkeys over a doorway at the Sacred Stable at Nikko in Japan (each in turn with paws covering ears, eyes and mouth). *Army and Navy Stores Catalogue*, 1926. *See also* HEAR all, see all, say nowt.

see. *See also* BELIEVE nothing of what you hear, and only half of what you see; there are none so BLIND as those who will not see; what the EYE does not see, the heart does not grieve over; HEAR all, see all, say nowt; they that LIVE longest, see most; LOOKERS-on see most of the game; see a PIN and let it lie, you'll want a pin before you die; see a PIN and pick it up, all the day you'll have good luck

seed. good seed makes a good crop *(English)* The quality of what you produce depends upon the quality of what you start out with. *Dialogue of Salomon and Marcolphus*, 1492. *See also* as you SOW, so shall you reap.

seed. *See also* the BLOOD of the martyrs is the seed of the Church; PARSLEY seed goes nine times to the Devil

seeding. *See* ONE year's seeding means seven years' weeding

seeing is believing *(Roman)* Only when a person sees something with his or her own eyes are they certain to believe it. S. Harward, *MS*, 1609 (also quoted by Plautus).

There's nothing like matter of fact; seeing is believing.
John Arbuthnot, *The History of John Bull*, 1712

seek and ye shall find *(Greek)* Those who actively pursue what they want are the most likely to be rewarded. Bible, Matthew 7:7 (also quoted by Sophocles in *Oedipus Tyrannus*). Related proverbs include 'as good seek nought as seek and find nought', 'who seeks what he should not, finds what he would not', 'seek that which may be found' and the worldly-wise 'he that seeks trouble never misses'.

Ask, and it shall be given you: seek, and ye shall find.
Bible, Matthew 7:7

seen. *See* CHILDREN should be seen and not heard

seldom comes a loan laughing home *(English)* Loans are rarely settled in full and on time. *Proverbs of Hending*, c.1300.
A borrow'd loan should come laughing home. What a man borrows he should return with thankfulness.
James Kelly, *A Complete Collection of Scotish Proverbs*, 1721

seldom seen, soon forgotten *(English)* When one is only rarely reminded of something it soon passes from one's memory altogether. *Douce MS*, c.1350. *See also* OUT of sight, out of mind.

self. self-praise is no recommendation *(English)* Those who speak well of themselves cannot be relied upon. T. Shelton, *Cervantes' Don Quixote*, 1612. Also encountered in the form 'self-praise comes aye stinking home'.

Self-praise is no recommendation, but I may say for myself that I am not so bad a man of business.
Charles Dickens, *Bleak House*, 1853

self-preservation is the first law of nature (English) The instinct to safeguard your own life and interests is paramount. R. Dallington, *Aphorisms*, 1613.

Self-preservation, Nature's first great Law.
Andrew Marvell, 'Hodge's Vision from the Monument', 1675

sell. See BUY in the cheapest market and sell in the dearest

seller. See the BUYER has need of a hundred eyes, the seller of but one

sends. See GOD never sends mouths but He sends meat; GOD sends meat, but the Devil sends cooks

September blow soft, till the fruit's in the loft (English) A mild and gale-free September allows fruit to be gathered in undamaged, so is much to be hoped for. T. Tusser, *Five Hundred Points of Husbandry*, 1571.

sermon. See SALMON and sermon have both their season in Lent

servant. a servant and a cock should be kept but a year (English) Servants should be dismissed before they become too well rooted in their post and cease to give of their best (as is also true of cocks). Thomas Fuller, *Gnomologia*, 1732. Other proverbs offering helpful advice on the management of servants (or employees) include 'don't take a servant off a midden', 'if you pay not a servant his wages, he will pay himself' and 'if you would have a good servant, take neither a kinsman nor a friend'. The ideal servant, another proverb states, has 'the back of an ass, the tongue of a sheep

and the snout of a swine'. Servants, for their part, are advised 'a good servant should never be in the way and never out of the way', 'servants should put on patience when they put on a livery' and 'servants should see all and say nothing'. Those who dream of better things will be encouraged by the proverb 'he that hath not served knows not how to command'.

serve. See you cannot serve GOD and Mammon; NO man can serve two masters

served. if you would be well served, serve yourself (English) If you want things done properly, the simplest course is to take matters into your own hands. G. Torriano, *English and Italian Dictionary*, 1659. See also if you WANT a thing done well, do it yourself.

served. See also FIRST come, first served; YOUTH must be served

service is no inheritance (English) No servant or employee has the right to hand on his post to his children. Thomas Hoccleve, *The Regiment of Princes*, 1412.

In Isbel's case and mine own. Service is no heritage.
William Shakespeare, *All's Well That Ends Well*, c.1602

set. See set a BEGGAR on horseback, and he'll ride to the Devil; set a THIEF to catch a thief

seven. See KEEP a thing seven years and you'll always find a use for it; you should KNOW a man seven years before you stir his fire; ONE year's seeding means seven years' weeding; RAIN before seven, fine before eleven; SIX hours' sleep for a man, seven for a woman and eight for a fool

shadow. *See* CATCH not at the shadow and lose the substance

shadows. *See* COMING events cast their shadows before; OLD sins cast long shadows

shame. *See* TELL the truth and shame the Devil

share and share alike (English) Divide everything equally. Randle Cotgrave, *A Dictionary of the French and English Tongues*, 1611.

They say, that a' man share and share equal-aquals in the creature's ulzie.
Walter Scott, *The Pirate*, 1821

shared. *See* a TROUBLE shared is a trouble halved

sharper. the sharper the storm, the sooner it's over (Roman) The more intense some experience or hardship is, the sooner it is likely to end. Francis Kilvert, *Diary*, 9 June 1872 (also quoted by Seneca in *Natural Questions*). Also encountered in the form 'the sharper the blast, the shorter 'twill last'.

sheep. if one sheep leap o'er the dyke, all the rest will follow (English) If one person does something many others are likely to follow suit. James Kelly, *A Complete Collection of Scotish Proverbs*, 1721.

Call in the other fellow, who has some common sense. One sheep will leap the ditch when another goes first.
Walter Scott, *Old Mortality*, 1816

sheep. *See also* there's a BLACK sheep in every family; a BLEATING sheep loses a bite; CARRION crows bewail the dead sheep, and then eat them; you might as well be HANGED for a sheep as for a lamb; one SCABBED sheep infects the whole flock

shepherd. *See* RED sky at night, shep-

herd's delight; red sky in the morning, sailor's warning

shift. you cannot shift an old tree without it dying (English) There comes a point where people or other things have become so firmly rooted over a long period of time that it becomes impossible to transplant them without destroying them completely. Alexander Barclay, *Mancinus' Mirror of Good Manners*, c.1518. *See also* you can't TEACH an old dog new tricks.

shines. *See* HAPPY is the bride the sun shines on; make HAY while the sun shines

shining. *See* the SUN loses nothing by shining into a puddle

ship. *See* one HAND for oneself and one for the ship; don't SPOIL the ship for a ha'porth of tar; a WOMAN and a ship ever want mending

shipwreck. let another's shipwreck be your sea-mark (English) Learn from others' mistakes in order to avoid repeating them. Thomas Fuller, *The History of the Worthies of England*, 1662. *See also* he COMPLAINS wrongfully on the sea who twice suffers shipwreck.

I am your sea-mark; and, though wrecked and lost,
My ruin stands to warn you from the coast.
John Dryden, *The Conquest of Granada*, 1670

shirt. *See* NEAR is my shirt, but nearer my skin

shirtsleeves. from shirtsleeves to shirtsleeves in three generations (English) The fruits of the hard work of one generation will be frittered away by the second, so that the subsequent generation is obliged to work as hard as the first. N. M. Butler, *True and False Democracy*, 1907 (attributed to US businessman Andrew Carnegie). *See also* from CLOGS to clogs is three generations.

shoe. a shoe too large trips you up (Roman) Over-ambition can lead to disaster. Often quoted as a warning to those who aim to tackle more than they can manage.

shoe. *See also* for want of a NAIL the shoe was lost

shoemaker. the shoemaker's son always goes barefoot (English) Those who concentrate their efforts on meeting the demands of others may neglect to direct their skill towards the interests of their own family. John Heywood, *A Dialogue containing … the Proverbs in the English Tongue*, 1546. Related proverbs include 'who is worse shod than the shoemaker's wife?'

shoes. *See* it's ILL waiting for dead men's shoes

shoot. he will shoot higher who shoots at the moon than he who aims at a tree (English) The person who has great ambitions will achieve more impressive results than the person who aims much lower. Philip Sidney, *Arcadia*, 1590. Also encountered with 'sun' in the place of 'moon'.

Who shootes at the mid-day Sunne, though he be sure he shall never hit the marke; yet as sure he is he shall shoote higher, than who ayms but at a bush.
Philip Sidney, *Arcadia*, 1590

shoots. he that shoots oft shall at last hit the mark (Roman) Anyone who makes many attempts at something is likely in the end to achieve what he or she is aiming at. Thomas More, *Utopia*, 1551 (also quoted by Cicero).

He that's always shooting, must sometimes hit.
Thomas Fuller, *Gnomologia*, 1732

shop. *See* KEEP your shop and your shop will keep you

shopkeepers. *See* the ENGLISH are a nation of shopkeepers

shorn. *See* GOD tempers the wind to the shorn lamb; many go out for WOOL and come home shorn

short. a short horse is soon curried (English) Minor tasks take little time. *Douce MS, c.*1350.

A short tale is soon told – and a short horse soon curried.
Walter Scott, *The Abbot*, 1820

a short prayer reaches heaven (English) Concise requests are likely to be better received than long rambling ones. *Good Wyfe wold a Pylgremage, c.*1460.

short counsel is good counsel (English) First thoughts are the most reliable. Roger of Wendover, *Chronicle*, 1235. The proverb is vividly illustrated in Roger of Wendover's *Chronicle* by the tale of Walcher, first Bishop of Durham, who fell into the hands of a mob in Gateshead in the year 1080: with the cry 'short rede, good rede, slay the bishop', his church was set ablaze and Walcher himself was put to death before anyone could voice any second thoughts.

short reckonings make long friends (English) Those who come to terms or settle their debts quickly are likely to enjoy lasting friendly relationships. R. Whitforde, *Work for Householders*, 1530. Also found with 'accounts' in the place of 'reckonings'.

the short cut is often the longest way round (English) What appears at first to offer a short cut in something may in the event turn out to require more time, effort or trouble.

Francis Bacon, *The Advancement of Learning*, 1605.

It is in life, as it is in ways, the shortest way is commonly the foulest, and surely the faire way is not much about.
Francis Bacon, *The Advancement of Learning*, 1605

short. *See also* ART is long, life is short; LONG foretold long last, short notice soon past

shortest. *See* BARNABY bright, Barnaby bright, the longest day and the shortest night; the LONGEST way round is the shortest way home

shot. *See* a FOOL's bolt is soon shot

shoulders. *See* you cannot put an OLD head on young shoulders

show. show me a liar and I will show you a thief (English) A person who is prepared to tell lies is also capable of stealing. R. West, *The Court of Conscience*, 1607. *See also* a LIAR is worse than a thief.

show me the man and I'll show you the law (Scottish) The impartiality of the law depends upon the impartiality of the judge. David Fergusson, *Scottish Proverbs*, 1641.

A case of importance scarcely occurred, in which there was not some ground for bias or partiality on the part of the judges, who were so little able to withstand the temptation, that the adage 'Show me the man, and I will show you the law', became as prevalent as it was scandalous.
Walter Scott, *The Bride of Lammermoor*, 1819

shower. *See* many DROPS make a shower

showers. *See* APRIL showers bring forth May flowers

shrew. every man can rule a shrew but he who has her (English) Everyone believes they would know what to do with an unruly wife, except those who are actually married

to one. John Heywood, *A Dialogue containing ... the Proverbs in the English Tongue*, 1546.

shrouds have no pockets (Italian) You cannot take your earthly wealth with you when you die. R. C. Trench, *On Lessons in Proverbs*, 1854.

shut. a shut mouth never fills a black coffin (US) A person who keeps his silence is unlikely to be murdered for being an informant. This proverbial piece of advice was widely heard in US cities during the gangster era of the 1920s and 1930s.

shut. *See also* a DOOR must either be shut or open; it is too LATE to shut the stable-door after the horse has bolted

shuts. *See* when one DOOR shuts, another opens

shy. *See* once BITTEN, twice shy

sick. *See* the DEVIL sick would be a monk; HOPE deferred makes the heart sick

sickness. sickness comes on horseback, but goeth away on foot (English) Illnesses come quickly, but are slow to recede. Randle Cotgrave, *A Dictionary of the French and English Tongues*, 1611. *See also* AGUES come on horseback, but go away on foot.

sickness shows us what we are (Roman) Ill-health is reminder of our own mortality. Thomas Fuller, *Gnomologia*, 1732 (also quoted by Lucretius).

sickness. *See also* the CHAMBER of sickness is the chapel of devotion

side. *See* the BREAD never falls but on the buttered side; GOD is always on the side of the big battalions; the GRASS is always greener on the other side of the fence; always LOOK on the bright side; it is best to be on the SAFE side

sides. *See* there are TWO sides to every question

sight. *See* in vain the NET is spread in the sight of the bird; OUT of sight, out of mind

silence. silence catches a mouse (English) The silent, stealthy approach has the best results. J. Clarke, *Paroemiographia Anglo-Latina*, 1639. Related proverbs include 'silence doth seldom harm'. *See also* SOFTLY, softly catchee monkey.

Saying nothing, till you be ready to put in execution, is the way to shun prevention, and effect your business.
James Kelly, *A Complete Collection of Scotish Proverbs*, 1721

silence is a woman's best garment (Greek) It becomes a woman to keep her silence. R. Taverner, *Proverbs or Adages of Erasmus*, 1539 (also quoted by Sophocles in *Ajax*). Another proverb archly observes 'silence is a fine jewel for a woman, but it's little worn'.

Let your women keepe silence in the Churches, for it is not permitted unto them to speake.
Bible, 1 Corinthians 14:34

silence is golden (Swiss) Silence is precious. W. White, *Eastern England*, 1865. *See also* SPEECH is silver, silence is golden

Silence is golden, as her father used to say when she used to fly into tempers and wanted to say nasty things to everybody within range.
Aldous Huxley, *Antic Hay*, 1923

silence is wisdom (English) The wise man keeps his peace. Geoffrey Chaucer, *Troilus and Criseyde*, c.1385.

silence means consent (Roman) If a person remains silent in a particular set of circumstances their silence may be taken to mean they have no objections to what is taking place or being proposed. William Wycliffe, c.1380, quoted in *Select English Works*, 1871. The principle has long been quoted in courts of law. Occasionally encountered in Latin, '*qui tacet consentire videtur*' and also as 'silence gives consent'.

But that you shall not say I yield, being silent,
I would not speak.
William Shakespeare, *Cymbeline*, c.1610

silk. you can't make a silk purse out of a sow's ear (English) It is impossible to get perfect results when working with imperfect materials. Alexander Barclay, *Eclogues*, 1518. Sows' ears were once commonly used to make drawstring purses, but these were carried generally by the poor only, as the rich favoured purses made of silk and other much more delicate materials than sows' ears, which are coarse in texture and heavily bristled. Variants include 'you cannot make a horn of a pig's tail'.

He remembered his uncle's saying that it took three generations to make a gentleman: it was a companion proverb to the silk purse and the sow's ear.
W. Somerset Maugham, *Of Human Bondage*, 1915

silk. *See also* an APE's an ape, a varlet's a varlet, though they be clad in silk or scarlet

silly. *See* ASK a silly question and you'll get a silly answer

silver. he that has not silver in his purse should have silk on his tongue (English) Anyone who has no money needs all the advantages of a charming manner to improve their situation. J. Howell, *Paroemiographia*, 1659.

silver. *See also* every CLOUD has a silver lining; SPEECH is silver, silence is golden

sin. every sin brings its punishment with it (English) There is an appropriate punishment for every offence. T. Draxe, *Bibliotheca Scholastica*, 1616.

That is the punishment of making free with the bottle ... but if it is an offence, then it carries its own punishment.
Captain Frederick Marryat, *Jacob Faithful*, 1824

it is a sin to steal a pin (English) Stealing something of small value is just as serious as stealing something worth a lot more. R. Whitford, *Werke for Housholders*, 1537. Variants include 'he that will steal a pin will steal a better thing' and 'he that will steal an egg will steal an ox'.

Children were taught to 'know it's a sin to steal a pin' ... when they brought home some doubtful finding.
Flora Thompson, *Lark Rise to Candleford*, 1945

sincerest. *See* IMITATION is the sincerest form of flattery

sing. *See* a BEGGAR may sing before a pickpocket; LITTLE birds that can sing and won't sing must be made to sing

singly. *See* MISFORTUNES never come singly

sinner. *See* the GREATER the sinner, the greater the saint

sins. *See* CHARITY covers a multitude of sins; OLD sins cast long shadows

sit. better sit idly than work for nothing (English) There is no point working if you are not going to be paid. D. Rogers, *Matrimonial Honour*, 1642. Related proverbs include 'better sit still than rise up and fall'.

sit awhile and go a mile (English) Those who make sure they are well rested will perform best. J. Palsgrave,

L'Éclaircissement de la langue française, 1530.

sits. *See* where MACGREGOR sits is the head of the table

sitting. it is ill sitting at Rome and striving with the Pope (Scottish) It is bad policy to pick arguments with someone or cause them some offence when you are at their mercy. J. Carmichaell, *Proverbs in Scots*, 1628.

sitting. *See also* it is as CHEAP sitting as standing

six. six feet of earth make all men equal (English) All men are equal in death (when buried six feet down). J. Howell, *Paroemiographia*, 1659.

six hours' sleep for a man, seven for a woman and eight for a fool (Roman) Anyone who takes more than the amount of sleep appropriate to their sex is either lazy or a fool. J. Wodroephe, *Spared Hours of a Soldier*, 1623. It was a favourite saying of George III. The proverb is known in several variants, which include 'five hours' sleep for a traveller, seven for a scholar, eight for a merchant and eleven for a knave'. Also related is 'the sluggard makes his night till noon' and 'nature requireth five, Custom taketh seven, Idleness takes nine and Wickedness eleven'.

skin. *See* BEAUTY is only skin deep; NEAR is my coat, but nearer my skin

skittles. *See* LIFE isn't all beers and skittles

sky. if the sky falls we shall catch larks (Roman) If something that is unlikely happens we shall be able to get a certain benefit by it (usually quoted sarcastically in response to those who speculate about the benefits they would get if something that is actually highly improbable were to take place). *Peter Idley's Instructions to his Son*, c.1445 (also quoted by Terence). *See also* PIGS might fly, if they had wings.

I cannot be put off by the news that our system would be perfect if it were worked by angels ... just as I do not admit that if the sky fell we should all catch larks.
George Bernard Shaw, *Misalliance*, 1914

sky. *See also* RED sky at night, shepherd's delight; red sky in the morning, sailor's warning

slander leaves a scar behind it (Roman) Allegations always leave the taint of suspicion, even when the victim is officially cleared. T. Draxe, *Bibliotheca Scholastica*, 1616. *See also* FLING enough dirt and some will stick.

slave. *See* better be an OLD man's darling than a young man's slave

sleep. sleep is the brother of death (Greek) Sleep is akin to death. *The Mirror of Magistrates*, 1563 (also quoted by Homer in the *Iliad*). Also encountered as 'sleep is the cousin of death'. Related sayings include 'sleep is the image of death'.

How wonderful is Death, Death and his brother Sleep!
Percy Bysshe Shelley, *Queen Mab*, 1813

sleep. *See also* one HOUR's sleep before midnight is worth two after; SIX hours' sleep for a man, seven for a woman and eight for a fool

sleeping. let sleeping dogs lie (English/French) Avoid the provocation of potential trouble. Geoffrey Chaucer, *Troilus and Criseyde*, c.1385 (also recorded in French in the thirteenth century and found in other European languages). Variants include 'wake not a sleeping lion', in which form Sir Philip Sidney quoted it in *Arcadia* in

1580, and 'he that sleeps bites no body'. In *Henry IV, Part 2*, William Shakespeare quoted it in the form 'wake not a sleeping wolf'. Other less well-known proverbs warn of the dangers of disturbing hornets and stirring up stinking puddles. *See also* LEAVE well alone; LET well alone.

Take my advice, and speer as little about him as he does about you. Best to let sleeping dogs lie.
Walter Scott, *Redgauntlet*, 1824

there will be sleeping enough in the grave (English) No one should over-indulge in sleep, as they will have sleep enough when they are dead. Benjamin Franklin, *The Way to Wealth*, 1736.

sleeve. *See* STRETCH your arm no further than your sleeve will reach

slice. a slice off a cut loaf isn't missed (English) It is easy for something to be taken dishonestly, without being detected, from what is in the process of being properly dispersed. William Shakespeare, *Titus Andronicus*, c.1593. Also encountered in the form 'it is safe taking a shive of a cut loaf'. *See also* much WATER goes by the mill that the miller knows not of.

More water glideth by the mill
Than wots the miller of; and easy it is
Of a cut loaf to steal a shive.
William Shakespeare, *Titus Andronicus*, c.1593

slip. *See* there's MANY a slip 'twixt cup and lip

sloth is the key to poverty (English) Laziness inevitably leads to poverty. *Politeuphuia*, 1669. Other proverbs concerning sloth include 'sloth is the Devil's cushion', 'sloth, like rust, consumes faster than labour wears', 'the slothful man is the beggar's brother' and 'sloth turneth the edge of wit'.

slow but sure wins the race (English) Those who make steady, measured progress will in the end finish ahead of those who rush ahead too quickly. T. Draxe, *Bibliotheca Scholastica*, 1633. The moral behind the proverb was illustrated by one of Aesop's most famous fables, written in the sixth century BC, that of the fleet-footed hare and the plodding tortoise: the hare, confident of victory in a race against the tortoise, takes a rest, but wakes too late to catch up with the steadily plodding tortoise as it reaches the finishing post. Sometimes quoted in the abbreviated form 'slow but sure'. Variants include 'slow and steady wins the race'. Among related proverbs with similar meanings is 'the snail slides up the tower at last though the swallow mounteth it sooner'. *See also* LITTLE strokes fell great oaks.

What signifies minding her? ... if she be slow she's sure.
Oliver Goldsmith, *The Vicar of Wakefield*, 1768

slowly. *See* make HASTE slowly; the MILLS of God grind slowly, yet they grind exceeding small

small. small is beautiful (US) Small-scale things are preferable to things on a larger scale. E. F. Schumacher, *Small Is Beautiful*, 1973 (Schumacher himself attributed it to his publishers Anthony Blond and Desmond Briggs). The saying was adopted as a slogan by those opposed to attempts to combine small businesses in huge public conglomerations during the 1970s. *See also* the BEST things come in small packages.

small sorrows speak; great ones are silent (Roman) People will share their minor sorrows with everyone, but are more reluctant to discuss more serious grievances. T. Hughes, *The Misfortunes of*

Arthur, 1587 (also quoted by Seneca).

The grief that does not speak whispers the o'erfraught heart and bids it break.
William Shakespeare, *Macbeth*, c.1604

there is small choice in rotten apples (English) There is little scope for choice when all alternatives are equally unappealing. William Shakespeare, *The Taming of the Shrew*, 1592.

Faith, as you say, there's small choice in rotten apples.
William Shakespeare, *The Taming of the Shrew*, c.1592

small. *See also* the MILLS of God grind slowly, yet they grind exceeding small

smell. *See* MONEY has no smell

smells. she smells best that smells of nothing (Roman) The woman (or man) who wears no perfume at all smells the best. Meres, *Palladis*, 1598 (also quoted by Plautus). The idea behind the proverb is that any person who wears perfume must be suspected of wearing it to mask some personal odour that may well be offensive.

Mulier recte olet, ubi nihil olet; then a woman smells best, when she hath no perfume at all.
Richard Burton, *The Anatomy of Melancholy*, 1621

smelt. one is not smelt where all stink (English) A guilty man may conceal himself in a crowd of similarly guilty men. T. Adams, *Sermons*, 1629.

smile. *See* NEVER rely on the glory of the morning or on the smile of your mother-in-law

smoke. much smoke, little fire (English) When much fuss is made about something, the chances are there is very little substance to it. *Brewer's Phrase and Fable*, 1959.

the smoke follows the fairest

(*Greek*) Envy clusters around those who are the most beautiful, gifted, intelligent etc. *Berkeley MS,* 1639 (also quoted by Aristophanes).

The reek follows the fairest ... This is in Aristophanes, and signifies that envy is a concomitant of excellency.
James Kelly, *A Complete Collection of Scotish Proverbs,* 1721

smoke. *See also* there's NO smoke without fire.

smooth. *See* the COURSE of true love never did run smooth

sneeze on a Monday, you sneeze for danger (*English*) There is something to be gleaned from a sneeze, according to the day of the week on which it happens. Harland, *Lancashire Folk-Lore,* 1867. In full, the proverb is usually given as 'sneeze on a Monday, you sneeze for danger; sneeze on a Tuesday, you kiss a stranger; sneeze on a Wednesday, you sneeze for a letter; sneeze on a Thursday, for something better; sneeze on a Friday, you sneeze for sorrow; sneeze on a Saturday, your sweetheart tomorrow; sneeze on a Sunday, your safety seek, the Devil will have you the whole of the week'.

snow. a snow year, a rich year (*English*) A year in which much snow falls will, by way of compensation, see plentiful harvests a few months later. J. Frampton, *Monardes,* 1580. Another proverb insists 'if February give much snow, a fine summer it doth foreshow'.

snows. *See* many HAWS, many snows

so. *See* so many COUNTRIES, so many customs; so many MEN, so many opinions

sober. *See* WANTON kittens make sober cats

soft. a soft answer turneth away wrath (*Hebrew*) A calm, composed manner will blunt the anger of others. William Wycliffe, Bible, Proverbs 15:1, 1382.

a soft fire makes a sweet malt (*English*) Too much haste will spoil the final result (just as too hot a fire will ruin the refining of a good malt whisky). Rowland Hill, *Commonplace Book,* 1530.

Hold, hold (quoth Hudibras), soft fire,
They say, does make sweet malt.
Samuel Butler, *Hudibras,* 1663

soft and fair goes far (*English*) A calm and gentle demeanour will achieve more than a more brusque approach. *Beryn, c.* 1400.

Soft and fair, young lady. You that are going to be married think things can never be done too fast.
Oliver Goldsmith, *The Good-Natured Man,* 1768

soft. *See also* FAIR and soft goes far in a day; SEPTEMBER blow soft, till the fruit's in the loft

softly, softly, catchee monkey (*African*) A quiet, stealthy approach will result in success. G. Benham, *Cassell Dictionary of Quotations,* 1907. In the 1970s the proverb was adopted as the title of a highly popular British television police series.

softly. *See also* FAIR and soft goes far in a day

solano. *See* ASK no favour during the solano

soldier. every soldier has the baton of a field-marshal in his knapsack (*French*) Any soldier, however humble, may aspire to the rank of commander. Usually attributed to Napoleon, though also to Louis XVIII. First recorded in English in 1840.

soldier. *See also* the FIRST duty of a soldier is obedience

soldiers. soldiers in peace are like chimneys in summer (English) A soldier in peacetime has no role to play. A. Copley, *Wits, Fits, etc.*, 1594.

soldiers. *See also* OLD soldiers never die, they simply fade away

solution. if you're not part of the solution, you're part of the problem (English) If you are not in tune with what is perceived to be the solution to some problem then by implication you only contribute to the problem itself. Malcolm Bradbury, *The History Man*, 1975.

some. *See* you WIN a few, you lose a few

something. something is better than nothing (English) It is better to have something, however imperfect, than nothing at all. John Heywood, *A Dialogue containing ... the Proverbs in the English Tongue*, 1546. Also encountered as 'somewhat is better than nothing'.

you don't get something for nothing (English) Nothing comes without a price of some kind. P. T. Barnum, *Struggles and Triumphs*, 1870. Also encountered in somewhat jocular northern English dialect form, 'you don't get owt for nowt'. *See also* there is no such thing as a FREE lunch; NOTHING comes of nothing.

son. my son is my son till he gets him a wife, but my daughter's my daughter all the days of her life (English) Mothers relinquish influence over their sons when they get married and another woman intervenes, but retain a permanent leading role in the lives of their daughters. John Ray, *A Collection of English Proverbs*, 1670.

son. *See also* like FATHER, like son; the SHOEMAKER's son always goes barefoot

sons. *See* CLERGYMEN's sons always turn out badly

soon. soon hot, soon cold (English) Emotions that arise quickly subside equally quickly. Burgh and Lydgate, *Secrees*, c.1450.

soon learnt, soon forgotten (English) What is quickly learned or acquired is equally quickly forgotten or dissipated. Geoffrey Chaucer, *Troilus and Criseyde*, c.1385. Also encountered in the form 'soon gotten, soon spent'.

'Unless I heard the whole repeated, I cannot continue it,' she said. 'Yet it was quickly learned.' 'Soon gained, soon gone,' moralized the tutor.
Charlotte Brontë, *Shirley*, 1849

soon ripe, soon rotten (Roman) Anything that matures quickly will soon become over-ripe (often quoted in reference to the young). William Langland, *Piers Plowman*, 1393.

And that that rathest rypeth, roteth most saunest.
William Langland, *Piers Plowman*, 1393

soon todd, soon with God (English) Children whose milk teeth appear early are fated to die prematurely. J. Howell, *Paroemiographia*, 1659. Many people interpret an early toothed (or 'todd') baby differently, insisting that the infant somehow knows that the mother will quickly become pregnant again, so gets its teeth early so that it will be the better able to fend for itself when the new arrival diverts the mother's attention – a notion often expressed as 'soon teeth, soon toes'. Also encountered in the form 'soon todd, soon turfed'.

soon. *See also* as soon as MAN is born he begins to die

sooner said than done *See* EASIER said than done

sorrow. sorrow comes unsent for (English) Sorrows come, regardless of the fact that no one wants them. Edmund Spenser, *The Shepheardes Calendar*, 1579. Also found as 'sorrow and ill weather come unsent for'.

Sorrow, ne neede be hastened on:
For he will come without calling anon.
Edmund Spenser, *The Shepheardes Calendar*, 1579

sorrow is always dry (English) Those who are weighed down with sorrow frequently find respite in drink. John Bale, *Kynge Johan*, c.1540.

Deborah, my life, grief, you know, is dry.
Oliver Goldsmith, *The Vicar of Wakefield*, 1768

sorrow. *See also* HELP you to salt, help you to sorrow; ONE for sorrow, two for joy

sorrowing. *See* he that goes A-BORROW-ING, goes a-sorrowing

sorry. *See* better SAFE than sorry

sorts. it takes all sorts to make a world (Spanish) The mass of humanity includes characters of all shades and humours, who should be tolerated for their apparent eccentricities. T. Shelton, *Cervantes' Don Quixote*, 1620.

In the world there must be of all sorts.
Miguel de Cervantes, *Don Quixote*, 1615

soul. *See* BREVITY is the soul of wit; the EYES are the window of the soul ; OPEN confession is good for the soul; PUNC-TUALITY is the soul of business

souls. *See* CORPORATIONS have neither bodies to be punished nor souls to be damned

sound. *See* EMPTY vessels make the most sound

source. *See* a STREAM cannot rise above its source

south. *See* when the WIND is in the south it blows the bait into the fish's mouth

sow (noun). **a sow may whistle, though it has an ill mouth for it** (English) Someone may possess a basic skill, but is quite incapable of practising it with any distinction. Maria Edgeworth, letter, 19 October 1802.

sow. *See also* you can't make a SILK purse out of a sow's ear

sow (verb). **as you sow, so shall you reap** (Hebrew) In due course you will have to accept the consequences of your actions, good and bad. Bible, Galatians 6:7. Related proverbs include 'he that sows thistles shall reap prickles', 'he that soweth good seed shall reap good corn' and 'who sows little mows the less'. *See also* as you MAKE your bed, so you must lie in it.

According to the several seeds that we sow we shall reap several sorts of grain.
Walter Raleigh, *History of the World*, 1614

they that sow the wind shall reap the whirlwind (Hebrew) Those who live their lives recklessly, seeking to gain profit and ignoring risk to themselves, must face the possible consequences of their actions. Bible, Hosea 8:7.

Indiscriminate profusion ... is sowing the wind to reap the whirlwind.
Walter Scott, *The Black Dwarf*, 1816

spade. *See* CALL a spade a spade

span. *See* when ADAM delved and Eve span, who was then the gentleman?

spare. spare at the spigot, and let out at the bung-hole (English) While taking care not to lose some minor benefit, take care not to lose much more inadvertently in some other way. G. Torriano, *Select Italian Proverbs*, 1642. The proverb derives from the business of brewing, referring to the danger of a brewer paying so much attention to checking that the spigot, which regulates the flow from a cask via the tap, is completely sealed that he fails to notice that much more is being lost from the bung-hole, by means of which the cask is emptied. Also encountered in the form 'save at the spigot, and let out at the bung-hole'.

spare the rod and spoil the child (Greek) Those who fail to discipline their children will find their offspring become selfish and ungovernable. Bible, Proverbs 13:24 (also quoted by the Greek poet Menander)

Salamon seide ... Qui parcit virge, odit filium. The Englich of this latyn is ... Who-so spareth the sprynge, spilleth his children. William Langland, *Piers Plowman*, 1377

spare well and have to spend (English) Those who live economically and thriftily will find that in the long term they have more money to spend. Miles Coverdale, *H. Bullinger's Christian State of Matrimony*, 1541. Variants include 'spare well and spend well' and 'know when to spend and when to spare, and you need not be busy; you'll ne'er be bare'. Another proverb recommends 'spare when you are young and spend when you are old'.

speak. never speak ill of the dead (Greek) Never criticize those who are no longer living and are thus unable to defend themselves. R. Taverner, *Erasmus' Flores Sententiarum*, 1540. The saying is sometimes attributed to the Spartan lawgiver Chilon in the sixth century BC. Also encountered in the form 'speak well of the dead'. Related proverbs include 'speak not of a dead man at the table'.

He that has too much feeling to speak ill of the dead ... will not hesitate ... to destroy ... the reputation ... of the living. Samuel Johnson, *Lives of the Poets*, 1781

speak fair and think what you will (English) Maintain a civil and courteous manner in public, but think whatever you like in private. Sir R. Barckley, *Discourse of the Felicity of Man*, 1598.

speak not of my debts unless you mean to pay them (English) It is impolite to discuss another's debts unless you intend to do something about them. George Herbert, *Outlandish Proverbs*, 1640.

speak softly and carry a big stick (West African) Maintain a calm and moderate demeanour when tackling contentious issues with others, but also remind other parties of the influence you could wield. This proverb, closely associated with the business of international diplomacy, is commonly attributed to US President Theodore Roosevelt, who quoted it in a speech he gave at the Minnesota State Fair in 1901, when he was discussing Latin-American relations.

speak when you are spoken to (English) It is good manners (particularly in children) to speak only when invited to in reply to others. T. Bowes, *La Primaudaye's French Academy*, 1586.

speak. See also ACTIONS speak louder than words; SEE no evil, hear no evil, speak no evil; THINK first and speak afterwards

speaking. See it's ILL speaking between a full man and a fasting

species. See the FEMALE of the species is more deadly than the male

speech. speech is silver, silence is golden (Swiss) Speech may have great value, but silence, which allows time to think and ensures that secrets remain private, is much more precious. George Herbert, *Jacula Prudentum*, 1640 (some suggest an Oriental origin). A Hebrew equivalent runs 'if a word be worth one shekel, silence is worth two'. *See also* SILENCE is golden.

Sprechen ist silbern, Schweigen ist golden – speech is silver, silence is golden.
Thomas Carlyle, in *Fraser's Magazine*, June 1834

speech is the index of the mind (Greek) The way a person talks reveals their inner preoccupations. Brathwait, *The English Gentleman*, 1630 (also quoted by Erasmus). Also encountered in the forms 'speech is the picture of the mind' and 'speech shows what a man is'.

speed. *See* more HASTE, less speed

spend. spend and God will send (English) Spend your money as you will, for Providence will surely look after your interests. *Douce MS*, c.1350. The underlying message is not so much that a person should be profligate with their wealth, but that refusal to spend where modest spending is appropriate may only end up in reduction to poverty in the long run. Sometimes encountered in the fuller form 'spend and God will send; spare and ever bare'. Related proverbs include 'spend not where you may save; spare not where you must spend'.

Solomon says, There is that scattereth, and yet aboundeth: And there is some that withholdeth more than is meet, and it tendeth to poverty.
James Kelly, *A Complete Collection of Scotish Proverbs*, 1721

what you spend, you have (English) You cannot lose what you have already

spent or enjoyed. c.1300, quoted in M. R. James, *Catalogue of the Library of Pembroke College*, 1905. Sometimes given in the longer form 'what you spend, you have; what you give, you have; what you leave, you lose'.

Ho, ho, who lies here?
I the good Earle of Devonshire,
And Maulde my wife, that was ful deare …
That we spent, we had:
That we gave, we have:
That we lefte we lost.
Edmund Spenser, *The Shepheardes Calendar*, 1579

spend. *See also* SPARE well and have to spend

spent. *See* what is GOT over the Devil's back is spent under his belly

spice. *See* VARIETY is the spice of life

spider. *See* where the BEE sucks honey the spider sucks poison; if you WISH to live and thrive, let a spider run alive

spigot. *See* SPARE at the spigot, and let out at the bung-hole

spilt. *See* it's no use CRYING over spilt milk

spirit. the spirit is willing but the flesh is weak (Hebrew) Sometimes a person's physical attributes are not equal to their aspirations. Walter Scott, *Journal*, 23 July 1827.

spite. *See* don't CUT off your nose to spite your face

spits. who spits against heaven it falls in his face (English) Those who attack or insult God will find that their ill wishes rebound upon them. Thomas North, *The Diall of Princes*, 1557. Also encountered in the form 'who spits against the wind it falls in his face'.

For your names
Of whore and murderess, they proceed from you,

As if a man should spit against the wind;
The filth returns in's face.
John Webster, The White Devil, 1612

splash. See when the OAK is before the ash, then you will get only a splash

spoil. don't spoil the ship for a ha'porth of tar (English) If you neglect minor repairs then you risk losing everything. John Day, The Blind Beggar, 1600. Most people assume the proverb is of nautical origins, but it is in reality related to agriculture, with 'ship' being a dialectical version of 'sheep'. Tar was formerly pasted on any sores and wounds that sheep suffered in order to keep flies off; injuries left thus untreated could fester and become maggot-ridden, thus leading to the animal's death. See also a STITCH in time saves nine.

'Never tyne the ship for want of a bit of tar, Gerard', said this changeable mother.
Charles Reade, The Cloister and the Hearth, 1861

spoil. See also too many COOKS spoil the broth; SPARE the rod and spoil the child

spoiled. See better one HOUSE spoiled than two

spoken. See SPEAK when you are spoken to; there's many a TRUE word spoken in jest

spoon. See he who SUPS with the Devil should have a long spoon

spots. See a LEOPARD can't change its spots

sprat. throw out a sprat to catch a mackerel (English) Sacrifice something of minor value to obtain something of much greater worth. William Hone, Every-day Book, 1826. Variants include 'set a herring to catch a whale'.

It was their custom, Mr Jonas said ... never to throw away sprats, but as bait for whales.
Charles Dickens, Martin Chuzzlewit, 1850

spread. See in vain the NET is spread in the sight of the bird

spring. it is not spring until you can plant your foot upon twelve daisies (English) Only when the daisies are flourishing in close abundance can spring be properly said to have arrived. R. Chambers, Book of Days, 1863.

springs. See HOPE springs eternal in the human breast

spur. a spur in the head is worth two in the heel (English) A person will perform all the better for a drink beforehand. John Ray, A Collection of English Proverbs, 1670. The proverb related originally to riding, acknowledging the truth that a rider emboldened by drink will ride harder and more recklessly than a sober man would.

That's four good miles; but 'a spur in the head is worth two in the heel'.
Maria Edgeworth, The Absentee, 1812

squeaking. the squeaking wheel gets the grease (English) Those who complain the loudest are the first to get attention. J. Bartlett, Familiar Quotations, 1937.

stable. See it is too LATE to shut the stable-door after the horse has bolted; the MAN who is born in a stable is a horse

stalled. See better a DINNER of herbs than a stalled ox where hate is

stand. if you can't stand the heat, get out of the kitchen (English) If you cannot bear the pressure, do not put yourself in a position where you will exposed to it. The saying is commonly attributed to US President Harry S Truman, who quoted it when turning down the presidential nomination in 1952, though Truman himself credited Major-General Harry Vaughan as the originator. Truman quoted the proverb in his book *Mr Citizen* in 1960.

He got in the way of justice ... You know what they say, if you don't like the heat, get out of the kitchen.
Malcolm Bradbury, *The History Man*, 1975

stand. *See also* EMPTY sacks will never stand upright; a HOUSE divided against itself cannot stand; every TUB must stand on its own bottom; UNITED we stand, divided we fall

standing. standing pools gather filth (English) Dirt gathers on something (or someone) that is little used or disturbed. J. Clarke, *Paroemiologia Anglo-Latina*, 1639.

Standing pools gather mud.
James Kelly, *A Complete Collection of Scotish Proverbs*, 1721

standing. *See also* it is as CHEAP sitting as standing

starve. *See* FEED a cold and starve a fever

starves. *See* while the GRASS grows, the steed starves

stays. *See* the FAMILY that prays together stays together

steady. *See* FULL cup, steady hand

steal. one man may steal a horse, while another may not look over a hedge (English) Some people are in a position to take full advantage of the opportunities life offers (both legal and illegal) with impunity, while other less privileged people find they are scarcely in a position to do anything at all without being called to account. John Heywood, *A Dialogue containing ... the Proverbs in the English Tongue*, 1546. In *The Irish Widow*, in 1772, David Garrick adapted the

proverb to lampoon the Irish: 'but an Englishman may look over the hedge, while an Irishman must not stale a horse'.

Strange how one artist may steal a horse while another may not look over a hedge.
Arnold Bennett, *Things That Have Interested Me*, 1921

steal. *See also* HANG a thief when he's young and he'll no' steal when he's old; it is a SIN to steal a pin

steed. *See* while the GRASS grows, the steed starves

step. one step at a time (English) It is best to take things steadily, tackling each problem as it arises. Rudyard Kipling, *Kim*, 1901.

It's beyond me. We can only walk one step at a time in this world.
Rudyard Kipling, *Kim*, 1901

step after step the ladder is ascended (English) A man goes up in the world stage by stage rather than all in one go. Randle Cotgrave, *A Dictionary of the French and English Tongues*, 1611.

step. *See also* it is the FIRST step that is difficult; from the SUBLIME to the ridiculous is but a step

stern. a stern chase is a long chase (English) When two parties join in a bitter struggle the contest between them is likely to last a long time. James Fenimore Cooper, *The Pilot*, 1823.

The Aurora ... had neared the chase about two miles. 'This will be a long chase, a stern chase always is.'
Captain Frederick Marryat, *Mr Midshipman Easy*, 1836

stey. *See* put a STOUT heart to a stey brae

stick. it is easy to find a stick to beat a dog (English) It is no difficult task to find some way of attacking or criticizing an enemy if you are set on such action. T. Becon, *Early Works*, 1563.

A staff is quickly found to beat a dog.
William Shakespeare, *Henry VI, Part 2*, c.1591

stick. *See also* FLING enough dirt and some will stick; SPEAK softly and carry a big stick

sticks and stones may break my bones, but names will never hurt me (English) The criticisms, insults and taunts of others will never cause me any real hurt, as a beating with a stick or stone might. G. F. Northall, *Folk-Phrases*, 1894. Frequently heard between children in the course of playground squabbles. *See also* HARD words break no bones.

still. a still tongue makes a wise head (English) Those who keep their thoughts to themselves are wiser than those who share them with all and sundry. J. Heywood, *Works*, 1562.

still waters run deep (Roman) A placid surface may conceal turbulent emotions and complexities lurking beneath. *Cursor Mundi*, c.1400 (also found in the *Disticha*, written c.175 BC and attributed by some to Cato). The proverb is usually quoted in reference to people who appear remote and cool in demeanour, warning that they may easily turn out to be not at all what they appear. It is a fact that waters that appear calm and smooth flowing on the surface may well mask strong and even dangerous currents below. Also encountered in the form 'silent waters run deep'. Another proverb that hints at dangers lurking in still waters warns 'serpents engender in still waters'. Shallow waters, accordingly, are the noisiest – 'shallow waters make most din'.

Our passions are most like to floods and streams,

The shallow murmur but the deep are dumb.
Walter Raleigh, lines written to Elizabeth I, c.1599

sting. the sting is in the tail (English) Something that appears generally good may bring a nasty surprise that is revealed only at the end. William Shakespeare, *The Taming of the Shrew*, c.1592.

Who knows not where a wasp does wear his sting? In his tail.
William Shakespeare, *The Taming of the Shrew*, c.1592

sting. *See also* if you GENTLY touch a nettle it'll sting you for your pains

stings. *See* BEES that have honey in their mouths have stings in their tails

stink. *See* SO we get the CHINK, we'll bear with the stink; the DEVIL always leaves a stink behind him; FISH and guests stink after three days

stinking. *See* NO man cries stinking fish

stinks. *See* the FISH always stinks from the head downwards

stir. stir with a knife, stir up strife (English) It is risking dire bad luck to stir a drink or food in the pot with a knife rather than a spoon. *Transcripts of the Devonshire Association*, 1900.

the more you stir it, the worse it stinks (English) The more something corrupt or otherwise rotten is probed the worse the discoveries that are made. John Heywood, *A Dialogue containing ... the Proverbs in the English Tongue*, 1546.

stir. *See also* you should KNOW a man seven years before you stir his fire

stitch. a stitch in time saves nine (Roman) Making minor repairs promptly prevents having to make more major repairs later. Thomas

Fuller, *Gnomologia*, 1732 (also quoted in a variant form by Ovid). *See also* don't SPOIL the ship for a ha'porth of tar.

A word in time saved nine; and now she was going to live in the country there was a chance for her to turn over a new leaf!
John Galsworthy, *The Man of Property*, 1906

stolen. *See* FORBIDDEN fruit tastes sweetest

stomach. *See* an ARMY marches on its stomach; the WAY to a man's heart is through his stomach

stone. stone-dead hath no fellow (*English*) Death is the perfect solution (frequently voiced by proponents of the death penalty). *The Soddered Citizen*, c.1663.

stone. *See also* you cannot get BLOOD from a stone; CONSTANT dropping wears away the stone; a ROLLING stone gathers no moss

stones. *See* you BUY land you buy stones, you buy meat you buy bones; DRIVE gently over the stones; people who live in GLASS houses shouldn't throw stones; STICKS and stones may break my bones, but names will never hurt me

stools. *See* BETWEEN two stools you fall to the ground

store is no sore (*English*) There is no harm in storing up things for future use. John Heywood, *A Dialogue containing ... the Proverbs in the English Tongue*, 1546.

Let my dressers crack with the weight of curious viands.
Philip Massinger, *A New Way to Pay Old Debts*, 1633

storm. after a storm comes a calm (*English*) Peace inevitably follows trouble. *Ancrene Riwle*, 1250. Related proverbs include 'always a calm before a storm'.

The mingled, mingling threads of life are woven by warp and woof – calms crossed by storms, a storm for every calm.
Herman Melville, *Moby-Dick*, 1851

storm. *See also* any PORT in a storm; the SHARPER the storm, the sooner it's over

story. *See* every PICTURE tells a story

stout. put a stout heart to a stey brae (*Scottish*) Pluck up your courage to tackle a challenging task. A. Montgomerie, *The Cherry and the Cloe*, 1585. A 'stey brae' is, in Scottish dialect, a 'steep hill'.

He ... shouted to me ... to 'pit a stoot hert tae a stey brae'.
John Buchan, *Greenmantle*, 1916

strange. *See* ADVERSITY makes strange bedfellows

stranger. a stranger's eye sees clearest (*English*) It is often the case that it takes a stranger unfamiliar with the way things stand to see things as they really are. Charles Reade, *The Cloister and the Hearth*, 1860.

stranger. *See also* FACT is stranger than fiction

straw. *See* you can't make BRICKS without straw; a DROWNING man will clutch at a straw; it is the LAST straw that breaks the camel's back

straws tell which way the wind blows (*English*) It is possible to observe by minor or trifling changes the general direction in which events are going (just as one might tell the direction in which the wind is blowing by tossing loose straws into the air). John Selden, *Table-Talk*, 1654.

Such straws of speech show how blows the wind.
Charles Reade, *The Cloister and the Hearth*, 1860

stream. a stream cannot rise above its source (*English*) There are natural limitations to what can be achieved by anyone or anything. S. Tuke, *The Adventures of Five Hours*, 1663. Also encountered in the form 'the stream can never rise above the spring-head'.

Then what can Birth, or mortal Men bestow,
Since Floods no higher their Fountains flow?
John Dryden, *The Wife of Bath*, 1700

stream. *See also* don't CHANGE horses in mid-stream

street. *See* BY the street of by and by one arrives at the house of never

streets. *See* the streets of LONDON are paved with gold

strength. one has always strength enough to bear the misfortunes of one's friends (English) It is human nature to gain secret comfort from the misfortunes of others. Oliver Goldsmith, *She Stoops to Conquer*, 1773.

Ay, people are generally calm at the misfortunes of others.
Oliver Goldsmith, *She Stoops to Conquer*, 1773

strength. *See also* UNION is strength; WISDOM goes beyond strength

strengthens. *See* as the DAY lengthens, so the cold strengthens

stretch your arm no further than your sleeve will reach (English) Do not attempt to exceed your own capabilities or resources (especially financial). Miles Coverdale, *H. Bullinger's Christian State of Matrimony*, 1541.

Put your Hand no farther than your Sleeve will reach. That is, spend no more than your Estate will bear.
James Kelly, *A Complete Collection of Scotish Proverbs*, 1721

stretches. everyone stretches his legs according to the length of his coverlet (English) The sensible person adjusts his or her needs according to the resources available. Walter of

Henley, *Husbandry*, 1300. Also encountered in the form 'whoso stretcheth his foot beyond the blanket, shall stretch it in the straw'. *See also* CUT your coat according to your cloth.

strike while the iron is hot (French/English) Act before the opportunity to do something slips away. Geoffrey Chaucer, *Troilus and Criseyde*, c.1385. The proverb has its origins in the business of the blacksmith, who works metal while it is still red-hot and pliable. *See also* make HAY while the sun shines; TAKE time by the forelock.

Where's the good of putting things off? Strike while the iron's hot; that's what I say.
Charles Dickens, *Barnaby Rudge*, 1841

strikes. *See* LIGHTNING never strikes the same place twice

striving. *See* it is ill SITTING at Rome and striving with the Pope

stroke. *See* beware of the OAK, it draws the stroke; avoid the ash, it courts the flash

strokes. *See* LITTLE strokes fell great oaks

strong. *See* the RACE is not to the swift, nor the battle to the strong; YORKSHIRE born and Yorkshire bred, strong in the arm and weak in the head

stronger. *See* a CHAIN is no stronger than its weakest link

Stuarts. all Stuarts are not sib (Scottish) People who share the same surname are not necessarily related. James Kelly, *A Complete Collection of Scotish Proverbs*, 1721. The proverb was quoted originally with reference to the royal Stuart family, to which many Scots liked to claim a link.

stubborn. *See* FACTS are stubborn things

studies. a man's studies pass into his character (Roman) A man will be influenced by what he learns. Francis

Bacon, *Essays*, 1612 (also quoted by Ovid in his *Heroides*). Sometimes encountered in the form 'a man's character passes into his studies'.

study. *See* a BELLY full of gluttony will never study willingly

stumble. a stumble may prevent a fall (English) A minor mishap may prevent a more serious misfortune. Thomas Fuller, *Gnomologia*, 1732. One variant runs 'he that stumbles and falls not mends his pace'. Another less consolatory proverb remarks 'he who stumbles twice over the same stone deserves to break his shins'.

style. the style is the man (Roman) The quality of a man may be determined by the way in which he does things and in how he presents himself (often applied to literary style). Richard Burton, *The Anatomy of Melancholy*, 1621.

To the Reader *Stylus virum arguit*, our style bewrays us.
Richard Burton, *The Anatomy of Melancholy*, 1621

sublime. from the sublime to the ridiculous is but a step (French) It is all too easy to move from what is admirable to what is laughable. Thomas Paine, *The Age of Reason*, 1793. The proverb is commonly, but inaccurately, attributed to Napoleon, who is supposed to have quoted Paine's words when discussing the retreat from Moscow in 1812.

The sublime and the ridiculous are often so nearly related that it is difficult to class them separately. One step above the sublime makes the ridiculous, and one step above the ridiculous makes the sublime again.
Thomas Paine, *The Age of Reason*, 1793

substance. *See* CATCH not at the shadow and lose the substance

succeed. *See* if at FIRST you don't succeed, try, try, try again

succeeds. *See* NOTHING succeeds like success

suck. *See* don't TEACH your grandmother to suck eggs

sucker. *See* never GIVE a sucker an even break

sucklings. *See* out of the MOUTHS of babes and sucklings

sudden. a sudden rising hath a sudden fall (English) Those who rise up in the world very rapidly are liable to fall again just as quickly. John Lydgate, *The Fall of Princes*, c.1440.

suffering. it is not the suffering but the cause which makes a martyr (English) A martyr is created by his sacrifice for a particular cause, not by his sacrifice alone. S. Torshell, *The Hypocrite Discovered*, 1644.

sufficient unto the day is the evil thereof (Hebrew) Confine your worries to the present, rather than concern yourself with what might possibly go wrong tomorrow. Bible, Matthew 6:34. *See also* don't CROSS the bridge until you get to it; TOMORROW is another day; TOMORROW never comes.

Take, therefore, no thought for the morrow; for the morrow shall take thought for the things of itself. Sufficient unto the day is the evil thereof.
Bible, Matthew 6:34

summer. *See* the RICH man has his ice in the summer and the poor man gets his in the winter; one SWALLOW does not make a summer; WINTER finds out what summer lays up

sun. although the sun shine, leave not thy cloak at home (English) Do not trust the weather to stay fine just because the sun is shining at the present. George Herbert, *Jacula Prudentum*, 1640.

let not the sun go down on your wrath (Hebrew) Always repair any rifts or quarrels with others before retiring for the night. Bible.

the sun loses nothing by shining into a puddle (Greek) The good might be brought into contact with what is evil or loathsome and yet not be contaminated by it. R. Brunne, *Handlyng Synne*, 1303 (also quoted by Diogenes Laertius, who may have originated it, and Tertullian). Variants include 'the sun is never the worse for shining on a dunghill'.

Though that holy writ speke of horrible synne, certes holy writ may nat been defouled, na-moore than the sonne that shyneth on the mixne.
Geoffrey Chaucer, *The Canterbury Tales, c.* 1387

sun. *See also* HAPPY is the bride the sun shines on; make HAY while the sun shines; there is NOTHING new under the sun

Sunday. *See* COME day, go day, God send Sunday

sunny. *See* if CANDLEMAS Day be sunny and bright, winter will have another flight

supper. *See* after DINNER rest a while, after supper walk a mile; HOPE is a good breakfast but a bad supper

sups. he who sups with the Devil should have a long spoon (English) Those who enter into dealings with people of dubious reputation should take care not to get drawn in too deeply and must keep their wits about them. Geoffrey Chaucer, *The Canterbury Tales, c.* 1387.

He must have a long spoon that must

eat with the Devil. What tell'st thou me of supping?
William Shakespeare, *The Comedy of Errors, c.* 1593

sure. *See* SLOW but sure wins the race

surgeon. a good surgeon must have an eagle's eye, a lion's heart and a lady's hand (English) It takes keen eyesight, courage and delicacy of touch to make a man a good surgeon. L. Wright, *Display of Dutie*, 1589.

surrender. *See* a CASTLE that speaketh is near a surrender

suspicion. *See* CAESAR's wife must be above suspicion

Sussex won't be druv (English) Residents of Sussex are notoriously stubborn and cannot be persuaded to do anything against their own inclination. T. Wales, *Sussex Garland*, 1910.

swallow. it is idle to swallow the cow and choke on the tail (English) Only a fool gives up on a job when most of the work has already been done. J. Howell, *Paroemiographia*, 1659.

one swallow does not make a summer (Greek) It should not be assumed that because one good thing has happened that everything will go well from now on (just as the arrival of the first swallow does not necessarily mean summer is now properly under way). R. Taverner, *Proverbs or Adages of Erasmus*, 1539 (also quoted in Aristotle's *Nicomachean Ethics*, as 'one swallow does not make a spring'). Related proverbs include 'one fair day in winter makes not birds merry' and 'one fair day assureth not a good summer'.

One foul wind no more makes a winter, than one swallow makes a summer.
Charles Dickens, *Martin Chuzzlewit*, 1844

swarm. a swarm of bees in May is worth a load of hay (English) Some things are best done in their proper season and will not prosper if done at any other time. S. Hartlib, *Reformed Commonwealth of Bees*, 1655. As regards bees, swarms that take to the wing later than May are less likely to produce much honey because nectar-bearing flowers will shortly be past their best – as witnessed by the proverb in its fuller form: 'A swarm of bees in May is worth a load of hay; a swarm of bees in June is worth a silver spoon; a swarm of bees in July is not worth a fly'. It has been suggested that 'a swarm of bees in June is worth a silver spoon' was a later addition, probably from the nineteenth century.

As she reminded the children: A swarm in May's worth a rick of hay; and a swarm in June's worth a silver spoon; while a swarm in July isn't worth a fly.
Flora Thompson, *Lark Rise to Candleford*, 1945

swear. he that will swear will lie (English) A person who will readily swear to something is just as ready to tell a lie. A. Dent, *The Plain Man's Pathway*, 1601.

if you swear you will catch no fish (English) A foul-mouthed fisherman will never get a bite. Thomas Heywood, *Fair Maid of the Exchange*, 1607. In former times the skippers of trawlers often prohibited swearing on board their vessels in order to promote the chances of bringing home a good catch (though it is also on record that one skipper faced with empty nets actually ordered his crew to swear in the hope that this would change their luck for the better).

sweep. if every man would sweep his own doorstep the city would soon be clean (English) Great things would be accomplished if individuals could be persuaded to play their part (typically by living their lives honestly and decently). T. Adams, *The Temple*, 1624. The usual implication when the proverb is quoted is that it is only rarely that the mass of people are willing to sacrifice their own self-interest in order to promote a common cause.

sweeps. *See* a new BROOM sweeps clean

sweet. take the sweet with the sour (English) Every man must be prepared to accept bad times along with the good. Alexander Barclay, *The Ship of Fools*, 1509. Variants include 'he deserves not sweet that will not taste of sour' and 'sweet meat will have sour sauce'.

Thy wit is a very bitter sweeting; it is a most sharp sauce.
William Shakespeare, *Romeo and Juliet*, c. 1593

sweet. *See also* HOME, sweet home; LITTLE fish are sweet; REVENGE is sweet; a ROSE by any other name would smell as sweet

sweeter. *See* the DEEPER the sweeter; the NEARER the bone, the sweeter the flesh

sweetest. from the sweetest wine, the tartest vinegar (English) The bitterest experiences or emotions may stem from the most harmonious and pleasant sources (often quoted in reference to love that has turned sour). W. Painter, *The Palace of Pleasure*, 1567.

The sweetest wine tourneth to the sharpest vineger.
John Lyly, *Euphues: The Anatomy of Wit*, 1578

sweetest. *See also* FORBIDDEN fruit tastes sweetest

swift. *See* the RACE is not to the swift, nor the battle to the strong

swim. *See* how we APPLES swim; don't go

near the WATER until you learn how to swim

swimmers. it is the best swimmers who drown (*English*) Those who are over-confident in what they do are the most likely to come to grief. V. S. Lean, *Collecteana*, 1902.

swine. *See* don't CAST your pearls before swine; on SAINT Thomas the Divine kill all turkeys, geese and swine

swings. what you lose on the swings you gain on the roundabouts (*English*) What you lose in the course of one enterprise you will make up for in what you gain in the course of another. P. R. Chalmers, *Green Days and Blue Days*, 1912. Variant forms include 'what we lose in hake, but gain in herring', a saying once common among fishermen, who knew that if they caught no hake they stood a better chance of catching herring, which hake tended to drive away. *See also* every CLOUD has a silver lining.

Swithin. *See* SAINT Swithin's Day, if thou dost rain, for forty days it will remain; Saint Swithin's Day, if thou be fair, for forty days 'twill rain no more

sword. one sword keeps another in the scabbard (*English*) If one party makes a display of strength, another party is likely to be dissuaded from making a similar display. Samuel Purchas, *Hakluytas Posthumus, or Purchas his Pilgrimes*, 1625. Also found in the form 'one sword keeps another in the sheath'.

sword. *See also* whosoever DRAWS his sword against the prince must throw the scabbard away; he who LIVES by the sword dies by the sword; the PEN is mightier than the sword

sympathy without relief is like mustard without beef (*English*) Expressions of sympathy are empty words if they are not accompanied by active assistance. R. L. Gales, *Vanished Country Folk*, 1914.

t

---

table. *See* where MACGREGOR sits is the head of the table; a POOR man's table is soon spread

tace is Latin for candle (English) Silence is advisable. 'Tace' in Latin means 'be silent'. Thomas Shadwell, *The Virtuoso*, 1676. The proverb suggests that silence will actually promote understanding, thus 'lighting a candle' in the darkness. In former times, it was customary for audiences in English theatres to toss candles on to the stage when they did not like a play: the management were supposed to take the hint and to dowse the lights and close the curtains.

'Tace, madam,' answered Murphy, 'is Latin for a candle; I commend your prudence.'
Henry Fielding, *Amelia*, 1751

tail. *See* the HIGHER the monkey climbs the more he shows his tail; it is idle to SWALLOW the cow and choke on the tail

tailor. the tailor makes the man (English) A man must be judged by the work of his tailor – in other words, by the quality of his suit of clothes. William Shakespeare, *King Lear*, 1605. *See also* APPEARANCES are deceptive.

Believe it, sir, That clothes do much upon the wit ... and thence comes your proverb, The tailor makes the man.
Ben Jonson, *The Staple of News*, 1625

tailors. tailors and writers must mind the fashion (English) In order to prosper, tailors and writers must adapt to the latest fashions. John Lyly, *Euphues: The Anatomy of Wit*, 1578.

tailors. *See also* NINE tailors make a man

take. a man must take such as he finds, or such as he brings (English) A person must accept things as they are, unless he or she has better to offer. Geoffrey Chaucer, *The Canterbury Tales*, c.1387.

I have herd seyd, man sal taa of twa thinges, Slyk as he fyndes, or taa slyk as he bringes.
Geoffrey Chaucer, *The Canterbury Tales*, c.1387

take the goods the gods provide (Roman) Accept without demurring what comes to you for free. John Dryden, *Alexander's Feast* (also quoted by Plautus).

'It is only because I am the governor's son,' Silverbridge pleaded ... 'What of that? Take the goods the gods provide you.'
Anthony Trollope, *The Duke's Children*, 1880

take the hair of the dog that bit you (English) To counter the adverse effects of something the best policy is to take a little more of it (usually quoted in reference to over-indulgence in alcohol and treatment of consequent hangovers). The proverb has its roots in the traditional notion that consuming the burnt hair of a dog would prove an antidote to its bite. *See also* LIKE cures like.

take things as they come (*English*) Do not anticipate possible problems, but deal with them as they arise. J. Davies, *The Scourge of Folly*, 1611.

take time by the forelock (*Greek*) Seize the opportunity before it passes by. Richard Mulcaster, *Positions*, 1581. The proverb has its origins in the ancient legend of the statue of Time by Lysippus, which supposedly depicted him as 'Opportunity', complete with a drooping forelock which others might grasp (though it could only be reached by those in front of him). The saying – sometimes extended to 'take time by the forelock for she is bald behind' – has also been attributed to Pittacus of Mitylene, a wise man who lived in the sixth century BC. Variant forms include 'take occasion by the forelock' and 'seize time by the forelock'. *See also* make HAY while the sun shines; PROCRASTINATION is the thief of time; never PUT off till tomorrow what you can do today; STRIKE while the iron's hot.

Tell her the joyous time wil not be staid,
Unlesse she doe him by the forelock take.
Edmund Spenser, *Sonnets*, 1595

you can't take it with you (*English*) It is not possible to take your earthly riches with you when you die, so you might as well make the most of them while you are still living. Also encountered in the fuller form 'you can't take

it with you when you go'.
For we brought nothing into the world, and it is certain we can carry nothing out.
Bible, Timothy 6:7

take. *See also* GIVE and take is fair play; to GIVE a thing, and take a thing, is to wear the Devil's gold ring; look after the PENNIES and the pounds will look after themselves; take the ROUGH with the smooth

takes. *See* you PAYS your money and you takes your choice; it takes all SORTS to make a world; it takes THREE generations to make a gentleman; it takes TWO to make a bargain; it takes TWO to make a quarrel; it takes TWO to tango

tale. a tale never loses in the telling (*English*) Constant repetition of a story tends to lead to the exaggeration of its content. *The Schoolhouse of Women*, 1541. The notion is supported by another, less well-known, saying: 'the tale runs as it pleases the teller'. Similar sentiments are expressed by 'a good tale is none the worse for being twice told'. A proverb that finds fault with the frequent repetition of the same stories, however, runs 'a tale twice told is cabbage twice sold', while another warns 'it ought to be a good tale that is twice told'.

A Tale never loses in the telling. Fame or Report ... commonly receives an Addition as it goes from Hand to Hand.
James Kelly, *A Complete Collection of Scotish Proverbs*, 1721

tales. never tell tales out of school (*English*) Refrain from spreading abroad what has been told to you in confidence. William Tyndale, *The Practice of Prelates*, 1530.

Write us, my good girl, a long, gossiping letter ... tell me any silly thing you can

recollect ... we will never tell tales out of school.
Mary Lamb, letter, 1805

tales. *See also* DEAD men tell no tales

talk of the Devil and he is bound to appear (Roman) If you discuss someone when they are not present the chances are that they will unexpectedly appear. G. Torriano, *Select Italian Proverbs*, 1642 (also quoted by Terence and Cicero). Variants include 'talk of the Devil and he'll either come or send'.

They were the very men we spoke of – talk of the devil, and – humph?
Walter Scott, *The Fortunes of Nigel*, 1822

talkers. the greatest talkers are the least doers (English) Talkative people are the least likely to be high acheivers. William Shakespeare, *Richard III, c.* 1592.

Talkers are no good doers: be assur'd We go to use our hands and not our tongues.
William Shakespeare, *Richard III, c.* 1592

talks. he that talks to himself talks to a fool (English) Talking to yourself is the first sign of madness. Thomas Fuller, *Gnomologia*, 1732.

talks. *See also* MONEY talks

tango. *See* it takes TWO to tango

tar. *See* don't SPOIL the ship for a ha'porth of tar

Tartar. *See* SCRATCH a Russian and you find a Tartar

tartest. *See* from the SWEETEST wine, the tartest vinegar

taste. *See* EVERYONE to his taste

tastes. everything tastes of porridge (English) All our attempts to deceive ourselves will fail ultimately to mask the unpalatable truth. *Brewer's Phrase and Fable*, 1959.

tastes differ (English) Every man has his own individual tastes, which are often at variance to those of others. J. Davis, *Travels in the USA*, 1803.

Tastes differ ... I never saw a marine landscape that I admired less.
Wilkie Collins, *The Moonstone*, 1868

tastes. *See also* there is no ACCOUNTING for tastes

tattered. *See* there's many a GOOD cock come out of a tattered bag

taxes. *See* NOTHING is certain but death and taxes

teach. don't teach your grandmother to suck eggs (English) It is impertinent to attempt to correct your elders or betters concerning things of which they have long experience themselves. Randle Cotgrave, *A Dictionary of the French and English Tongues*, 1611. Alternatives include warnings against teaching your grandmother to spin, to handle ducks and to sup sour milk. One variant runs 'don't teach your father how to get children'.

A child may sometimes teach his grandmother to suck eggs.
Henry Fielding, *Tom Jones*, 1749

you can't teach an old dog new tricks (English) It is impossible to persuade the old, who are established in their ways of life, to adopt new habits. J. Fitzherbert, *Husbandry*, 1530.

The same renitency against conviction which is observed in old dogs, 'of not learning new tricks'.
Laurence Sterne, *Tristram Shandy*, 1767

teacher. *See* EXPERIENCE is the best teacher; EXPERIENCE is the teacher of fools

teaches. he that teaches himself has a fool for his master (English) Those who try to teach themselves rather than consult proven teachers are fools. Ben Jonson, *Timber, of Discoveries*, 1640.

Learn of the skilful: He that teaches himself, hath a fool for his master.
Benjamin Franklin, *Poor Richard's Almanack*, 1741

teaches. See also he who CAN does, he who cannot teaches

tears. nothing dries sooner than tears (Roman) Grief soon exhausts itself.

teeth. See the GODS send nuts to those who have no teeth

tell. tell me with whom thou goest, and I'll tell thee what thou doest (English) A man, and his actions, will be influenced by the company he keeps. George Pettie, *Guazzo's Civil Conversation*, 1581.

tell money after your own father (English) Check money received from your relatives to ensure you have not been cheated. S. Hieron, *The Preacher's Plea*, 1604.

Reckon money after all your kin.
James Kelly, *A Complete Collection of Scotish Proverbs*, 1721

tell not all you know, nor do all you can (English) Never divulge the full extent of your private self and capabilities or knowledge to others. Benjamin Franklin, *Poor Richard's Almanack*, 1739.

tell the truth and shame the Devil (English) Those who admit their faults should be encouraged by the thought that in so doing they heap shame on the Devil who tempted them in the first place. W. Patten, *Expedition into Scotland*, 1548.

And I can teach thee, coz, to shame the Devil
By telling truth: tell truth, and shame the Devil.
William Shakespeare, *Henry IV, Part 1*, c.1597

tell. See also BLOOD will tell; CHILDREN

and fools tell the truth; DEAD men tell no tales; every PICTURE tells a story; STRAWS tell which way the wind blows; never tell TALES out of school; TIME will tell

telling. See a TALE never loses in the telling

tells. he that tells a secret is another's servant (English) A person who divulges his or her secrets to another is at that person's mercy. George Herbert, *Jacula Prudentum*, 1640.

temperance is the best physic (English) Abstinence from alcohol is the best way to promote good health. H. G. Bohn, *A Handbook of Proverbs*, 1855.

tempers. See GOD tempers the wind to the shorn lamb

tempus fugit. See TIME flies

thaw. See ROBIN HOOD could brave all weathers but a thaw wind

themselves. See GOD helps those who help themselves; LISTENERS never hear any good of themselves

thicker. See BLOOD is thicker than water

thief. once a thief, always a thief (English) A person once guilty of theft will always be dishonest. J. Stevens, *Spanish and English Dictionary*, 1706. Historical variants include 'once a knave, always a knave' and 'once a devil, always a devil'. Another colourful saying alleges 'the thief is sorry he is to be hanged, but not that he is a thief'.

one thief robs another (English) Thieves are not above stealing from one another. *Sir John Oldcastle*, 1600. See also there is HONOUR among thieves.

set a thief to catch a thief (Greek) In order to detect those guilty of wrongdoing the best policy is to recruit someone experienced in such wrong-doing themselves. E. Gayton, *Pleasant Notes upon Don Quixote*, 1654 (similar thoughts were voiced centuries earlier by Callimachus, Cato the Younger and Geoffrey Chaucer among others). Related proverbs include 'a thief knows a thief, as a wolf knows a wolf'.

A theef of venisoun, that hath forlaft
His likerousnesse, and al his olde craft,
Can kepe a forest best of any man.
Geoffrey Chaucer, *The Canterbury Tales*, c.1387

thief. See also CALL a man a thief and he will steal; HANG a thief when he's young, and he'll no' steal when he's old; OPPORTUNITY makes a thief; a POSTERN door makes a thief; PROCRASTI-NATION is the thief of time; if there were no RECEIVERS, there would be no thieves

thieves. all are not thieves that dogs bark at (English) It does not follow that a person is guilty of something just because everyone says he or she is. Henry Peacham, *The Garden of Eloquence*, 1577. See also GIVE a dog a bad name and hang him.

when thieves fall out honest men come by their own (English) When criminals fall out among themselves, good men come back to the fore. John Heywood, *A Dialogue containing … the Proverbs in the English Tongue*, 1546.

Thanks to this quarrel, which confirms the old saying that when rogues fall out, honest people get what they want.
Charles Dickens, *Martin Chuzzlewit*, 1850

thieves. See also there is HONOUR among thieves; LITTLE thieves are hanged, but great ones escape

thing. if a thing is worth doing, it's worth doing well (English) It is always worth taking a little extra effort

when doing something that is worth doing. Lord Chesterfield, letter, 9 October 1746.

thing. See also there is no such thing as a FREE lunch; to GIVE a thing, and take a thing, is to wear the Devil's gold ring; KEEP a thing seven years and you'll always find a use for it; you can have TOO much of a good thing; if you WANT a thing done well, do it yourself; the WORTH of a thing is what it will bring

things. all things are possible with God (Hebrew) With God's assistance there is no limit to what can be achieved. Bible, Matthew 19:26 (also quoted by Homer).

Jesus … said unto them, With men this is unpossible, but with God al things are possible.
Bible, Matthew 19:26

things at the worst will mend (English) When matters reach their lowest ebb they are bound to start improving. William Shakespeare, *King John*, c.1595.

Things at the worst will cease, or else climb upward
To what they were before.
William Shakespeare, *Macbeth*, c.1604

things done cannot be undone (English) There is no altering what is already done. *Good Wyfe wold a Pylgremage*, c.1460.

when things are at the worst they soon begin to mend (English) Just when it seems that things can get no worse they are likely to improve. G. Whetstone, *Heptameron of Civil Discourses*, 1582. See also the DARKEST hour is just before the dawn.

Things being at the worst, begin to mend.
John Webster, *The Duchess of Malfi*, 1623

things. See also the BEST things come in

small packages; the BEST things in life are free; all things COME to those who wait; never DO things by halves; FACTS are stubborn things; FIRST things first; all GOOD things must come to an end; LITTLE things please little minds; there is MEASURE in all things; things PAST cannot be recalled; to the PURE all things are pure; THREE things are not to be trusted: a cow's horn, a dog's tooth and a horse's hoof

think. think first and speak afterwards (English) Always think before you speak. H. G. Bohn, *A Handbook of Proverbs*, 1855. Variants include 'think to-day and speak to-morrow'.

think much, speak little and write less (English) Think as much as you like but exercise great self-restraint when it comes to actual expression of those thoughts. John Lydgate, *Minor Poems*, c.1430.

think on the end before you begin (English) Never do anything without having a clear idea of what you want to acheive in the end. *Cursor Mundi*, c.1300.

Thus human life is best understood, by the wise man's rule, of regarding the end.
Jonathan Swift, *Tale of a Tub*, 1704

think. *See also* GREAT minds think alike

thinks. he thinks not well that thinks not again (English) The person who allows no opportunity for second thoughts is unlikely to come out with the best ideas. Randle Cotgrave, *A Dictionary of the French and English Tongues*, 1611.

third. the third time pays for all (English) A third attempt at something, if successful, makes up for previous failures. J. Higgins, *Mirror for Magistrates*, 1574.

Primo, secundo, tertio, is a good play; and the old saying is, 'the third pays for all'.
William Shakespeare, *Twelfth Night*, c.1601

third time lucky (English) Difficult challenges are often successfully met on the third attempt. Robert Browning, letter, c.1840. Three is the number of the Holy Trinity and has long been considered lucky.

thirty. a man at thirty must be either a fool or a physician (Roman) Any man who has not learned to look after his health by the age of thirty is a fool. Tacitus, *Annals*, first century AD. Tacitus attributed the saying to the Emperor Tiberius, who lived to the ripe old age of seventy-eight. When Plutarch cited the proverb he altered the relevant age to sixty.

thistles. *See* as you SOW, so shall you reap

Thomas. *See* on SAINT Thomas the Divine kill all turkeys, geese and swine

thought. thought is free (English) There are no limitations on what a man may think. John Gower, *Confessio Amantis*, c.1390. The saying was a particular favourite of William Shakespeare and it appears in various guises in *Twelfth Night*, *Hamlet*, *Measure for Measure*, *Othello* and *The Tempest*.

Fair lady, do you think you have fools in hand? – Now, sir, thought is free.
William Shakespeare, *Twelfth Night*, c.1601

thought. *See also* the WISH is father to the thought

thoughts. *See* SECOND thoughts are best

thousand. *See* one PICTURE is worth ten thousand words; a thousand PROBABILITIES do not make a truth

thread. the thread breaks where it is weakest (English) A single flaw will compromise the strength of a thread – or anything else. George Herbert, *Outlandish Proverbs*, 1640. *See also* a CHAIN is no stronger than its weakest link.

threatened men live long (English) Those whose lives are in some way endangered often live longest, as though in defiance of the threat made against them. Lady E. Wheathell, quoted in M. Saint C. Byrne's *Lisle Letters*, 1534.

'The proverb says that threatened men live long,' he tells her lightly.
Charles Dickens, *The Mystery of Edwin Drood*, 1870

three. it takes three generations to make a gentleman (English) A genteel nature cannot be acquired but comes by birth and takes at least three generations. James Fenimore Cooper, *The Pioneers*, 1823.

He remembered his uncle's saying that it took three generations to make a gentleman: it was a companion proverb to the silk purse and the sow's ear.
William Somerset Maugham, *Of Human Bondage*, 1915

three may keep a secret, if two of them are dead (English) It is part of human nature to find the keeping of secrets well nigh impossible. John Heywood, *A Dialogue containing ... the Proverbs in the EnglishTongue*, 1546. Also found as 'three may keep counsel if two be away' and as 'two may keep counsel, if one of them's dead'. Variants include 'three are too many to keep a secret, and too few to be merry' and 'the secret of two no further will go, the secret of three a hundred will know'.

Is your man secret? Did you ne'er hear say Two may keep counsel, putting one away?
William Shakespeare, *Romeo and Juliet*, c.1593

three removals are as bad as a fire (English) Moving house three times results in as much damage to one's belongings as a fire. Benjamin Franklin, *Poor Richard's Almanack*, 1758.

I never saw an oft removed Tree, Nor yet an oft removed Family, That throve so well, as those that settled be. And again, Three Removes are as bad as a Fire.
Benjamin Franklin, *Poor Richard's Almanack*, 1758

three things are not to be trusted: a cow's horn, a dog's tooth and a horse's hoof (French) Never trust something or someone who could cause you potential harm. John of Fourdun, *Scotichronicon*, c.1383 (recorded in French in the thirteenth century). The proverb exists in several variant forms. As well as advising against trusting animals that might suddenly turn against a man, other versions warn against trusting the weeping of a woman, the oaths of a merchant, the prayers of a drunkard and the laugh of an Englishman.

three. *See also* two BOYS are half a boy, and three boys are no boy at all; from CLOGS to clogs is only three generations; one ENGLISHMAN can beat three Frenchmen; FISH and guests stink after three days; from SHIRTSLEEVES to shirtsleeves in three generations; TWO's company, but three's a crowd

thrift is a great revenue (Roman) Careful control of expenditure may contribute substantially to a person's wealth. J. Howell, *Paroemiographia*, 1659 (also quoted by Cicero).

thrive. he that will thrive must first ask his wife (English) Before a man can prosper he must win the approval of his wife. 1500, quoted in R. L.

Greene, *Early English Carols*, 1935. Related proverbs include 'first thrive and then wive'.

He that would thrive, must ask his wife. It was lucky for me that I had one as much dispos'd to industry and frugality as myself.
Benjamin Franklin, *Autobiography*, 1790

he that will thrive must rise at five (English) Those who wish to get on in life must rise early. G. Harvey, *Marginalia*, c.1590. A fuller version of the proverb runs 'he that will thrive must rise at five; he that hath thriven may lie till seven'.

throw. *See* don't throw the BABY out with the bathwater; don't throw out your DIRTY water until you get in fresh; people who live in GLASS houses shouldn't throw stones; throw out a SPRAT to catch a mackerel

thyself. *See* KNOW thyself; PHYSICIAN, heal thyself

tide. *See* TIME and tide wait for no man

tiger. *See* he who RIDES a tiger is afraid to dismount

time. all things grow with time, except grief (Yiddish) Grief will lessen with the passage of time. A Latin proverb on similar lines runs 'time tames the strongest grief'. *See also* TIME heals all wounds.

he that hath time hath life (English) A man with expectations of much time ahead of him may rejoice in life. John Florio, *First Fruites*, 1578.

Then do not squander time, for that is the stuff life is made of.
Benjamin Franklin, *The Way to Wealth*, 1736

there is a time for everything (Hebrew) There is an appropriate time for all things. Bible, Ecclesiastes 3:1. Recorded in English literature since at least the fourteenth century (it was quoted by Geoffrey Chaucer in *The Canterbury Tales* and subsequently by William Shakespeare). Also found in the form 'there is a time and a place for everything'.

To everything there is a season, and a time to every purpose under the heaven.
Bible, Ecclesiastes 3:1

there is a time to speak, and a time to be silent (Hebrew) In some circumstances it is appropriate to speak out, in others it is best to keep your silence. Bible, Ecclesiastes 3:7. Related proverbs include 'there is a time to wink, as well as to see'.

there is no time like the present (English) Do not delay doing things that can be done at once. G. Legh, *The Accidence of Armoury*, 1562.

'There is no time like the present', cried Mr Bramble.
Tobias Smollett, *Humphry Clinker*, 1771

time and tide wait for no man (English) Do not delay doing something, as the chance to do it will pass. Geoffrey Chaucer, *The Canterbury Tales*, c.1387. Also found in the form 'time and tide stay for no man' and, in Scotland, as 'time bides na man'.

Time and tide will wait for no man, saith the adage. But all men have to wait for time and tide.
Charles Dickens, *Martin Chuzzlewit*, 1844

time flies (Roman) Time, and with it the life of man, passes very quickly. Geoffrey Chaucer, *The Canterbury Tales*, c.1387 (also quoted in variant forms by Horace and Ovid among others). Often encountered in its original Latin form, '*tempus fugit*'. Equivalents include 'time fleeth away without delay' and 'take time when time cometh, for time will away'.

In reality, killing time

Is only the name for another of the multi-
farious ways
By which Time kills us.
Osbert Sitwell, 'Milordo Inglese'

time heals all wounds (Greek) All
injuries heal with the passing of time.
Geoffrey Chaucer, Troilus and Criseyde,
c.1385 (also quoted by Euripides in
Alcestis, c.438 BC, by Menander and by
Seneca). Often quoted in reference to
the recently bereaved. Also found as
'time cures all things' and as 'time is
the great healer'. A jovial modern
reworking of the proverb runs 'time
wounds all heels'.

Time is the great physician.
Benjamin Disraeli, Henrietta Temple, 1837

time is money (Greek) Time is an asset
with its own monetary value – so it
should not be wasted. T. Wilson,
Discourse upon Usury, 1572 (also quoted
by Antiphon as far back as 430 BC and
subsequently by Theophrastus).

'You don't come often to the club, Stout?'
... 'No, time is money'.
Edward Bulwer-Lytton, Money, 1840

time tries all things (English)
Everything is subject to the processes
of time. Republica, 1553. Variants
include 'time trieth truth'.

Time, I, that please some, try all.
William Shakespeare, The Winter's Tale, c.1611

time will tell (English) All things will
be revealed with the passage of time.
R. Taverner, Proverbs or Adages of Erasmus,
1539. Less concise versions include
'time revealeth all things'.

The doctor had looked very grave ... and
had said that time alone could tell.
E. H. Porter, Pollyanna, 1913

time works wonders (English) The
passage of time can acheive remarkable changes for the better. A. Marten,
Exhortation to Defend the Country, 1588.

Time does wonders.
Lord Byron, letter, 7 January 1815

time. See also you may FOOL all of the
people some of the time, some of the
people all of the time, but not all of
the people all of the time; NEVER is a
long time; PROCRASTINATION is the thief
of time; one STEP at a time; a STITCH in
time saves nine; TAKE time by the forelock; the THIRD time pays for all; THIRD
time lucky; WORK expands so as to fill
the time available

**times. times change and we with
time** (Roman) All things, including
ourselves, are changed by the passage
of time. John Lyly, Euphues: The Anatomy
of Wit, 1578.

The tymes are chaunged as Ovid sayeth,
and wee are chaunged in the times.
John Lyly, Euphues: The Anatomy of Wit, 1578

times past cannot be recalled
(English) Once time has passed by it
cannot be lived again. Geoffrey
Chaucer, Troilus and Criseyde, c.1385.

Volat irrevocabile tempus, time past cannot be
recal'd.
Richard Burton, The Anatomy of Melancholy,
1621

times. See also ACCUSING the times is but
excusing ourselves; OTHER times, other
manners; PARSLEY seed goes nine times
to the Devil

tinkers. See IF ifs and ands were pots and
pans, there'd be no work for tinkers'
hands

**today. one today is worth two
tomorrows** (English) A single good
deed done today is better than the
promise that you will do two good
deeds tomorrow. W. Secker, Nonsuch,
1660.

today you, tomorrow me (Roman) It
is your turn to do something today,
but it will be my turn tomorrow.

Ancrene Wisse, 1250. Also encountered in the reverse form, as 'today me, tomorrow you'.

What haps to-day to me to-morrow may to you.
Edmund Spenser, *The Faerie Queene*, 1596

today. *See also* HERE today, gone tomorrow; JAM tomorrow and jam yesterday, but never jam today; what MANCHESTER says today, the rest of England says tomorrow; never PUT off till tomorrow what you can do today

Tom. *See* MORE people know Tom Fool than Tom Fool knows

tomorrow. tomorrow is another day (*Spanish*) Things may improve on the morrow. J. Rastell, *Calisto and Meliboea*, c.1527 (also quoted by Fernando de Rojas in *La Celestina* in 1499 and subsequently by Cervantes). In the twentieth century the proverb provided the last line of the celebrated Hollywood movie *Gone with the Wind*, 1936. *See also* don't CROSS the bridge until you get to it; SUFFICIENT unto the day is the evil thereof.

We will say no more of it at present ... To-morrow is a new day.
Walter Scott, *St Ronan's Well*, 1824

tomorrow never comes (*English*) Things delayed until another day are unlikely ever to get done. Lord Berners, *Froissart*, 1523. Equivalents in other languages include the Spanish 'tomorrow is often the busiest day of the year'.

To-morrow every fault is to be amended; but that To-morrow never comes.
Benjamin Franklin, *Poor Richard's Almanack*, 1756

tomorrow. *See also* JAM tomorrow and jam yesterday, but never jam today; what MANCHESTER says today, the rest of England says tomorrow; never PUT off

till tomorrow what you can do today; TODAY you, tomorrow me

tongue. the tongue ever turns to the aching tooth (*English*) A person's attention will always be diverted to whatever irritates them the most. George Pettie, *Guazzo's Civil Conversation*, 1581.

the tongue is not steel yet it cuts (*English*) A person may make a sharp impression with the words he or she speaks. Geoffrey Chaucer, *The Canterbury Tales*, c.1387. Variants include 'the tongue breaketh bone and herself hath none' and 'a tart temper never mellows with age; and a sharp tongue is the only edged tool that grows keener with constant use'.

tongue. *See also* a STILL tongue makes a wise head

too. you can have too much of a good thing (*English*) It is possible to have too much of anything, however desirable it may originally be. B. Burgh, *Cato*, 1483. Also found in the form 'too much of a thing is good for nothing'. *See also* ENOUGH is as good as a feast.

Why then, can one desire too much of a good thing?
William Shakespeare, *As You Like It*, c.1599

too. *See also* too many COOKS spoil the broth

tools. *See* a BAD workman blames his tools; CHILDREN and fools must not play with edged tools

tooth. *See* an EYE for an eye, and a tooth for a tooth

top. *See* there is always ROOM at the top

touch. touch wood, it's sure to come good (*English*) Potential misfortune may be avoided by touching wood without delay. R. Anderson, *Ballads in*

Cumberland Dialect, 1805. This ancient superstition may go back to pagan tree worship, reinforced by reverence for the wooden Cross on which Christ was crucified. Tradition has it that it is not enough just to say the words, but that wood (preferably that of the sacred oak or ash) should actually be touched – though this stipulation is often ignored nowadays.

you should never touch your eye but with your elbow (English) The eyes are delicate and should never be touched. George Herbert, *Jacula Prudentum*, 1640. The same advice was sometimes extended to the ears and the teeth. There is some evident good sense behind the proverb, as eye diseases are often highly contagious and easily exacerbated by rubbing and so forth. Also found in many other European languages.

touch. *See also* if you GENTLY touch a nettle it'll sting you for your pains

touches. he that touches pitch shall be defiled (Hebrew) Those who mix with bad company are bound to be tainted themselves. Bible, Ecclesiasticus 13:1. *See also* if you PLAY with fire you get burnt.

'There,' John would add, 'you can't touch pitch and not be mucked.'
Robert Louis Stevenson, *Treasure Island*, 1883

tough. *See* when the GOING gets tough, the tough get going

town. *See* GOD made the country, and man made the town

trade follows the flag (English) The expansion of national influence around the world will be rewarded by increased opportunities for trade. J. A. Froude, *Fraser's Magazine*, 1870. Many observers have refuted the accuracy of the proverb, alleging that the reverse is more usually true, with national influence being achieved through increased trade. Related proverbs include 'the flag protects the cargo'.

trade is the mother of money (English) There are always fortunes to be made through trade. T. Draxe, *Bibliotheca Scholastica*, 1633.

trade. *See also* every MAN to his trade; there are TRICKS in every trade; TWO of a trade never agree

trades. *See* JACK of all trades is master of none

travel. it is better to travel hopefully than to arrive (English) It is often better to have something to aim for than actually to acheive it. Robert Louis Stevenson, *Virginibus Puerisque*, 1881.
To travel hopefully is a better thing than to arrive, and the true success is to labour.
Robert Louis Stevenson, *Virginibus Puerisque*, 1881

travel broadens the mind (English) Exposure to different cultures, peoples and landscapes is always educational. Anthony Powell, *Venusberg*, 1933. Another proverb supports this view 'he that travels knows much', but another questions the worth of travel, thus: 'travel makes a wise man better, but a fool worse'.

traveller. a traveller may lie with authority (English) Those who have travelled extensively may boast of their exploits without fear of contradiction. William Langland, *Piers Plowman*, c. 1362.
A good traveller is something at the latter end of a dinner; but one that lies three thirds ... should be once heard and thrice beaten.
William Shakespeare, *All's Well That Ends Well*, c. 1602

travels. he travels fastest who travels alone (English) A traveller who goes without companions will experience fewer delays. Henry David Thoreau, *Walden, or Life in the Woods*, 1854.

Down to Gehenna, or up to the Throne,
He travels fastest who travels alone.
Rudyard Kipling, *The Story of Gadsby*, 1888

travels. See also BAD news travels fast

tread. See FOOLS rush in where angels fear to tread

tree. as a tree falls, so shall it lie (Hebrew) Do not allow death or other extremities dissuade you from long-held beliefs. Bible, Ecclesiastes 11:3.

Where the tree falleth there it lyeth ... and every ones deathes daye is his domes day.
John Lyly, *Euphues: The Anatomy of Wit*, 1578

the tree is known by its fruit (Hebrew) A person, organization, idea or other entity may be judged by the results that flow as a consequence. Bible, Matthew 12:33.

If then the tree may be known by the fruit ... there is virtue in that Falstaff.
William Shakespeare, *Henry IV, Part 1*, c.1597

when the tree is fallen, all go with their hatchet (Greek) Many people will gather round where there is hope of possible gain for little effort. George Pettie, *Guazzo's Civil Conversation*, 1581 (also quoted by Menander).

tree. See also the APPLE never falls far from the tree; he that would EAT the fruit must climb the tree; you cannot SHIFT an old tree without it dying; as the TWIG is bent, so is the tree inclined; a WOMAN, a dog and a walnut tree, the more you beat them the better they be

tricks. there are tricks in every trade (English) There are ways to cheat in every trade and occupation. M. Parker, *Knavery in all Trades*, 1632.

tricks. See also you can't TEACH an old dog new tricks

trouble. a trouble shared is a trouble halved (English) Talking through your troubles with others makes them seem less daunting. Dorothy L. Sayers, *Five Red Herrings*, 1931.

never trouble trouble till trouble troubles you (English) Never provoke trouble unnecessarily. *Folk-Lore Journal*, 1884. See also do not MEET troubles halfway.

true. there's many a true word spoken in jest (English) Very often a comment intended humorously turns out to be (or may turn out to be) more accurate than anyone expected. Geoffrey Chaucer, *The Canterbury Tales*, c.1387. In some circumstances the proverb may be quoted when a serious intended comment that has been delivered in a lighthearted fashion seems likely to be dismissed as a joke.

There actually are Johannis churches here ... as well as Apollinaris ones ... There is many a true word spoken in jest.
George Bernard Shaw, *Widowers' Houses*, 1898

true blue will never stain (English) True honesty and intregrity will never be corrupted. *Roxburghe Ballads*, c.1630. The colour blue is traditionally associated with the Virgin Mary, herself deemed incorruptible. More likely, however, is the suggestion that the proverb is derived from the blue aprons worn by butchers, which, being dark in colour, tend not to show bloodstains. Variants include 'true blood may not lie'.

true. See also the COURSE of true love never did run smooth; what EVERYBODY says must be true; MORNING dreams come true; what is NEW cannot be true

trust. if you trust before you try, you may repent before you die (English) Never trust those of whom you are not certain. c.1560, quoted in Huth, *Ancient Ballads*, 1867. Also heard in the more succinct form 'try before you trust'.

put your trust in God and keep your powder dry (English) Put your faith in God to help you out of difficulty, but to be on the safe side also make preparations to intervene more actively to defend your interests. Colonel Blacker, *Oliver's Advice*, 1834. Commonly attributed to the English Parliamentarian leader Oliver Cromwell, addressing troops under his command during a river crossing at the time of the English Civil War. A more recent, equally down-to-earth, version of the old proverb was voiced during the Japanese attack on Pearl Harbor in the Second World War, when an unidentified chaplain in the US navy is alleged to have exhorted fellow-sailors with the words 'praise the Lord and pass the ammunition'. Another variation was repeated during the same conflict between Londoners who, realizing that German buzz bombs fell shortly after their engines cut out, would pray 'praise the Lord and keep the engine running'.

trust is the mother of deceit (English) When a person puts their trust in someone else the other person may be tempted to betray that trust. *The Romance of the Rose*, c.1400. Similar thoughts are expressed in the proverbs 'he who trusteth not is not deceived' and 'in trust is treason'.

My trust, like a good parent, did beget of

him a falsehood in its contrary as great as my trust was.
William Shakespeare, *The Tempest*, c.1610

trust not a new friend nor an old enemy (English) Never place your trust in those you hardly know or in those with whom you were once on bad terms. *Ballad*, 1450.

truth. there is truth in wine (Greek) Wine encourages those who drink it to reveal truths they might otherwise keep hidden. Roger Taverner, *Proverbs or Adages of Erasmus*, 1545. Often attributed to Alcaeus.

There is no saying truer than that ... there is truth in wine. Wine ... has the merit of forcing a man to show his true colours.
Anthony Trollope, *He Knew He Was Right*, 1869

truth fears no trial (English) What is true will withstand all tests. William Shakespeare, *Love's Labour's Lost*, c.1594. Variants include 'truth fears no colours'. Among related proverbs is 'truth is truth to the end of the reckoning'.

Sir, I will be as good as my word ... Fear no colours.
William Shakespeare, *Henry IV, Part 2*, c.1598

truth is no slander (English) Criticism of another must be allowed if it is true. B. Melbancke, *Philotimus*, 1583.

But that slander, sir, is found a truth now.
William Shakespeare, *Henry VIII*, c.1612

truth is stranger than fiction (Roman) What happens in real life can be much more extraordinary than anything that would be countenanced by writers of fiction. Lord Byron, *Don Juan*, 1823. *See also* FACT is stranger than fiction.

'Tis strange – but true; for truth is always strange, –

Stranger than fiction.
Lord Byron, *Don Juan*, 1823

truth lies at the bottom of a well
(Greek) The truth is often to be found
deep down, well hidden. J. Wigand, *De
Neutralibus*, 1562 (also quoted by
Diogenes Laertius and Cicero). The
proverb is often attributed to
Democritus. A contrary view is
expressed by the proverb 'truth lies on
the surface of things'.

Whilst the unlearned ... were all busied in
getting down to the bottom of the well,
where Truth keeps her little court ...
Laurence Sterne, *Tristram Shandy*, 1758

**truth should not always be
revealed** (English) Sometimes it is
for the best to keep the truth
hidden. Thomas Usk, *The Testament
of Love*, c.1387. Variants include
'all truth is not to be told at all
times'.

truth will out (English) The truth will
always come out in the end. John
Lydgate, *The Life of St Alban*, 1439.
Variants include 'truth will prevail',
'truth and sweet oil always come to
the top' and 'truth will sometimes
break out, unlooked for'. A Spanish
equivalent runs 'truth and oil always
come to the surface'. *See also* MURDER
WILL OUT.

Truth will come to light; murder cannot be
hid long; a man's son may, but in the end
truth will out.
William Shakespeare, *The Merchant of Venice*,
c.1596

truth. *See also* CHILDREN and fools tell
the truth; the GREATER the truth, the
greater the libel; HALF the truth is often
a whole lie; a LIE travels around the
world while truth is putting on her
boots; TELL the truth and shame the
Devil

try. *See* if at FIRST you don't succeed, try,
try, try again; you never KNOW what
you can do till you try

**tub. every tub must stand on its own
bottom** (English) Every person must
defend their own independence and
stand on their own merits (just as the
most humble tub must rest on its own
bottom). W. Bullein, *Dialogue against
Fever*, 1564.

I have nothing to do with that ... Let every
Tub stand on its own Bottom.
Colley Cibber, *The Refusal*, 1721

tug. *See* when GREEK meets Greek, then
comes the tug of war

tune. *See* a DRIPPING June sets all in tune;
when the FURZE is in bloom, my love's
in tune; there's many a GOOD tune
played on an old fiddle; he that LIVES in
hope dances to an ill tune; he who PAYS
the piper calls the tune

tunes. *See* why should the DEVIL have all
the best tunes?

**turkey, heresy, hops and beer came
into England all in one year**
(English) Legend has it that turkeys,
hops and beer, and with them heresy,
were all imported to England in the
same year – according to some, in
1524. H. Buttes, *Diet's Dry Dinner*, 1599.
Variants add carp and pike to the list.
In fact there seems to be little historical basis for the tradition, hops for
instance having come centuries earlier
with the Romans.

turkeys. *See* on SAINT Thomas the Divine
kill all turkeys, geese and swine

turn. turn about is fair play (English)
As long as each party gets their turn,
then the rules of fair play are deemed
to be satisfied. *The Life of Captain Dudley
Bradstreet*, 1755.

You had your chance then; seems to me it's

mine now. Turn about's fair play.
Robert Louis Stevenson, *The Wrecker*, 1892

turn. *See also* CLERGYMEN's sons always turn out badly; one GOOD turn deserves another; even a WORM will turn

turneth. *See* a SOFT answer turneth away wrath

turning. *See* it is a LONG lane that has no turning

turns. *See* a BAD penny always turns up

twelve. *See* it is not SPRING until you can plant your foot upon twelve daisies

twenty-four. there are only twenty-four hours in the day (English) There is a limit to how much can be achieved in the course of a day's work. V. S. Lean, *Collecteana*, 1902–04.

twice. *See* once BITTEN, twice shy; CABBAGE twice cooked is death; he GIVES twice who gives quickly; LIGHTNING never strikes the same place twice; OPPORTUNITY seldom knocks twice at any man's door

twig. as the twig is bent, so is the tree inclined (English) By influencing someone or something at an early age it is possible to influence how they develop later on (just as a tree will grow in the direction in which it is trained as a sapling). Alexander Pope, *Epistles to Several Persons*, 1732. A Scottish version runs 'thraw the wand while it is green'. Related proverbs concerning trees include 'a tree falls the way it leans'. *See also* GIVE me a child for the first seven years, and you may do what you like with him afterwards.

'Tis Education forms the common mind,
Just as the Twig is bent, the Tree's inclined.
Alexander Pope, *Epistles to Several Persons*, 1732

two. if two ride on a horse, one must ride behind (English) If two people participate in an enterprise together one inevitably must take the lead. William Shakespeare, *Much Ado About Nothing*, c. 1598.

An two men ride of a horse, one must ride behind.
William Shakespeare, *Much Ado About Nothing*, c.1598

it takes two to make a bargain (English) The agreement of both sides must be obtained before any bargain can be sealed. John Lyly, *Euphues and His England*, 1580.

'Hold, hold, Sir,' cried Jenkinson, 'there are two words to that bargain.'
Oliver Goldsmith, *The Vicar of Wakefield*, 1766

it takes two to make a quarrel (English) There can be no argument unless at least two parties disagree. J. Stevens, *Spanish and English Dictionary*, 1706.

There must always be two parties to a quarrel, says the old adage.
Charles Dickens, *Oliver Twist*, 1838

it takes two to tango (US) Many activities, including dancing the tango, necessarily require the participation of two people. Hofmann and Manning, 'Takes Two to Tango', 1952.

There are lots of things you can do alone,
But it takes two to tango.
Hofmann and Manning, 'Takes Two to Tango', 1952

of two evils choose the lesser (Greek) When faced with a choice of two unattractive alternatives, select the less risky course. Aristotle, *Nicomachean Ethics*, c.335 BC. Plutarch turned the proverb to comic use in telling the story of a Spartan who, obliged to marry, chose a small wife, explaining he was thereby choosing the lesser of two evils. The proverb is found in several European languages. One

Hebrew variant runs 'he is not called wise who knows good and ill, but he who can recognize of two evils the lesser'. Film star Mae West famously added her own version of the proverb when she quipped 'whenever I'm caught between two evils, I take the one I've never tried'.

Since it is the lesser evil of the two, it is to be preferred.
Henry Fielding, *The Temple Beau*, 1730

there are two sides to every question (Greek) There are always two ways of looking at things in any debate. Joseph Addison, the *Spectator*, 1711 (also quoted by Diogenes Laertius in the third century BC and attributed by him to Protagoras two centuries before that).

Let them recollect this, that there are two sides to every question, and a downhill as well as an uphill road.
Charles Kingsley, *The Water Babies*, 1863

two and two make four (English) Logic dictates that something must be so, despite all attempts to prove otherwise. Jeremy Collier, *Essays on Moral Subjects*, 1697.

Even in the valley of the shadow of death two and two do not make six.
Leo Tolstoy, attributed on his death when reconciliation with the Church was suggested, 1910

two blacks don't make a white (English) A wrong deed cannot be justified on the grounds that this is not the first time such a crime has been committed. James Kelly, *A Complete Collection of Scottish Proverbs*, 1721. *See also* TWO wrongs don't make a right.

But whatever satisfaction the pot may have in calling the kettle blacker than itself the two blacks do not make a white.
George Bernard Shaw, *The Intelligent Woman's Guide to Socialism and Capitalism*, 1928

two dogs fight for a bone, and a third runs away with it (English) While two parties quarrel over something, a third party may find the opportunity to snatch what is argued over for themselves. Geoffrey Chaucer, *The Canterbury Tales*, c.1387.

I pray you, sirs, list to Esop's talk: Whilest two stout dogs were striving for a bone, There comes a cur and stole it from them both.
Arden of Feversham, 1592

two fools in a house are too many (English) No household will prosper where both husband and wife are fools. John Lyly, *Euphues and His England*, 1580. Also encountered in the form 'two fools in a bed are too many'.

two heads are better than one (Greek) When two people apply themselves to a problem they are more likely to come up with a solution than one person tackling it alone. John Gower, *Confessio Amantis*, c.1390 (also quoted by Homer). Fuller versions of the proverb run 'two heads are better than one – or why do folks marry?', 'two heads are better than one, even if the one's a sheep's' and 'two heads are better than one quoth the woman when she had her dog with her to the market'. Formerly also found in the form 'two have more wit than one' and occasionally encountered as 'two eyes can see more than one'. *See also* too many COOKS spoil the broth; FOUR eyes see more than two.

Here comes brother Thomas; two heads are better than one; let us take his opinion.
Samuel Foote, *The Nabob*, 1778

two of a trade never agree (Greek) Different practitioners in the same trade will always be at odds with each other. Thomas Dekker, *The Honest Whore, Part 2*, c.1605 (also quoted by Hesiod in *Works and Days*).

It is a common rule, and 'tis most true,
Two of one trade never love: no more do
    you.
Thomas Dekker, *The Honest Whore, Part 2*, 1630

two wrongs don't make a right (English) Committing an offence on the grounds that this is not the first time the offence has been committed or that it is retaliation for some other wrong is not a legitimate defence. B. Rush, letter, 2 August 1783. Representing another view of affairs is the contrasting 'two negatives make an affirmative', which was quoted by William Shakespeare in *Twelfth Night* in 1601. *See also* TWO blacks don't make a white.

two's company, three's a crowd (English) Two people may enjoy a flourishing, intimate relationship, but the presence of a third party might hinder such enjoyment. John Heywood, *A Dialogue containing ... the Proverbs in the English Tongue*, 1546. Usually quoted by lovers whose privacy is threatened by the unwanted presence of a third person. A less well-known proverb relates to somewhat larger numbers, observing 'seven may be company but nine are confusion' (or, alternatively, 'seven make a banquet, nine a riot'). Also found in the form 'two is company, but three is none'.

two. *See also* BETWEEN two stools you fall to the ground; a BIRD in the hand is worth two in the bush; two BOYS are half a boy, and three boys are no boy at all; FOUR eyes see more than two; one HOUR's sleep before midnight is worth two after; better one HOUSE spoiled than two; NO man can serve two masters; ONE for sorrow, two for joy; if you can't RIDE two horses at once, you shouldn't be in the circus; if you RUN after two hares you will catch neither; THREE may keep a secret, if two of them are dead; one VOLUNTEER is worth two pressed men

tyrants. 'tis time to fear when tyrants seem to kiss (English) It is always an ominous sign when tyrants agree. William Shakespeare, *Pericles*, c.1608.

u

uncle. See CALL the bear 'uncle' till you are safe across the bridge

undone. See what's DONE cannot be undone

unexpected. the unexpected always happens (*Roman*) The unforeseen is bound to come to pass. E. J. Hardy, *How to be Happy though Married*, 1885 (also found in the writings of Plautus). Variants include 'the unlooked for often comes'. See also NOTHING is certain but the unforeseen.

unforeseen. See NOTHING is certain but the unforeseen

union is strength (*Greek*) Those who work together will find they have more influence than if they work separately. R. Williams, *Complete Writings*, 1654 (also found in Homer's *Iliad* and attributed to Periander, the tyrant of Corinth in the sixth century BC). Also encountered as 'unity is strength'. See also UNITED we stand, divided we fall.

This union shall do more than battery can to our fast-closed gates.
William Shakespeare, *King John*, c. 1595

united we stand, divided we fall (*US*) Those who stand together will remain strong, while those who quar-rel among themselves will never prosper. John Dickinson, 'Liberty Song', 1768. The slogan was taken up by American troops during the War of Independence and it later became the motto of the US state of Kentucky. See also a HOUSE divided against itself cannot stand; UNION is strength.

Then join Hand in Hand brave Americans all,
By uniting we stand, by dividing we fall.
J. Dickinson, 'Liberty Song', 1768

unlucky. See LUCKY at cards, unlucky in love

untaught. better untaught than ill taught (*English*) It is better to remain in ignorance than to be taught things that are wrong. John Ray, *A Collection of English Proverbs*, 1670.

up. what goes up must come down (*English/US*) Nature dictates that all things must in time be brought back down to earth. L. I. Wilder, *By the Shores of Silver Lake*, 1939.

up. See also up CORN, down horn

upright. See EMPTY sacks will never stand upright

use. See it's no use CRYING over spilt milk; KEEP a thing seven years and you'll always find a use for it

used. a used key is always bright (English) Constant use of something keeps it in good repair. Benjamin Franklin, *The Way to Wealth*, 1736. The proverb is sometimes quoted in condemning laziness or sloth.

V

vacuum. *See* NATURE abhors a vacuum

vain. *See* in vain the NET is spread in the sight of the bird

valet. *See* NO man is a hero to his valet

valour. *See* DISCRETION is the better part of valour

variety is the spice of life (English) A wide range of experience or interests enriches life. William Cowper, *The Task*, 1784.

Variety's the very spice of life,
That gives it all its flavour. We have run
Through every change that fancy at the loom,
Exhausted, has had genius to supply.
William Cowper, *The Task*, 1784

varlet. *See* an APE'S an ape, a varlet's a varlet, though they be clad in silk or scarlet

ventured. *See* NOTHING ventured, nothing gained

vessels. *See* EMPTY vessels make the most sound

vicar. the vicar of Bray will be vicar of Bray still (English) No matter what happens, the person spoken of will cling to his office or privilege. Thomas Fuller, *The History of the Worthies of England*, 1662. The proverb refers to a vicar of Bray who in former times famously vowed to retain his post regardless of whether the Church of his day was Protestant or Catholic in persuasion. *See also* not every man can be vicar of BOWDEN.

vice is often clothed in virtue's habit (German/English) Evil often appears in the guise of goodness. Cornelius Agrippa, *Vanity of Arts and Sciences*, 1569. Related proverbs include 'vice makes virtue shine'.

view. *See* DISTANCE lends enchantment to the view

vinegar. *See* HONEY catches more flies than vinegar; from the SWEETEST wine, the tartest vinegar

virtue. virtue is its own reward (Greek) Good behaviour is an end in itself and should not be judged merely by its consequences. John Dryden, *The Assignation*, 1673 (also found in various forms in the Stoical writings of Zeno in the fourth century BC and in Ovid, Seneca and Epictetus among others). Related proverbs include 'virtue has all things in itself', 'virtue is a jewel of great price' and 'virtue is the only true nobility'.

Your vertue selfe her owne reward shall breed,

Even immortall praise, and glory wyde.
Edmund Spenser, *The Faerie Queene*, 1596

virtue. *See also* BEAUTY without virtue is a flower without perfume; PATIENCE is a virtue

visit your aunt, but not every day of the year (Spanish) To maintain a friendship, do not meet too often. *See also* a HEDGE between keeps friendship green.

voice. the voice of the people is the voice of God (English) The voice of the masses is as undeniable as the will of God, however mistaken it may be. Alcuin, letter, 804. Sometimes encountered in Latin, as '*vox populi, vox Dei*'. In the fourteenth century Archbishop of Canterbury Walter Reynolds quoted the proverb in reference to the deposition of Edward II, when preaching at the coronation of Edward III. Not everyone in history has respected the notion: in 1863 US general W. T. Sherman quipped in a letter to his wife '*vox populi, vox humbug*'.

All this may be; the people's voice is odd,
It is, and it is not, the voice of God.
Alexander Pope, *Imitations of Horace*, 1738

volunteer. one volunteer is worth two pressed men (English) A person who gives his services voluntarily is much more valuable than a person who is forced to work against his will. T. Hearne, *Journal*, 1705. The saying dates from the days of the press gangs, when unwilling men were kidnapped ('pressed') and obliged to do service in the Royal Navy.

vomit. *See* the DOG returns to its vomit

W

wading. no safe wading in an unknown water (English) There is risk involved in entering unknown territory of any kind. *Manifest Detection*, c. 1552.

No safe wading in uncouth waters. It is no wisdom to engage with dangers that we are not acquainted with.
James Kelly, *A Complete Collection of Scotish Proverbs*, 1721

wag. *See* 'tis MERRY in hall when beards wag all

wait. *See* all things COME to those who wait; TIME and tide wait for no man

waiting. men count up the faults of those who keep them waiting (French) It is bad policy to keep others waiting, as they will while away the time considering your faults.

waiting. *See also* it's ILL waiting for dead men's shoes

waits. *See* EVERYTHING comes to him who waits

walk. we must learn to walk before we can run (English) A person must learn basic skills before going on to more complex challenges. *Douce MS*, c. 1350.

Ffyrst must us crepe and sythen go.
Towneley Play of the First Shepherds, c. 1450

walk. *See also* after DINNER rest a while, after supper walk a mile

wall. *See* the WEAKEST go to the wall; a WHITE wall is a fool's paper

walls have ears (English) Be careful what you say, even to friends, as shared secrets may easily be overheard. Geoffrey Chaucer, *The Canterbury Tales*, c. 1387. The proverb was widely heard during the years of the Second World War when it was adopted by the British government as part of the propaganda campaign to warn people to be on their guard against the German 'fifth column' (infiltrators and spies) who might be listening out for clues about troop movements and so forth. An equivalent proverb is also known in France, where Catherine de' Medici is said to have had the walls of the Louvre specially constructed so that she could hear through them the conversations of unsuspecting courtiers. A Hebrew equivalent of the proverb warns 'do not speak of secrets in a field that is full of little hills'. *See also* FIELDS have eyes, and woods have ears.

'She's told me. She's very particular' – he looked around to see if walls had ears.
Arnold Bennett, *The Old Wives' Tale*, 1908

walnut. See a WOMAN, a dog and a walnut tree, the more you beat them the better they be

walnuts and pears you plant for your heirs (Greek) Slow-growing trees, and other projects of long gestation, must be planned with the knowledge that they will only reach fruition in subsequent generations. George Herbert, *Outlandish Proverbs*, 1640 (also found in a variant form in the writings of Cicero). The proverb is supported by the related saying 'he who plants a walnut tree expects not to eat of the fruit'.

want. if you want a thing done well, do it yourself (English) Others will never satisfy your own standards as well as you will yourself, so you might as well do it yourself in the first place. Miles Coverdale, *H. Bullinger's Christian State of Matrimony*, 1541. See also if you would be well SERVED, serve yourself.

That's what I always say; if you want a thing to be well done, You must do it yourself.
Henry Wadsworth Longfellow, *Poems*, 1858

want is the whetstone of wit (English) The wits are sharpest when one is under pressure from hunger or poverty. *Tarlton's Jests*, 1611. A variant of the proverb, however, runs 'wine is a whetstone to wit'.

want of care does us more damage than want of knowledge (English) Carelessness can be more harmful than ignorance. Nathan Bailey, *An Universal Etymological English Dictionary*, 1736.

want. See also the MORE you get, the more you want; for want of a NAIL the shoe was lost; if you want PEACE, prepare for war; WASTE not, want not

wanton kittens make sober cats (English) Those who are wild and reckless in their youth may yet turn out sober and responsible as adults. Thomas Fuller, *Gnomologia*, 1732.

war. war makes thieves, and peace hangs them (English) Villains are created by war and punished when peace is restored. George Herbert, *Jacula Prudentum*, 1640.

when war begins Hell opens (English) Warfare brings forth horror. G. Torriano, *Select Italian Proverbs*, 1642. Related proverbs include 'war is Death's feast' and 'he that preaches war is the Devil's chaplain'.

war. See also COUNCILS of war never fight; all's FAIR in love and war; when GREEK meets Greek, then comes the tug of war; if you want PEACE, prepare for war

warm. he that is warm thinks all so (English) When a person is comfortable he or she finds it hard to imagine that others are not so. George Herbert, *Jacula Prudentum*, 1640. See also COLD hands, warm heart.

warned. be warned by others' harm (Roman) Learn from the mistakes of others. Rowland Hill, *Commonplace Book*, c.1500 (also encountered in the writings of Plautus).

wars are sweet to those that know them not (English) To those who have never experienced it, warfare is exciting and alluring. R. Taverner, *Proverbs or Adages of Erasmus*, 1539.

It's a rough trade – war's sweet to them that never tried it.
Walter Scott, *The Antiquary*, 1816

wash. don't wash your dirty linen in public (French) Do not sort out your problems under the public gaze. T. G.

Fessenden, *Pills* (previously it had been quoted by Voltaire in 1720). In 1815 Napoleon quoted it – as 'people wash their dirty linen at home' – in the course of a celebrated address to the French Assembly when he reclaimed power following his escape from Elba.

I do not like to trouble you with my private affairs; – there is nothing ... so bad as washing one's dirty linen in public.
Anthony Trollope, *The Last Chronicle of Barset*, 1867

washes. *See* one HAND washes the other

waste not, want not (English) Those who make the best use of what they have will never be short of what they need. John Wesley, letter, 10 August 1772.

Helping her to vegetable she didn't want, and when it had nearly alighted on her plate, taking it across for his own use, on the plea of waste not, want not.
Thomas Hardy, *Under the Greenwood Tree*, 1872

waste. *See also* HASTE makes waste

watched. a watched pot never boils (English) Those who wait impatiently for something to happen will find their impatience does nothing to hasten proceedings (and even seems to stretch the time of waiting). Elizabeth Gaskell, *Mary Barton*, 1848. Variants include 'a watched phone never rang'. An opposite view is expressed by the proverb 'long looked for comes at last'.

What's the use of watching? A watched pot never boils.
Elizabeth Gaskell, *Mary Barton*, 1848

water. don't go near the water until you learn how to swim (English) Do not undertake any risky enterprise until you have acquired the skills necessary to accomplish it. H. G. Bohn,

Hand-Book of Proverbs, 1855. *See also* it is the best SWIMMERS who drown.

don't pour water on a drowned mouse (English) Do not bring further trouble to those who are already suffering. J. Clarke, *Paroemiologia Anglo-Latina*, 1639.

Take pity on poor miss; don't throw water on a drownded rat.
Jonathan Swift, *Polite Conversation*, 1738

much water goes by the mill that the miller knows not of (English) Many more things go astray or are stolen than the owner is aware of. John Heywood, *A Dialogue containing ... the Proverbs in the English Tongue*, 1546. A Scottish equivalent runs, 'mickle water goes by the miller when he sleeps'.

What, man! more water glideth by the mill than wots the miller of.
William Shakespeare, *Titus Andronicus*, c.1593

water. *See also* BLOOD is thicker than water; COME with the wind, go with the water; DIRTY water will quench fire; don't throw out your DIRTY water until you get in fresh; you can lead a HORSE to water, but you can't make him drink; the MILL cannot grind with the water that is past; you never MISS the water till the well runs dry

waters. *See* STILL waters run deep

way. the way to a man's heart is through his stomach (English) The best way to win the love of a man is to offer him a plentiful supply of appetizing food. J. Adams, letter, 15 April 1814. Also encountered as 'the way to an Englishman's heart is through his stomach'.

way. *See also* the LONGEST way round is the shortest way home; LOVE will find a way; STRAWS tell which way the wind blows; a WILFUL man must have his way; where there's a WILL there's a way

ways. there are many ways of dressing a calf's head (English) There are many ways of saying or doing a foolish thing (or, if one way of doing something does not work, there is always another way that may be tried next). Seventeenth century. The proverb is an allusion to the banquets held by members of the Calves' Head Club, which was dedicated to ridiculing the memory of Charles I, deemed by his enemies to have been a 'foolish' king, whose folly expressed itself in many and varied forms. The club first met in 1693; at its annual banquet on the anniversary of the king's execution, 30 January, those present enjoyed a large dish of calves' heads dressed in different ways to represent Charles and his closest supporters. The last banquet was held in 1735.

Their bill of fare was a large dish of calves' heads, dressed several ways, by which they represented the king and his friends who had suffered in his cause; a large pike with a small one in its mouth, as an emblem of tyranny; a large cod's head by which they intended to represent the person of the king singly; a boar's head with an apple in its mouth, to represent the king as bestial ...
Ned Ward (attributed), *Secret History of the Calves' Head Club, or the Republicans Unmasked*, c.1700

there are more ways of killing a cat than choking it with cream (English) There is more than one way of doing something. Sydney Smith, *John Smith's Letters*, 1839. Also encountered in the variant form 'there's more than one way to skin a cat'. 'Butter' sometimes replaces 'cream'.

Hold on yet awhile. More ways of killing a cat than choking her with cream.
Charles Kingsley, *Westward Ho!*, 1855

there are more ways of killing a dog than choking it with butter (English) There are many alternatives when it comes to doing something. W. T. Thompson, *Chronicles of Pineville*, 1845.

A proverb always had to be capped. No one could say, 'There's more ways of killing a dog than hanging it' without being reminded, 'nor of choking it with a pound of fresh butter.'
Flora Thompson, *Lark Rise to Candleford*, 1945

there are more ways of killing a dog than hanging it (English) There is more than one way to do something. John Ray, *A Collection of English Proverbs*, 1670.

ways. *See also* you can't have it BOTH ways

weak. *See* YORKSHIRE born and Yorkshire bred, strong in the arm and weak in the head

weakest. the weakest go to the wall (English) Those who are weakest or least effective will be sacrificed first. *The Coventry Plays*, 1534. Tradition has it that the central image of 'going to the wall' derives not from the wall that a condemned man might be leaned against before execution but to the practice in former times of putting the most vulnerable in the safest beds (closest to the wall) or else to medieval churches, where seating for the elderly and infirm was arranged around the walls, while the more able stood. Variants include 'the weaker goes to the pot'.

That shows thee a weak slave; for the weakest goes to the wall.
William Shakespeare, *Romeo and Juliet*, c.1593

weakest. *See also* a CHAIN is no stronger than its weakest link

wealth is enemy to health (*English*) A wealthy man lives lazily, surrounded by luxury, and thus becomes unfit and prone to illness. John Gower, *Confessio Amantis*, c. 1 390.

wealthy. *See* EARLY to bed and early to rise, makes a man healthy, wealthy and wise

wear. it is better to wear out than to rust out (*English*) It is better to die sooner after a busy life than to decay gradually with nothing to do. The proverb is usually ascribed to Bishop Cumberland around 1 700, when he quoted the line to a friend who suggested that he was wearing himself out through overwork. Similar sentiments are to be found in a number of other European languages; centuries before Bishop Cumberland coined the English version Martin Luther included among his favourite quips, 'If I rest, I rust'.

> If ye will needs say I am an old man, you should give me rest … I were better to be eaten to death with a rust than to be scoured to nothing with perpetual motion.
> William Shakespeare, *Henry IV, Part 2*, c. 1 598

wear. *See also* if the CAP fits, wear it; to GIVE a thing, and take a thing, is to wear the Devil's gold ring

wears. *See* CONSTANT dropping wears away the stone

weather. *See* ROBIN HOOD could brave all weathers but a thaw wind

weathercock. *See* a WOMAN is a weathercock

wed. better wed over the mixen than over the moor (*English/Scottish*) It is safer to marry someone from your own neighbourhood than someone from farther afield, of whom you inevitably know less. 1 628, quoted in M. L. Anderson, *Proverbs in Scots*, 1 957. 'Mixen' signifies midden or dunghill.

> He might hae dune waur than married me … Better wed over the mixen as over the moor, as they say in Yorkshire.
> Walter Scott, *The Heart of Midlothian*, 1 8 1 8

wedding. one wedding brings another (*English*) When one wedding takes place it is almost inevitable that another will quickly follow. M. Parker, *Wooing Maid*, 1 6 3 4. *See also* one FUNERAL makes many.

> The cook says at breakfast-time that one wedding makes many.
> Charles Dickens, *Dombey and Son*, 1 848

wedlock. *See* AGE and wedlock bring a man to his nightcap

Wednesday. *See* MONDAY's child is fair of face

weds. he that weds before he's wise shall die before he thrive (*English*) The man who gets married young before he has had a chance to gain any experience of the world will not prosper. John Heywood, *A Dialogue containing … the Proverbs in the English Tongue*, 1 546.

weeding. *See* ONE year's seeding means seven years' weeding

weeds. *See* ILL weeds grow apace

week. *See* if you would be HAPPY for a week take a wife

weep. *See* LAUGH and the world laughs with you; weep and you weep alone

weepers. *See* FINDERS keepers, losers weepers

welcome. *See* when all FRUIT falls, welcome haws

well. all's well that ends well (*English*)

If something comes out right at the end then this justifies or compensates for all actions taken or sacrifices made to achieve this end result. *Proverbs of Hending*, c.1250. The phrase is most familiar as the title of one of William Shakespeare's comedies, written in 1602. One version of the proverb extends it thus: 'all's well that ends well, as the peacock said when he looked at his tail'. *See also* the END justifies the means.

All's well that ends well: still the fine's the crown.

William Shakespeare, *All's Well That Ends Well*, c.1602

well begun is half done (Greek) If you get a job off to a good start you will find half the most difficult work is already done. *Proverbs of Hendyng*, c.1300 (also found in the *Epistles* of Horace).

well done is twice done (English) A thing well done stays done for twice as long. John Day, *The Ile of Gulls*, 1606.

what is well done is done soon enough (English) If something is correctly completed then it is not important how long it takes. Roger Ascham, *Toxophilus*, 1545.

well. *See also* if a JOB's worth doing, it's worth doing well; LEAVE well alone; he LIVES long who lives well; you never MISS the water till the well runs dry; the PITCHER goes so often to the well that it is broken at last; if you would be well SERVED, serve yourself; SPARE well and have to spend; if a THING is worth doing, it's worth doing well; TRUTH lies at the bottom of a well; if you WANT a thing done well, do it yourself

west. the west wind is a gentleman and goes to bed (English) A westerly wind is civilized enough to drop in

the evening and allow men to go peacefully to sleep. M. A. Denham, *A Collection of Proverbs ... relating to the Weather*, 1846.

west. *See also* EAST, west, home's best; the west WIND always brings wet weather; when the WIND is in the west the weather is at the best

wet. a wet May brings plenty of hay (English) Rain in the month of May is a sign of a good harvest of hay to come. M. A. Denham, *A Collection of Proverbs ... relating to the Weather*, 1846.

wet. *See also* all CATS love fish, but fear to wet their paws

what. what's mine's mine own (English) What belongs to me is mine alone. H. Parrot, *Laquei ridiculosi*, 1613.

What's yours is mine, and what's mine is my own.

Jonathan Swift, *Polite Conversation*, 1738

what. *See also* what can't be CURED, must be endured; what's DONE cannot be undone; what you don't KNOW can't hurt you; what MUST be, must be; what a NEIGHBOUR gets is not lost; what you lose on the SWINGS you gain on the roundabouts; what goes UP must come down

wheel. *See* the SQUEAKING wheel gets the grease

whelps. *See* the HASTY bitch brings forth blind whelps

when. *See* when the BELLY is full the mind is among the maids; when the CAT's away, the mice will play; when one DOOR shuts, another opens; when the GOING gets tough, the tough get going; when POVERTY comes in at the door, love flies out of the window; when the WINE is in, the wit is out

where. *See* where the BEE sucks honey

the spider sucks poison; where there's a WILL there's a way

while there's life there's hope. *See* where there's LIFE there's hope

whirlwind. *See* they that SOW the wind shall reap the whirlwind

whistle. *See* a SOW may whistle, though it has an ill mouth for it

whistling. a whistling woman and a crowing hen are neither fit for God nor men (English) A woman who whistles offends nature, as does a crowing hen, and both threaten bad luck. James Kelly, *A Complete Collection of Scotish Proverbs,* 1721. In former times a woman heard whistling might be accused of witchcraft, whistling up storms to endanger ships at sea, while the crowing of a hen signified that someone nearby was close to death.

'A whistling woman and a crowing hen are neither fit for God nor men,' is a mild English saying.
Rudyard Kipling, *Beast and Man,* 1891

white. a white wall is a fool's paper (Italian) A blank wall is an open invitation to the graffiti artist, who knows no better but to scrawl upon it. John Florio, *First Fruites,* 1578.

he that hath a white horse and a fair wife is never without trouble (English) Those who possess white horses and pretty wives will find themselves in constant difficulty from those who are envious of them. G. Pettie, *Guazzo's Civil Conversation,* 1581.

white. *See also* TWO blacks don't make a white

whole. *See* HALF the truth is often a whole lie; the HALF is better than the whole

whom. *See* whom the GODS love die young

whore. once a whore, always a whore (English) Prostitutes (and by extension, politicians and others who 'sell' themselves to others) can never be redeemed, as they are inclined to such immorality by nature. H. Parrot, *Laquei Ridiculosi,* 1613.

why. every why hath its wherefore (English) There is reason behind everything. George Gascoigne, *Supposes,* 1566.

For they say every why hath a wherefore.
William Shakespeare, *The Comedy of Errors,* c.1593

why. *See also* why BUY a cow when milk is so cheap?; why KEEP a dog and bark yourself?

wide will wear but narrow will tear (English) Clothing that is too big or too wide will serve well enough, but if it is too tight it will tear. John Ray, *A Collection of English Proverbs,* 1678.

widow. *See* he that MARRIES a widow and three children marries four thieves

wife. *See* a BLIND man's wife needs no paint; CAESAR's wife must be above suspicion; a DEAF husband and a blind wife are always a happy couple; there's one GOOD wife in the country, and every man thinks he hath her; if you would be HAPPY for a week take a wife; my SON is my son till he gets him a wife, but my daughter's my daughter all the days of her life; he that will THRIVE must first ask his wife

wilful. a wilful man must have his way (English) A determined man cannot be denied. Walter Scott, *The Antiquary,* 1816. A related proverb cautions 'a wilful man had need be very wise' as, according to yet another ancient saying, 'a wilful man never wants woe'.

The Hecate ... ejaculated, 'A wilfu' man will hae his way.'
Walter Scott, Rob Roy, 1818

will. he that will not when he may, when he will he shall have nay (English) Those who do not seize opportunities when they are offered will find they get no second chance. AD 1000, quoted in Anglia, 1889. See also make HAY while the sun shines; STRIKE while the iron is hot.

That young lady, with whom I so much desired to be alone again, sang ... 'He that will not when he may, When he will he shall have nay.'
R. L. Stevenson, Catriona, 1893

where there's a will there's a way (English) Those who are determined enough will always find a way to achieve what they desire. George Herbert, Jacula Prudentum, 1640.

Please do not suppose ... that I do not know how difficult it is ... But when there's a will there's a way.
George Bernard Shaw, Fanny's First Play, preface, 1911

will. See also if ANYTHING can go wrong, it will; there are none so BLIND as those who will not see; he that COMPLIES against his will is of his own opinion still; there are none so DEAF as those who will not hear; what MUST be must be

willing. a willing mind makes a light foot (English) Enthusiasm for some task, such as a long journey, makes its achievement much easier. Philip Massinger, The Picture, 1629.

willing. See also all lay LOADS on a willing horse; the SPIRIT is willing but the flesh is weak

wills. he who wills the end, wills the means (English) Those who dictate an end result also dictate, or should

dictate, how it must be achieved. R. South, Twelve Sermons, 1692. See also where there's a WILL, there's a way.

win. you can't win them all (US) Everyone loses sometimes. Raymond Chandler, The Long Good-bye, 1953.

you win a few, you lose a few (US) No one wins at everything, and those who win must accept that there will also be times when they lose. P. O'Donnell, Sabre-Tooth, 1966. Usually voiced as consolation to someone who has just been defeated at something, or else in resigned acceptance of failure. Often encountered as 'win some, lose some'.

win. See also let them LAUGH that win

wind. after wind comes rain (English) Rain comes in the wake of a fresh wind. Edward Hall, Hall's Chronicle, 1542. Such predictions were regarded with particular seriousness by seafarers in the days of sail. One more specific elaboration of the proverb among seamen ran 'when the wind comes before the rain, you may hoist your topsails up again; but when the rain comes before the winds, you may reef when it begins'.

the west wind always brings wet weather, the east wind wet and cold together, the south wind surely brings us rain, the north wind blows it back again (English) The direction in which the wind blows is a sure indication of the kind of weather shortly to be expected. Mrs Bray, Traditions of Devon, 1838. Of all winds, a north-easterly wind is generally agreed to promise the best prospects.

when the wind is in the east, 'tis neither good for man nor beast

(English) An easterly wind, which can be very cold and piercing, threatens the welfare of all living creatures. R. Cawdrey, *Treasury of Similes*, 1600. Another proverb draws a more detailed conclusion about an easterly wind that blows on Easter Day: 'if the wind is in the east on Easter Day, you'll have plenty of grass, but little good hay'. *See also* if it RAINS when the wind is in the east, it will rain for twenty-four hours at least.

When the wind's in the East, It's neither good for man nor beast ... The East-wind with us is commonly very sharp, because it comes off the Continent.
John Ray, *A Collection of English Proverbs*, 1670

when the wind is in the south it blows the bait into the fish's mouth (English) A southerly wind brings the fish to the fishermen's lines. Izaak Walton, *The Compleat Angler*, 1653. Fishermen are less likely to prosper when the wind is in the north, however: 'when the wind is in the north the skilful fisher goes not forth'.

when the wind is in the west the weather is at the best (English) A westerly wind accompanies balmy weather. Thomas Fuller, *Gnomologia*, 1732.

wind. *See also* COME with the wind, go with the water; GOD tempers the wind to the shorn lamb; it's an ILL wind that blows nobody any good; the NORTH wind doth blow, and we shall have snow; a REED before the wind lives on, while mighty oaks do fall; ROBIN HOOD could brave all weathers but a thaw wind; they that SOW the wind shall reap the whirlwind; STRAWS tell which way the wind blows; the WEST wind is a gentleman and goes to bed; WORDS are wind

window. *See* the EYES are the window of the soul; when POVERTY comes in at the door, love flies out of the window

wine. when the wine is in, the wit is out (English) Subtle, clever humour must not be expected from those freely indulging in alcohol. John Gower, *Confessio Amantis*, c.1390. Also encountered in the forms 'wine in, truth out' and 'ale in, wit out'. *See also* when the DRINK is in, the wit is out.

Whan the wyne were in and the wyt out, wolde they take uppon them ... to handle holy scrypture.
Thomas More, *Dialogue of Images*, 1529

wine hath drowned more men than the sea (English) More men have perished through over-indulgence in wine than have died at sea. *Politeuphuia*, 1669.

wine savours of the cask (English) The origins of something may often be detected in the finished product. John Lyly, *Euphues: The Anatomy of Wit*, 1578. *See also* the CASK savours of the first fill.

As wine savours of the cask wherein it is kept, the soul receives a tincture from the body, through which it works.
Richard Burton, *The Anatomy of Melancholy*, 1621

wine wears no breeches (English) Niceties of language are cast aside when wine is freely indulged in. Randle Cotgrave, *A Dictionary of the French and English Tongues*, 1611.

you cannot know wine by the barrel (English) Outward appearances are no indication of inner quality. Randle Cotgrave, *A Dictionary of the French and English Tongues*, 1611. *See also* APPEARANCES are deceptive.

wine. *See also* GOOD wine engendereth good blood; GOOD wine needs no bush; you can't put NEW wine in old bottles; from the SWEETEST wine, the tartest vinegar; there is TRUTH in wine

wing. *See* a BIRD never flew on one wing; the MOTHER of mischief is no bigger than a midge's wing

wink. wink at small faults (English) Ignore minor offences or flaws. William Shakespeare, *Henry V*, c.1598.

If little faults, … shall not be wink'd at, how shall we stretch our eye when capital crimes … appear before us?
William Shakespeare, *Henry V*, c.1598

wink. *See also* a NOD IS as good as a wink to a blind horse

winter. winter finds out what summer lays up (English) The stores that are laid up when the weather is fine are soon exhausted when the weather turns cold. *The Good Wyfe wold a Pylgremage*, c.1460.

winter. *See also* if CANDLEMAS Day be sunny and bright, winter will have another flight; if Candlemas Day be cloudy with rain, winter is gone, and won't come again; a GREEN winter makes a fat churchyard; the RICH man has his ice in the summer and the poor man gets his in the winter

wisdom. wisdom goes beyond strength (English) Brains will always beat brawn. T. Draxe, *Bibliotheca Scholastica*, 1616.

wisdom. *See also* EXPERIENCE is the mother of wisdom

wise. a wise head makes a still tongue (English) The wise man keeps his thoughts to himself. Thomas Fuller, *Gnomologia*, 1732. Also found in the form 'a wise head makes a close mouth'. Another proverb on similar lines runs 'he hath wisdom at will that

with angry heart can hold his tongue still'.

a wise man changes his mind, a fool never will (English) A wise man is prepared to admit it when he has made a mistake. James Mabbe, *Celestina*, 1631. Related proverbs include 'a wise man ought not to be ashamed to change his purpose'.

a wise man is never less alone than when he is alone (Roman) A wise man is never alone when he has his thoughts to accompany him. George Pettie, *Guazzo's Civil Conversation*, 1581. The proverb is generally attributed to Scipio Africanus the Elder, though others have also ascribed it to Themistocles.

a wise woman is twice a fool (English) A wise woman is still only the equal of two fools. Roger L'Estrange, *Select Colloquies out of Erasmus*, 1680.

he is not a wise man who cannot play the fool on occasion (Roman) A truly wise man may enjoy a little folly now and then. *Precepts of Cato*, 1553.

I have reade in a booke, that to play the foole wisely, is high wisdome.
Ben Jonson, *Poetaster*, 1601

he is not wise that is not wise for himself (Greek) A person is not wise who is incapable of looking after his own interests. Anthony Rivers, translation of C. de Pisa's *Moral Proverbs*, 1478.

it is a wise child that knows its own father (Greek) A child who claims to know who for certain who is its father is wise indeed, bearing in mind the speed with which the world (and its inhabitants) change. J. Withals, *Dictionary*, 1584 (similar sentiments are voiced by Homer in the *Odyssey*). William Shakespeare turned the proverb on its head in *The Merchant of Venice*, writing 'it is a wise father that knows his own child'.

The children of this age must be wise children indeed if they know their fathers.
William Wycherley, *The Gentleman Dancing Master*, 1673

it is easy to be wise after the event (English) It is easy to see things more clearly with the benefit of hindsight. G. Harvey, *Marginalia*, c. 1590.

Away, thou strange justifier of thy selfe, to bee wiser then thou wert, by the event.
Ben Jonson, *Epicoene*, 1616

wise men learn by others' faults, fools by their own (English) The wise do not repeat the mistakes of others. Geoffrey Chaucer, *Troilus and Criseyde*, c. 1385.

Wise men, as Poor Dick says, learn by others' harms.
Benjamin Franklin, *Poor Richard's Almanack*, 1758

wise. *See also* EARLY to bed and early to rise, makes a man healthy, wealthy and wise; a FOOL may give a wise man counsel; FOOLS ask questions that wise men cannot answer; FOOLS build houses and wise men live in them; where IGNORANCE is bliss, 'tis folly to be wise; one cannot LOVE and be wise; PENNY wise, pound foolish; a STILL tongue makes a wise head; a WORD to the wise is enough

wish. if you wish to live and thrive, let a spider run alive (English) No one who kills a spider will prosper. *Notes & Queries*, 1863. Spiders have always been considered to be lucky (one legend credits a spider with spinning a web to conceal the entrance to the cave in which the Holy Family were hiding from their persecutors). Spiders are also said to have saved the

lives of Mohammed and Frederick the Great in a similar manner. In medieval times spiders were encouraged to enter homes as they preyed on disease-spreading flies; it was thus very unlucky to kill one.

the wish is father to the thought (Roman) It is easy to believe what one wants to believe. William Shakespeare, *Henry IV, Part 2*, c. 1598 (also quoted by Julius Caesar in *The Gallic Wars*).

The wish might be father to the thought … but the thought was truly there.
Anthony Trollope, *Framley Parsonage*, 1860

wishes. if wishes were horses, beggars would ride (English) If wishes came true life would be very different from what it really is. J. Carmichaell, *Proverbs in Scots*, 1628. One variant runs 'if wishes would bide, beggars would ride'. Another proverb advises 'if wishes were thrushes beggars would eat birds'.

If wishes were horses,
Beggars would ride;
If turnips were watches,
I would wear one by my side.
J. O. Halliwell, *The Nursery Rhymes of England*, 1844

wishes won't wash dishes (US) It takes more than mere hope or good intentions to get something done. Historical variants include 'wishes never can fill a sack', which was recorded in the seventeenth century.

wit. wit without wisdom is but little worth (English) Humour without intelligence is of little value. *Proverbs of Alfred*, c. 1270. Also encountered in the form 'wit without learning is like a tree without fruit'.

wit. *See also* BOUGHT wit is the best; BREVITY is the soul of wit; when the

DRINK is in, the wit is out; WANT is the whetstone of wit; when the WINE is in, the wit is out

wive. it's hard to wive and thrive both in a year (English) A man cannot expect to get married and at the same time expect his business not to be disrupted. *Towneley Plays, c.*1410.

You can't expect to wive and thrive in the same year.
Jonathan Swift, *Polite Conversation,* 1738

wiving. *See* HANGING and wiving go by destiny

wolf. who keeps company with the wolf will learn how to howl (Spanish) Those who mix with bad company will learn their evil ways. John Florio, *Second Fruites,* 1591.

Tho' you have kept company with a wolf you have not learnt how to howl of him.
Samuel Richardson, *Clarissa,* 1748

wolf. *See also* a GROWING youth has a wolf in his belly; HUNGER drives the wolf out of the wood; he that goes to LAW holds a wolf by the ears

woman. a woman, a dog and a walnut tree, the more you beat them the better they be (English) Women, dogs and walnut trees benefit from harsh treatment, which will curb their natural tendency to excess. G. Pettie, *Guazzo's Civil Conversation,* 1581. It was once common practice to thrash walnut trees to shake loose the fruit and also to snap long shoots and thus encourage the growth of new fruiting spurs. It has also been suggested that beating a walnut tree encouraged the spread of the sap and thus promoted the health of the whole tree.

Do you think that she is like a walnut-tree? Must she be cudgelled ere she bear good fruit?
John Webster, *The White Devil,* 1612

a woman and a ship ever want mending (Roman) Women, like ships, require constant attention and – in the case of women – regular supplies of luxuries, new clothing etc. John Florio, *First Fruites,* 1578 (also quoted by Plautus).

Whoever wants to acquire a lot of trouble should get himself a ship and a woman. For neither of them is ever sufficiently equipped, and there is never enough means of equipping them.
Plautus, *Poenulus,* second century BC

a woman is a weathercock (English) Women are easily swayed, changing their mind at the slightest persuasion (just as a weathercock responds to the wind). T. Draxe, *Bibliotheca Scholastica,* 1616. Other proverbs that support the same notion include 'a woman's mind and winter wind change oft' and 'women, wind and fortune are given to change'.

a woman is an angel at ten, a saint at fifteen, a devil at forty and a witch at fourscore (English) The character of a woman degenerates with age. *Swetnam the Woman Hater,* 1620.

a woman's place is in the home (English) A woman should confine her attentions to domestic tasks about the house, looking after the welfare of her family. 'J. Slick', *High Life,* 1844. Another proverb dictates that 'a woman is to be from her house three times; when she is christened, married and buried'.

a woman's strength is in her tongue (English) The prime weapon of a woman is her tongue. J. Howell, *Paroemiographia,* 1659. Other equally misogynistic proverbs allege 'one tongue is enough for a woman', 'a woman's heart and her tongue are not relatives', 'women's tongues wag like lambs' tails' and 'a woman's tongue is the last thing about her that dies'.

a woman's work is never done (English) Women face a never-ending cycle of housework, from which there is no respite. T. Tusser, *Five Hundred Points of Husbandry*, 1570.

If you go among the Women, you will learn ... that a Woman's Work is never done.
Benjamin Franklin, *Papers*, 1722

woman. *See also* a BAD woman is worse than a bad man; BECAUSE is a woman's reason; HELL hath no fury like a woman scorned; a MAN is as old as he feels, and a woman as old as she looks; SILENCE is a woman's best garment; SIX hours' sleep for a man, seven for a woman and eight for a fool; a WHISTLING woman and a crowing hen are neither fit for God nor men; a WISE woman is twice a fool

women. many women, many words (English) Where women congregate there will always be plenty of chatter. *The Castle of Perseverance*, c.1425.

women are saints in church (English) Women seem saintly in church, but behave quite differently in other situations. *School House of Women*, 1542. Fuller versions of the proverb vary somewhat, but one typical variant runs 'women are saints in church, angels in the street, devils in the kitchen and apes in bed'.

women must have the last word (English) Women insist upon having the last word in any argument. *School House of Women*, 1542.

She was like the rest of your sex, ma'am — she went her own way, and had the last word.
Eden Phillpotts, *Yellow Sands*, 1926

women. *See also* never CHOOSE your women or your linen by candlelight

won. *See* FAINT heart ne'er won fair lady

wonders. wonders will never cease (English) The unexpected and the remarkable can always happen and does so from time to time. H. Bates, 1776, quoted in T. Boaden, *The Private Correspondence of D. Garrick*, 1823.

wonders. *See also* TIME works wonders

wood. *See* don't HALLOO till you are out of the wood; HUNGER drives the wolf out of the wood

woods. *See* FIELDS have eyes, and woods have ears

wool. many go out for wool and come home shorn (Spanish) Those who set out to acquire some benefit for themselves may only end up worse off. J. Minsheu, *Dialogues in Spanish*, 1599.

To wander through the world ... without once considering how many there goe to seeke for wooll, that returne againe shorne themselves.
T. Shelton, *Cervantes' Don Quixote*, 1612

no wool is so white that a dyer cannot blacken it (English) No person or thing is so perfect that it is entirely invulnerable to criticism. G. Pettie, *Petite Pallace*, 1576.

wool. *See also* MUCH cry and little wool

word. a word spoken is past recalling (Greek) Once something has been said it is impossible to unsay it. Geoffrey Chaucer, *The Canterbury Tales*, c.1387 (also quoted by Horace).

a word to the wise is enough (Roman) A wise man needs no more than a hint to do whatever is necessary. William Dunbar, *Poems*, 1513 (also quoted by Plautus).

But what sayeth the proverb, *verbum sapienti* —

a word is more to him that hath wisdom than a sermon to a fool.
Walter Scott, *The Bride of Lammermoor*, 1819

word. *See also* an ENGLISHMAN's word is his bond; there's many a TRUE word spoken in jest

words. words are wind (*English*) Words have no substance compared to actual deeds. *Ancrene Riwle, c.*1225. Contrasting proverbs include 'words cut more than swords', 'words bind men' and 'a word spoken is an arrow let fly'. *See also* STICKS and stones may break my bones, but names will never hurt me.
Words are wind; but deeds are mind.
Samuel Richardson, *Clarissa*, 1748

words. *See also* ACTIONS speak louder than words; FINE words butter no parsnips; HARD words break no bones; one PICTURE is worth ten thousand words

work. all work and no play makes Jack a dull boy (*English*) Those who spend all their time working and allow no time for other interest make dull company. J. Howell, *Proverbs*, 1659.

if you won't work you shan't eat (*Hebrew*) Those who do not put in some effort cannot expect any reward. Bible, 2 Thessalonians 3:10.
If you won't work you shan't eat ... You're a wild elephant, and no educated animal at all. Go back to your jungle.
Rudyard Kipling, *Life's Handicap*, 1891

it is not work that kills, but worry (*English*) It is not overwork that is harmful to health, but stress. D. M. Mulock, *Young Mrs Jardine*, 1879. *See also* it is the PACE that kills.

work expands so as to fill the time available (*English*) Any task may be stretched to take up all the time that has been allotted

to it ('Parkinson's Law'). Cyril Northcote Parkinson, in *The Economist*, 19 November 1955.
It is a commonplace observation that work expands so as to fill the time available for its completion.
Cyril Northcote Parkinson, in *The Economist*, 19 November 1955

work. *See also* the DEVIL finds work for idle hands; the END crowns the work; the EYE of the master does more work than both his hands; FOOLS and bairns should never see half-done work; IF ifs and ands were pots and pans, there'd be no work for tinkers' hands; MANY hands make light work; as good PLAY for nought as work for nought; a WOMAN's work is never done

workman. as is the workman so is the work (*English*) The quality of work done depends upon the calibre of the workman doing it. Randle Cotgrave, *A Dictionary of the French and English Tongues*, 1611.

workman. *See also* a BAD workman blames his tools

works. *See* TIME works wonders

workshop. *See* an IDLE brain is the Devil's workshop

world. *See* GOD's in his heaven; all's right with the world; HALF the world doesn't know how the other half lives; the HAND that rocks the cradle rules the world; LAUGH and the world laughs with you; weep and you weep alone; LOVE makes the world go round; MONEY makes the world go round; better be OUT of the world than out of fashion; it takes all SORTS to make a world

worlds. *See* all's for the BEST in the best of all possible worlds

worm. even a worm will turn (*English/French*) Given sufficient cause, even the most retiring person will eventually turn on an aggressor. John Heywood, *A Dialogue containing … the Proverbs in the English Tongue*, 1546. A worm when trodden upon will turn back on itself, as though to menace an attacker.

The smallest worm will turn, being trodden on.

William Shakespeare, *Henry VI, Part 3*, c.1591

worm. *See also* the EARLY bird catches the worm

worry. *See* it is not WORK that kills, but worry

worse. worse things happen at sea (English) However bad things might be, there is always the consolation of knowing that they could have been even worse. Charles Spurgeon, *John Ploughman's Talk*, 1869.

worse. *See also* NOTHING so bad but it might have been worse; the REMEDY may be worse than the disease

worst. *See* HOPE for the best and prepare for the worst; when THINGS are at the worst they soon begin to mend

worth. the worth of a thing is what it will bring (French/English) The value of something depends upon how much it can be sold for. J. Sanforde, H. C. Agrippa's *Vanity of the Arts and Sciences*, 1569. Equivalent proverbs include 'the worth of a thing is known by its want'.

For what is Worth in any thing, But so much Money as 'twill bring?

Samuel Butler, *Hudibras*, 1664

worth. *See also* a BIRD in the hand is worth two in the bush; an OUNCE of practice is worth a pound of precept; a PECK of March dust is worth a king's ransom; one PICTURE is worth ten thousand words; a SWARM of bees in May is worth a load of hay; if a THING is worth doing, it's worth doing well; one VOLUNTEER is worth two pressed men

worthy. *See* the LABOURER is worthy of his hire

wrath. *See* a SOFT answer turneth away wrath

wren. *See* the ROBIN and the wren are God's cock and hen

wrinkled purses make wrinkled faces (English) Lack of money prematurely ages a person. Thomas Fuller, *Gnomologia*, 1732.

wrong. no wrong without a remedy (English) There is, or should be, a remedy for every offence. *Spectator*, 10 December 1910. The sentiment in the proverb has long been enshrined as a legal maxim.

wrong. *See also* the ABSENT are always wrong; if ANYTHING can go wrong, it will; the KING can do no wrong

wrongs. *See* TWO wrongs don't make a right

y

year. *See* there are no BIRDS in last year's nest; a CHERRY year, a merry year; a plum year, a dumb year; ONE year's seeding means seven years' weeding; TURKEY, heresy, hops and beer came into England all in one year

years. **years know more than books** (English) More knowledge comes with experience than through academic study. George Herbert, *Outlandish Proverbs*, 1640.

years. *See also* KEEP a thing seven years and you'll always find a use for it; you should KNOW a man seven years before you stir his fire

yesterday. *See* JAM tomorrow and jam yesterday, but never jam today

Yorkshire born and Yorkshire bred, strong in the arm and weak in the head (English) Those born in Yorkshire are physically strong but mentally weak. *Notes & Queries*, 1852. Over the years the proverb has been applied to the inhabitants of many other counties and towns. Other insulting proverbs aimed at Yorkshiremen include 'shake a bridle over a Yorkshireman's grave, and he will arise and steal a horse'.

Manchester bred: Long in the arms, and short in the head.
W. C. Hazlitt, *English Proverbs*, 1869

young. **a young physician fattens the churchyard** (English) The mistakes of an inexperienced doctor will lead to the deaths of many of his patients. Variants include 'a young doctor makes a humpy churchyard'. Another proverb stresses the advisability of 'a young barber and an old physician'.

young folks think old folks to be fools, but old folks know young folks to be fools (English) Those with long experience know better than the young or less experienced, even though this may not be recognized. J. Grange, *Golden Aphroditis*, 1577. Variants include 'of young men die many, of old men scape not any'.

You *think* us old fellows are fools; but we old fellows *know* young fellows are fools.
Jonathan Swift, *Polite Conversation*, 1738

young men may die, but old men must die (English) The young must accept that the threat of death is always a risk, but the elderly must expect imminent death as a certainty.

Thomas More, *Dialogue of Comfort*, 1534.

As the younge man maye happe some time to die soone, so the olde man can never live long.

Thomas More, *Dialogue of Comfort*, 1534

young. *See also* whom the GODS love die young; only the GOOD die young; HANG a thief when he's young, and he'll no' steal when he's old; better be an OLD man's darling than a young man's slave; you cannot put an OLD head on young shoulders

youth. youth and old age will never agree (English) The old and the young will never see things in the same way. Geoffrey Chaucer, *The Canterbury Tales*, c.1387. Another proverb underlying the different attitudes of the young and old runs 'young men forgive, old men never'.

Crabbed age and youth cannot live together.

William Shakespeare, *The Passionate Pilgrim*, c.1599

youth must be served (English) The young, with their natural vigour and freshness, are at a natural advantage in certain circumstances and cannot be denied. John Lyly, *Euphues: The Anatomy of Wit*, 1578. Variants include 'youth will have its day', 'youth will have its course' (in which form it was usually quoted in the sixteenth century) and 'youth will have its fling'.

When all the world is young, lad
And all the trees are green:
...Young blood must have its course, lad
And every dog his day.

Charles Kingsley, *The Water Babies*, 1863

youth. *See also* a GROWING youth has a wolf in his belly

Yule. *See* a GREEN winter makes a fat churchyard